Humour in Chinese Life and Letters

T0351817

Humour in Chinese Life and Letters

Classical and Traditional Approaches

Edited by

Jocelyn Chey and Jessica Milner Davis

香港大學出版社
HONG KONG UNIVERSITY PRESS

Hong Kong University Press
14/F Hing Wai Centre
7 Tin Wan Praya Road
Aberdeen
Hong Kong
www.hkupress.org

ISBN 978-988-8083-51-0 *(Hardback)*
ISBN 978-988-8083-52-7 *(Paperback)*

British Library Cataloguing-in-Publication Data
A catalogue record for this book is available from the British Library.

10 9 8 7 6 5 4 3 2 1

Printed and bound by Goodrich International Co. Ltd., Hong Kong, China

This book is dedicated to Jeremy Guy Ashcroft Davis
and to the late Hans Moon-lin Chey 齊夢麟,
both husbands without peer.

Contents

List of Figures

Contributors

Shirley Chan 陳 慧 lectures in Chinese Studies in the Department of International Studies at Macquarie University, Sydney. She has a B.A. in Asian Studies and a Master's degree in International Studies from the University of Sydney. She was awarded her Ph.D. from the University of Sydney for a thesis on early Confucianism and the Confucian *Analects*. She has taught a wide range of Chinese courses to background Chinese-speaking and non-background Chinese-speaking students, including at the University of Sydney and the University of New South Wales. Her major research interests are traditional Chinese thought, Chinese philosophy, Chinese intellectual history and Chinese early texts. Her current research deals with the Confucian texts contained in the corpus of texts excavated at Guodian, China. She is a member of Macquarie University's Ancient Cultures Research Centre.

Jocelyn Chey 梅卓琳 is a Visiting Professor in the School of Languages and Cultures, University of Sydney, and a consultant on Australia–China relations. She received her Master's degree from the University of Hong Kong and her doctorate from the University of Sydney. She has held senior positions in both the Australian diplomatic service and academia. After lecturing in Chinese Studies at the University of Sydney, she joined the Australian Commonwealth Public Service in 1973, contributing to the development of Australia–China relations for over 20 years in the Departments of Trade and Foreign Affairs. She was posted three times to China and Hong Kong, including as Consul-General in Hong Kong 1992–95. At the foundation of the Australia–China Council in 1979, she served as Executive Director, building the Council's activities and reputation. Dr Chey is an Honorary Fellow of the Oriental Society of Australia and Fellow of the Australian Institute of International Affairs. She received a medal from the Australia–China Council and was presented with the Order of Australia in 2009 for her contributions to the Australia–China relationship.

Jessica Milner Davis is an Honorary Research Associate in the School of Letters, Art and Media, University of Sydney and convenes the Australasian Humour Studies Network (http://www.sydney.edu.au/humourstudies). She received her B.A. and Ph.D. degrees from the University of New South Wales, and served as its Deputy Chancellor and Pro-Chancellor between 1981 and 2006. Dr Davis has been a Visiting Scholar at Bristol and Stanford Universities, All Souls College, Oxford and Università di Bologna at Forlì, and is a Life Member at Clare Hall, Cambridge. In 2001 she was President of the International Society for Humor Studies and is a member of the Editorial Board for *Humor: International Journal for Humor Research*. Her research areas are the history and theory of comedy and cross-cultural studies in humour. Her edited volume, *Understanding humor in Japan*, won the 2008 Association for Applied and Therapeutic Humor book prize for humour research.

Andy Shui-Lung Fung 馮瑞龍 is an Associate Professor of Chinese Language and Comparative Literature at the Beijing Normal University–Hong Kong Baptist University, United International College. He received his B.A. (Hons), M.Phil. and Postgraduate Certificate of Education from the University of Hong Kong and his Ph.D. from Griffith University, Brisbane. His doctoral thesis dealt with theories of Chinese drama from a comparative literary perspective, and his areas of research and publication are Chinese language, literature, culture and teaching methods. Previously, he was Course Director and Assistant Professor for the B.Ed. program and supervisor of research students in the Faculty of Education at the University of Hong Kong. He has been a Council Member of the Hong Kong Chinese Language Society and Executive Committee Member, Hong Kong Federation of Education Workers.

Lily Xiao Hong Lee 蕭虹 received her Ph.D. from the University of Sydney. Her 1984 thesis was entitled "A Study of *Shih-shuo hsin-yü* (*Shishuo xinyu*)". She taught in the Department of Oriental Studies, which was later incorporated into the School of Asian Studies and then the School of Languages and Cultures, at the University of Sydney, and is currently Honorary Associate of that school. She has taught and researched in the areas of classical fiction, vernacular fiction and the writings of Chinese women, and her research into Chinese women's history and literature has recently expanded to include the women of Tibet and those living along the Silk Road. She is co-editor-in-chief with the late Agnes Stefanowska of the multi-volume reference work *Biographical dictionary of Chinese women* (Hong Kong University Press, 2007).

Qian Suoqiao 錢鎖橋 is an Assistant Professor in the Department of Chinese, Translation and Linguistics, City University of Hong Kong. He holds the degrees of M.A. and Ph.D. in Comparative Literature from the University of California, Berkeley, and a B.A. in English from Beijing Foreign Studies University, China. He has been Assistant Professor, Department of Comparative Literature, Hamilton College, Clinton, NY, was a Mellon Fellow in the Humanities, Barnard College, New York and in 2009 held a Fulbright Senior Research Award in Comparative Literature at Harvard University. He is the author of many articles in both English and Chinese, and his most recent book is *Liberal cosmopolitan: Lin Yutang and middling Chinese modernity* (Brill, 2011). He is also editor of *Selected bilingual essays of Lin Yutang* (Chinese University of Hong Kong Press, 2010).

Joseph C. Sample teaches in the Department of English at the University of Houston-Downtown. He first encountered Lin Yutang's writings in graduate school nearly 20 years ago, when he was told that Lin was a minor figure who did not merit sustained study: since then he has waited patiently for the world to catch up. Formerly at Clemson University in Clemson, South Carolina, he taught courses in American humour, served as a research associate with the Pearce Center for Professional Communication and directed the Cultures and Languages Across the Curriculum program. He received his doctorate in English from Iowa State University, an M.A. in East Asian Studies from the University of Minnesota and a second M.A. in English from Texas A&M University. He studied Chinese at National Taiwan Normal University and at Shanghai International Studies University. His current book project deals with written and visual discourses commonly found in English-language writings on China and the Chinese and the "rhetoric of things Chinese".

Rey Tiquia 第紀亞 雷毅 is an Honorary Fellow in the School of Historical Studies, Faculty of Arts, University of Melbourne and a qualified practitioner of Traditional Chinese Medicine (TCM). He received his B.A. from Manuel Luis Quézon University, Manila, the Philippines, and completed his M.Sc. and Ph.D. degrees in the history and philosophy of science at the University of Melbourne. His dissertation was entitled "Traditional Chinese medicine as an Australian tradition of health care", and he has lectured on the history and philosophy of TCM at both the University of Melbourne and Victoria University. In 2000, the Wellcome Trust invited him to facilitate a workshop for the Closed-Door Research Conference on Complementary and Alternative Medicine in London. Since 1997, he has been an Honorary Professor at the Shanxi College of TCM, Taiyuan.

Weihe Xu 許衛和 is an Associate Professor of Chinese at Middlebury College, Vermont, where he teaches Chinese language and literature. He received his M.A. in English and American Literature and his Ph.D. in Chinese and Comparative Literature from Washington University in St Louis, MO. His research concentrates on traditional Chinese prose fiction and humour in traditional China. He has published articles on the eighteenth-century novel *Honglou meng* (The dream of the red chamber), literary studies and Confucian influences on Chinese humour. He is currently preparing a monograph about humour in *Honglou meng* and late imperial Chinese literati sentiments for the Edwin Mellen Press.

Zhan Hang-Lun 詹杭倫 is an Associate Professor in the School of Chinese, Faculty of Arts, University of Hong Kong, and is a former professor and supervisor of M.A. and Ph.D. students in the

Renmin University of China, Beijing (formerly known as the People's University). He received a B.A. from China West Normal University, Nanchong, Sichuan, M.A. from Sichuan Normal University, Chengdu and Ph.D. from Hong Kong Baptist University. His areas of research are classical Chinese literature, Chinese literary theory and the study of overseas sinology. He has published widely, including on the literary history and thought of the Jin dynasty, and on Qing dynasty theories of *fu* prose poems from the Tang and Song dynasties, as well as releasing a monograph on *James J. Y. Liu, dealing with the synthesis of Chinese and Western theories of literature.*

Preface

Preparing this volume has been a labour of love for the co-editors and an attempt to combine our specialized knowledge in two seemingly different fields — comedy and humour for Jessica Milner Davis and Chinese culture and history for Jocelyn Chey. Decades ago, in Sydney, we pursued doctoral studies in these quite separate fields. Then we went our separate ways — Jocelyn to Canberra, Beijing and Hong Kong, and Jessica to Bristol, Paris and America. In the first decade of a new century and having returned once more to Sydney, we came together at a conference of the Oriental Society of Australia and realized that before us was a project we seemed fated to undertake in partnership.

We are sincerely grateful to our co-authors for making this project possible. We thank them also for their patience while we explored what it meant to combine so many different perspectives, disciplines and periods (not to mention so many variants in spelling of proper names or fonts and styles for Chinese characters). Each author has endeavoured to make his or her own expertise accessible to the general reader without conceding scholarly values in the process, a difficult and time-consuming task. We believe the result is an excellent introduction to an important and much misunderstood topic, presented in a way we hope our readers will enjoy. This volume includes studies to illustrate some of the traditional concepts, themes and forms of humour in Chinese life and letters and a projected companion volume reflecting modern and contemporary approaches in preparation. Even within this scope, it has not been possible to address fully every topic and period (the contemporary art scene, for example, remains a significant omission), but we hope others will be inspired to fill such gaps.

We also hope this work will contribute to cross-cultural understanding. Humour is often dangerous, since — like many other forms of human behaviours, both innate and learned — it may be used for both good and ill. While it is an important survival technique for those under personal stress or in subordinate positions, and an excellent adjunct to teaching and learning when well used, humour can also wound and exclude. Further, it represents a challenge to authority of all kinds. Different cultures and times have evolved a range of protocols and social conventions for channelling and containing humour-making and humour-appreciation. Every country — especially Australia — has its own approach to what it is possible for one to get away with in humour, when and with whom. In Australia, you can pretty much "take the mickey" out of anyone, almost at any time. When abroad, Australians quickly learn that this does not always work elsewhere and that humorous behaviour needs to be modified. Equally, people from more reserved cultures soon discover what to expect from Aussies in their own environment. A deeper awareness of such cultural differences can only enhance international understanding.

De gustibus non est disputandum: even when better understanding exists, personal differences in tastes and attitudes regarding humour will remain. But what these chapters show is that East and West have more in common when it comes to humour and laughter than is commonly thought. Beneath superficial differences in topics and styles of joking and comedy, or in public laughter and the shape of linguistic puns, this book reaffirms the commonality of human attitudes to enjoying (and censoring) humour. Such insights are, to us, a source of satisfaction. And we urge our readers always to remember *xue wu zhi jing* 學無止境 (there are no boundaries in study) — especially about humour.

We thank our families for their support and enthusiasm about this project and record our appreciation for expert assistance from colleagues in the East Asian Collection of Fisher Library at the University of Sydney, the Harvard-Yenching Library and the Chinese Department of the University of Cambridge Library; also from our Hong Kong University Press editorial team, Michael Duckworth, Dennis Cheung and Jessica Wang.

Jessica Milner Davis
Jocelyn Chey
Sydney, August 2011

1

Youmo and the Chinese Sense of Humour

Jocelyn Chey

Humour in China

Was there no humour or general concept of humour in China before 1923? That was when the Chinese writer, translator and inventor Lin Yutang 林語堂 (1895–1976) claimed that "orthodox Chinese literature did not allow for humorous expression, so the Chinese people did not understand the nature of humor and its function".[1] While *youmo* 幽默 is now standard usage in everyday Chinese, having replaced other earlier neologisms, what has happened to the faculty of "humorous expression" and its social functions since then? Did they emerge under Lin's care and did they survive subsequent massive social changes intact, or were they suppressed or changed beyond recognition?[2]

Some scholars claim that humour was never absent from Chinese life and letters, referring in particular to the ancient term *huaji* 滑稽, which elsewhere in this book is variously translated as laughable, funny, just funny, and so on. If *huaji* and related terms such as laughter (*xiao* 笑) indicate humour, or are subsumed within the meaning of that term,[3] then they certainly provide evidence of humorous traditions in China that date back more than 2000 years. Setting aside the scope and meaning of *huaji* for the moment, let us examine the intellectual context within which Lin was working, particularly in the English language.

Humour is a slippery concept. In this book, the editors and authors adopt the widest possible interpretation in line with current humour scholarship. This avoids the danger of disagreements about definitions, but some discussion of terms is necessary before we engage with the evolving concept of humour in Chinese life and letters.

The *Shorter Oxford English dictionary* (SOED, 3rd ed., 1955) defines humour as "the faculty of observing what is ludicrous or amusing, or of expressing it; jocose imagination or treatment of a subject". This entry further states that humour is "less purely intellectual than wit and often allied to pathos". In English usage, humour frequently has a visual or non-verbal component. It can be silly or playful. Wit, by contrast, is defined in the same edition of the SOED as "quickness of intellect or liveliness of fancy, with capacity of apt expression", and has been greatly admired by European intellectuals over many centuries. References to wit appear in classic literary sources such as the works of William Shakespeare (1564–1616), who made Polonius, his comically didactic and long-winded character in *Hamlet*, ironically instruct his charge that "brevity is the soul of wit";[4] and Samuel Johnson (1696–1772), who gave as his first definition of wit "powers of the mind; mental faculties; intellects", following this with six other related definitions, including "quickness of fancy" and "man of fancy or genius (real or supposed)".[5] European wit was certainly humorous, even if it made its intellectual appeal to the hearer or reader through literary technique rather than through what English speakers like to call "the funny bone" — that is, an instinctive reaction to something funny.

During the nineteenth century, the distinction between wit and humour seems to have become less marked on both sides of the Atlantic. The American humorist Mark Twain (1835–1910) noted to himself, "Wit & Humor — if any difference it is in *duration* — lightning & electric light. Same material, apparently; but one is vivid, brief, & can do damage — tother [the other] fools along & enjoys the elaboration."[6] This more catholic interpretation inspired Lionel Strachey (1864–1927), the American writer and translator (a cousin of the more famous Lytton Strachey), to translate and compile a compendium he called *The world's wit and humor*, in 15 volumes published in New York between 1905 and 1912. He drew distinctions between differing European traditions but did not extend his sampling into Asian languages, beyond Omar Khayyam whose work was well-known in translation.

Mark Twain's contemporary, the English poet and writer George Meredith (1828–1909), made an in-depth study of humour in European literature and philosophy. His work was influential around the world, including on Lin Yutang, inspiring him to introduce his new perspective on humour to the Chinese literary consciousness and more broadly to Chinese society.

In his *Essay on comedy* (published in 1877, having been delivered in lecture form to the London Institute earlier that year) Meredith wrote, "To touch and kindle the mind through laughter, demands more than sprightliness, a most subtle delicacy."[7] It celebrated an English approach to humour in which comedy combined emotion with intellectual wit or incongruity — something he opposed to the great French concepts of *l'ésprit* or *le comique*, a pure comedy of the intellect. The latter reached its apotheosis in the vitalist philosophical writings of Henri Bergson, especially his book *Le rire* (which also began life as a lecture as early as 1884, and was finally published in 1900).[8] Meredith chose the terms "the Comic spirit" and "the Comic muse", personified as "the Comic", to indicate the distinction. In a very British Empire way, he also saw comedy as a tool to promote reason and civilization, and to control the excesses of government and factional groups in society.[9]

Adopting Meredith's definitional approach and applying it in the Chinese context, Lin Yutang concluded that *huaji* was not worthy to be dignified as work inspired by the Comic muse. Lin saw that Meredithian humour however could be a civilizing tool for the modernization of Chinese society, and proposed that if humour took root among the people, China could be a country where courtesy and common sense prevailed and where the excesses of corrupt government and overweening local officials would be kept in check. He was not thinking of promoting humour in the villages and factories; rather, his *youmo* humour was bourgeois, belonging essentially to the literate class.

Chinese discourse about humour in the 1930s divided into pro-British, French and German factions. Lin followed Meredith and Croce in preference to Bergson. He also set aside the psychoanalytic views of Sigmund Freud, as formulated in *Jokes and their relation to the unconscious* (1905) and *Humour* (1928). The "Continental" view of humour was espoused by other scholars, notably Qian Zhongshu 錢鐘書 (1910–98). There was a highly charged political dimension to this discourse, reflecting the Nationalist government's[10] preoccupation with eradicating the influence of the Chinese Communist Party (CCP) during the 1930s. Humour is never fully comprehensible apart from its social and political context. This is particularly true in modern

China and has been for some time, as Qian Suoqiao makes evident in Chapter 10.[11] The political dimension of modern Chinese humour draws on ancient sources and rival ideologies. Lin Yutang, seeking a native heritage, linked it with the Daoist rather than the Confucian tradition, creating an artificial distinction between the two, which has lain at the heart of debates and misunderstandings of the nature of Chinese humour ever since.[12] During the Nationalist period, scholars blamed Confucianism for contemporary social problems, labelling it the ethical system of the establishment. Daoism, as they interpreted it, had historically been the vehicle for anti-establishment thinking. Since Daoism actually advocates disassociation from the grubbiness of officialdom, one might well ask why Lin proposed the use of humour to improve society. However, the destabilizing social changes of the 1920s and 1930s made him agree with Meredith that humour should have a didactic purpose — to correct the whims, ailments and "strange doctors" of the day — and he believed this made *youmo* essentially Daoist rather than Confucian. Such humour was clearly superior to the *huaji* funny stuff of dirty jokes, slapstick and nonsense — it was a serious matter of national importance.

It is also noteworthy that when Lin translated Meredith, he took the word "comedy" to refer to comedy on the stage and translated Meredith's Comic spirit as *paidiao* 俳調 (joking), the title of a chapter in the fifth-century *Shishuo xinyu* 世說新語 (A new account of tales of the world).[13] The performance aspect is central to Lin's philosophy of humour. Whether written, spoken or performed, the humour he proposed was to be targeted and was an active process rather than a passive response.

Translation added a further layer of complication. Meredith's purple prose presented challenges, and the English concept of humour is complex, varying in usage, purpose and definition, with many terms ranging from amusement and badinage to wisecracking and wit. Some have obvious equivalents in Chinese and others are more difficult to distinguish from one another.[14] Exact equivalents are *not* provided by terms such as *xue* 謔 (joking), *xie* 諧 or *guji* or *huaji* 滑稽 (glib or laughable), *ji* 譏 (to ridicule), *chao* 嘲 (derision) or *paidiao* (mentioned above).

Lin published his Meredith-inspired essay "On humour" in the magazine that he helped found in 1932, *Lunyu banyuekan* 論語半月刊 (Analects Fortnightly),[15] modelled on *Punch* and devoted, as that English magazine was, "to hold the balance fairly between the parties, to avoid fixed and bitter partisanships, to 'hit all round' as occasion seemed to demand, and to award praise where it appeared to be deserved".[16] The *Lunyu* aimed to take the middle road in support of freedom, the poor and the oppressed against abuses of political privilege. Lin wrote:

> Any country's culture, lifestyle, literature, or thought needs to be enriched by humour. If a people do not have this enrichment of humour, their culture will become more hypocritical with each passing day, their lives will be closer and closer to cheating, their thought pedantic and outdated, their literature increasingly withered and their spirit increasingly obstinate and ultraconservative.[17]

Since Meredith and Lin, understanding of humour has been liberalized greatly by scholarly investigation around the world. The general category is now seen as having many sub-categories, including jokes, wit, satire and many other forms of mirthful expression. Humour is known from recent brain research to involve not just cognition, but also emotional responses and a range of laughing responses. The experience of humour may extend to other species, such as the great apes and even rats.[18] Research in social psychology has shown that purposes, available forms of expression and circumstances all help determine what type of humour is used, indicating the importance of comparative studies. *Youmo* or "Daoist" humour with educational and improving intent, when seen in this context, obviously is only one of many types. Again, since individual psychological make-ups differ, as do societies and conventions, it follows that types of humour and styles of usage will vary from time to time and place to place. In order to study humour, an inclusive approach and the use of broad concepts and definitions are vital.

It is therefore instructive to consider the history of humour in China without insisting on a break between *huaji* and *youmo*, but rather by placing both in their proper positions in one long tradition. Little detailed study has been done on the earliest examples of humour in China, despite the fact that written collections of humour probably predate comparable European works such as the Byzantine *Philogelos* (compiled around 400 CE).[19] Brief selections of the earliest *huaji* stories have been made available in translation.[20] I include them in the general category of humour rather than the sub-category of wit or *huaji*.

Humour in ancient China certainly extended beyond documented stories of *huaji*. In examining connections between humour and national (including ethnic) culture and history, it is important to remember that in former times literary records belonged to the elite and to those whose native language was Chinese (including all dialects) or who were educated to read Chinese, but that the elites were not the sole proprietors of humour. Humour must also have been then, as it is today, a tool of the oppressed and the underdog, not didactic but closer to the category of protest humour.[21] Voiceless and unrecorded ordinary people throughout history certainly had jokes and merriment, drew humorous graffiti and thumbed their noses at scholars and officials, even if very few of their quips and pranks were recorded for posterity. Reviewing the history of humour, we tend to over-estimate the importance of types favoured by the literati and the elites. In China, enormous differences persist today between ethnic and dialect groups, and between urban and rural populations, and no doubt these were even more pronounced in the past. Where Chinese dialect groups had orthographic tools to record their language, they preserved jokes and humour that record local perspectives, as demonstrated for example by Marjorie Chan's ongoing research[22] mining the rich lode of Cantonese-language humour in one of its modern expressions, the pop song. The ancient merriment and subaltern humour of other ethnic minorities in China has almost entirely lapsed into oblivion, and little work has been done to collect relevant historic materials. It is hoped that this book will stimulate more attention to this aspect of humour studies.

The Chineseness of Chinese Humour

This book has adopted liberal definitions of China and of Chinese, as well as of humour, because current political divisions are not paralleled by equal cultural divides. A few studies of Chinese humour have extended to Hong Kong, Taiwan and the Chinese diaspora generally, but further work is needed to establish whether the findings of this book apply equally to these communities. Studies of attitudes to humour in Taiwan were pioneered by Chao-Chih Liao and have been followed by recent psychological studies.[23] In addition, as Weihe Xu notes in Chapter 4, important questions exist about differences in humour types and usages in the light of cross-cultural influences and parallels between China and other Confucian societies such as Korea and Vietnam. Indeed, China itself is a multi-ethnic nation and it is regrettable that we have not been able to include more material on the humour of the ethnic minorities. Other areas awaiting fuller treatment include humour in the contemporary novel, in poetry and on the stage; humour in art and architecture; and many earlier periods of literature. This book presents itself as a pioneering effort, not a definitive review.

Of the many types or forms of humour found in Chinese literature, in popular sayings and informal jokes, and in art and daily life, some are more prevalent than elsewhere, and such distinctions are worth noting. Language is the vehicle for preserving and communicating culture, and the Chinese language is a particularly apt vehicle to convey humour, being rich in homophones that have great potential for punning humour. A wide variety of puns are found in classical Chinese texts and also in contemporary spoken and written Chinese.

Two examples suffice to show the continuity of this tradition. In the eighth century, the Tang dynasty poet Liu Yuxi 劉禹錫 (772–842) wrote:

東邊日頭西邊雨，
道是無晴却有晴。
The east is sunny and the west is raining,
So it seems there is no fine weather and still fine weather.

Here Liu uses *qing* 晴 (fine weather) as a homophone for *qing* 情 (love, affection), so that the second line may also be read as "So it seems that there is no love but there is still love." The second example comes from the 1930s, when the Nationalist government embarked on a campaign to exterminate Communist bases in south China. It promulgated the slogan *Sha Zhu ba Mao* 殺朱罷毛, meaning "Kill (Marshal) Zhu (De) and eliminate Mao (Zedong)". The slogan was memorable because *Zhu* 朱 is a homophone for *zhu* 豬 (pig), *ba* 罷 is a homophone for *ba* 拔 (pull out) and *mao* 毛 is not only a surname but also means hair, so that the phrase can also mean "Kill the pig and pluck its hair".

Such verbal puns may be complemented by visual material, and while such reification in accompanying illustrations is by no means exclusive to Chinese humour, its prevalence is encouraged by the nature of the language itself. The widespread practice of blogging in contemporary China provides one example. A blogger posting under the name of Zhang Facai 張發財, who has published many visual puns, has one that is a picture of a clock face where all the numbers are 3 (see Figure 1.1). There is no accompanying text but the reader who verbalizes the picture will understand the visual pun on a current slogan used in official anti-pornography texts, *san dian quan kai* 三點全開 (three [vital] points in full view) — a reference to full-frontal nudity.[24]

Figure 1.1   Clock-face joke by Beijing graphic designer Zhang Facai 張發財. Black and white copy of image from Joel Martinsen, "Joke advertising", *Danwei*, 28 December 2008 (accessed 4 June 2009). Originally downloaded from a blog that later closed down: http://blog.sina.com.cn/s/blog_49b5a8160100bfds.html. Reproduced with the permission of the artist.

Another type of linguistic punning humour uniquely connected to the Chinese language is called in Chinese *xiehouyu* 歇後語 (sometimes translated as "a saying with the latter part suspended"). Only the first part of the saying is spoken, leaving the hearer to extrapolate the second part and interpret it as a pun for another word or phrase with a different meaning. This linguistic pattern resembles rhyming slang but is different in both usage and intent. One theory about the origins of Cockney and other rhyming slang is that it is a secret language intended to deceive non-initiates.[25] While *xiehouyu* are certainly dependent upon cultural familiarity (as the examples below demonstrate), they do not share this secretive character. In fact, many are part of everyday Chinese vocabulary, while others are used as a humorous way of demonstrating the speaker's linguistic competence. Here are two examples:

> 外甥打燈籠：照舅 （照舊）
>
> Keep to the same. (literal meaning: When a sister's son holds a lantern, he is to light up [the way] for his maternal uncle).

Here the speaker says "Sister's son holds a lantern" and the hearer intuits "Giving light to his uncle". The humour resides in the fact that in the second part of the saying *zhao* 照 has two meanings, "to light up" and "in accordance with", while *jiu* 舅 (maternal uncle) is a pun for *jiu* 舊 (former time).

> 老包染頭髮：越描越黑
>
> The more one works on it, the worse it becomes. (literal meaning: Old Bao is dyeing his hair and the more he touches it up, the darker it becomes.)

In this case, the spoken part is "Old Bao dyes his hair"; in the second part, while the word *hei* 黑 means dark or black, it also has the connotation of bad or evil, suggesting that the flaw becomes more and more evident. The person referred to in this saying is Bao Zheng 包拯, a high official of the Song dynasty who was famous for his sense of justice. He is the hero of many well-known operas and, significantly, in Peking Opera his face is painted black with a crescent-shaped white birthmark on his forehead, reflecting the close connection in the popular mind between his character and his black hair.

Because young people today are less familiar with classical sayings and historical allusions than the older generations were, *xiehouyu* are becoming less common. These proverb-forms can be found in many dialects, however, including Cantonese. Very likely their persistence in Cantonese culture is due to the continuing popularity of local opera and consequent general familiarity with the legends and historical plots. To give one example:

花旦生仔： 謝天謝地

Thank God. (literal meaning: When the *fataan* 花旦 (heroine) gives
birth to a son, she thanks Heaven and Earth.)

The *fataan* is the young female character in Cantonese Opera. In any
plot that involves a mother giving birth, this naturally happens off-
stage but immediately afterwards the actress will come to the front of
the stage and bow, saying *Tse t'in tse tei!* 謝天謝地 (Thank Heaven and
Earth), so these words are familiar to all opera aficionados.

While technical aspects of the Chinese language influence the mode
or expression of humour, they do not affect its substance, nor are they
responsible for any unique or absolutely different "Chinese" quality
of humour. As Nagashima has noted in the case of Japanese linguistic
punning,[26] other languages with similar characteristics evolve similar
formats of humorous word play to share and enjoy. Nevertheless,
these forms importantly derive from the nature of the language itself,
not from any introduction of an accepted type of humour from the
West. They are home-grown exemplars of a Chinese sense of humour,
without essentially differing in their nature from other classes and
types of linguistic puns.

Comparative humour studies reveal that different topics may be
regarded as fit for humour, deriving from aspects of daily life that may
be significant in one society but not elsewhere. C. T. Hsia noted in 1953
that Chinese people do not value privacy and idiosyncrasy as highly
as most Europeans do. He acknowledged some politically incorrect
realities of the time:

> The Chinese still retain a childish delight in taking notice of any
> physical and moral deviation from the norm; their fellow creatures,
> so unfortunate as to be physically deformed and disabled, are
> usually objects of ridicule. Thus the blind, the deaf, the hunchback,
> the bald, and the pock-faced are laughed at openly. This sense
> of ridicule is also directed against persons who claim to possess
> special knowledge or power or who live an abnormal existence:
> the doctor, the teacher, the magistrate, the monk.[27]

Hsia also referred to the Confucian principle that each should behave
appropriately according to his or her station. He believed this gave
rise to traditional and current jokes about cuckolds and henpecked

husbands. He noted the provincialism of humour, characteristic of rural communities where few people travelled outside their native districts, which elicited urban jokes about people from other provinces or language groups or country bumpkins.[28] The work of Christie Davies on bodies of popular jokes from cultures around the world has shown that such joke-types are common to most nations — jokes about sub-groups characterized by stupidity, filth, meanness, sexual availability, and so on.[29] There is nothing exclusively Chinese about them. It would be more surprising — as Davies points out in his methodological essay on studying humour, "The dog that didn't bark in the night" — *not* to find a particular category.[30]

As for laughter at the physically deformed and disabled, one is inescapably reminded of European precedents, ranging from the ubiquitous mediaeval and renaissance comic playlets at the expense of the blind and the lame to more contemporary examples of black humour, no doubt controversial but nevertheless widespread. The debate over taste and propriety in humour is as old as society itself. Context is all.

Understanding social context is essential in order to appreciate humour, and indeed motivates this book. Naturally humour has as many complexities as a society itself does. One of the earliest international scholars to study Chinese humour, Henry Wells, made the point that it could not be understood apart from its cultural context:

> Much of the finest Chinese humor is remarkably sophisticated and cultured, expression proceeding from a state of mind where delicate shades of thought and feeling are apprehended and amusement derived from incongruities within an advanced stage of society . . . The Chinese take humor seriously. It not only signifies happy surprise but happy intuition, a form of insight above or at least beyond logic . . . Even in the earliest recorded times, the Chinese people, whether in towns or in the countryside, appear both uncommonly humorous and urbane . . . The incongruity at the root of all humor lies peculiarly at the root and germ of Chinese humor . . . The refractions are peculiarly delicate, the emanations singularly subtle.[31]

Wells also wrote that, "As horizons in the twentieth century expand, pictures hitherto unfamiliar to the world at large are mounted on the walls."[32] While it is certainly true that Western horizons have expanded to encompass some view of Chinese and Asian humour, and in particular easily accessible types such as comic action films (so-called "kung-fu movies"), which are universally appreciated, Chinese horizons have likewise expanded successively to include Japanese, Russian and European humour. At the same time, Chinese society itself has changed — sometimes convulsively so. As a result, new targets and new vehicles for humour have continuously been thrown up at many levels of society, drastically changing the face of the humour that this book attempts to study.

In the last few decades, psychologists and sociologists worldwide have turned their attention to the phenomenon of humour and, as noted earlier, comparative international studies are now being carried out in China and other "Confucian" societies into attitudes to humour. These include the use of humour in university teaching, its relationship to mental outlook, creativity and personality traits.[33] Attention is being given to conceptual issues in this cross-cultural research since it is important that studies of humour cover not only the various types and range of content of humour, but also its social uses and the connections between it and personality types, all of which benefit from using a cross-cultural perspective. Such studies accumulate firm empirical data about contemporary Chinese values and attitudes, including the relationship between humour and optimism, attitudes to laughter itself and the various uses of humour — for example, in advertising and in the classroom by both students and lecturers.

Such studies so far have covered humour styles and usage among the educated and more cosmopolitan elites in the countries concerned. More work clearly remains to be done in the rural areas of China, which despite increasing urbanization still account for a major proportion of the whole population today. Where research projects have included cross-cultural comparisons, however, they generally confirm (unsurprisingly, given the connections already noted between culture and humour) that there are significant differences between, for example, typical responses from China and Canada, and between Taiwan and Switzerland, in general attitudes to humour and in respondents' self-assessments of their use of humour in daily life. The authors speculate that these differences are not just matters of personality, but of culturally based differences at many levels, including different relations between students and teachers, different gender expectations, and so on. It is here, perhaps, that the "Chineseness" of humour lies.

The History of Humour (*huaji* and *youmo*)

Traditional Chinese medicine (TCM) as a system of understanding human physiology and treating human ailments can be traced back to the time of Confucius, *Kongzi* 孔子 or *Kongfuzi* 孔夫子 (551–479 BCE). Because TCM links emotions with bodily organs and functions, it describes humour as an emotional and natural part of the human make-up in a way that is deeply rooted in Chinese beliefs and culture. In setting out these theoretical and philosophical understandings of the place of humour and emotions generally in the physical make-up of humans, Chapter 3 by Rey Tiquia casts interesting light on the lost European tradition of the bodily humours. According to the ancient text known as the *Huangdi neijing* 黃帝內經 (Inner canon of the Yellow Emperor), mentioned in the *Han shu* 漢書 (Book of Han), humour is physically located in the "endogenous heart".[34] Because the circulation of *qi* 氣[35] in the body is crucial to health and good humour, laughter can help unblock this circulation when needed. The parallels with Galen's "humorism" are striking, despite one principal difference: the way TCM conceives of and propounds the meridian *qi* circulation system. Such concepts are fundamental for the many who practise and consume TCM today, certainly in China and increasingly in the West. Tiquia also notes that TCM long ago linked humour, emotions and diseases with the seasons, anticipating modern Western medical understanding of affective disease patterns. Thus, from a very early date, TCM set boundaries for humour that have always influenced its expression and application. Importantly, TCM does not distinguish between high and low humour as beneficial stimuli, and thus embraces both *huaji* and *youmo* — both Confucian and Daoist approaches.

In any understanding of the cultural background to humour in China, it is difficult to under-estimate the importance of Confucius, thinker and social philosopher. From his time onwards, Chinese society had set rigid standards for proper behaviour and established moral imperatives. Inappropriate levity and laughter was frowned upon, especially after the tenth century under the influence of the philosophical reforms commonly known as Neo-Confucianism. Accordingly, Chapter 4 by Weihe Xu underpins many others in this book by outlining the framework of the Confucian world-view and the proper conduct of a Chinese gentleman in relation to humour. Once again, significant parallels emerge with classical tradition in the West. Xu's later Chapter 8, discussing the ways in which humour is linked to character portrayal in the hugely influential mid-eighteenth-century novel *Honglou meng* 紅樓夢 (Dream of the red chamber), shows how underlying beliefs in Confucian norms influenced literary and popular models of behaviour and how humour was used artistically to humanize a female paragon of virtue.

Despite this, Chinese social philosophy has never been uniform or unvarying. Daoism, deriving from the teaching of the possibly mythical Laozi 老子 and various Daoist canonical texts, including the *Liezi* 列子 (attributed to Lie Yukou 列圄寇 c. 400 BCE), represents an alternative view of life and propriety, and has a history that equals Confucianism in antiquity. Chapter 5, by Shirley Chan, describes the tradition of Daoist humour as distinctly more carefree than that circumscribed by Confucian conventions; it was often used for purposes of veiled social criticism, although going nowhere close to Lin Yutang's definition of didactic *youmo*. Chinese religious traditions also reveal links between Buddhist and Daoist tenets that influence the practice and expression of humour. The Zen use of humour to produce sudden enlightenment dates back to the ninth century. From this time on, jokes could be used to communicate religious truth to disciples at a level deeper (or perhaps higher) than intellectual understanding.[36]

From the time that Confucianism became the ideology of imperial rulers and governments, it was disseminated through the education and examination system, and provided both a tool for the rulers and a system restricting autocracy; however, it never represented the whole spectrum of Chinese humour, ranging from Confucian decorum to Daoist subversion. That the gulf separating these two conventions nevertheless could be, and was, bridged by humour is shown in collections of anecdotes about *huaji* wits who lived as early as the Zhou dynasty (1045–256 BCE). They represent a type of palace humour encapsulated in dialogues between the ruler and court jesters, in which quick wit was necessary for survival in murky political waters. Several scholars have noted the importance of the *Huaji liezhuan* 滑稽列傳 (Biographies of the *huaji*-ists)[37] contained in the *Shiji* 史記 (Records of the Grand Historian), by Sima Qian 司馬遷 (145?–86? BCE), a chronicle of history and the lives of notable figures since the founding of the Chinese empire by the legendary Yellow Emperor. It contains four biographies: those of Chunyu Kun 淳于髡, who lived in the state of Qi during the Warring States period (471–221 BCE); You Meng 優孟, jester to the court of King Zhuangwang of the state of Chu (reign period 613–591 BCE); You Zhan 優旃, jester to the court of the first Emperor of the Qin dynasty (676–652 BCE); and Dongfang Shuo 東方朔, who served in the court of Han Wudi (156–87 BCE).[38]

A biography of Dongfang Shuo is also included in the official history of the Han dynasty. From this comes an anecdote that illustrates the essence of *huaji* (it may have appeared much funnier to contemporaries than to modern readers because the social context was so different from ours). It is a levelling joke in which the emperor thinks he has ultimate authority and power but in fact is no more immune to being tricked than anyone else. As Kowallis points out, this story contains a moral: that filial piety ranks higher as a moral responsibility than do court rules.

The story concerns the origin of the Lantern Festival held on the fifteenth day of the first month of the year. When one of the emperor's palace women was unable to carry out her filial duty of visiting her parents after the New Year, she threatened to drown herself in a palace well. Dongfang decided to help her avoid this fate. He told the emperor that the Jade Emperor (king of the Daoist gods) had ordered the Fire God to burn down the capital on the sixteenth day. The emperor asked Dongfang what he should do to prevent this disaster. Dongfang suggested that since the Fire God loved red lanterns, the streets should be hung with them. This might distract the god from carrying out his wicked plan. The emperor followed his advice. Then, while everyone was out viewing the lanterns, the young lady was able to escape from the palace and pay her respects to her parents.[39]

The lives recorded by Sima Qian (and Ban Gu) are in effect those of the earliest individual humorists recorded in the Chinese literary corpus: the court jesters of those times. They certainly predate parallel records from the West,[40] and demonstrate the pragmatic use of humour for didactic purposes or as a means for scholars to veil attacks on persons in privileged positions. Both of these are long-standing traditions in Chinese philosophy and history, and they are Daoist *youmo* as much as they are Confucian *huaji*.[41]

In its original context, *huaji* was a form of humour relating to sharpness of intellect — a desirable quality for court advisers and scholars and one having subversive potential. Subversive humour certainly exists in China as it does around the world. It is impressive that it managed to flourish even under the autocracy of the Han rulers. As noted by Lily Lee in Chapter 5, the oldest collection of jokes and witty stories in the world may well be the *Xiao lin* 笑林 (Forest of laughter), ascribed to Handan Chun 邯鄲淳, a native of Yingchuan in north-west China who lived during the Han dynasty in the second century CE. The complete collection is no longer extant, but a small number of stories were included in two tenth-century encyclopaedias, the *Taiping yulan* 太平御覽 (Imperial encyclopaedia) and the *Taiping guangji* 太平廣記 (Taiping miscellany). These are sufficient to give some idea of the original contents. Lu Xun 魯迅 (1881–1936) noted in his *Zhongguo xiaoshuo shi lüe* 中國小說史略 (Brief history of Chinese fiction)[42] the importance of the *Xiao lin* and quoted its most famous joke. It is an example of jesting at the expense of a regional sub-group characterised by stupidity:

> 魯有挈長竿入城門者，初，堅执之不可入，橫执之亦不可入，計無所出。俄有老父曰，"吾非聖人，且見事多矣，何不以鋸中裁而入！" 遂依而裁之。

> In the land of Lu [present-day Shandong province] there was once a man who tried to enter a city gate while carrying a long pole. If held vertically, the pole was too high to make it under the gate; if held horizontally, the gate was too narrow to allow him to advance. Unable to think of any other way to get it through, the man was presently approached by an elderly gentleman, who announced: "Though sage I be none, I have witnessed many things in my lifetime. Pray, couldst thou not saw thine staff in half and then clear the limits of the portal with it in hand?" The man then acted accordingly and split his own pole in two![43]

Huaji wit was applied not only to rulers but also to the state-supported education system and to the often-problematic relationship between teacher and student. Lily Lee recounts several such stories from the *Shishuo xinyu*, generally attributed to Liu Yiqing 劉義慶 (403–444 CE), another early collection of *huaji* and historical anecdotes.[44] Intellectual circles at this time were strongly influenced by Daoism, and several stories in the collection concerned well-known Daoists. The humour, however, is not Daoist in Lin Yutang's sense but rather served to consolidate in-circle relations between scholar/officials educated in the Confucian classics.

Although most early recorded Chinese literary humour tended to fall into the category of *huaji* wit that appealed to the literati, when in the Yuan dynasty (1271–1368) their social standing changed — with ethnic Chinese being relegated to subordinate roles and the Mongol rulers preferring to rely on allies and "Semuren" (Persians, Muslims and Christians) — recorded humour changed too. Culturally, there was increased use of vernacular language, particularly in novels and operas. Advances in printing technology helped to disseminate texts, while operas entertained, educated and instructed villagers and townsfolk in the same way as medieval miracle plays functioned in Europe. Comic drama blossomed, bequeathing scripts that demonstrate sophisticated use of a wide variety of comedic techniques, described in Chapter 7 on Yuan love-comedies, by Andy Shui-lung Fung and Zhan Hang-Lun. Stories from these operas, along with folk tales, popular jokes and other comic tales were also retailed in the market place by professional storytellers. The tradition, known as *shuo gu* 説鼓 or *shuo guzi* 説鼓子, of metrical recitation with accompaniment of drum and other instruments has continued up to the present day, particularly in the Yangzhou region.[45]

By the Ming dynasty (1368–1644), when the market for printed books had expanded even further — especially in towns where small-scale industries developed and there was a growing educated middle class — the distinction between high and low comedy became further blurred. Collections of *huaji*, jokes and humorous stories flourished, distributed sometimes as money-spinning ventures, but often also with subversive intent. Author-collectors, including retired officials and unsuccessful examination candidates who were often veering away from orthodox Confucianism in the direction of subversive Daoism, indulged in humorous writing and exacted revenge for grievances. Attacks were often veiled behind stereotypes and the identification of targets reveals as much about Ming society as the topics and named public figures in contemporary political jokes do about theirs.

Confucianism remained the official ideology of China for 2000 years, until the late nineteenth century, when intellectuals became convinced that the nation needed to modernize and began to regard Confucian teaching as supporting the status quo and inhibiting reform. Japanese and European ideas spread (in translation), and many students learned foreign languages and travelled overseas. Early in the twentieth century, the written language was reformed and came to approach the spoken language more closely, enabling literature and art to embrace a wider section of the community.

Nationalist (Republican) China proved an important transitional period for humour, including the "Year of Humour" declared by Lin Yutang in 1933.[46] The foreign colonial administration of Shanghai provided a sanctuary for scholars and writers, where they felt safe to poke fun or launch barbed humour at the follies and foibles of the old society and the corrupt administrations of officials and warlords. As literacy levels rose with the spread of modern education, appreciation of written humour spread to a wider audience. Newspapers and film opened up new media, including the advent of cartooning, combining verbal and visual humour. Aspects of these new media such as the work of early cartoonists are attracting increased attention in academic studies of humour in China.[47] In this era Japan, the Soviet Union and Western countries inspired and encouraged Chinese artists and writers to try new artistic forms of expression, including new approaches to wit and humour. Their success led to the government appropriating them for propaganda purposes, sometimes diluting or distorting the original free Daoist-type humour. One might say that they were conscripted for new Confucian-type uses. Also at this time Western theories of literature, aesthetics and humour inspired Chinese scholars, and lively debates ensued between the followers of Meredith — like Lin Yutang — and those of Bergson, like Qian Zhongshu and Lao She 老舍 (original name Shu Qingchun 舒慶春, 1899–1966).[48]

Another major influence on the expression of humour in the Republican period was the rise of the Chinese film industry, presenting new opportunities for both verbal and visual humour. A rich tradition of comic film drama arose, reflected for instance in the emergence in the 1990s of the "Happy-New-Year" movie.[49] Again, since the economic reforms of the 1980s in mainland China, the development of professional public relations has given rise to the technical preparation of propaganda, paralleling increasing use of propaganda by Western nations. Here humour — in the form of cartoons, slogans and officially disseminated jokes — was quickly identified as a useful sugar-coating for government propaganda, making it more memorable and easily digested. While Japan led the way in Asia, as Barak Kushner has shown,[50] China was not far behind. Chinese humour was sanctioned and promoted as propaganda aimed at the Japanese colonial power. More recently, the internet has added breadth and new forms to humour in Chinese society — especially parody in the form known as *e'gao* 惡搞.[51] Since China is reputed to have the world's greatest number of bloggers and mobile phones, it is not surprising that new forms of humour have also taken advantage of these new communication tools. Jokes and stories circulating in these media may often attack political phenomena or contribute to nationalist or chauvinist campaigns as the subversive power of humour exploits new forms.

Humour in China today is also reacting to and being transformed by trends towards commodification and commercialization. As part of the global community, young Chinese audiences respond to humour in advertising, just as their counterparts do elsewhere and with results very similar to those of other cultures around the world.[52] Local and state interests have followed this trend and promoted humour as a business enterprise. For instance, a museum of jokes opened recently in Wanrong, Shanxi province as a tourist business, displaying humorous sculptures and handcrafts, and selling joke books and other souvenirs.[53]

Humour Topics and Targets

C. T. Hsia referred to Chinese mentality being inspired by distrust of the use of brute force, as inculcated by Daoist principles, so that Chinese people admired *huaji* stories that demonstrated how quick and clever ideas got results while military and official demarches were fruitless. He quoted a story from the classic novel *San guo yanyi* 三國演義 (The

romance of the Three Kingdoms) about how General Zhuge Liang 諸
葛亮 (181–234 CE) acquired an arsenal of arrows from his enemy by
launching boats manned by straw men on a foggy night — the enemy
shot at the phantom army and the arrows stuck fast in the straw figures.[54]
This type of witty story is not unique to China, of course. The tales of
Till Eulenspiegel, the medieval German trickster, and his nineteenth-
century Czech parallel, the subversive Good Soldier Schweik, come
to mind. European wit, like its Chinese counterpart, consists of verbal
quickness and repartee. It is the special Chinese context — with its
cultural assumptions, topics and targets — that characterizes such *huaji*
stories, rather than any innately Chinese quality.

It is impossible to list all the other common butts of Chinese jokes
without the benefit of further detailed research, so three examples are
selected here. Firstly — and not surprisingly, given the potential for
observations about hypocrisy and incongruity — many traditional
jokes concern the role and habits of Buddhist and Daoist priests and
monks, such as the following:

> A Daoist priest, who was walking through the burial ground of a
> prince's palace, was bewitched by a host of evil spirits. He obtained
> the help of a passer-by, who saw him safely home. Said the priest
> to his rescuer: "I am deeply indebted to you for rescuing me, but
> I have no means of rewarding you. Here is an amulet which will
> keep off evil spirits. I beg you to accept it with my best thanks."[55]

The preponderance of jokes against the religious in classic collections
surely indicates not only their powerful status in society but also the
inability of lay people to counter-attack in any other way when venal
monks and abbots railed in their sermons against moral turpitude.
Similar pressures, of course, produced the comic diatribes of Chaucer,
Erasmus, Rabelais and Cervantes, among many others.

Another category of jokes, both old and new, concerns henpecked
husbands. A story from Feng Menglong 馮夢龍 (1574–1645), *Xiao fu*
笑府 (Treasurehouse of funny stories), illustrates men's difficulties in
maintaining socially approved gender roles:

> A group of henpecked husbands met to discuss ways of asserting
> the authority of the husband and maintaining masculine dignity.
> To give them a good scare, a certain busybody came up to inform
> them: "Your wives have got wind of this. They're coming up here

in a gang to give you fellows a good beating." Scared out of their senses, they all fled helter-skelter with the exception of one who just sat tight. People thought that he was the only one who was not afraid of his wife. A closer look revealed that he had already died of fright.[56]

Again, it is easy to find similar examples of jokes about henpecked husbands from other periods and other cultural traditions, including Jewish, British, Australian and Indian. Many cultures have ambivalent attitudes to gender roles and the taboos surrounding them.

Joking in China is not exempt from the use of ethnic or national stereotype characteristics. While a European joke may recount how Europe would be hell if Germans were the policemen, Swiss the lovers, English the cooks, Italians the bankers, and so on, similar geographical and racial out-groups provide butts for many similar Chinese jokes. One from the time of the 1911 Revolution asserted that Cantonese gave the money and Hunanese provided the army, but Zhejiang people became government officials. This highlighted how Chiang Kai-shek, a Zhejiang native, used many fellow provincials in his new government. Another joke says it is better to fight with people from Suzhou than to talk with people from Ningbo — it is generally held that Suzhou people talk quietly while those from Ningbo shout.[57] Such comic stereotypes demand the kind of collation and investigation afforded to collections in the West — a task that is, sadly, beyond the scope of the present volume.

Differences in style and content also reflect regional priorities and preoccupations. What is funny in Shanghai may be incomprehensible in Hong Kong or Taiwan, or in Overseas Chinese communities. While the differences are compounded by linguistic variation, as exemplified by the fact that Cantonese verbal puns simply do not make sense outside the Cantonese-speaking world, the gap is not simply linguistic. Absent cultural and/or local knowledge will affect the funniness of such regional jokes, in the same way it affects our ability to appreciate China's most ancient *huaji* collection, *Xiao lin*, because of the cultural gap that has occurred over time. Here, for instance, is a Taiwanese joke, the humour of which depends on knowing the names of Taiwanese political leaders in the 1980s. It will lose its significance entirely without this background knowledge:

Deng Xiaoping (the architect of mainland China's economic reforms) is being interviewed about the current political situation in Taiwan.

Interviewer: "Who is the current president of Taiwan?"

Deng (stalling for time): "Wait a moment!" *Deng huir!* 等回兒 [sounds like the personal name of the actual president, Li Teng-Hui 李登輝].

Interviewer: "And who do you think should be the next president?"

Deng (reaching for a cigarette): "Whoever you like." *Suibian* 隨便 [sounds like Chen Shui-bian 陳水扁, who did become the next president].[58]

There are differences in the topics of humour that appeal to Chinese men and women, but these are probably neither more nor less than in the rest of the world. Many Chinese men, like Australians or Americans, appreciate crude jokes about sex and other taboo subjects. One literary example is a parody of the *San zi jing* 三字經 (Three-character classic), a text traditionally used to teach Confucian morality.[59] It plays on a *double entendre,* where the Chinese character *xing* 性 means both nature and sex (this may be difficult to convey in translation):

人之初 性本善 性相近 習相遠

Original text: People at birth are naturally *xing* 性 good. Their natures *xing* are similar; their habits become different.

New reading: At the beginning of life, sex *xing* is good. Basically all sex *xing* is the same, it depends how you do it.

苟不教 性乃遷 教之道 貴以專

Original text: If neglected and not taught, nature *xing* deteriorates. The right way to teach it is with absolute concentration.

New reading: If you do not practise it all the time, sex *xing* will leave you. The way of learning it is basically to do it with only one person.

昔孟母 擇鄰處 子不學 斷機杼

Original text: Formerly the mother of Mencius chose her neighbourhood. When her child would not learn, she broke the shuttle *zhu* 杼 on her loom.

New reading: Once the mother, Mrs Meng, chose her neighbour to avoid bad [sexual] influences. If you don't study hard, your tool *zhu* will become useless.[60]

To sum up, Chinese humour topics are generally similar to humour topics elsewhere, but when one turns to the psychology and sociology of humour and laughter interesting differences do emerge, deriving from Confucian social etiquette that requires adult persons to exercise self-discipline. For instance, smiling in company is not encouraged. People having their photos taken straighten their mouths so as to appear serious. On the other hand, Chinese people often laugh when a serious mistake is discovered, and will laugh even more if the situation seems life-threatening — for example, a driver might well laugh if a wheel was about to fall off his vehicle. This kind of laughter is used involuntarily to cover up embarrassment. It does not indicate enjoyment of discomfort or other people's misfortune, but in the European cultural tradition it seems misplaced and inappropriate. Studying it with modern psychological tools represents a challenge that is being addressed by scholars in cross-cultural collaboration.

Naturally, not all Chinese people have the same taste in humour. Humour is an integral part of personality, and some individuals have greater sensitivity to or predisposition for finding humorous situations than others. Such personality differences mean that in all cultures some people will enjoy humour more than others in any given situation. Outliers, such as the well-known blogger and *Time* Person of the Year 2006, Wang Xiaofeng 王小峰, maintain that Chinese people in general have no sense of humour. According to Wang, their laughter is either in obedience to command or social expectation, or it is involuntary, like a hiccup or a fart.[61] Wang's view is a minority one, perhaps simply intended to be provocative. As the psychological studies referred to earlier are starting to show, personality differences in China are in fact alive and well, even if there is still much to learn about them.

Humour Types and Modes

Since humour in China can be found in many forms, both literary and conversational, this book does not pretend to do more than scrape the surface of a rich lode. As in the West, humorous literature (in both the broad and narrow senses) has always (*pace* the efforts of Qian Zhongshu, Lao She and Lin Yutang) been regarded as of lesser value than serious literature. As early as the Yuan dynasty, it nevertheless gave rise to specialized dramatic forms, such the theatrical comedy known as *xiangsheng* 相聲 (cross-talk) as well as to popular storytelling. Some of these forms might perhaps be called typically Chinese, but that claim must await appropriate cross-cultural studies. Another possibly unique humour mode is a tradition of amusing doggerel called *dayou shi* 打油詩, a Chinese literary game between friends where each picks up a thought or expression from the last and twists the meaning in an unexpected and therefore funny way.[62] Traditionally, scholar friends used *dayou shi* to cement relationships, and the practice is still widespread in the modern age, aided by the convenience of postings on blogs and websites. An anonymous example of *dayou shi* from a contemporary website goes as follows:

> "A" (in a female persona) writes:
> 打雷下雨狂风吹，心惊肉跳咋能睡？
> 老公短信送温情，独身一人自陶醉！
> Thunder and lightning and a wild wind blowing;
> Fearful and jumpy, how can I sleep?
> My old man sends me a love note;
> Left on my own, I become drunk.
>
> "B" responds:
> 陶醉之時人已睡，夢中與夫來相會。
> 睜眼雨停陽光照，老公早在身邊醉。[63]
> By the time she is drunk, she is already asleep.
> In her dream she meets her husband.
> When she opens her eyes, the rain is over and the sun out.
> And her husband is there at her side, drunk.

Less formal doggerel rhymes known as *shunkouliu* 順口遛 — something like folk rhymes — are surely paralleled by comparable forms in other languages and cultures; nevertheless, China has an infinite variety, often targeting social or political phenomena. One example will suffice:

> 打麻將三天五天不睡，
> 喝茅台三瓶五瓶不醉，
> 干正事三年五年不會。

> He can play mahjong for three to five days without sleep,
> And drink three to five bottles of Maotai liquor without a hangover,
> But he can't do anything properly in three to five years.

The *xiangsheng*, a comedic performance type mentioned above, is a dramatic exchange — usually between two actors — that makes extensive use of puns and allusions.[64] Originating in the Ming dynasty, *xiangsheng* became very popular in the twentieth century. It provided a vehicle for satirizing contemporary follies. Colin Mackerras reports that *xiangsheng* performer Hou Baolin 侯寶林 (1917–93) and others said these were "works of comic nature which use satire and humour as their principal base. Their satirical content strikes home at contemporary malpractices and also often includes political satire."[65] Recognizing their popularity, the propaganda department of the Chinese Communist Party regulated content, banning subversive and critical materials and proposing topics designed to support ideological campaigns. From the 1960s Cultural Revolution period onwards, *xiangsheng* thus lost their cutting edge and the original actors were replaced in their old age by younger Party-trained artistes. Not surprisingly, the artform then became stale and lost its popular appeal.

In twentieth-century films, radio and TV, humour has often depended on linguistic plays on words and *double entendres*, to which the Chinese language lends itself admirably, as already noted. The introduction of foreign films such as Chaplin's silent comedies, Laurel and Hardy, and Disney cartoons, along with the translation into Chinese of foreign humorous texts, reshaped the boundaries of what might be imagined as humorous. As in Japan and elsewhere, avant-garde novels, poetry and art reached out to humour and nonsense to express and respond to the ambivalences of modern life.[66] Forms of humour introduced from the West, such as cartooning, comic strips and humorous columns in newspapers and magazines, spread rapidly throughout China. Political lampooning through caricatures became common from the Nationalist period onwards, often directed or inspired by Soviet models.[67]

Common visual jokes in China today include cartoons, posters and sculpture. Contemporary art often incorporates humorous comment on social attitudes, consumerism and the political system, as typified by the work of performance artist Han Bing 韓冰 (b. 1974), whose

"Walking the cabbage movement" 遛白菜運動, in which he pulled a Chinese cabbage on a lead around various public arenas including Beijing streets, highlighted the urban revolution in material culture where households now rank pedigree pets more highly than staple foodstuffs.[68] Visual jokes in architectural form also have a long history in China, particularly in classical gardens, where follies such as teahouses and garden features often use oddities of scale and placement to poke fun at establishment values.[69] Visual jokes are also found in art history, including paintings, drawings and crafts such as porcelain, from very early times. This again deserves a study of its own.

Humour Under Changing Social Conditions

Humour has long given a voice to political protest, in China as elsewhere. As is well known, subversive use of humour was commonplace in Eastern Europe and the Soviet Union before the collapse of communism and studies of jokes from former Soviet-dominated countries show that underground jokes circulate among people who are not allowed to criticize publicly the government and ruling party.[70] Humour often turns against what Hsia calls "the powerful repressive forces of society"[71] in both a coping and a retaliatory fashion. Much Jewish humour falls into this category.[72] Although this topic has not yet been fully studied in China, Xue-liang Ding has pioneered the way and a forthcoming study addresses this aspect of humour, placing it in the context of relaxation of political control after a prolonged repression.[73] Ding's observations suggest that when censorship and social control were most rigid in China, humour could not be used at all; when some latitude is allowed, however, it seems to fulfil a need for self-expression and acknowledgement of unspoken truths.

Political controls were in fact gradually relaxed after the death of Mao Zedong in 1976. In 2004, the SARS epidemic presented a challenge to the Chinese government's information policies and became an economic as well as a health crisis. A crop of jokes circulated on the internet. Here is one example:

> What the Party couldn't fix, SARS did: The Party couldn't stop extravagant banqueting but SARS did; the Party couldn't stop

tourist travel using government funds but SARS did; the Party couldn't stop conferencing in scenic spots, but SARS did; the Party couldn't stop officials handing out false information, but SARS did; the Party couldn't stop prostitution but SARS did.[74]

Humour is risky in any situation where politics is highly charged, in China as elsewhere. In 2004, a Taiwan blogger published a "Happy anti-Bian guide", listing a hundred ways in which then President Chen Shui-bian might be deposed. All proposals were clearly jokes, many absolutely ridiculous; however, official attention focused on one suggestion that homemade bombs could be put on remote-controlled, miniature-model airplanes and directed at the presidential office. This was no joke to the police, who summoned the blogger for interrogation.[75]

Since humour belongs to the elites as well as the underdogs, it has always served to reinforce elite bonds, as in the case of the *Shishuo xinyu*, discussed by Lee. Members of the ruling classes may express their humour in a more relaxed way than common people, confident they themselves will be immune from criticism. Zhou, Mao and other political leaders did use humour, even in official meetings. The following anecdote was recorded during Zhou Enlai's meeting with the long-winded US envoy Henry Kissinger in 1972:

> *Kissinger:* I think the Prime Minister notices that I am especially inhibited in his presence right now.
>
> *Zhou Enlai:* Why?
>
> *Kissinger:* Because I read his remarks to the press that I am the only man who can talk to him for a half hour without saying anything.
>
> *Zhou Enlai:* I think I said one hour and a half.[76]

Although neither political jokes nor social satire are unique to China, the severity of repercussions they may incur underlines the continuing marginality of humour as a mode of discourse.[77] Admittedly, over recent years the CCP has relaxed censorship so that artists and writers have lost some fear of retribution if they cross agenda boundaries, either explicit or hidden. New forms of broad, gentle humour such as that of Lin Yutang are emerging in newspapers, television programs and writing, both fiction and non-fiction. It has become possible to critique social behaviour in general, as well as the interaction between social norms and political control. There are still, however, limits to freedom of expression and on some topics caution still prevails. In his regular column in the popular *Qingnian bao* 青年報 (Youth daily), the writer Wang Xiaobo 王小波 (1952–97) poured scorn on the attitude prevalent in China which assumed that only one side of any debate could be correct,[78] recounting what he called a well-known Western joke about a missionary who was captured by cannibals, trussed and roasted over an open fire. The missionary noticed that he was only roasting on one side and not the other and called out to his captors, "Turn me over, otherwise one side will be too well done and the other side will still be raw." Wang continued:

> The moral is: If you are not afraid to become a kebab, then there is nothing to stop you making jokes. But most of the savages who hear (you) do not laugh: there must be a certain level of civilization before people understand this kind of humour — and for this reason the disciples of humour get eaten by those with no taste and no sensibility.

Conclusion

Is there such a thing as a Chinese sense of humour? Clearly, humour and wit are appreciated and have flourished for centuries, continuing to thrive while adapting to profound changes. Although particular topics and formats may be more common and there are definite regional differences, the essence of humour in China is the same as elsewhere. It is neither Daoist nor Confucian. The frailty of humankind and the gap between expectations and reality are basic human dilemmas for all peoples. Rather than speaking of a peculiarly Chinese sense of humour, it may be useful to speak of humour "with Chinese characteristics". To do so would be to borrow a familiar contemporary Chinese political term and adapt it for the purposes of studying humorous ambiguity, irony and wit. "Socialism with Chinese characteristics" was an official term applied to policies developed by Deng Xiaoping to combine a market economy with political socialism.[79]

Social conventions about when, where, with whom and under what circumstances humour may be introduced are one significant area of difference in sense and style of humour between cultures. The uses and abuses of humour differ, as does the individual perception of the importance and relevance of humour in daily life. Globalization and increased communication with the outside world, especially via the internet, have internationalized forms of humour in China as elsewhere, but have not affected social conventions to the same degree. Differences remain. Comparative humour between China and other countries certainly needs better understanding and analysis. In terms of accessing Chinese humour by non-Chinese literate audiences, the need for translation — particularly of literary jokes and humorous writing — adds a level of difficulty (as well as itself contributing many examples of unintended funniness). What is most evident from our work preparing this book is that there is a continuous line of development from "classical" Chinese humour to the present day, so that many aspects of contemporary humour — and indeed contemporary society — can only be appreciated if they are seen in their historical and philosophical contexts.

This line of development now connects with other national and global types of humour but culture-specific themes persist (jokes about henpecked husbands originating from ancient joke books, for instance, have not died off but now circulate on the internet) and some themes have been dropped (such as jokes about randy monks, no longer relevant in today's secular society). New material is constantly added and old material discarded; international jokes are revised and localized; new formats invented, rediscovered, transformed. New media replace old, but humour — whether *huaji* or *youmo* — continues to evolve its vital role for Chinese culture.

2

The Theory of Humours and Traditional Chinese Medicine: A Preamble to Chapter 3

Jessica Milner Davis

All thinking and writing about humour sooner or later confronts issues of terminology and concepts relating to this complex form of human behaviour. In English, "humour" has shifted its meaning considerably down the centuries. Other times have privileged words such as "jest", "mirth", "wit" and even "the comic" (borrowed from the French expression *le comique*, meaning the essence of what is amusing) above "humour" as the general term for things related to laughter and amusement. The most important antecedent to present day usage is the ancient medical "theory of the humours", where the Latin word *humores* denoted the four primary body fluids or "humours": *chole* (yellow bile); *melanchole* (black bile); *flegma* (phlegm); and *sanguis* (Latin for blood). The first three are Greek names for the "surplus" fluids that are discharged in illness while the last, blood, causes illness when insufficient (as in anaemia or severe blood loss). These four were understood "in terms of a general cosmological theory in which fire, earth, air and water were the four basic elements of all things [and] physical constitution and psychological characteristics were determined by the balance or blend (L. *temperare*) of the humours".[1] Hence a humour defined a person's basic constitutional temperament, or type of personality, not just their evanescent mood or an experience of "humour" in the modern sense.

When the word came into English, as Willibald Ruch has pointed out, it "entered as *humour* into Middle English via French (responsible for the *ou*), still primarily a technical term, associated with the humor theory of temperament and humoral pathology".[2] It remained largely so until the late eighteenth and early nineteenth centuries, when "being humorous" became inextricably bound up with the idea of the even-tempered, wryly amused English gentleman (exemplified by *Punch* magazine[3]). The word then returned to modern French with precisely this connotation of gentle, *humour à l'anglais* (as opposed first to *humeur*, which retained the medical sense of character or mood as in *mauvaise humeur*, bad-tempered; and second to *esprit*, or lively wit, characteristically French).[4] From these antecedents, humour has now grown internationally to embrace all aspects of whatever is amusing, provoking laughter and smiles, regardless of mood or purpose.

In both its old and modern senses, humour has an important part to play in Traditional Chinese Medicine (TCM) and the traditional Chinese world-view of temperament and bodily health, as Rey Tiquia explains in Chapter 3. For this reason, it is important to explore the subject of the "humours". In fact, the two classical views — Eastern and Western — of the physical elements, of bodily "humours", of character and of health have much in common — although, as Jocelyn Chey notes in Chapter 1, it is also important that students of humour in its modern sense understand the differences. One obvious variation is that in TCM there are five elements (*wu xing* 五行),[5] not four; and since these affect both physical body and emotions, the two views of how the body operates and of appropriate therapies necessarily differ somewhat. This is particularly reflected in the way TCM conceives of, and is designed to promote, the centrality of the body's meridian *qi* 氣 circulation system (as stressed by Tiquia). Nevertheless, both theories rest upon the concept of balance in bodily and emotional health, and seek the goal of harmony for its essential contribution to health. In so doing, both seem to anticipate some aspects of modern psychology. To explore this intriguing idea a little further, I shall briefly sketch the development of the Western theory of humours and its connections with modern psychological thought.

Deriving from ancient Egyptian and Greek holistic concepts of the body and of temperament, this theory was expounded by Galen of Pergamon (129–199/217 CE),[6] himself greatly influenced by Hippocrates of Cos (c.460–c.370 BCE), the "father of medicine". By the late sixteenth century, it was the prevailing medical paradigm across Europe. Ruch describes how physiological theory at that time assumed that the mixture (*L. temperare* = to combine or blend in proper proportion) of the four humours in the make-up of a person was expressed in physical appearance, physiognomy and proneness to disease. Optimally, the humors are balanced, but a predominance of blood, phlegm, yellow bile or black bile yields, respectively, the sanguine, phlegmatic, choleric, and melancholic temperament.[7]

If the humours were not well balanced — allowing for a natural predominance of the one determining a particular character — then corrective treatment was prescribed, tailored to that patient's character.

The role of humour in the modern sense was also well understood by practitioners, in terms of its formative impact on character and also as a potential remedy. It was particularly endorsed by the French doctor and classical scholar Laurent Joubert (1529–83), who translated and published the relevant classics to correct what he saw as contemporary misunderstandings about the body. His pioneering *Traité du ris* (Treatise on laughter) was published originally in Latin and then in French in 1579, and its full title illustrates his positive evaluation of laughter.[8] In it, Joubert discusses many disability cases of persons unable to enjoy laughter (he terms them "agelasts") and the importance of attitude to laughter in identifying temperament, as well as in offering positive mood-enhancement. In England, as across the Channel, these concepts formed the basic belief-system for works which are still read as classics, such as Richard Burton's *Anatomy of melancholy* (1621) and Ben Jonson's pair of popular plays for the Elizabethan stage, *Everyman in his humour* (1598) and its sequel, *Everyman out of his humour* (1599).[9]

The vitality of the idea of "the humours" is shown by the longevity of the terms they generated. Noga Arikha's masterly study, *Passions and tempers: A history of the humours*,[10] points out that we continue to speak of melancholic and sanguine temperaments, even if the associated medical treatments such as administering things that are bitter or cold or their opposites died out long ago. While today's remedies for emotional distress are most likely to be defined in chemical terms, the old-fashioned selection did include "sending a patient to a different location", which sounds pretty much like a rest cure or modern respite care.

The theory went out of favour in the West generally with the advent of notions of strict dualism of mind and body promulgated by influential French philosopher René Descartes (1596–1650). Chronicling these matters in appreciative detail, Arikha explores many forgotten authorities hugely influential in their time, including Joubert. Importantly, her narrative concludes by reflecting on post-Cartesian attempts to reunite the mind and the body, beginning with Thomas Willis (1621–75), who pioneered investigations of the brain's neural anatomy,[11] and ending with today's explorations of positive psychology and its very practical messages embracing both cognition and emotion.[12]

Psychologists studying humour today strive to bring effective and practical approaches to the investigation and measurement of its various aspects and contemporary uses in personality, social life, politics, entertainment, education, the health professions, organizational behaviour and communications of all kinds, including advertising and informal internet groups. Their research corrects any lingering view from modern rationalists that humour, or "having a sense of humour", is purely a cognitive function. Experiencing things that make one laugh — or being repelled by them, as some people are (more extreme cases than Joubert's agelasts, these unfortunates are termed gelotophobes) — clearly involves emotion as well as cognition. Definitive evidence of this now comes from brain studies using functional magnetic resonance imaging (fMRI) to record activation of both affective and cognitive neural pathways when subjects respond to humorous stimuli such as cartoons.[13]

Modern scientific studies tend to focus on a descriptive approach to humour rather than investigating its prescription as therapy. Here the anticipatory significance of the theory of the humours for modern psychological symptomatology has been noted by Robert Stelmack and Anastasios Stalikas. Although Galen's own observations on character were few and did not correspond very well to the later four classic types, these researchers see his true legacy as a "descriptive typology of character that emerged in the eighteenth and nineteenth centuries [and] bears a remarkable resemblance to the extraversion and neuroticism dimensions".[14] Thus a line of inheritance runs from Galen, via Kant and Eysenck to today's *Diagnostic and Statistical Manual of Mental Disorders* (DSM).[15] Modern parallels to Joubert's case-studies of unbalanced agelasts take the shape of studies on gelotophobia and on humour in combination with the DSM-IV.[16]

The role of humour in therapy is, however, more complex. Despite some tentative progress and the emergence of popular movements such as "laughter yoga" and clown doctors, it is still hedged with scientific uncertainty.[17] What is agreed to be important is the need to clarify the models and types of humour and their uses, and correlations with good and bad outcomes. Thus we see the emergence of studies focusing on styles of use of humour in daily life, interpersonal behaviour, coping behaviour, self-esteem, and so on.[18] However, if questions still surround the applications of humour — particularly in physical health or in televised violence[19] — the more general point is nevertheless accepted: that good emotional balance is needed. Here the importance of ancient ways of thinking should not be under-estimated for providing insight into modern problems and lives.

At the heart of Rey Tiquia's chapter lies the notion of the elements (however computed and identified) as the "ultimate roots of all natural things": this carries with it the implication that what has been cast out of balance can, by the same means (or adaptations of it), be restored to balance. Methodologies may differ; however, in addressing health, today's professionals would surely agree. For good health of mind and body, we should emulate the ancient wisdom of the Golden Mean and seek the balance of equanimity, or *xin ping qi he* 心平氣和, that allows free-flow to the all-important *qi* 氣, the animating principle beyond all elements. We should ignore neither joy nor sorrow, anger nor compassion, humour nor seriousness, but equally should not allow any to master us for too long. We should also remember that experiencing humour is in itself both a positive and a negative emotion — delight mixed with shock or transgression — and that laughter can be used for both good and ill, to include and to exclude. Hence we see the importance of investigating the full range of types of humour and the most adaptive ways of using it beneficially today. The use of humour therapy in TCM reminds us that these very contemporary approaches share much with an older approach that is now attracting wider interest than in the past, not only among those in the Chinese diaspora, but also among a wide variety of patients seeking balance and wholeness in their lives and minds.

3

The *Qi* That Got Lost in Translation:
Traditional Chinese Medicine, Humour and Healing

Rey Tiquia

This chapter argues that there is a physical basis for humour according to traditional Chinese medicine (TCM), in which humour — that is, those funny stories or jokes that make one break into smiles or laughter — is linked with the emotion of happiness or joy. This makes humour a function of the operations of what I will call the "endogenous heart",[1] and I will outline why this should be so in TCM and explore the clinical consequences that flow from conceptualizing humour in this way. To some extent, such an understanding of humour may be compared with European theories in classical and medieval times of the four "humours" constituting the human body (yellow bile, blood, phlegm and black bile, which correlate with the four elements of fire, air, water and earth respectively). This Western notion of the four elements is comparable to the *wu xing* 五行 (five elements) of TCM — *mu* 木 (wood), *huo* 火 (fire), *tu* 土 (earth), *jin* 金 (metal) and *shui* 水 (water) — in the sense that in both philosophical systems the elements constitute the ultimate roots of all natural things.[2]

In making such a comparison, there is a risk of confusing the various meanings of the English word "humour", which then included not only the four cardinal humours of the body determining temperament but also the mental or temperamental states themselves, and now extends to the more general meaning of funny things and the experience of them. In the case of Chinese medical theory and the role of humour in maintaining good health, there is an additional confusion that derives from poor translation of Chinese terms involving *qi* 氣, which can be identified as "the circulating life force whose existence and properties are the basis of much of Chinese philosophy and medicine".[3] Accurate translation of this key term is essential, I believe, to grasping the essence of the connection between *qi* and humour and its role in TCM therapies.

Chinese medical healing emphasizes the need for balance between different types of *qi*, a balance that must vary according to season and environment. Although Western medicine now accepts the prevalence of affective as well as physical disorders, and Western psychology has turned at last from a preoccupation with negative affect to study hedonics or positive psychology,[4] these discoveries were anticipated centuries ago in China, where good humour and happiness have always been considered a requisite for the maintenance of good health. Such an approach suggests that laughter may indeed be good — perhaps the best — medicine. Good humour in the affective and bodily senses depends upon balance or equanimity, a state that is usually described in Chinese as *xin ping qi he* 心平氣和 or *xin he qi ping* 心和氣平 — that is, having a calm mood, being quiet in mind, having a peaceful disposition, having one's heart feel lighter, etc.[5] Although there are many such phrases in English that are roughly equivalent in meaning, if we analyse the original Chinese phrase, we can see that in each instance the word *qi* "got lost in the process of translation" and the translators have universally failed to understand the importance of *qi* in the TCM theory of human physiology.

To take one specific example, John DeFrancis translates *xin ping qi he* into a human ontology of someone "being even-tempered and good-humoured",[6] overlooking the role of *qi* in determining such bodily health and humour. Qi, together with the *yin* and *yang* 陰陽, the five elements/agents/phases and the eight trigrams of the *Book of changes* 八挂易經,[7] animates both our human bodies and the bodies of the universe around us. All these Chinese concepts carry complex metaphoric allusions that resist easy translation. Following the work of Leibniz (to be discussed below), they have sometimes been presented by European scholars as if they were scientific theories; in practice, however, they constitute the framework of TCM treatments and invoke notions of balance, opening up manifold possibilities for therapeutic intervention designed to redress imbalance.

In its earliest usage, *qi* referred to floating clouds, the breath and the atmosphere between heaven and earth. Chinese origin stories relate how the universe emerged from cosmological confusion when the bright, light *yang qi* ascended to become Heaven, and the thick, heavy *yin qi* descended to become Earth. Properly understood, therefore, *qi* is the origin of the entire universe. The chapter "Disquisition on astrology" (Tianwen xun 天文訓) in the second-century BCE work of philosophy *Huainanzi* 淮南子 (which blends Confucian, Daoist and Legalist thought) states:

> In the beginning, nothing had physical shape, and the first spontaneous formations were the continua of space and time. Out of these were produced the original *qi*.[8]

In the Song dynasty, Neo-Confucianism[9] drew on the Confucian classics as well as early texts such as the *Huainanzi* to formulate a cosmogony predicated on the "Dichotomy of principle", contrasting *li* 理 and *qi*; this in turn gave way to a new vitalist ontology that emerged in the seventeenth century. Founded on materiality and the actualities of life, this new way of thinking gave rise to a vitalism centred upon *qi*, which came to dominate the century's thinking and created a monistic philosophy of *qi* that "stressed the vivid, immediate and ultimate completion of a concrete and dynamic life expressed in terms of *Qi* (material force) and *Qi* (concrete things and implements)".[10] These views have prevailed since that time, at least among theoreticians of TCM. Dai Zhen 戴震 (1724–77), one of the main proponents of this new philosophical school, identified *qi* with the *dao* 道, contending that:

> *Dao* is like movement (*xing* 行). The evolutionary operations (*hua* 化) of the Ether (*qi*) produce and reproduce without pause. That is why this process is called the *Dao*.[11]

This new philosophy had found an early resonance in the practice of medicine and helped innovate the *Wen bing* (Warm febrile diseases) school of medicine founded by Wu Youxing 吳有性 (c. 1580–1660). In *Wen yi lun* 瘟疫論, first published in 1642, Wu stated that *qi* is "a boat with oars (i.e. a vessel) that moves and transports fire",[12] and elaborated this material nature of the *qi*:

> Things or matter are products of the transformation (*hua* 化)[13] of *qi*, while *qi* is a resultant product of changes in things. Hence we can say that *qi* is matter while matter is *qi*. Knowing that *qi* can put matter into order (*zhi* 治)[14] then we know that matter can put *qi* into order. Matter or things that put *qi* into order are referred to as *yaowu* 藥物 [medicinal] matter.[15]

From this simple, irreductionist understanding of medicinal matter, or *yaowu*, derive routine therapeutic practices designed to move and transform a patient's *qi*. From the larger "natureworld" of Heaven-Earth (*tiandi* 天地) and its five locales (north, south, east, west and centre) flow the movements[16] of the five elements (wood, fire, earth, metal, water) and their five transformations and changes (birth [breeding and growth], growth, transformation, harvest and storing). These in turn generate the five seasons (spring, summer, long summer, autumn and winter) and the five *qi* (cold, heat, dryness, damp and wind).[17] Since the human world and the nature world are of one *qi*,[18] the human world arouses (*gan* 感) and responds to (*ying* 應)[19] the five *qi* from Heaven. The *qi* presence is thus something to be "felt", and TCM practitioners who have been trained to feel its presence can detect its movement in their own bodies as well as in other "bodies". The practitioners embody the *qi* and thus the *qi* can assume life as a balancing tool. "Sensing" its presence in their own bodies and its "projection" into ordinary medical tools such as the acupuncture needle or herbs, practitioners help other bodies feel and be aware of the presence of their own *qi*, thus assisting them to put their own disharmonious *qi* into balance and creating an environment for good humour in body and affect.

On the basis of information from European missionaries in China, the philosopher and mathematician Gottfried Leibniz (1646–1716) put forward a commentary emphasizing the subtle nature of *qi*. He equated it with "ether" or "matter in its original form", and thus afforded *qi* a place in Western reasoning. He wrote:

> It seems that this *qi*, or this primitive air, truly corresponds to matter, just as it corresponds to the instrument of the first principle, which moves matter; just as the artisan moves his instrument, producing things. This *qi* is called air, and for us could be called ether [in original translation spelt AETHER] because matter in its original form is completely fluid, without bonds or solidity, without any interstices and without limits which could distinguish parts of it from the other. In sum, this matter (*qi*) is the most subtle one can imagine.[20]

In TCM practice, *qi* needs to be understood as an ontological entity that is enacted or performed. In clinical encounters, *qi* is performed to differentiate between clinical patterns and to associate the appropriate *yaowu.* The natural body (which is alive and full of *qi*) is enacted in practices that are a natural part of the whole body. The medical treatments and materials include acupuncture, traditional Chinese massage (*tuina* 推拿), food therapy (*shiliao* 食療), the use of *materia medica*, emotional counter-therapy and *qi* exercises, such as *qigong* 氣功 and tai chi (*taijiquan* 太極拳). The varied *qi* motions of individual *yaowu*, or of a group of them collected in a standardized formula known as a *fang* 方, are chosen to fit the clinical pattern of imbalance or disequilibrium in the uneasy body of the patient. *Qi* exercises, Chinese herbal medicine, acupuncture and emotional counter-therapy all act in the same way to rebalance the *qi*. Emotional counter-therapy realizes its medicinal objective by using one of the seven recognized emotions to counter-balance any extreme emotion that manifests clinically as an abnormal flow of *qi*. The concepts and rationale behind this line of therapy will be dealt with in more detail below, but here it is enough to say that in this way correct balance and good humour can be restored and the patient's bodily ailments will benefit from such treatment.

One Western authority, Joseph Needham, has referred to the *qi* as the "doctrine of pneuma" and concluded that it evolved during the thirteenth century to mean:

> all forms of matter, from the most condensed to the most tenuous; in ancient China it referred rather to subtle matter (comprising what we should now think of as gases and vapours, radioactive emanations, radiant energy, etc.) and invisible biological influences (including nerve influences, hormonal actions, infection and contagion). In medical thought *qi* was something like a vital force in living mind–body organisms, acted upon favourably or unfavourably by other *qi* from the environment, but also itself sometimes capable of spontaneous malfunction.[21]

His description underlines the wide scope of *qi* as it affects body, mind and mood (or humour), for both good and bad.

As an ontological entity, *qi* animates the human body in four directional states of orientation: upwards, downwards, inwards and outwards. In this way, the normal distribution, circulation and metabolism of not only the body's *qi*, but also blood, thin and thick body fluids, spirit, refined *qi* and so on can all be ensured. If this animating *qi* flow is disrupted, then bad humour, illnesses and disease may result. Yanhua Zhang, who has collected material about contemporary mainland practice in *qi* treatments, describes the process as follows:

> What is central about *qi* is what it does — its functions. They are summarized as promoting human physiological activities, keeping up the body's temperature, defending the body from invasion of "heteropathic *qi*", reinforcing and conserving the vital substance of the body, and transforming bodily substances. Normal functions are achieved through orderly motions of *qi* characterized as moving up, going down, coming in and going out. The dynamic balance is upset if certain *qi* is supposed to go up but goes down instead, or if certain *qi* moves too fast or too slow. For example, the heart *qi* goes down, while the kidney *qi* is going up. The liver *qi* spreads out while the lung *qi* clears downward. When the movement is obstructed, the result is the disordered *qi* mechanism, such as stagnation, congestion, blockage, and closure of *qi*, which lead to all kinds of somatic and psychological symptoms.[22]

The impact of *qi* upon mental and mood states is also noted by Ma Zhongxue, who claims that changes in human emotional/affective states exert significant influence upon the various endogenous organ-systems.[23] As indicated at the outset of this chapter, by the endogenous heart I mean not only the physical heart but also its animating forces that generate emotions. It is best conceptualized as the internal, metaphoric equivalent of the "exogenous fire element" (*huo xing* 火行) within the human body. As we shall see, other organs besides the heart can also be termed endogenous.[24]

On the other hand, the endogenous organ-systems also function in synchronicity with the rhythms of growth and decline as well as the rise and fall of the *yin* and *yang* energies and the cycle of the four seasons. Hence the harm that emotion/affect can inflict will depend on variations in the flow of the temporal rhythm. Generally speaking, during any specific season, when a particular emotion/affect is generated from a specific endogenous organ-system, the flow of *qi* and blood towards this inner organ will thrive and thus emotion will not harm that organ — but it may sometimes harm the organ that it "restrains", resulting in what is known as a deficient clinical pattern. For instance, when an emotion/affect emerges from one endogenous organ-system that can be "overcome" by another, the second organ is said to be "easily bullied". Even when the emotion/affect occurs in an inner organ that cannot actually be overcome by another, the latter will still bully the former, producing injury to both. For example, happiness is the emotional aspiration of the heart and the heart is the "son" of the liver/wood element (which can thus be bullied by the heart). Thus, when a person is "injured" by being excessively happy during the spring season, clinical symptoms emerge whereby the heart *qi* slackens in its flow, together with manifestations of liver–blood depletion and deficiency. Other temporally related emotional changes involving different inner organs will follow a similar logic, which offers practitioners valuable insights into the treatment and adjustment not only of physical ailments, but also of emotional instabilities. Emotion is in fact the key. As the Japanese philosopher Yuasa Yasuo observed: "Eastern medicine's theory of the body takes emotion as the flow of *qi*."[25] The schema in Figure 3.1 provides help in visualizing these complex interactions.

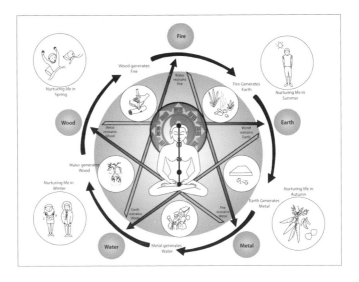

Figure 3.1 Temporally related emotional changes involving different inner organs of the body, shown in a diagrammatic representation of "Nature according to the five elements". Artwork by Ana Marikit Tiquia, based on conceptualizations widely used in TCM.

As positive psychology continues its investigations into positive mood and affect and what supports them, perhaps we may see a reappraisal of the ancient but fruitful concepts outlined above. For TCM, human emotions are conceived of as generated from the five endogenous visceral organs. When emoting, however, an experiential response to given stimuli may be disproportionate or excessive in terms of affect. If so, this can interfere with the normal operation of the *qi* flow and therefore cause illness. As Nathan Sivin points out, this has been understood since the foundations of TCM:

> Abnormal emotion could affect *qi* functions, as [detailed] in a tractate on the causes of pain in the Basic Question of the Inner Canon of the Yellow Lord: "I know that all medical disorders arise from the *qi*. Anger *nu* 怒 makes the *qi* rise; joy *xi* 喜 relaxes it; sorrow *bei* 悲 dissipates it; fear *kong* 恐 makes it go down; cold contracts it; heat makes it leak out; fright *jing* 驚 makes its motion chaotic; exhaustion consumes it; worry *si* 思 congeals it." The results are physical; for instance, "Anger reverses the flow of the *qi*. When it is extreme (the patient) will vomit blood or void 'rice-in-liquid' diarrhoea."[26]

Thus the story behind TCM is a composite one, integrating a number of ways of capturing the concept of balance. Together, these methods sensitively detect imbalance and provide a framework for recommendations to restore balance.[27] In TCM, health is defined as a balance between the *yin* and the *yang*, and a healthy body is one where there is balance between body and mind, as well as between the human body and the body of the environment. Health means having a life free from discomfort, pain and suffering, which are seen as indices on a scale of deviation from balance. The ideology of health-as-balance is actually enshrined in the character for medicine, *yi* 醫, as well as in the character for balance, *ping* 平. *Ping* means free expansion on all sides, level-headed or tranquil. Thus a balanced and healthy person is referred to as a *ping ren* 平人, level-headed, calm and in harmony with themselves and the world around. Such a person enjoys freedom from extremes and deviations. When the balance of *yin* and *yang* is disrupted, dis-ease (*bing* 病) and its clinical patterns emerge. In TCM, therefore, the general therapeutic approach to clinical patterns of imbalance is to restore the balance (*yi ping wei qi* 以平為期). Parallel to the recognition of health as balance and illness as imbalance is the utilization of the balancing attributes (therapeutic action or *gong xiao* 功效) of thousands of TCM remedies.

TCM identifies the seven emotions of happiness, anger, worry, pensiveness, sadness, fear and terror as normal human spiritual expressions. As described above, under certain circumstances sudden emotional fluctuations that exceed the normal sphere of control — such as being too angry, too sad, too terrified and so on — can affect the circulation of *qi* and will eventually affect the normal functioning of the endogenous organs and the acu-tract system of the body. The acu-tracts (*jingmai* 經脈) are the pathways (*lujing* 路經) of *qi* transformations, originating from the visceral or hollow organs.[28] Excessive anger, for example, makes the *qi* surge upwards; excessive worry depresses its flow; too much joy or happiness (as discussed above) slows its circulation; excessive grief dispels it; excessive pensiveness makes it coalesce into a knot and cause obstruction; fear makes it descend dramatically; while terror or fright creates chaotic *qi* movement. Extreme anger can affect the endogenous liver organ-system as it may make the liver *qi* rise dramatically, bringing about a clinical pattern with symptoms of chest congestion, pain, congestion along the flanks of the body, dizziness and loss of appetite. Grief or extreme sadness can affect the normal functioning of the endogenous lung system — which, in addition to respiratory functions, is also responsible for the circulation of *qi* all over the body. Extreme sadness can thus bring about a clinical pattern with symptoms of lack of energy, discomfort in breathing and coughing.

Other examples of emotional imbalance include extreme worry and inescapable pensiveness, which can harm the spleen system responsible for the transformation and transportation of food. Constant brooding and worrying cause "idleness of the stomach", another recognizable clinical pattern characterized by loss of appetite. Excessive fright can affect the normal functioning of the kidney system, which in TCM is considered to be responsible for reproduction, regeneration and excretion of body waste. Excessive fright also often leads to general weakness all over the body, and sometimes to stool and urine incontinence — a phenomenon known in TCM as "fright bringing about the downward movement of the *qi*". Terror can likewise affect the normal functioning of the heart system that houses the spirit, causing a loss of tranquillity and leading to nervous disorders. Although happiness is the manifestation of pleasant feelings that are beneficial to the body, in extremes it too can be harmful to the heart system, as it can lead to disturbance and loss of tranquillity, sleep and even appetite.

To address clinical patterns brought about by such extremes of emotions, TCM naturally prescribes careful balancing. Since the *qi* dramatically surges upwards in the body as a result of anger, the countering emotional therapy of grief is used to dispel it. Excessive worry will lead to a depressed or trapped *qi*; hence happiness is prescribed to facilitate the *qi*'s smoother flow. Excessive grief and sadness that dispel *qi* can be rectified by the emotion of pensiveness or reflection, which knots the flow of *qi* in order to restore harmony. Excessive pensiveness and brooding over a particular problem can obstruct the free flow of *qi* by stagnating it, so the counter-balancing emotion of anger, which moves the *qi* upwards and dispels any *qi* obstruction, is used. Finally, fright, which causes the *qi* to move in chaotic directions, can be balanced by the emotion of worry, which traps and depresses the *qi*.[29]

In the case of the emotion of happiness or joy (thus humour), TCM practitioners such as Yang Yongxuan 杨永璇 (1901–81) have taken the view that this cannot possibly harm the endogenous heart. Thus they privilege the emotion of happiness above the other six emotions. Yang based his views on the Ming dynasty scholar Yang Jizhou 杨继洲 (1522–1620), author of the acupuncture classic *Zhenjiu dacheng* 針灸大成 (The compendium of acupuncture and moxibustion), first published in 1601, who said, "People who are happy suffer from less illness because their *qi* flows harmoniously and in a relaxed manner along the acu-tracts" — that is, they come to have a balance of heart and mind and a *qi* (*yang*) and blood (*yin*) that flow in harmony with the world around them (*xin he qi ping* 心和氣平).[30] When dealing with clients whose endogenous organs had been harmed by excessive emotional stimulus, on the other hand, Yang would guide them patiently and systematically, while consoling and helping them see what was right and sensible. He took the view that it was right to "humour them [*yi yan xi zhi* 以言戲之] so that they can smile through their tears [*po ti wei xiao* 破涕為笑]",[31] and he related jokes to such patients to help restore the right flow of *qi*. As Needham puts it:

> When one feels naturally happy, and free from self-seeking and upsetting personal desires or greedy ambitions, then the salutary *qi* of necessity responds and follows. Vitality thus guarding from within, how can diseases originate?[32]

This explanation of the practical functioning of *qi* serves to demonstrate how, in TCM, humour in both its bodily and emotional senses can be seen as linked to the presence or absence of good health. It also shows how, according to classical Chinese medical theory, good humour (in the modern Western sense) is a natural effect of the alignment of emotions and seasons, which if absent should be restored. Such views are shared by most TCM authorities, even if their own clinical practices of emotional counter-therapy may differ from those of Yang Yongxuan. When the balance of emotions has been disturbed due to endogenous or exogenous factors, humour and its accompanying laughter can and do have a therapeutic function, serving to ease the flow of *qi* in the body. Perhaps in laughter and humour, then, we can hope to find a rapprochement between ancient and modern approaches to health and positive mood.

4

The Classical Confucian Concepts of Human Emotion and Proper Humour

Weihe Xu

In considering the Confucian concept of proper humour, this chapter makes three arguments. First, its rationale is the same as that underpinning Confucian regulation of human emotions, since humour was seen as deriving from a basic human passion, delight (*le* 樂). Second, the Confucian touchstone of propriety is "the mean", embodied by the Confucian Rites (*li* 禮).[1] Third, in accordance with the spirit of the Rites, proper humour should be moderate, private, tasteful, useful and benign.

The concept of proper humour is termed "classical Confucian" because it derives predominantly from the 13 Confucian classics (*shisan jing* 十三經). Although not necessarily identical with the views of the historical Confucius 孔子 (551–479 BCE), this concept nevertheless reflects the beliefs and value systems of a Confucian or Ruist (*rujia* 儒家)[2] world-view, rather than a Daoist, Moist, Legalist or Buddhist outlook. Strictly speaking, it is anachronistic to talk about ancient notions of humour, since even in the West such a concept did not really exist until the seventeenth century; in China it did not appear until the early 1930s, when the modern English term "humour" was transliterated into Chinese as *youmo* 幽默. Yet much of what we now call humour must have existed in Chinese antiquity, just as trees existed before the word *mu* 木 or *shu* 樹 was invented. Certainly special words were coined to designate such pleasurable experiences.

One of the earliest such terms was *xue* 謔 (joking), and terms for other kinds of the laughable include *guji* or *huaji* 滑稽 (the glib or laughable),[3] *xie* 諧 (jest), *ji* 譏 (to ridicule) and *chao* 嘲 (to deride). The ancient Chinese also developed etiquettes (often tacit) of laughter and joking. These inchoate ethics of mirth are reflected in the Confucian classics, from which we can infer the Confucian concept of proper humour. It must be deduced because the ancient Chinese — albeit a humorous people[4] — hardly ever theorized their mirthful experiences. There was no Chinese equivalent of Plato's comments on laughter and the laughable in *Philebus*, of Aristotle's discussion of comedy in *Poetics* or of Cicero's treatise on the rhetoric of wit and jest in *De oratore*. The first Chinese essay on jesting appeared six centuries after Cicero, at the turn of the sixth century CE. Written by Liu Xie 劉勰 (465–522), it forms Chapter 15 of *Wenxin diaolong* 文心雕龍 (The literary mind and the carving of dragons).[5] Even this is descriptive or prescriptive rather than analytical. More theoretical Chinese discourse of humour would have to wait another millennium until the Ming–Qing period (1368–1911).[6] Forced by such reticence, we must extrapolate ancient Chinese thought on humour from a few scattered remarks on mirth or from recorded examples of conduct.

Early Confucian classics often enumerate basic human feelings. The shortest of these inventories consists of only *hao* 好 (like) and *wu* 惡 (dislike),[7] while the longest contains 11;[8] the usual number ranges from four to seven.[9] Almost all such lists include *xi* 喜 (joy), but many also include *le*, a passion born of joy (*le sheng yu xi* 樂生於喜),[10] usually rendered in English as "delight". Just as "delight" connotes feeling or giving great joy, *le* was regarded as one of the two strongest human emotions, the other being *ai* 哀 (grief).[11] And laughter was seen as a common expression of such joy and delight — for instance, "laughter is the sound of joy" (*xiao, xi sheng ye* 笑，喜聲也); "when people feel joy, they laugh" (*renqing xi ze xiao* 人情喜則笑); and "when their thoughts are moved by delight, they will laugh" (*si she le qi bi xiao* 思涉樂其必笑).[12] Hence joy and delight are mirthful pleasures. Had the modern concept of humour been available to the ancient Chinese, it would probably have been classified as a kind of mirthful amusement, since joking (*xue* 謔) was already conceptualized as a way of making sport (*xi* 戲) by using speech (*yan* 言) to express malice (*nue* 虐) and get a laugh.[13] In other words, *xue* was already treated as a delightful form of emotional expression.

The Classical Confucian Position on Human Emotion

Since mirthful amusement was regarded as an emotion, outlining the classical Confucian position on emotion will reveal the philosophical, ethical and political underpinnings for the Confucian concept of proper humour. Advocated by Confucius, his grandson Zi Si 子思 (c.483–402 BCE), Mencius 孟子 (390–305 BCE) and Xunzi 荀子 (340–245 BCE), this position has been greatly clarified by one of the pre-Qin (221–206 BCE) texts recently discovered at Guodian 郭店, entitled *Xing zi ming chu* 性自命出 (Human nature comes from the decree of Heaven; hereafter *XZMC*). Its alleged author, Zi Si, supposedly also wrote the *Zhongyong* 中庸 chapter in the *Liji* 禮記 (The Book of Rites).[14] These two texts (*XZMC* and *Zhongyong*) cast especially valuable light on the conservative Confucian attitude towards emotion, which can be characterized succinctly as *containment through regulation*. As Confucius observed, "It is rare that people err because of self-restraint" 以約失之者鮮矣 (*Lunyu*, 4.23),[15] and he was also quoted as asserting the necessity of regulating one's life.[16] Xunzi similarly admonished that "although desires cannot be uprooted, we should seek to restrain them" 慾雖不可去，求可節也 (*Xunzi*, 243).

In ancient China, emotion (*qing* 情) was believed to be part and parcel of human nature (*xing* 性), as early usage of *qing* connoted basic instincts, exemplified in the *Liji*: "What are called human *qing*? Joy, anger, sorrow, fear, love, dislike and desire. Humans are capable of these seven feelings without learning." 何謂人情？喜，怒，哀，懼，愛，惡，慾，七者弗學而能 (*Liji*, 164). In sources such as *Xunzi* and *Da Dai Liji* 大戴禮記 (The Book of Rites by Dai De), *xing* denotes *qing* and vice versa.[17] The *XZMC* construes this integral nature and the genesis of *qing* as follows:

> 喜怒哀悲之氣，性也。及其見於外，則物取之也 … 情生於性。The ethers of joy, anger, sorrow, and grief are human nature. When they are manifested outwardly, it is because they are brought out by [external] things . . . *Qing* issues from human nature. (*XZMC*, 134)

The implications here are radical and profound. First, since humans are emotional beings, their primeval, non-deliberative reactions to the outer world will be emotional as well as physical. Second, since emotion is integral to humanity, without it we cannot be completely human. Third, since human nature is irreducible and bound to manifest itself, trying to eradicate emotion or forbid its expression is futile. Therefore, the Confucians believed in balancing physical (or psychological) tension with relaxation and in channelling emotion towards propriety through the Rites (*Liji*, 254, 272, 294). Constant suppression of emotion was seen as harmful to health and dangerous to society, since when pent-up emotions erupt they can disrupt personal or social life. This assumption underlies, for instance, Xunzi's repudiation of Mozi's 墨子 (468–376 BCE) opposition to music, since that is an indispensable means of guiding people to express their emotions properly in order to avoid social chaos (*Xunzi*, 214–17).

Just as humans are fundamentally emotional beings, the Confucian Way (*Rudao* 儒道) is fundamentally an emotive way (*qingdao* 情道), rooted in human nature. The syllogism behind the classical Confucian outlook on emotion (*qingdaoguan* 情道觀) can be constructed by rearranging statements from the *XZMC* and the *Zhongyong*: (a) following human nature is called the Way (*shuai xing zhi wei dao* 率性之謂道); (b) emotion [first] comes out of human nature (*qing chu yu xing* 情出於性); therefore, (c) the Way starts with emotion (*Dao shi yu qing* 道始於情).[18]

This does not mean that one should follow emotion wherever it leads, for the Confucians also believed in building the Way (*xiu dao* 修道) so that it ends in righteousness (*yi* 義).[19] Michael Puett aptly paraphrases: "*Qíng* . . . is how one would spontaneously respond to a situation, while *yì* is how one ought to respond."[20] Here, *yi* represents the aggregate of all that is good (*qunshan zhi jue ye* 群善之絕也), or what refines human nature (*li xing zhe* 厲性者) (*XZMC*, 144). Hence the Confucian Way is ultimately a moral path that aims to elevate humankind from emotional being to moral being.

Depending on the view one takes of human nature, there are three major Confucian arguments against untrammelled emotion. First, if human nature is innately evil (as Xunzi contended), then blindly following emotion (or, worse, desire) will lead to social chaos and animalistic degeneration (*Xunzi*, 42). Second, if human nature is innately good (as Mencius maintained), one still should not follow emotion freely because external forces can corrupt original goodness and pollute one's feelings. Finally, if human nature is inherently neither evil nor good (as deemed by Gaozi 告子, c.420–c.350 BCE),[21] there are still the dangers of either deficiency or excess in emotion. For classical Confucians, therefore, the wisest way of dealing with emotion was to *regulate* it by providing an adequate outlet and setting bounds to expression, thereby guiding it towards righteousness.

In the Confucian view, righteousness, propriety and the mean (*zhongyong*) are one and the same. Thus the *XZMC* uses *yí* 宜 (propriety) and *yì* 義 (righteousness) interchangeably;[22] the *Liji* defines righteousness as propriety (*yì zhe yí ye* 義者宜也) (376); and the *Baihu tong* 白虎通 (The comprehensive discourse on the classics in the White Tiger Hall) states that righteousness is proper, which means that judgements and decisions all attain the mean (*yi zhe yi ye, duan jue de zhong ye* 義者宜也，斷決得中也).[23] Therefore, the way to guide emotion towards righteousness is to make its expression proper or moderate, since going too far is just as bad as falling short (*guo you buji* 過猶不及) (*Lunyu*, 11.16). A popular analogy for the perfect balance between excess and deficiency is the precisely level (*ping* 平) arm of a steelyard (*heng* 衡).[24]

Confucius lamented that human attainment of constant moderation was rarely seen (*Lunyu*, 6.29), and that even when the wish was present, people could not achieve it for long unless they were sages (*Liji*, 370, 371, 372). This is particularly true of finding and keeping the mean of one's emotions, which was imperative for Confucians wishing to act properly since passion spurs action. As the *XZMC* observed, one would not act (*xing* 行) on one's will (*zhi* 志) until one's nature and heart/mind were pleased (*dai yue er hou xing* 待悦而後行).[25] This seems to say that propriety in action is determined by balance in passion.

Accordingly, before exhorting constant practice of moderation, the *Zhongyong* defines the mean in terms of basic human passions.[26] It posits two kinds of emotion, the not-yet-aroused (*weifa* 未發) and the aroused (*yifa* 已發) (recalling the *XZMC*'s ethereal and manifest emotions). As a result, there are two kinds of emotional balance: the natural equilibrium (*zhong* 中) of not-yet-aroused emotions, and the harmony (*he* 和) of emotions aroused in due proportion through artificial rebalancing. The natural equilibrium is "the all-inclusive ground of existence of the universe as a cosmic whole" (*daben* 大本), while the human-made harmony constitutes "the unimpeded path of the fullest attainment in the world of human experience" (*dadao* 達道).[27] This duality — echoing the *XZMC*'s suggestion that the Confucian (and humane) Way starts with emotion and ends in righteousness — implies that one key to adhering to the Way lies in constantly rebalancing aroused passions and their expressions: the lifelong task of building the Way, which is called education (*xiu dao zhi wei jiao* 修道之謂教) (*Liji*, 370).

The ultimate instrument of Confucian education is the Rites, which are all-encompassing guidelines for human conduct, embodying righteousness, propriety and the mean. The *Liji* declares, "Without the Rites, there would be no attainment of the Way, virtue, humaneness or righteousness." (*Dao de ren yi, fei li bu cheng* 道德仁義，非禮不成) Asked what represents the mean, Confucius replied, "It's the Rites, the Rites! The Rites make the mean." (*Li hu li! Fu li suo yi zhi zhong ye* 禮乎 禮！夫禮所以制中也) (*Liji*, 14, 163, 164, 344, 352) He defined the sagely virtue of *ren* 仁 (humaneness) as the ability to discipline oneself so as never to do anything against the Rites (*Lunyu*, 12.1; cf. also 8.2). Hence to be righteous and proper in expressing one's (aroused) emotions is to rebalance them according to the Rites.

The intimate correlation between the Rites and emotion is not only because the Confucian Way was believed to start with emotion and end in righteousness, but also because the Rites were believed to be the substance of righteousness (*Li ye zhe, yi zhi shi ye* 禮也者，義 之實也). It was even claimed that the sage kings had established the essence of righteousness and the order of the Rites so as to govern human emotion (*Shengren xiu yi zhi bing, li zhi xu, yi zhi renqing* 聖人 脩義之柄，禮之序，以治人情) by ordering (*zhi* 治), regulating (*jie* 節), patterning (*wen* 文), adorning (*shi* 飾) and balancing (*ping* 平) it (*Liji*, 160, 164, 167). Although imposed from without, the Rites were never viewed as alien to humanity, since their invention was based on, or stemmed from, human emotion (*li zuo yu qing, li sheng yu qing* 禮作 于情, 禮生于情) (*XZMC*, 151, 49n). Thus, being in accord with human nature, they can guide people to reach the Heavenly Way by following the general course of human emotion (*Suo yi da tiandao, shun renqing zhi dadou* 所以達天道, 順人情之大竇) (*Liji*, 167). An underlying assumption here is that anything against human nature is doomed to fail. Thus the Rites were regarded as the most effective instruments to civilize and sublimate human nature; to regulate and discipline emotion; to order and harmonize the family, the state and the world; and to make people *junzi* 君子 (gentlemen).[28] Poem 52 in the *Shijing* 詩經 (Book of songs) derides those who fail to observe the Rites as worse than rats and deserving an early death.[29]

The ethics and politics of this classical Confucian philosophy of rebalancing aroused emotions (*qingdao zhongyong guan* 情道中庸觀) are summarized by the *Liji* in the following way: the purpose for which the sage kings created the Rites and music (the harmoniser of emotions) was to teach people how to balance their likes and dislikes so as to return them to the rectitude of the human way (*jiang yi jiao min ping hao wu er fan rendao zhi zheng ye* 將以教民平好惡而反人道之正也) (*Liji*, 256). The initial formulation of the conservative position on emotion can now be expanded as *containment through regulation by constantly re-balancing emotional expressions on the scales of the Rites*. The same principle underlies the Confucian ethics of mirth.

The Confucian Concept of Proper Humour

Like all emotions, laughter and humour are indispensable and often irrepressible. The *Lunyu* records that, having heard that the late Gongshu Wenzi 公叔文子 had never laughed, Confucius asked one of Gongshu's retainers whether this was true. The latter replied that it was an exaggeration: in fact, his master had laughed, but only when he was delighted, so that nobody ever became weary of his laughter (*Le ran hou xiao, ren bu yan qi xiao* 樂然後笑，人不厭其笑). "So he was like that," Confucius responded. "But how could he be like that?" (*Qi ran, qi qi ran hu* 其然，豈其然乎) (*Lunyu*, 14.13). The incident is significant because, despite Confucius' palpable reservations, Gongshu Wenzi's apparent eccentricity later became a norm: that one should never be too free with laughter (*bu gou xiao* 不苟笑).[30] This was due to concern that frequent mirth would not only weary others but also give rise to undue familiarity (*xia* 狎 or *jin* 近), which would in time breed insolence (*jian* 簡 or *bu xun* 不遜).[31] As I have shown elsewhere, from a Confucian point of view this might eventually have dire sociopolitical consequences.[32]

Confucius's initial inquiry nevertheless evinces disbelief in the possibility of a mirthless life, while his final response betrays doubt that laughter or smiling is always tractable. He, in fact, could not help breaking into a smile and teasing Zi You 子游 when he heard singing accompanied by stringed instruments in a little town in Zi You's charge. His impulsive mirth was apparently triggered by the incongruity he perceived in Zi You teaching high-brow music to his small-town rustics, which Confucius compared to using an ox-butchering knife to kill a chicken (*Lunyu* 17.4). Both traditional and modern commentators have noted that Confucius's humour may also have been prompted by subtle self-satire — he might have been doing much the same thing himself.[33]

Confucius's suspicion that the "funny ha-ha" is sometimes irresistible may also have stemmed from his observation of others' mirthful behaviour. The *Liji* recounts that Zi Lu 子路 (also known as You 由) burst into laughter at a man who one morning held a tearful sacrificial ceremony known as *daxiang* 大祥 to mark the beginning (twenty-fifth month) of the third and last year of the official three-year mourning period for his deceased parents, but was then heard singing in the evening (*Liji*, 45). Presumably, Zi Lu found the man's mood swing too dramatic to be proper, and so he laughed. This seems quite natural and justifiable.

Surprisingly, Confucius scolded him, "Oh, You 由! You'll never stop criticising others, will you? You do know that three years of mourning is a long time, don't you?" After Zi Lu left, Confucius told the others present that he didn't think that the singing mourner had done anything too improper. After all, as prescribed by the Rites, he could legitimately sing in a month's time.[34] Not only was Confucius in effect telling Zi Lu to give the bereaved man a break; he also implied that some amusement was necessary in order to maintain emotional balance. This view is articulated in another incident recorded in the *Liji*: Confucius asked Zi Gong 子貢[35] whether he had had a good time at a year-end sacrificial feast put on by the community to give thanks to the harvest gods. Zi Gong replied that he had found nothing at all delightful about the whole country getting drunk and running wild with jollity. In return, Confucius virtually called him a bore, telling him that he failed to understand that, after a year's hard work, people needed a day off to enjoy themselves with drinks and fun; more importantly, he also failed to grasp the political importance of this thanksgiving party.

To enlighten him, Confucius drew an analogy with how an archer maintains a good bow — by alternately tightening and relaxing its string (*Liji*, 294), suggesting how people can be properly governed.[36] Such psychological politics presupposes a necessary balance between tension and relaxation, both physical and psychological.

From balancing physical exertion or emotional strain with amusement, it is only a short step to balancing gravity with humour. This virtue is embodied by a gentleman alluded to in several of the 13 Confucian classics as an example of persistent learning and self-cultivation.[37] He is the hero of poem no. 55, "Qiyu" 淇澳 (Little bay of the Qi), in the *Shijing*, traditionally identified as Duke Wu of Wei 衛武公 (d. 758 BCE). The poem lauds him with the refrain, "Oh how grave and yet tolerant, / How magnificent and awe-inspiring! / So refined a gentleman, / For ever unforgettable!", but it concludes: "Oh, how magnanimous and amicable, / As he leans on the rail of his chariot. / Oh, how good he is at chaffing and joking, / But never crude or rude."[38]

Commenting on these lines, Zheng Xuan 鄭玄 (127–200 CE) wrote: "The virtues of the *junzi* include both tension and relaxation. Rather than being always grave and solemn, he sometimes chaffs and jokes as well." This means, as Kong Yingda 孔穎達 (574–648 CE) later explained, that the poem's hero has attained the mean of tension and relaxation (*zhang chi de zhong* 張弛得中).[39] Both commentators thus justify the gentleman's humour by Confucius's strung-bow analogy — perhaps with Confucius' authority, since he also regarded the poem's hero as an exemplar of virtue.[40] It seems reasonable, therefore, to infer Confucius's own endorsement of the latter's good-natured and moderate humour. After all, Confucius himself used and appreciated humour. In any event, all of these provided later Confucians such as Han Yu 韓愈 (768–824) and Liu Zongyuan 柳宗元 (773–819), and semi-Confucians such as Su Shi 蘇軾 (1037–1101), with authoritative support for humour.[41]

That one can and ought to have fun does not mean that one should have it whenever or wherever one pleases. Although humour as an irreducible human passion is bound to express itself, its expression should be proper. This sense of propriety is most succinctly articulated in a story by Pu Songling 蒲松齡 (1640–1715), in which a mother reprimands her constantly giggling daughter: "There is no-one

who does not laugh, but one must laugh at an appropriate time."
(*Ren wang bu xiao, dan xu you shi* 人罔不笑，但須有時)[42] Indeed, the
realization that there are appropriate times and places to pull a long
face or to relax it, unless (as with unregulated emotions) undesirable
consequences ensue, gave rise to some tacit precepts of proper humour
for a gentleman.

First, public levity was taboo. As dictated by the Confucian politics
of appearances, the Rites required the *junzi* to look grave and reverent
in public.[43] Chapter 10 of the *Lunyu* provides ritualistic portrayals of
Confucius's public deportment, such as the following:

On going through the outer gates to his lord's court, he drew himself
in, as though the entrance was too small to admit him.

> When he stood, he did not occupy the centre of the gateway; when
> he walked, he did not step on the threshold.
>
> When he went past the station of his lord, his face took on a serious
> expression, his step became brisk, and his words seemed more
> laconic.
>
> When he lifted the hem of his robe to ascend the hall, he drew
> himself in, and stopped inhaling, as if he had no need to breathe.
>
> When he had come out and descended the first step, relaxing his
> expression, he seemed no longer to be tense.
>
> When he had reached the bottom of the steps he went forward
> with quickened steps as though he was gliding on wings.
>
> When he resumed his station, his bearing was respectful.[44]

Here before us is a reverent, punctilious, almost trembling Confucius.

On the other hand, Confucius could feel murderous towards those
he thought had publicly insulted his lord with their humour and
laughter. Allegedly, he once had some court jesters executed, and their
severed limbs scattered, because they had performed their acts during a
meeting between his lord and theirs.[45] Although modern scholars tend
to dismiss this as fiction, the story illustrates the Confucian tendency to
view *public* humour as inappropriate. It is quite conceivable that such
open mirth would be repulsive to anyone who had internalized the
Rites' prescriptions for public reverence and gravity (feelings that are
as inimical to humour as fear and outrage).

There were exceptions to the rule, however, since a gentleman could employ humour at court to induce his lord to change his mind and mend his ways. Mencius, for instance, was noted for his forensic wit.[46] Courtly persuasion like this usually took the form of *jian* 諫 (admonition), *shui* 説 (persuasion) or *bian* 辯 (argumentation). Such public humour was tolerated in the Chinese tradition of indirect admonition — that is, *juejian* 譎諫 (crafty admonition) and *fengjian* 諷諫 (allegorical admonition) as opposed to *zhijian* 直諫 (direct admonition).[47] A crafty or allegorical admonisher resembles a court jester whose official responsibilities include warning his lord through laughter.[48] Though the jester might escape punishment if his humour displeased his lord, the gentleman admonisher could lose his head. Since, sadly, there was no guarantee that his jokes would work, he must always engage gingerly: "Be fearful, be careful, / As if approaching a ravine; / Fear and tremble, / As if treading on thin ice." (*Shijing*, no. 196)

Although humour is (generally) inappropriate in public, a Confucian gentleman could indeed lighten up in private. Despite the solemnity of traditional representations of the revered Teacher as shown in Figure 4.1, at home, or with his students for instance, a smiling Confucius often emerged. The *Lunyu* reports that he was informal at home (*Lunyu*, 10: 24), while Chapter 7 says that in his leisure hours he looked relaxed and amicable (*Lunyu*, 7.4). In so doing, he exemplified another ritual prescription that [when] at leisure, one should be mild (*yan ju gao wenwen* 燕居告溫溫) (*Liji*, 218, 219).

Mildness (*wen* 溫) here means gentleness (*rou* 柔).[49] This gentleness is not merely an attitude assumed by the *junzi* but, according to the Confucian classics, one of his basic qualities.[50] Thus, despite his grim demeanour in public, the *junzi* is actually gentle at heart. As another student of Confucius, Zi Xia 子夏, observed, one can feel this gentle-heartedness when one gets close to the *junzi* (*Lunyu*, 19.9), and his classmates would gladly testify that their teacher was just like this (*Lunyu*, 7.38).[51] Arguably, the *junzi*'s inherent amiability should dispose him to be affable and friendly. After all, a supreme Confucian virtue is *ren* (humaneness), which connotes human fellowship.[52] And the foundation of *ren* is gentleness and good-heartedness (*Wen liang zhe, ren yi zhi ben ye* 溫良者，仁義之本也) (*Liji*, 434).

Figure 4.1   "Portrait of the revered master Confucius teaching" (先師孔子行
教像 *Xian shi Kongzi xing jiao xiang*) by Wu Daozi 吳道子 (c. 685 – 758 CE).
Rubbing made in the first half of the twentieth century (1912 – 1945) from a
Qing dynasty (1644 – 1911) stele located in Qufu, Shandong Province, China.
Reproduced courtesy of the Harvard-Yenching Library, Harvard University.

Christoph Harbsmeier's insightful study of Confucius's humour
demonstrates that an "atmosphere of intellectual friendship"
pervaded Confucius's relationship with his students, giving rise to the
"remarkable humane sensibility of Confucius's moral thinking", which

fostered both his humour and that of his students.[53] This seems to suggest that, while the Rites' emphasis on gravity and reverence curbed a gentleman's public humour, his intrinsic gentle-heartedness and amicability would encourage a genial private environment in which humour could flourish. Thus, with his students, Confucius was still a dignified teacher but more spontaneous, playful and even jocose than he was in public. Consider the following story:

> Zi Gong asked Confucius, "Do dead people have consciousness or not?" Confucius replied, "If I say they do, I'm afraid filial sons and obedient grandsons will send off the dead in ways that will impede the living. If I say they don't, I'm afraid unfilial sons and grandsons will discard their deceased parents without burial. Ci [Zi Gong], if you want to know whether or not the dead have consciousness, you'll find out when you die. It won't be too late then."[54]

But will Zi Gong be able to know anything when he's dead and done? Confucius's witty and brainteaser-like response is consistent with his "agnostic humanism",[55] which made him more interested in life than the afterlife (*Lunyu*, 11.12).

If one teases others, others will sooner or later tease back, even if they are one's most reverent students. This seems to have happened when Confucius was under siege in the town of Kuang. Yan Hui 顏回 fell behind; when he finally caught up, Confucius said, "I thought you were dead." Yan Hui responded, "Master, while you are alive, how would I dare to die?" (*Lunyu*, 11.23) Although traditional Chinese commentators tended to take this tit-for-tat seriously, as representing Yan Hui's eternal loyalty and utter respect for his teacher, modern readers may see a subtle humour exchanged here between teacher and student,[56] especially in the light of their close friendship. Yan Hui's sarcastic remark may even have been encouraged by Confucius's fondness for self-satire — hence this private tit-for-tat joke between them.

As Harbsmeier notes, much of Confucius's humour belongs to this kind of subtle self-irony, which can be detected even in his most cocky moments. Hearing Confucius say that he wanted to go and live among the barbarians, someone warned him, "Think about their crudity. What are you going to do about that?" Confucius replied, "You see, once a gentleman lives among them, what crudity will there be?" (*Lunyu*, 9.14).

This sounds very much like wishful thinking, since ridding the world of its crudity was precisely what he had so far failed to accomplish (*Lunyu*, 18.6); otherwise, he would not have had to travel from state to state or even consider fleeing the world, perhaps in a moment of despair (*Lunyu*, 5.7). In a much-recycled amusing story, moreover, a contemporary described Confucius as a homeless dog (*sangjia zhi gou* 喪家之狗), and when Zi Gong relayed this to Confucius he laughed heartily and said that appearances were not important, but to say he was like a homeless dog, "how true it is, how true it is!" (*Ran zai! Ran zai!* 然哉! 然哉!)[57] His mirthful appropriation of an apparent insult makes a good sense in the light of his active sense of humour and the fact that he actually left his home state of Lu in search of a ruler who would put his ideas of good government into practice, but to no avail. While this much-loved story may well be fictional, it is not necessarily untrue: some factual basis is indicated by *Lunyu*, 14.32, which seems to suggest that the historical Confucius was probably aware of the simile as well as its aptness. In any case, what is evident (for instance, *Lunyu*, 9.8, 9.13) is his capability and fondness for what today's psychologists call self-defeating humour.[58]

Although private mirth is permissible, one should not over-indulge, since intemperance would be as improper as a perpetual long face. The Rites advocate constant practice of the mean, but actually encourage more vigilance against excess than deficiency. The perception is that over-indulgence is more dangerous to a virtuous life than under-indulgence because humans are more prone to being carried away by desires and to indulging in, rather than refraining from, pleasures, thereby losing their senses more quickly. This approach has much in common with Western classical attitudes,[59] as seems to have been appreciated by early Jesuit missionaries to China who chose to portray Confucius in a Graeco-Roman classical setting in a seventeenth-century book on his life and thought (Figure 4.2).

The Confucian classics teem with warnings against immoderation. Confucius, for instance, commended "Guanju" 關雎 (Osprey's cry), the first poem in the *Shijing*, because it expressed delight without abandon and sorrow without (emotional) self-injury (*Le er bu yin, ai er bu shang* 樂而不淫，哀而不傷) (*Lunyu*, 3.20). On the other hand, he deemed three kinds of delight harmful: delight in extravagant amusements;

Figure 4.2   Image of Confucius, facing the title-page of *Lunyu* in *Confucius Sinarum philosophus*, 1687, a Latin translation of classical Confucian works, printed in Paris under special licence from King Louis XIV. Reproduced by kind permission of the Syndics of Cambridge University Library.

delight in dissolute adventures; and delight in lavish feasting (*Le jiaole, le yiyou, le yanle* 樂驕樂，樂佚游，樂晏樂) (*Lunyu*, 16.5) — for such delights tend to go overboard easily. It is no accident that the *Liji* opens with these proscriptions: never become arrogant; never indulge desires; never gratify the will to the full; and never enjoy pleasures to

the extreme (*Ao bu ke zhang, yu bu ke zong, zhi bu ke man, le bu ke ji* 敖
不可長，慾不可從，志不可滿，樂不可極) (*Liji*, 13). When Mencius said
that Confucius never did anything immoderate (*Zhongni bu wei yishen
zhe* 仲尼不為已甚者) (*Mengzi*, 4B: 10), the "anything" should include
humour. It follows, then, that the second precept for proper humour is
moderation, to which I will return later.

Although it confirms the Confucian wariness of excess, Mencius's
assertion above is not entirely accurate, since in the *Lunyu* Confucius
appears as a short-tempered and sometimes abusive man, prone to
emotional outbursts and occasionally engaging in insulting humour.[60]
He once declined Ru Bei's invitation to a meeting by lying that he
was sick, but as soon as Ru Bei's messenger stepped out of the door,
Confucius took up a lute and sang loudly so as to be heard (*Lunyu*,
17.20). Maybe there were good reasons for being rude,[61] but Confucius's
humour here seems less exemplary than the legendary hero of "Qiyu",
whose humour was "never crude or rude".[62]

The "Qiyu" poem is highly significant for studies of Chinese humour.
Besides supplying later Confucians with powerful ammunition for
their defence of humour, it is the earliest direct portrayal in Chinese
literature of a sense of humour as a virtuous personality trait. More
importantly, the poem's description of its hero as "Good at chaffing
and joking, / But never crude or rude" (*Shan xi xue xi, bu wei nue xi* 善
戲謔兮，不為虐兮) verbalizes the third Confucian precept for proper
humour: it should be benign.

Ironically, this requirement seems to have stemmed from a deep-
seated negativism in the early Chinese concept of joking, as is betrayed
by the formation of the character *xue* 謔 = *yan* 言 (speech) + *nue* 虐
(cruelty or malice). Such negativism is confirmed and reinforced by
subsequent pejorative usage of *xue* and by its close association with
negative emotions such as derision (*chao* 嘲), resentment (*yuan* 怨)
and anger (*nu* 怒).[63] The inherent malice in humour is most vividly
envisaged in a Chinese metaphor for hurtful jokes, *xiaozhongdao* 笑中
刀 (dagger wrapped in laughter).[64] This perception of the embedded
blades in joking seems to have prompted a desire for kinder and gentler
jokes by extracting the innate spite of *xue*. In yearning for and extolling
this kinder form of humour, "Qiyu" is very much in tune with a host of
Confucian virtues, such as benevolence, moderation and unremitting
self-refinement through ritual discipline.

As a result, "never crude or rude" became a dictum for proper humour, evidenced in dramaturgical treatises and prefaces or postscripts to the traditional Chinese joke books that flourished in late imperial China.[65] Discussing humour in drama, for instance, Su Shi 蘇軾 (1037–1101) recommended that one proper way to enhance the mirth of the sovereign and his subjects was through amiable humour (*yu zuo huansheng, yi chen shanxue* 欲佐歡聲，宜陳善謔).[66] Similarly, in his collection of jokes, *Gujin xiao* 古今笑 (The laughable of the past and the present), Feng Menglong 馮夢龍 (1574–1646) observed in a brief preface to a section on *yalang* 雅浪 (refined hilarity) that tasteful jokes never hurt feelings (*yaxue bu shang xin* 雅謔不傷心).[67] Later, in an appendix to his own joke collection, *Xiao dao* 笑倒 (Falling over with laughter), Chen Gaomo 陳皋谟 (fl. 1718) set forth ten kinds of taboo jokes, such as those that are insensitive, gossipy, embarrassing, etc., and topped his list with the "dagger wrapped in laughter".[68]

Li Yu 李漁 (1611–80) also warned against certain kinds of jokes in drama, foremost among them the salacious (*yinxie* 淫藝), because it was both crude and cruel. He advised that if the plot called for erotic humour, the proper way to present it was by "being 'good at chaffing and joking, / But never crude or rude'" (*shan xi xue xi, bu wei nue xi zhi fa* 善戲謔兮，不為虐兮之法). He not only quoted "Qiyu" but also alluded to Confucius's praise of the "Guanju" poem's balanced expression of delight without abandon when recommending that erotic but not lascivious humour could be produced by leaving juicy details unsaid or employing metaphors to let the audience's imagination do the dirty work.[69] Such techniques recall crafty remonstration (*juejian* 譎諫), instanced by a joke he cited as a model of appropriate dramatic humour:

> Owing to a severe drought, the king of Shu prohibited people from making wine (in order to save water). One day the police found equipment for distilling and arrested the owner. Just then, Jian Yong, one of the king's advisors, was accompanying the king on a tour and, noticing a man and a woman walking in the street, he said to the king, "Please have that man and that woman arrested, for they are about to start an affair." "How do you know?" asked the king. "Because they both have the equipment, just like the distilling equipment owner. That is how I know it." The king laughed and ordered the owner of the distilling equipment to be released.[70]

Such an indirect approach returns us to the precept of moderation, since Li Yu implies that lasciviousness results from licence. Feng Menglong even saw intemperate or immoderate humour as leading to cruelty:

> 謔浪，人所時有也。過則虐，虐則不堪，是故雅之為貴。
>
> Hilarious jokes are what people enjoy from time to time. But if they exceed bounds, they become cruel; if cruel, they become insufferable. This is why tasteful humour is most appreciated.[71]

This principle of moderation in humour also informed traditional Chinese dramaturgy. According to Li Yu, dramatic humour should never be pedantic or too vulgar, although the best kind approximates the common.[72] Here, he echoed Liu Xie's characterization of jests as a minor literary genre using as its medium the simple language of the common people (*WXDL*, 169). It seems that Li Yu also heeded the stipulation by Wang Jide 王驥德 (d. 1623) that humorous songs (*paixie zhi qu* 俳諧之曲) in drama:

> …… 著不得一個太文字，又著不得一句張打油句；須以俗為雅，而一語之出輒令人絕倒，乃妙。
>
> . . . must never use a single too literary word nor a single doggerel sentence. They should transform rusticity into elegance, so that as soon as they are sung, the audience will fall over with laughter. That is most admirable.[73]

Hence both of these critics saw proper dramatic humour as resulting not from a simple combination of the crude and the sophisticated but from moderation in refining crudity — a very different thing.

This delicately balanced synthesis is often characterized as *ya* 雅 (refined, tasteful or elegant). The definition given by Yang Xiong 揚雄 (53 BCE–18 CE) makes it clear that *ya* connoted propriety: "What is balanced and upright is tasteful, and what is excessive and wayward is licentious." (*Zhongzheng ze ya, duowa ze zheng* 中正則雅，多哇則鄭)[74] Even the Daoist thinker Ge Hong 葛洪 (284–364 CE) advocated proper humour as refined and risible, moderate and never hurtful (*ya er ke xiao, zhong er bu shang* 雅而可笑，中而不傷).[75] And repeated calls were made for *yaxue* 雅謔 (tasteful jokes), especially in the late Ming and early Qing periods (roughly the sixteenth to early eighteenth centuries), betraying a widespread concern about threats of rampant hilarity and vulgarity then. This was a period of "lively controversy and intellectual diversity",[76] in which literati appreciation of humour peaked, but many jokes produced at the time were unpalatable and offended their collectors' Confucian sensibilities, alerting them to the danger to social order posed by unbridled levity. Hence the emergence of a more theoretical discourse of humour in dramaturgy and the hortatory prefaces to joke books in which authors contemplated the values of humour, proffered joke techniques and formulated taboos.[77]

Another aspect of such literary negativism towards humour is an abiding perception of its inferiority. Bias is patent in Liu Xie's definition of jesting as an expression of resentment or anger by means of a shallow language catering to the common people so as to amuse all to laughter (*ci qian hui su, jie yue xiao ye* 辭淺會俗，皆悅笑也). Owing to their base nature and crude medium, jests are susceptible to frivolity, abuse or indecency. Therefore, Liu Xie classified jesting as a minor genre like that of *xiaoshuo* 小說 (literally, small talk, or fiction), the lowest in the hierarchy of Chinese letters: while the other genres were valued as "silk and hemp", jokes (and riddles) were looked down upon as "straw and rush" (*WXDL*, 169, 170, 177).

This prejudice was reinforced by the low social status of professional jesters (*paiyou* 俳優 or *paichang* 俳倡), including court jesters. Despite enjoying imperial favour, the latter were essentially slaves — some were former prisoners of war or criminals, and some of them were also dwarves. Consequently, they were despised[78] and not to be associated with. Mei Gao 枚皋 (b. 153 BCE), a court poet noted for his jests, became ashamed of resembling and being treated like a jester (*zi hui lei chang* 自悔類倡 *jian shi ru chang* 見視如倡).[79] Hence advocating *yaxue* may well betray an inferiority complex, and the desire to elevate humour by refining its crudity into elegance may be based on the assumption that, although innate, the (base) nature of humour is transformable — just as human nature is.

The call for *yaxue* also shares much with an apologetic tradition that sought to justify humour from philosophical, psychological and pragmatic angles by stressing its irrepressibility, its indispensable role in emotional balance and its utility. Thus the last Confucian precept for proper humour is that it should be useful — or, stated more precisely, the benefits of humour depend on proper usage. This utilitarian defence first emerged in the reasons given by Sima Qian 司馬遷 (145?–86? BCE) for including biographies of *huaji* 滑稽 (humorists) in the *Shiji* 史記 (Records of the Grand Historian). He believed that, as it was part of the Heavenly Way (*tiandao* 天道), humour was useful in resolving disputes through subtle and incisive words. His biographies of three court jesters in particular describe how they used jests to admonish their rulers to prevent stupidity, unkindness, misconduct, even political, military or diplomatic disasters, to help them to realize their hegemonic ambitions. "How can one not see," Sima Qian asked, "the greatness of what these jesters accomplished?" (*Qi bu yi wei zai* 豈不亦偉哉) For him, proper humour follows the great Way (*he yu dadao* 合於大道), and moderation (in humour, as in all things) is a virtue — as he suggested when describing how the jester Chunyu Kun 淳于髡 admonished King Wei of Qin 秦威王 against over-indulgence in drinking.[80]

It was Liu Xie, however, who was the first to articulate fully the utilitarian argument for humour. Besides mirth's value in assisting reconciliation, he pointed out another common use: to relieve fatigue. Yet he vehemently opposed humour for humour's sake (*kong xi huaji* 空戲滑稽), because frivolous jests might damage social mores. Morally useful humour, on the other hand, was endorsed, since by aiming at righteousness and rectitude it could help with current situations, give advice or admonition, rectify the wayward, and prevent or stop foolishness and violence. And he saw subtle satire (*weifeng* 微諷) as the main form of useful humour, since it could save a person or even a country from danger. In a concluding verse, he summarized the values of proper humour thus: "Righteous and opportune, / Jests (and riddles) help by giving satirical warnings." (*hui yi shi shi, po yi fengjie* 會義適時，頗益諷戒) (*WXDL*, 167–77)

Underpinning Liu Xie's argument is the belief that proper humour is used to instruct. He and Sima Qian both effectively agree that humour — whether seen as a peripheral genre of literature or as a means of moral, political or diplomatic persuasion — ought to be didactic. This accords with Confucianism, which attaches such importance to teaching (*jiao* 教), regarded as integral to moral education, that all writings are viewed as instructive vehicles of the Confucian Way. Therefore, Liu Xie pointed out, "as long as [humour] admonishes or warns, it is duly recorded in the *Liji*" (*gou ke zhen jie, zai yu Lidian* 苟可箴戒，載於禮典) (*WXDL*, 168).

This utilitarian didactic position was inherited and developed by Ming and Qing proponents of humour. In a preface to his joke collection *Xiao zan* 笑贊 (An accolade for humour), Zhao Nanxing 趙南星 (1550–1627) noted that not only could one divert oneself by reading or recalling jokes when feeling lonely or bored, but one could also use jokes to discuss Confucian principles and understand the ways of the world (*ke yi tan mingli, ke yi tong shigu* 可以談名理，可以通世故).[81] Similarly, Feng Menglong wrote that laughter could remove worries, pacify anger, smooth away troubles and resolve puzzlement (*po fan juan fen, yi nan jie huo* 破煩蠲忿，夷難解惑). Emphasising the didactic function of humour, he chastised "rotten Confucians" for opposing humour and recommended it as an efficacious remedy of their rottenness.[82] Furthermore, Li Yu regarded the best but most difficult kinds of humour as possessing *guanxi* 關係 (moral pertinence), saying that the laughable and humour should contain great lessons so as to make more pre-eminent the virtues of loyalty, filial piety, moral integrity and righteousness (*Xixiao huixie zhi chu, baohan jueda wenzhang, shi zhong xiao jie yi zhi xin, de ci yu xian* 嬉笑詼諧之處, 包含絕大文章，使忠孝節義之心，得此愈顯). In this way, humour is not merely humour but a convenient gate of dharma that ushers people to the Way (*ze kehun fei kehun, nai yin ren ru dao zhi fangbian famen* 則科諢非科諢，乃引人入道之方便法門).[83] Drawing on Mencius's philosophy (that human nature was originally good), Li Yu's contemporary Shi Chengjin 石成金 (b. 1659) even maintained that, like strong medicine, good satirical humour could help people see their waywardness and "recover their innate goodness" (*Renxing zhi tianliang dun fu* 人性之天良頓複).[84]

Shi Chengjin saw humour as capable of these profound effects because people, while averse to straight-faced homilies, were drawn to jokes: "they tend to fall asleep when listening to serious words, yet fear to fall behind in hearing a joke. This is an invariable fact about people nowadays" (*Zhengyan wen zhi yu shui, xiaohua ting zhi kong hou, jinren zhi hengqing* 正言聞之慾睡，笑話聽之恐後，今人之恆情).[85] Understanding the same pragmatics of audience psychology, Wang Jide and Li Yu had also stressed the utility of humour in drama since it could keep the audience awake and attentive. Li Yu had even likened dramatic humour to "ginseng soup" (*renshentang* 人參湯) — an attention tonic, so to speak.[86] Later, Wu Jianren 吳趼人 (1866–1910), the author of *Ershinian mudu zhi guai xianzhuang* 二十年目睹之怪現狀 (An eyewitness account of strange things in the past 20 years), observed that "in terms of influencing people, grave words are not as powerful as humorous remarks: this is why jokes and fiction are in vogue" (*Qi suo yi ru ren zhe, zhuangci bu ru xieyu, gu xiaohua xiaoshuo shang yan* 其 所以入人者，莊詞不如諧語，故笑話小説尚焉). He also recognized that jokes were a double-edged sword, since uncouth or malicious jokes (*e'xue* 惡謔) could corrupt morals.[87] In short, because it appeals to people's attention and because people are partial to it, humour can be a potent didactic tool.

Beyond the moral, the goals of Confucian didacticism also extended to the sociopolitical, thanks to the belief that learning and moral cultivation can bring about familial, social and universal order, peace and happiness (*Liji*, 436). For if every member of the human family became a virtuous person, there would be fewer causes of suffering, discontent or unrest. Guo Zizhang 郭子章 (1542–1618) was probably very sincere in his belief that useful and superior humour was concerned not only with teaching Confucian morals (*mingjiao* 名教) but also with helping to restore order to the world (*li luan* 理亂),[88] a distant echo of Liu Xie's earlier assertion that proper humour could help save the world from danger.

Conclusion

Proper humour, seen from the Confucian perspective, means a form of private, moderate, good-natured, tasteful and didactically useful mirth. This humour ethic stems from the belief that emotion is indispensable, and that unbridled passions are dangerous and must be expressed in a balanced way. It also stems from a profound concern for social morality, order and harmony.

There are intriguing similarities between the Confucian and ancient Greek and Roman conceptions of humour and civilized behaviour — their negativity towards laughter and the laughable, their rationales for regulating them, their justifications for jesting and their precepts for proper humour. The Greeks and Romans believed humour should be moderate, good-natured, urbane and useful in epistemological, psychological, oratorical or moral terms (since a concern about conduct is essentially a moral one and all etiquettes are steeped in moral values).[89] Certainly there are many differences between the Chinese and the Greco-Roman views of humour, but it is thought-provoking (even comforting) to see that two peoples devoid of mutual knowledge and living in very different epochs shared surprisingly similar attitudes.

Perhaps such parallels have to do with what Karl Jaspers called the axial period, which human history entered between the ninth and the third centuries BCE. This was the era when wise human beings such as Confucius, Buddha, Jeremiah, Zarathustra and Plato lived, learned, thought, taught, and also laughed and joked. Leaving open the causes of the "axis of world history", since "no one can adequately comprehend what occurred here",[90] Jaspers suggested that we should nevertheless try to understand this wondrous period from all sides. This should surely include human commonalities such as a sense of humour. Different peoples laugh at different jokes, of course, but we all do laugh and crack jokes; we even make and laugh at the same kinds of jokes, if not the same jokes (give or take some specialized cultural knowledge).

Another human commonality is surely the *sense of propriety*, which at its best can transcend time, race and culture — we all have it, more or less. But what is deemed proper will differ from culture to culture and from time to time. In today's China, for instance, public humour coming from a statesman or a stateswoman hardly raises an eyebrow. In fact, a sense of humour has become so admirable a trait that everyone wishes to show it. Concepts of public and private, too, have altered since cyberspace became available to all: the internet seems a twilight zone where one can disclose (often under the cloak of anonymity or pseudonymity) the most private aspects of one's life in a global public park. The Chinese *seem* to have thrown most Confucian precepts for proper humour out the window — consider, for instance, Chinese humour websites where almost anything goes.[91] One might then ask whether there are any (implicit or explicit) precepts for proper humour in modern China. If so, what are they? How widely do they differ from Confucian tenets? What do the two approaches share in common (if anything)? How have the differences evolved? Clearly, answering these questions requires further research and analysis, to which this book is designed to contribute.

5
Identifying Daoist Humour: Reading the *Liezi*

Shirley Chan

About 20 years ago, an important article was published by Christoph Harbsmeier concerning the sense of humour displayed in some of the canonical texts of classical Chinese philosophy, such as the *Lunyu* 論語 (Confucius's *Analects*), the *Mengzi* 孟子 (Works of Mencius), the *Hanshi waizhuan* 韓詩外傳, the *Zhanguo ce* 戰國策, the *Lüshi chunqiu* 呂氏春秋, the *Hanfeizi* 韓非子 and the *Zhuangzi* 莊子.[1] Harbsmeier did not, however, include the Daoist text the *Liezi* 列子 in his discussion; nor has it since been addressed, despite the richness of its ironic devices and its vividly humorous character sketches. In this chapter, I focus on the various styles of *huaji* 滑稽[2] found in the *Liezi* that contribute to its humorous sensibilities, arguing that *huaji* does not differ in essence from what is now generally understood as humour in contemporary China. The *Liezi* helped establish a Daoist tradition of using wit and humour as didactic and critical tools for awakening the sensibilities of its audience to the falsity and ridiculousness of contemporary mundane events that they otherwise would have accepted as inevitable parts of human life.

It is well known that the English word "humour" was translated and introduced to Chinese readers by Lin Yutang 林語堂 in 1924 as *youmo* 幽默.[3] *You* 幽 denotes something dim, dark, quiet and weak that leads to a hidden deeper level, and *mo* 默 means silent and mute. This term thus indicates that the whole matter does not simply end with laughter, but invites reflection in order to penetrate the humanistic or philosophical realities involved.[4] Lin also suggested that humour possessed a philosophical perspective on matters such as the way of life, contentment and leisure, and the tolerance of vice and evil. Following Lin Yutang's introduction of the term *youmo* and its gradual adoption, modern Chinese generally use this word to refer to sophisticated ways of conveying social and cultural values understood and shared by educated people.

The English word "humour", embracing all types of funniness, does not therefore have an exact Chinese equivalent. The older Chinese term *huaji* is the expression closest to it in meaning, and its long history certainly indicates that Chinese culture contains a rich tradition of wit, jokes and humour.[5] Compared with its modern connotations of farcicality or tomfoolery / pranks,[6] *huaji* was originally much broader in meaning. The characteristics of *huaji* can be recognized epistemologically in the two characters with which it is written: *hua* 滑 (also pronounced *gu*) means fluent, glib, subtle and smooth; *ji* 稽 means recrimination and discussion. In this sense, *huaji* is discourse intertwined with wit, subtlety and humour.[7] Some artistic forms traditionally attributed to the development of *huaji* include the later development of comedy and farce, or what was traditionally referred to as *paixie* 俳諧 during and before the Qin and Han periods. In *paixie*, the rich imagining and visualization of mythologies, folklore, fables and ancient writings were the sources used by authors to convey a philosophical argument.

Huaji was specially employed in argumentation in intellectual discourse, and the meaning of the term was set in the Warring States period in pre-Qin China, when society and culture were undergoing more rapid and drastic changes than ever before. The warfare and political crises that marked the period led to the flourishing of different schools of thought, responding to the need for solutions to sociopolitical issues. Thinkers, itinerant scholars and masters of different schools all came into contact with exponents of rival systems of thought and felt compelled to promote their own ideas. They had not only to face competition between the different schools, but also to convince the feudal lords or state rulers to embrace the political ideals they espoused. The way in which teachers and strategists presented or defended their ideas had therefore to be engaging, interesting and convincing, while aiming to provide solutions for social conflict. This indeed is what the Grand Historian Sima Qian 司馬遷 (145?–86? BCE) expressed at the beginning of the chapter *Huaji liezhuan* 滑稽列傳 (Collective biographies of the *huaji*-ists), when he explained the reason for including this particular category in his *Shiji* 史記 (Records of the Grand Historian):

天道恢恢，豈不大哉！談言微中，亦可以解紛。

The Way of Heaven is grand and embracing! One can reduce conflict and disturbance by being circumspect yet at the same time pointed in speech.[8]

The *Huaji liezhuan* records episodes from the lives of three *huaji*-ists: Chunyu Kun 淳于髡, You Meng 優孟 and You Zhan 優旃 from the Spring and Autumn and Warring States periods (722–221 BCE) and Qin dynasty (221–206 BCE). These humorists speak wittily and relevantly to persuade their lords to accept their advice. They know very well what to say, when to say it and how to speak convincingly.[9] Examining these examples of *huaji* expressed in the speech and/or writings of the *huaji*-ists, we see that their key technique is in fact euphemism, as direct criticism is mostly avoided despite the humorous tone of the arguments. Instead, the speakers present their views by drawing upon relevant stories, mythologies, anecdotes and allegorical tales. In the process, they may employ irony, satire, similes, metaphors and exaggeration. Readers are invited to connect their own situation or activity with that alluded to in the story being recounted. While the author does not limit the force of the argument by the use of such literary devices, members of the target audience are unconsciously seduced by the humorous sensibility of the story, which persuades them to identify their own situation as readers with the context of the anecdote.

The writing of the *Liezi*, together with that of the *Zhuangzi*, has been referred to as the period in which Daoism was developed. Unlike the *Daode jing* 道德經, a treatise attributed to Laozi 老子, the founder of Daoism, the *Liezi* and the *Zhuangzi* are both characterized by rich imagination and a *huaji* style in writing, so that they present their teachings under the guise of fable and story.[10] Sima Qian refers to Zhuangzi as a philosopher who criticized Confucian social conventions by being a *huaji*-ist.[11] And indeed, a large proportion of both the *Liezi* and the *Zhuangzi* is made up of legends, jokes, parables and allegorical tales, all laced with humour and paradox. Although the individual stories are short, pithy and philosophical, they evince a keen sense of dramatic effect — indeed, some appear fantastic and rather wildly imaginative. The *Zhuangzi*, which is attributed to Zhuang Zhou 莊周, was composed by several different hands under the general themes of living as part of nature and freeing oneself from society and its conventions. As is the case with Laozi, it is hard to determine exactly when Zhuang Zhou lived, although it is commonly accepted, following Sima Qian, that he may have been a contemporary of Mencius (fourth century BCE).[12]

Very little is known of Liezi either. His full name was Lie Yukou 列 禦寇, and it appears that he was living in Zheng 鄭 State in the early Warring States period — that is, some time in the fourth century BCE. Liezi figures prominently in the pages of the *Zhuangzi*, from which we learn that he could "ride upon the wind", indicating that he had supernatural powers or had been empowered by embodiment of the Way (*dao* 道), the constant, active force preceding and filling the universe.[13] In fact, both the *Liezi* and the *Zhuangzi* share some common themes and have some obvious analogies.[14] This chapter will focus on the book that appropriates the name of *Liezi*, although I will also refer to the *Zhuangzi* when it becomes relevant. As far as timing is concerned, while the predominant scholarly view is that the *Liezi* was written as late as 300 CE, it has also been argued that it could well have originated as early as the third century BCE.[15]

Thematically, the *Liezi* presents Daoist ideas and teachings that involve such matters as reconciliation with the vicissitudes of life, the value of spontaneity and effortlessness, the relationship between dream and reality, the acceptance and following of nature, the relativity of standards and the formation of cosmology.[16] Presenting these themes with humorous elements or components was a deliberate tactic to enable readers to share the perspective of the writer or writers in an effective and affective way. The humour appeals to readers' emotions as well as to their rationality, and its surprising twists of logic must help retain attention. The following is a brief examination of some of the principal rhetorical methods employed in the text of the *Liezi*. Although they include hyperbole, metaphor, recasting[17] and *reductio ad absurdum*, none defeats the fundamentally serious messages of the text; rather, they are emotionally appealing and effective ways of communicating the important philosophical messages of the author(s).

One of the most noticeable features of the *Liezi* is that the masters of rival schools, such as Confucius and Yang Zhu 楊朱, do not appear in the text as opponents of Daoism, but are recast as spokesmen for and devotees of Daoist teachings. While this could simply be taken as examples of Daoist reconciliation with other schools, by putting Daoist theories into the mouths of their representatives, it was also intended to dramatize the powerful influence of Daoist ideas by presenting the two sages and others as converts. Further, by using a humorous style of anecdote and argumentation, the author(s) may in fact succeed in refuting such intellectual adversaries. As an example, we see in the *Liezi* that Confucius himself appears as one who preaches the Daoist attitude towards death:

> 子貢倦于學，告仲尼曰：“愿有所息，”仲尼曰：“生無所息。”子貢曰：“然則賜息于所乎？”仲尼曰：“有焉耳，望其壙，睪如也，宰如也，墳如也，鬲如也，則知所息矣。”子貢曰：“大哉死乎！君子息焉，小人伏焉。”仲尼曰：“賜！汝知之矣。人胥知生之樂，未知生之苦；知老之憊，未知老之佚；知死之惡，未知死之息也。”[18]

> Zigong grew weary of study, and told Confucius: "I want to find rest." "There is no rest for the living." "Then shall I never find it?" "You shall. Look forward to the lofty and domed mound of your tomb, and know where you shall find rest." "Great is death! The gentleman finds rest in it, the petty man submits to it!" "Zigong, you have understood. All men understand the joy of being alive but not its misery; the weariness of growing old but not its ease; the ugliness of death but not its repose."[19]

It is generally accepted that Confucius committed himself entirely to learning, and that he spent his whole life studying Zhou dynasty culture and self-cultivation. He described himself as one who was so fond of learning that he did not realize he was approaching old age.[20] However, the above conversation in the *Liezi* between Confucius and his disciple suggests that, to the contrary, both men had grown weary of study. When the disciple complains of its arduousness and wants to find some rest, the master, unexpectedly, does not criticize him. Instead, he explains that death is something one should look forward to in order to end this laborious process of learning! This ironically humorous conversation not only reverses the conventional image of Confucius as one who found joy only in education and learning, but it also shrewdly promotes the ecstatic Daoist acceptance of death.

The *Liezi* also argues that one should not be perplexed by outer form or judge with the eyes alone because the beauty and nobility that derives from the innermost heart when one avoids self-indulgence is true natural beauty and as such is the most beautiful of all. In the extract below, the one who is presented as having learnt this lesson best from the Daoist teaching is Yang Zhu, and he ironically instructs his pupils:

> 楊朱過宋東之于逆旅。逆旅人有妾二人，其一人美，其一人惡；惡者貴而美者賤。楊子問其故。逆旅小子對曰：「其美者自美，吾不知其美也；其惡者自惡，吾不知其惡也。」楊子曰：「弟子記之！行賢而去自賢之行，安往而不愛哉！」
>
> When Yang Zhu was passing through Song, he spent the night at an inn. The innkeeper had two concubines, one beautiful and the other ugly. The ugly one he valued, the beautiful one he neglected. When Yang Zhu asked the reason, the fellow answered: "The beautiful one thinks herself beautiful, and I do not notice her beauty. The ugly one thinks herself ugly, and I do not notice her ugliness." "Remember this, my disciples," said Yang Zhu. "If you act nobly and banish from your mind the thought that you are noble, where can you go and not be loved!"[21]

The school of Yang Zhu (c. 350 BCE) is described as advocating full enjoyment during one's life. Its followers believed that life was short and one should not permit the least injury to the wholeness of the body for the sake of any external benefit, nor should one submit to moral conventions merely through an idle desire to win reputation and fame. The best way to preserve life and the natural order was through refusing any involvement in the struggle for wealth and power. In the *Liezi*, Yang Zhu's well-known aphorism of "not plucking one hair" is cited to explicate the Daoist belief that "all under Heaven will be in order when it is ruled with effortlessness":

> 楊朱曰：「．．．古之人損一毫利天下，不與也；悉天下奉一身，不取也。人人不損一毫，人人不利天下：天下治矣。」禽子問楊朱曰：「去子體之一毛，以濟一世，不汝為之乎？」楊子曰：「世固非一毛之所濟。」禽子曰：「假濟，為之乎？」楊子弗應。禽子出，語孟孫陽。孟孫陽曰：「子不達夫子之心，吾請言之。有侵苦肌膚獲萬金者，若為之乎？」曰：「為之。」孟孫陽曰：「有斷若一節得一國。子為之乎？」禽子默然有間。孟孫陽曰：「一毛微于肌膚，肌膚微于一節，省矣。然則積一毛以成肌膚，積肌膚以成一節。一毛固一體萬分中之一物，奈何輕之乎？」
>
> Yang Zhu said, ". . . A man of ancient times, if he could have benefited the Empire by the loss of one hair, would not have given it; and if everything in the Empire had been offered to him alone,

he would not have taken it. When no one would lose a hair, and no one would benefit the Empire, the Empire was in good order." Qin Guli asked Yang Zhu: "If you could help the whole world by sacrificing one hair of your body, would you do it?" "The world certainly will not be helped by one hair." "But supposing it did help, would you do it?" Yang Zhu did not answer him. When Qin Guli came out, he told Meng Sunyang who said, "You do not understand what is in my Master's mind. Let me explain. If you could win ten thousand pieces of gold by injuring your skin and flesh, would you do it?" "I would." "If you could gain a kingdom by cutting off one limb at the joint, would you do it?" Qin Guli was silent for a while. Meng Sunyang continued, "It is clear that one hair is a trifle compared with skin and flesh, and skin and flesh compared with one joint. However, enough hairs are worth as much as skin and flesh, enough skin and flesh as much as one joint. You cannot deny that one hair has its place among the myriad parts of the body; [so] how can one treat it lightly?"[22]

Here, the story about Yang Zhu is utilized by the compiler(s) (if not the original author) of the *Liezi* as an extreme example to advocate the Daoist ideal of freeing oneself from state office. The theme of this parable is not really advocating the hedonistic principle of pleasure. Rather, through Yang Zhu and his disciple's analogy, we are told that we should take seriously a minor act such as "plucking one hair", which seems insignificant but can so accumulate as to make one take one's own life lightly, and thus would not only cause injury to individuals' bodies but also create social disorder if everyone should compete in doing the same.

If readers remain critical of this Yang Zhu philosophy, which seems on the surface to be one of "self-centredness", the next argument presented in the same chapter might change that opinion, for in it the writer explains that our life — like that of all other species and things lying between heaven and earth — belongs to the world itself (i.e. to nature) and should thus be treated as a communal possession. Accordingly, one should avoid doing harm to one's own body.[23]

Preserving one's life by retiring from official life is, of course, a familiar Daoist theme. A chapter in the *Zhuangzi*, appearing under the name of Liezi and titled *Lie yukou*, runs as follows:

或聘於莊子，莊子應其使曰：「子見夫犧牛乎？衣以文繡，食以芻叔，及其牽而入於太廟，雖欲為孤犢，其可得乎！」

Some [ruler] having sent a message of invitation to him, Zhuangzi replied to the messenger, "Have you seen, Sir, a sacrificial ox? It is robed with ornamental embroidery, and feasted on fresh grass and beans. But when it is led into the grand ancestral temple, though it wished to be (again) a solitary calf, would that be possible for it?"[24]

Official service is generally regarded by Confucians as a solemn and noble pursuit. Yet here the *Zhuangzi* compares officials to sacrificial oxen and elsewhere (as we shall see below) to a sacred tortoise — that is, to things naturally rejected as life-models on account of their inevitable loss of life and freedom. The paradox is startling, as shown in the following passage, where we are told how Zhuangzi refused to take up office when he was approached by an emissary from the King of the powerful Chu State:

> "吾聞楚有神龜，死已三千歲矣，王巾笥而藏之廟堂之上。此龜者，寧其死為留骨而貴乎，寧其生而曳尾於塗中乎？"二大夫曰："寧生而曳尾塗中。"莊子曰："往矣！吾將曳尾於塗中。"

> "I have heard," said Zhuangzi, "that in your king's possession [there] is a sacred tortoise, dead these three thousand years, but still lying in the king's treasure chest. Now, were the tortoise to have his choice, would he die so as to leave his bones as relics to be treasured by men, or would he rather live and wag his tail in a mud pool?" "He would rather live and wag his tail in the mud pool," said the messenger. Whereupon Zhuangzi dismissed him, saying, "Please be gone. I want to wag my tail in the mud pool."[25]

This passage no doubt leaves a deep and lasting impression on readers' minds on account of Zhuangzi's humorous comparison of himself to the tortoise that would choose to live freely rather than be caged up in a box, even after death. While smiling ruefully at Zhuangzi's self-mocking metaphor, readers are more likely to be drawn into and convinced by the argumentation than they would be if the discourse were more direct and employed no such ironic literary devices.

In the *Liezi*, it is not just ordinary people or the masters of the different schools who convert to Daoism; there are also such ancient heroes and mythical figures as Huangdi (the Yellow Emperor) and the emperors Shun and Yu. This all-embracing approach gives the author(s) and readers more imaginative space, and delivers a greater impact by making it appear that the messages being taught have been known by many famous figures down the ages. These figures are recast and described as having very human qualities and feelings. Some are transformed into ideal rulers — but only when they have been inspired by Daoist ideas of the effective and natural way of government. For instance, the Yellow Emperor is shown as having suffered physical weakness from exerting all his knowledge and strength to rule his people — "his ravaged flesh grew darkened and his dulled senses were stupefied" (焦然肌色皯，昏然五情爽惑).[26] After he changed his way of ruling to a natural and effortless Daoist way of action, however, the empire was better governed. Even more dramatically, the parable suggests that the Daoist way of ruling was in fact the reason the emperor himself became immortal, and we are told that he was so beloved that the people did not cease wailing for him for more than 200 years after he finally "ascended into the sky"![27] This possibly unintentionally humorous remark about the people's lengthy mourning for their departed emperor not only prompts readers to speculate that the Daoist way of ruling was excessively well received by his people, but also implies that his people lived very long lives since they continued wailing for more than 200 years.

Intentional comic irony and metaphor are used frequently in the *Liezi*. One example occurs in a story that begins with Mr Guo of Qi, who is very rich, telling Mr Xiang of Song, who is very poor, that stealing is in fact what made him rich. Just as readers are beginning to regard Mr Xiang as ridiculous because he tries to get rich by becoming a thief but is caught, the narrative continues, making it clear that Mr Guo's Way of stealing in fact means something else: it is the Daoist injunction to produce wealth by utilizing what is afforded by nature and Heaven. The irony deepens as the story continues, promoting the true Way of stealing, which is based on knowing what *should* be stolen and what *should not*; what is common property and what is private property:

> 齊之國樂大富，宋之向氏大貧；自宋之齊，請其術。國氏告之曰：「吾善為盜。始吾為盜也，一年而給，二年而足，三年大壤。自此以往，施及州閭。」向氏大喜，喻其為盜之言，而不喻其為盜之道，遂踰垣鑿室，手目所及，亡不探也。未及時，以贓獲罪，沒其先居之財。向氏以國氏之謬己也，往而怨之。國氏曰：「若為盜若何？」向氏言其狀。國氏曰：「嘻！若失為盜之道至此乎？今將告若矣。吾聞天有時，地有利。吾盜天地之時利，云雨之滂潤，山

澤之產育，以生吾禾，殖吾稼，筑吾垣，建吾舍。陸盜禽獸，水盜
魚鱉，亡非盜也。夫禾稼、土木、禽獸、魚鱉，皆天之所生，豈吾
之所有？然吾盜天而亡殃。夫金玉珍寶穀帛財貨，人之所聚，豈天
之所與？若盜之而獲罪，孰怨哉？"

Mr Guo of Qi was very rich. Mr Xiang of Song, who was very
poor, travelled from Song to Qi to inquire about his methods.
"I am good at stealing," Mr Guo told him. "After I first became
a thief, within a year I could keep myself, within two I was
comfortable, within three I was flourishing, and ever since then
I have been the benefactor of the whole neighbourhood." Xiang
was delighted; he understood from what Guo said that he was a
thief, but misunderstood his Way of being a thief. So he climbed
over walls and broke into houses, and grabbed anything in reach
of his eye and hand. Before long, he was found guilty of possessing
stolen goods, and lost his whole inheritance. Thinking that Guo
had deceived him, he went to him to complain. "In what way have
you been stealing?" Guo asked him. Xiang described what had
happened. "Alas!" Guo said. "Have you erred so far from the true
Way of stealing? Let me explain. I have heard it said: 'Heaven has
its season, earth has its benefits.' I rob heaven and earth of their
seasonal benefits, the clouds and rain of their irrigating floods, the
mountains and marshes of their products, in order to grow my
crops, plant my seed, raise my walls, build my house. I steal birds
and animals from the land, fish and turtles from the water. All this
is stealing; for crops and seed, clay and wood, birds and animals,
fish and turtles, are all begotten by heaven, and how can they
become my possessions? Yet I suffer no retribution for robbing
heaven. On the other hand precious things such as gold and jade,
and commodities such as grain and silk, are collected by men, and
how can we claim that it is heaven which provides them? When
you steal them, why should you resent being found guilty?"[28]

Metaphorical teaching with humorous irony is also employed in a
fable about how a monkey keeper cheats his monkeys. This fable is not
simply about the cleverness of the animal keeper. It can also be read
as dry mockery of ordinary people who are driven by greed and self-
interest, and who are thus too easily deceived by social rules imposed
by the authorities:

宋有狙公者，愛狙，養之成群，能解狙之意；狙亦得公之心。損其
家口，充狙之欲。俄而匱焉，將限其食。恐眾狙之不馴于己也，
先誑之曰："與若芧，朝三而暮四，足乎？"眾狙皆起而怒。俄而

曰：“與若芋，朝四而暮三，足乎？”眾狙皆伏而喜。物之以能鄙
相籠，皆猶此也。聖人以智籠群愚，亦猶狙公之以智籠眾狙也。名
實不虧，使其喜怒哉！

There was a keeper of monkeys in [the kingdom of] Song who loved monkeys so much that he reared flocks of them. He could interpret the monkeys' thoughts, and the monkeys also caught what was in his mind. He made his own family go short in order to give the monkeys whatever they wanted. Before long he found himself in need, and decided to give them less to eat. Fearing that the monkeys would not submit to this tamely, he played a trick on them beforehand: "If I give you three chestnuts in the morning and four in the evening, will that be enough?" The monkeys all rose in a rage. "Will it be enough if I give you four in the morning and three in the evening?" The monkeys were all pleased and lay down again . . . The sage by his wisdom gets all the fools into his cage, just as the keeper did to the monkeys. Without taking anything away, in name or reality, he can either please them or enrage them![29]

In its exploration of important themes, the *Liezi* employs exaggeration and heightened contrast to depict limited human knowledge and values. Philosophical ideas are presented via bizarre and vivid anecdotes that lead readers to ruminate upon them while entering into the playful humour of the stories. One example is a tale about the value of mental "fasting" so as to achieve a state in which one no longer feels the obstruction of external things but develops the capacity to deal effortlessly with situations. This is illustrated in a story about practising archery on a cliff in order to overcome the innate human fear of danger. It describes how Liezi was confidently demonstrating his archery to Bohun Wuren, showing that he could perform very skilfully, and Bohun Wuren asked Liezi to fire his arrows from the top of a high mountain while treading a perilous cliff which overlooked an abyss 1000 feet deep. Liezi ascended the mountain and was asked to move forward to the edge. At this point, the story presents us with the comic figure of Liezi so terrified of falling off the cliff that he is not even able to stand on his own feet, let alone shoot his arrow:

御寇伏地，汗流至踵。

Liezi lay on his face with the sweat streaming down to his heels . . . [30]

Responding to this picture of fear, Bohun Wuren draws out the moral for his readers:

夫至人者，上窺青天，下潛黃泉，揮斥八極。神氣不變。今汝怵然
有恂目之志，爾于中也殆矣夫！

The highest man peers at the blue sky above him, measures the
Yellow Spring below him; tossed and hurled to the Eight Corners,
his spirit and his breathing do not change. Now you tremble and
would like to shut your eyes. Isn't there danger within you?[31]

Dream and reality are used in both the *Zhuangzi* and the *Liezi* to
demonstrate that illusion, personal beliefs and one's own world-
view have a deep impact upon perceptual certainty. The *Liezi* also
draws attention to the relative magnitude of time and space, arguing
that ordinary human life exists in such arbitrary dimensions of space
and duration that we should be ready to accept experience from very
different perspectives, including living in our dreams as well as in
reality. Once we liberate ourselves from temporo-spatially determined
illusion, we will gain the true happiness that is not confined to any one
particular perception. Liezi offers an example of the contrasting worth
of dream and reality in a story where one is so diverted by the down-
to-earth, comical situation that it is almost impossible to question the
validity of the moral conclusion:

周之尹氏大治產，其下趣役者，侵晨昏而弗息。有老役夫，筋力竭
矣，而使之彌勤。晝則呻呼而即事，夜則昏憊而熟寐。精神荒散，
昔昔夢為國君。居人民之上，總一國之事。游燕宮觀，恣意所欲，
其樂無經。覺則復役。人有慰喻其懃者，役夫曰："人生百年，晝
夜各分。吾晝為仆虜，苦則苦矣；夜為人君，其樂無比。可所怨
哉？"

Mr Yin of Zhou ran a huge estate. The underlings who hurried
to serve him never rested from dawn to dusk. There was an old
servant with no more strength in his muscles, whom he drove all
the harder. By day the servant went to work groaning, at night
he slept soundly dulled by fatigue. Losing consciousness, every
evening he dreamed that he was lord of the nation, enthroned
above the people, with all affairs of state under his control. He gave
himself up to whatever pleased him, excursions and banquets,
palaces and spectacles; his joy was incomparable. Waking, he was
a servant again. When someone condoled with him for having to
work so hard, the servant said: "Man's term of life is a hundred
years, divided between day and night. By day I am a bondman and
my life is bitter indeed; but at night I become a prince, and my joy
is comparable. Why should I complain?"[32]

It is generally recognized that the focus of Daoism is upon the individual in nature rather than the individual in society. Daoism holds that the goal of life for each of us is to find one's own personal adjustment to the rhythm of the natural (and supernatural) world, and thus to follow the Way (*dao*) of the universe. This is a highly abstract concept to communicate. As we have seen, the *Liezi* frequently resorts to metaphor to bring such high matters down to earth for its readers. A special case is the use of logical argumentation by analogy in *reductio ad absurdum*, which also entertains while it teaches. The following story sets out to show that by becoming unconscious and adapting to nature, humans can survive even in an environment in which it is impossible for other species to live, despite supposedly being adapted to it. The story presents a dream-like world, yet one that is wholly solid in its concrete and detailed observation — for example, describing the swimmer's lank hair as he walks along the bank. Such a technique manages to make the high ideal believable by reifying the absurdly impossible challenge:

> 孔子觀于呂梁，懸水三十仞，流沫三十里，黿鼉魚鱉之所不能游也。見一丈夫游之，以為有苦而欲死者也，使弟子并流而承之。數百步而出，被髮行歌，而游于棠行。孔子從而問之曰：「呂梁懸水三十仞，流沫三十里，黿鼉魚鱉所不能游，向吾見子道之，以為有苦而欲死者，使弟子并流將承子。子出而被髮行歌，吾以子為鬼也。察子則人也。請問蹈水有道乎？」曰：「亡，吾無道。吾始乎故，長乎性，成乎命，與齊俱入，與汨偕出，從水之道而不為私焉。此吾所以道之也。」

> Confucius was looking at Lüliang waterfall. The water dropped two hundred feet, streaming foam for thirty miles; it was a place where fish and turtles and crocodiles could not swim, but he saw a man swimming there. Taking him for someone in trouble who wanted to die, he sent a disciple along the bank to pull him out. But after swimming a few hundred yards the man came out, and strolled along singing under the bank with his hair hanging down his back. Confucius proceeded to question him: "I thought you were a ghost, but now I can look you over I see you are human. May I ask whether you have a Way to tread in water?" "No, I have no Way. I began in what is native to me, grew up in what is nature to me, matured by trusting destiny. I enter the vortex with the inflow and leave with the outflow, follow the Way of the water instead of imposing a course of my own; this is how I tread it."[33]

We smile as we picture the discomfiture of the great sage who thought he was performing a meritorious act of saving a life.

This story is an example of teaching the Daoist precepts of adaptability to nature and natural response to the physical environment, but such adaptability and response also apply to human emotional reactions. These precepts directly contradict traditional Confucian teaching, which holds that virtue consists of expressing human emotions properly, in accordance with ritual codes and social conventions.[34] The Confucian virtues particularly point to our "feelings" towards our parents, and as such they have been considered the root of humanism. To the authors of the *Liezi*, on the other hand, human emotion was a natural and spontaneous response to the external environment. The following story is clearly intended as mockery of what would, in Confucian terms, be called proper human emotion:

> 燕人生於燕，長於楚，及老而還本國。過晉國，同行者誑之；指城曰：「此燕國之城。」其人愀然變容。指社曰：「此若里之社。」乃喟然而歎。指舍曰：「此若先人之廬。」乃涓然而泣。指壠曰：「此若先人之冢。」其人哭不自禁。同行者啞然大笑，曰：「予昔紿若，此晉國耳。」其人大慚。及至燕，真見燕國之城社，真見先人之廬冢，悲心更微。

> There was a man who was born in Yan but grew up in Chu, and in old age returned to his native country. While he was passing through the state of Jin his companions played a joke on him. They pointed out a city and told him: "This is the capital of Yan." He composed himself and looked solemn. Inside the city they pointed out a shrine: "This is the shrine of your quarter." He breathed a deep sigh. They pointed out a hut: "This was your father's cottage." His tears welled up. They pointed out a mound: "This is your father's tomb." He could not help weeping aloud. His companions roared with laughter: "We were teasing you. You are still only in Jin." The man was very embarrassed. When he reached Yan, and really saw the capital of Yan and the shrine of his quarter, really saw his father's cottage and tomb, he did not feel it so deeply.[35]

Significantly, the old man whose instinctive behaviour was to show solemnity and sorrow towards his birthplace and his father's tomb tended to lose such profound feelings after being fooled and embarrassed by others. Confucians, of course, upheld the idea that virtuous feelings should be continuously cultivated to the point at which they were so unswerving that they were not easily removed or changed.[36] The fact that such changes in an old man's feelings could take place exposes the flimsiness of the cardinal Confucian virtue of filial piety. The outcome of the story not only has us laughing at the old man but also leads us to question whether human emotions are in fact truly escapable and unchangeable, and thus whether conventional values should really be set in stone and used to judge all moral standards, as Confucians advocated.

For their part, Daoists believed that one should rely not so much on human skill as upon the operations of the Way. Given this premise, it is not surprising to find the *Liezi* expressing a sarcastic and critical attitude towards human efforts to create and reproduce nature. This view produces in readers some darkly humorous and perhaps surprising judgements about the nature of human folly, even in the service of art, as in the following excerpt:

> 宋人有為其君以玉為楮葉者，三年而成。鋒殺莖柯，毫芒繁澤，亂之楮葉中，而不可別也。此人遂以巧食宋國。子列子聞之，曰：「使天地之生物，三年而成一葉，則物之葉者寡矣。故聖人恃道化而不恃智巧。」

> There was once a man from Song who carved a mulberry leaf out of jade for his prince. It took him three years to complete; and it imitated nature so exquisitely that if it was put among real mulberry leaves its indentations, stalk, veins and lustre were indistinguishable from those of the rest. The man's skill won him a regular salary from the government of Song. When Liezi heard about this he commented: "If Heaven and Earth grew things so slowly that it took them three years to finish a leaf, there would not be many things with leaves. Therefore the sage trusts the transforming process of the Way, and puts no trust in cunning and skills."[37]

The examples I have discussed show how different devices in the *Liezi* — metaphor, exaggeration, hyperbole and *reductio ad absurdum* — all contribute to the humour throughout the text. Clearly, their use of surprising contrast and an ironic tone is designed to grasp the attention of readers and provoke reflection on the implications of what is being recounted. The spirit of the unconventional mind(s) of the author(s) captured in these devices provides amusement for readers as well as instruction in the tenets of Daoism. This is what contributes to the *Liezi*'s effectiveness as a text that entertains while it teaches. It is true that not all the anecdotes appear to be humorous at first sight. This is because they depend, like all humour, on a great deal of "local knowledge" about assumptions, conventions and historical figures and places.[38] As Harbsmeier has noted, however, while jokes from a different culture and from a different time may not strike modern readers as uproariously funny, as long as we possess shared feelings of sympathy with the all-too-human figures of their narratives, we may begin to understand not only their humour but also their wisdom.[39]

The impact of Daoist humour is not confined to the ancient texts themselves: over the ages it has continued to provide direct authority for humour to teach ethical, moral and philosophical lessons. Thus this subtle and ironic humour has had a far-reaching effect on Chinese culture, and has provided inspiration to artists and writers in establishing some well-known styles of portraying comic characters and situations. While there is insufficient space here to illustrate this heritage, perhaps one example from modern times could be the well-known figure of Ah Q in Lu Xun's comic masterpiece *Ah Q zhengzhuan* 阿Q正傳 (The true story of Ah Q), originally published in 1921–22.[40] This story portrays someone unable to face up to reality who succeeds, ironically, through self-deception, highlighting the falsities and failings of his contemporary society. It might be going too far to suggest that Ah Q is a modern parable drawing on the *Liezi* tradition, but it certainly shares a similar kind of sardonic humour and could expect its audience to recognize and be influenced by such echoes. The popular Hong Kong comic, Old Master Q (*Lao Fuzi* 老夫子), likewise mocked social change and social problems in Hong Kong between the 1960s and the 1980s. More recent examples include the contemporary Taiwanese artist Tsai Chih-chung (Cai Zhizhong 蔡志忠 b. 1948), whose work includes cartoon versions of Daoist texts such as *Liezi*,[41] and the satirical artist Yue Minjun 岳敏君 (b. 1964), whose exaggeratedly grinning figures are famous internationally. Yue Minjun in particular belongs in the Daoist humour tradition of gently mocking contemporary society.[42] The full impact on later Chinese art and writing of teaching truth in this way through irony and humour remains an area that deserves further attention and evaluation.

6

Shared Humour: Elitist Joking in *Shishuo xinyu* (A New Account of Tales of the World)

Lily Xiao Hong Lee

To write about humour in *Shishuo xinyu* 世説新語 (A New Account of Tales of the World, hereafter *Shishuo*),¹ one must first examine the appropriateness of applying such a modern Western concept to a work compiled in medieval China. The Chinese term *youmo* 幽默, a transliteration of the English word "humour", has come to mean both anything that amuses or entertains and the various amused reactions to such stimuli. Did humour in either of these senses exist in ancient China? More specifically, can we tell whether early medieval Chinese people had humour and enjoyed it? Accepting the most general interpretation of humour as it is now understood helps avoid the pitfalls of theoretical arguments and provides a straightforward answer: if humour is what provides amusement and brings a shadow of a smile or provokes laughter, then it is indeed possible to talk about humour in this remarkable classical text, which is neither moralistic nor sentimental but rather full of humour. Since it was created and enjoyed in those times, then the answer to the questions posed above must be "Yes".

Background and Origins

Over the centuries, *Shishuo* has been a very popular text, especially among Chinese literati — that is, the gentry or landowners from whom were drawn the officials in successive imperial governments. In the traditional division of classes or occupations, scholar-officials ranked highest, above farmers, craftsmen and merchants. The popularity of *Shishuo* spread outwards, particularly following the growing availability of writing materials — especially paper, which was comparatively easy and cheap to produce in larger quantities using a method developed by Cai Lun 蔡倫 (50–121 CE).[2] Writing styles also became more diversified over the centuries, and affected the ways in which scholarship was conducted.[3] The act of putting pen or brush to paper had once been carefully guarded, only to be used for texts considered to be beneficial to statecraft and the edification of the mind — in other words, for historical and philosophical writing. Writing later branched off to include texts that amused and fascinated. Although the genre of *xiaoshuo* 小說 (fiction — literally "small talk"), under which *Shishuo* was traditionally classified, thus had humble origins; it may nevertheless have been of benefit to the ruler,[4] and by the time *Shishuo* itself appeared the genre had developed to serve many causes. *Shishuo*'s aims were aiding those who wished to polish the art of conversation, and simply providing enjoyment through amusing anecdotes and examples of clever repartee; it has always been regarded as amply fulfilling both.[5] The work has survived through more than a millennium and a half to the present day, not because it was on the reading list for the imperial civil examinations but because of its readers' affection and the pure enjoyment it afforded them.

The actual date of *Shishuo*'s compilation is not recorded. Fan Ziye argued that it was probably completed around 439–40 CE; Mather puts it around 430.[6] I, on the other hand, have extended the time of *Shishuo*'s compilation to 435; however, I agree that, given the many projects Liu Yiqing initiated and the fact that he and his literary aides could not have devoted themselves full time to the compilation of these works, it was probably completed about 439–40.[7] Judging by the fact that at least one edition known to us appeared in the same Liu Song dynasty (420–78) in which Liu Yiqing lived, it soon became popular, while imitations and commentaries began to appear within 80 years of his death.[8] The best commentary was written by Liu Jun 劉峻 (462–521), who incorporated the many sources on which *Shishuo* had relied and provided background for its often-cryptic entries, to the benefit of readers and scholars of later ages. New editions appeared in almost every dynasty from then on, often several in one period. The early editions before the age of printing were necessarily manuscripts. The earliest and only remnant of a hand-copied *Shishuo*, dated to the Tang dynasty, is in the possession of collectors in Japan. A photographic edition of this fragment was taken back to China in the twentieth century. The earliest recorded printed edition is a Song edition printed in 1138, but it is no longer extant. The earliest surviving printed copy is also a Song edition: the Maeda edition, preserved in Japan. This edition contains a great number of errors, however, and therefore the modern Chinese edition — whose distant provenance is a Song-dynasty edition, which in turn was based on an edition of a century earlier — is considered better than the Maeda edition.[9]

After having circulated for a millennium, *Shishuo*'s popularity seems to have waned after the Yuan dynasty (1279–1368), but it was revived with the publication in 1556 of an abridged edition entitled *Shishuo xinyu bu* 世說新語補 (Addended *Shishuo xinyu*), which combines the original text with entries of the same nature relating to later ages penned by others. This new edition became so popular that it threatened the continued existence of the original *Shishuo*. Fortunately, despite the popularity of this new edition, the original edition managed to survive into modern times. The inclusion of the original *Shishuo* in the *Siku quanshu* 四庫全書, a collection copied under imperial decree in the eighteenth century, no doubt ensured this. It was not only popular throughout China; numerous imitations over the ages also appeared in other East Asian countries such as Japan and Korea. In Japan, seven imitations are reported by Qian Nanxiu,[10] while in Korea examples of works considered to have been written in the *Shishuo* genre include Lee In-ro's *Pahan jib* 破閒集 and Choe Ja's *Bohan jib* 補閒集.[11]

Although compiled in the fifth century, *Shishuo*'s sources are earlier: *Shishuo* is in fact a collection of anecdotes and quotations about historical figures dating mainly from the third and fourth centuries. Its pages reflect an important shift from orthodox Confucianism to Daoism in the outlook of the literati during this Wei–Jin period. Many of its personages espouse Daoist ideas or display these ideas in their behaviour, and it often illustrates a close link between Daoist thought and humour.[12] The compiler is traditionally given as Liu Yiqing 劉 義慶 (403–44), Prince of Linchuan in present-day Jiangxi Province, of the southern Liu Song (420–79) dynasty. However, later research has shown that it could have been compiled by scholars under his sponsorship.[13] The educated elite provided the audience for *Shishuo*. In most cases, no background is provided for the anecdotes and even full

names of the people referred to are not given, on the understanding
that to refer to them by their official title, courtesy name or even
nickname was sufficient to identify them to readers. This has made the
text difficult for later readers, and even more so for readers from the
West. The definitive English translation by Richard Mather, published
in 1976, provides detailed explanations and references to assist English-
speaking readers in understanding the text.

Liu Yiqing was enfeoffed as prince by his uncle, the first and
founding emperor of the Liu Song dynasty,[14] and was thus trained
to govern from a young age. However, we are told that he was also
particularly interested in literature — though not really blessed
with a gift for writing. In adulthood, he was entrusted by his cousin,
a later emperor, with the task of controlling large areas of the state;
being officially responsible for both political and military affairs, he
would have been kept very busy. Bibliographical works covering
the times in which he lived credit him with other voluminous works
comprising hundreds of *juan* 卷 (chapters). All this has caused later
scholars to call his authorship into doubt. The literary scholar Lu Xun
魯迅 (1881–1936) surmised that the real compilers of *Shishuo* were
the literary aides mentioned in Liu's official biography.[15] Following
this lead, I investigated the lives of his four aides/protégés, and have
argued on the basis of their personalities and surviving fragments of
their work that two of them — He Changyu 何長瑜 (d. c. 445) and Yuan
Shu 袁淑 (408–53) — in fact exhibited the kind of open-mindedness and
irreverence that also characterizes *Shishuo*, and were thus most likely
involved in its compilation.[16]

Shishuo can loosely be described as a cross between an unofficial
history, a biography and a gossip page. It embraces telling details about
historical figures and events not important enough to have entered the
pages of the official histories, but nevertheless interesting because such
details reveal the deep psychology of these historical figures, affording
insight into their interactions. The principal criterion for inclusion
seems to have been that the material was of general interest. If that is so,
then humour probably earned its inclusion in this way. Looked at from
another angle, *Shishuo* is a book about human traits. This is made clear
by the titles of the chapters, such as "The square and proper", "The

free and unrestrained" and "Stinginess and meanness", which seem to attempt to embody the entire spectrum of human characteristics. If *Shishuo* were indeed intended to cover all angles of human nature, it could not afford to leave out humour.

Sharing jokes among an in-group is naturally found in many cultures. A Greek manuscript entitled *Philogelos*, or "Laughter-lover", is dated not earlier than the tenth century CE; however, like *Shishuo*, it contains earlier material from as early as the third century.[17] This collection contains jokes made at the expense of intellectuals: the pedantic student, the lawyer, the doctor and the professor. Although it is not clear who the author or authors were, it is thought to have been created by the "lower urban classes".[18] The similarity between this work from the world of Greek Byzantium and *Shishuo* lies in both works having the educated or intellectuals as their subject. However, they differ in that the creators of *Shishuo* were themselves literati, rather than members of the lower urban classes. Evidently, however, gentlemen in the West — like the Chinese educated elite — read and enjoyed joke books from early times. A later example, from sixteenth-century England, is a compilation entitled *A hundred mery talys*, which circulated widely in England and is said to have been the product of a highly educated Humanist circle,[19] just as *Shishuo* was. It also shares similarities and differences with *Shishuo*. Derek Brewer has observed of the jesting in European Renaissance and early modern works like *A hundred mery talys* that "it promotes humour and harmony of the group who share it and its implications", and this seems to apply to *Shishuo*; however, his further comment proves quite opposite to what *Shishuo* stands for: "Traditionally jests tend to endorse popular prejudice, as with the universally practised ethnic joke, or almost equally universal anti-feminism in many forms, or mockery of physical handicaps."[20]

Shishuo and Joke Books

Shishuo does not purport to be a jest book: humour is only a by-product of its *raison d'être*, which is to be a collection of elegant and interesting sayings and anecdotes. Also, the compilers of *Shishuo* were aiming at an elite group whose taste may well have been opposite to that of the popular culture of the time. China certainly also had its jest books. Roughly two centuries before the compilation of *Shishuo*, there appeared a book entitled *Xiao lin* 笑林 (The forest of laughter). The reputed author, Handan Chun 邯鄲淳 (fl. c.220 CE), was a writer, calligrapher and specialist in Chinese written characters. When the Cao Wei dynasty was established (221), he was given the prestigious title of erudite (*boshi* 博士). His *Xiao lin*, originally in three *juan*, is no longer extant and only 29 of its entries are still preserved today.[21] The work has been described as a joke book and is clearly devoted to humour and laughter, as indicated by its title and the remaining contents, which seem to focus directly on exposing human folly and frailties. The main difference between this work and *Shishuo* is that the people who appear in the *Xiao lin* entries are commoners rather than the elite. The jokes are less subtle and more suited to popular taste. We can deduce, therefore, that it was compiled as a work for a popular or wider audience, whereas *Shishuo* was a work for the literati. There is no discernible link between the two.

We can only speculate about why *Shishuo* survived intact while *Xiao lin* was largely lost. The fate of a work in pre-modern China depended largely on the literati, who were not only the creators of texts but also their chief consumers. Texts not continually used by them were apt to disappear, and many did just that over the centuries. Elsewhere, I have argued that *Shishuo* survived because it incorporated many earlier texts and thus acted as a kind of storehouse for its own genre. Knowing nothing more about *Xiao lin* and its compiler, we cannot be sure it functioned in the same way. The extant fragments of *Xiao lin* have been culled from early reference books known as *leishu* 類書, a type of work unique to China. Works in this category were encyclopaedic, but differed from the Western concept of encyclopaedias in that they collected quotations from other books and arranged them under topics, rather than composing their own summaries of what was known about a topic. Consequently, these *leishu* are treasure houses of lost books. Scholars in the eighteenth century first started to cull snippets of lost books from *leishu*, and this work was continued sporadically in the nineteenth century. An illustrious twentieth-century scholar of this kind was Lu Xun, who culled fragments of many ancient works of fiction in his compilation *Gu xiaoshuo gouchen*, published after his death in the first edition of his complete works in 1938.

Types of Humour in *Shishuo*

Shishuo was compiled and worked on the assumption that certain books and their contents were a commonality within the literati group; it could be enjoyed only by those who had studied and internalized the Confucian classics and official histories. It contains many in-jokes to be shared by these privileged readers, but also seemingly universal jokes that can be enjoyed by everyone. Certain jokes have a child confronting an adult, or a man a woman. Some passages ridicule human weakness, poking particular fun at country bumpkins in the way noted by Brewer. A number of jokes document a lack of reverence and respect for social status, and established behaviour and attitudes. The types of humour classified and illustrated below give an idea of the range in this work. Types do sometimes overlap, and one passage may represent several approaches to humour. Moreover, the humour may be situated in what people say as well as in their behaviour — sometimes in a combination of both.

Literati In-Group Jokes

Literati in-group jokes are created by and for the literati. Their premise is that speaker and listener share knowledge of a body of literature and that, without any explanation or reminder by the "speaker" in the written joke, the "listener" (reader) will be able to recall the passages referenced and grasp the intended humour. For Chinese speakers and readers in the fifth and later centuries, this body of literature included the Confucian classics, especially the *Shijing* 詩經 (Book of songs), *Shujing* 書經 (Book of history), *Chunqiu* 春秋 (Spring and autumn annals) and *Zuo zhuan* 左傳 (Commentary [on the annals] according to Master Zuo). All literati who hoped to be recommended for official positions were also expected to be familiar with two official histories: the *Shiji* 史記 (Records of the Grand Historian) and *Han shu* 漢書 (Book of Han). Although students were not necessarily required to learn these by heart, they were expected to be familiar with the events and characters mentioned in them. Without this knowledge and a grasp of the archaic language in which it was couched, the audience would be unable to get the point of the jokes in *Shishuo*. This type of humour is so characteristic of *Shishuo* that it recurs at least as a side aspect to many of the passages below.

In some cases, the humour arises simply from quoting classics appropriate to a certain situation:

> 簡文作撫軍時，嘗與桓宣武俱入朝，更相讓在前。宣武不得已而先之，因曰：「伯也執殳，為王前驅。」簡文曰：「所謂『無小無大，從公于邁』。」

When Emperor Jianwen[22] was serving as Generalissimo Controlling the Army, he once came into the audience hall with Huan Wen. After the two had repeatedly yielded precedence to each other, Huan finally had no recourse but to go first. In so doing he said:

"The earl grasps his spear
And goes ahead as the king's fore-rider."

Jianwen countered with:

"There are no small and no great;
All follow the duke in his travels."[23]

Understanding the archaic language of this joke may be just as difficult for Chinese readers not fluent in classical Chinese as for non-Chinese readers, although the English translation removes this barrier for some. Readers must also know who these two men were, and understand their relative standing in their own world. Emperor Jianwen, personal name Sima Yu [Ssu-ma Yü] 司馬昱 (320–72, reign period 372) had not yet ascended the throne at the time of this episode. He was then Prince of Kuaiji, representing the interests of the imperial house. Huan Wen (312–73), on the other hand, was a dominant minister in control of the army with ambitions of replacing the imperial house with his own. Their potential conflict lay somewhat beneath the surface, as in this episode the two are very cautious in dealing with each other. Huan Wen's quotation from the *Book of songs* expresses his respect as a feudal lord for the imperial house. In reply, Sima Yu quotes the same work to indicate his reluctance to take precedence over Huan Wen, since he wishes to follow Huan's leadership as "the duke" — a reference to the Duke of Zhou, a famous character from what was then already ancient history. The Duke of Zhou was the brother of King Wu, founder of the Zhou dynasty, serving as regent for his son King Cheng, still a minor when he succeeded to the throne. On the surface, the narrative seems simply to be about someone of higher official position being courteous to his senior in age (Huan Wen was undoubtedly older than Sima Yu) and/or the senior in age being courteous to someone who holds a higher position; however, understanding the background politics reveals a deeper significance and underlying hostility. Since Huan Wen did not wish to expose his ambition openly, he chose a quotation to demonstrate his loyalty while Sima Yu chose a quotation that revealed — albeit subtly — his awareness of Huan's ambition. The story could not have failed to elicit knowing smiles from those who understood its nuances.

A similar story about two different people in the same situation has an opposite twist, so that instead of being self-deprecatory, their remarks are self-congratulatory:

> 王文度、范榮期俱為簡文所要。范年大而位小，王年小而位大。將前，更相推在前。既移久，王遂在范後。王因謂曰：「簸之揚之，糠秕在前。」范曰：「洮之汰之，沙礫在後。」
>
> Wang Tanzhi [Wang T'an-chih] and Fan Qi [Fan Ch'i] were once summoned simultaneously by Emperor Jianwen. Fan was older but lower in rank, while Wang was younger but higher in rank. As they were about to go in, each more and more insistently urged the other to go first.
>
> After this had gone on for some time, Wang finally ended up behind Fan, where he quipped, "Winnow it and toss it; the chaff and unripened kernels fall in front."[24] Fan retorted, "Sift it and wash it; the sand and gravel remain behind."[25]

The classical references are here used rather differently. First, the quotations are not exact but contain invented material; second, although modelled on the *Book of songs*, they use material from other classics. The clever composition of each two-line set is elegant enough to lead readers/listeners to think they might indeed be part of the classic 300 songs in the *Book of songs*. What is more, both of Fan's lines match Wang's completely in sound and sense. Although the writing of matching literary couplets was still in the future and had probably not yet begun, Chinese people have long appreciated clever line-matching in prose or poetry, and literati with a penchant for this art form would certainly have admired Fan's repartee.

When such repartee comes not from highly educated adults but from the mouths of children, there is an additional element of surprise and astonishment deriving from the difference in age. Here, humour acts as an equaliser. An outright and direct answer from a young person or a subordinate, when funny, is not simply acceptable to a superior; if successful, it may delight. Here is one good example from among many (an attractive aspect of the collection for young readers):

> 鍾毓、鍾會少有令譽。年十三，魏文帝聞之，語其父鍾繇曰：「可令二子來。」於是敕見。毓面有汗，帝曰：「卿面何以汗？」毓對曰：「戰戰惶惶，汗出如漿。」復問會：「卿何以不汗？」對曰：「戰戰慄慄，汗不敢出。」

> Zhong Yu [Chung Yü] and his younger brother Zhong Hui [Chung Hui] both enjoyed excellent reputations in their youth. When they were around thirteen years old, Emperor Wen of Wei heard of them and said to their father, Zhong You [Chung Yu], "You may bring your two sons to see me sometime."

> Accordingly an imperial audience was arranged for them. Yu's face was covered with sweat, and the emperor asked, "Why is your face sweating?"

> Yu replied:

> "Tremble, tremble, flutter, flutter;

> My sweat pours out like so much water."

> Turning to Hui, the emperor asked, "And why are you *not* sweating?"

> Hui replied:

> "Tremble, tremble, flutter, fall;

> My sweat can't even come at all."[26]

What does not quite come through in translation is that both boys' responses are in the archaic language and style of the *Book of songs*. Moreover, Zhong Yu's response rhymes and Zhong Hui's response follows the same format but varies it slightly in order to achieve rhyme for his lines as well. The elegance of the archaic language and the quick wit and ingenuity coming from two children are surprises that must provoke a smile in readers.

Quick-witted stylish repartee could also come from underlings and be equally funny:

習鑿齒、孫興公未相識，同在桓公坐。桓語孫「可與習參軍共語。
」孫云：「『蠢爾蠻荊』，敢與大邦為讎？」習云：「『薄伐獫
狁』，至于太原。」²⁷

Xi Zuochi [Hsi Tsuo-ch'ih] and Sun Chuo [Sun Ch'o] had not
previously known each other. Both were present at a gathering of
Huan Wen's staff. Huan said to Sun, "You may converse with my
aide, Xi Zuochi."

Sun began:

"Stupid the southern boors of Jing
Who dare oppose a mighty state."²⁸

Xi countered:

"In punishing the northern hordes,
Our troops have come to Taiyuan town."²⁹

What needs to be known is that Sun Chuo was from the northern
city of Taiyuan, while Xi Zuochi was from Xiangyang towards the
south, in the region known from ancient times as Jing. In referring to
northern hordes, the southerner Xi associates the northerner Sun with a
ferocious and bellicose minority people from the north-west mentioned
in the *Book of songs*. Since both quotations are from the *Book of songs*, this
verbal battle between southerner and northerner is waged through the
words of the classics.

Such use of well-chosen quotations by educated aides-de-camp is
not so surprising, but in the mouths of slaves in disgrace its comic force
is certainly stronger:

鄭玄家奴婢皆讀書。嘗使一婢，不稱旨，將撻之。方自陳説，玄
怒，使人曳箸泥中。須臾，復有一婢來，問曰：「胡為乎泥中？」
荅曰：「薄言往愬，逢彼之怒。」³⁰

In Zheng Xuan [Cheng Hsüan]'s household, the male and female
slaves were literate. Once when Xuan was being waited on by a
female slave, she failed to satisfy his wishes. He was on the point of
flogging her, when she began making excuses for herself. In a rage,
Xuan had her dragged through the mire. A moment later another
female slave came by and asked in the *Song* "Shiwei":³¹

"What are you doing in the mire?"

She replied, from the *Song* "Bozhou":³²

"I went to him and pled my cause,
But there met only with his wrath."

The fact that the slave girls are depicted as capable of quoting from the classic text is evidence of *Shishuo*'s relaxed attitude to social distinctions. It allows the collection to embrace a more extreme form of the humour, which is rooted in the incongruity between quoting the classics or imitating their pompous style and being immersed in everyday situations. This creates a strong contrast between the pompous and the mundane where the audience is amused by recognizing the sources and evaluating the new uses to which the speakers put them.

On a slightly different level, there are jokes not related to the classics but still qualifying as in-jokes of the literati. One kind is a quip deriding current fads among the literati themselves, such as the following, which concerns the eccentric scholar-official and artist Gu Kaizhi 顧愷之 (c.344–406 CE), sometimes described as the father of Chinese painting:

> 人問顧長康：「何以不作洛生詠？」答曰：「何至作老婢聲！」
>
> Someone asked Gu Kaizhi [Ku K'ai-chih], "Why don't you ever chant poems in the manner of the scholars of Luoyang?"
> Gu replied, "Why should I make a noise like an old slave woman?"[33]

This entry does not actually quote lines from the classics, yet it is essential for the listener to know that the Luoyang scholars' chant, while very popular among the Jin literati, tended to be quite nasal. The joke is an in-group put-down that only insiders could really enjoy. They would also be aware that Gu himself was adept at in-group humour, evidenced not only in the above story but perhaps also in his most famous painting, "Admonitions of the instructress to the palace ladies" 女史箴图 (see Figure 6.1), which was created as an illustration to an account of the life of Jin dynasty Empress Jia (257–300).[34]

Another example appealing to in-group knowledge is the following:

> 高坐道人不作漢語，或問此意，簡文曰：「以簡應對之煩。」
>
> The monk Gaozuo [Kao-tso] did not speak Chinese. Someone inquired about the significance of this, and the future Emperor Jianwen replied, "It's to save himself the trouble of answering questions."[35]

Figure 6.1   Painting of a palace lady by Gu Kaizhi 顧愷之 (c.344–406 CE).
Detail from "Admonitions of the instructress to the palace ladies" 女史箴圖
(probably a copy dating from seventh or eighth century CE). Handscroll, ink
and colour on silk. © The Trustees of the British Museum, reproduced in black
and white with permission.

During the Eastern Jin dynasty, monks from India and Central Asia
travelled to China to spread Buddhism. They were well received by
the literati, who showed interest in their religion and thought, and they
often attached themselves to local powerful men. Gaozuo, for example,
often kept company with Chancellor Wang Dao (王導 276–339) and
other notables in the Eastern Jin court. Conversation was one of the
main activities in these gatherings, and it was inevitable that the monk
would be bombarded with questions from inquisitive literati about his
foreign looks and customs as well as about Buddhist thought. However,
he was a native of the "western regions" (present-day Central Asia)
and had not learned to speak Chinese as some of his fellow monks
had done, and always communicated with Chinese scholars through
interpreters. The future Emperor Jianwen amusingly attributed this to
an ulterior but pragmatic motive — not wanting to be pestered with
stupid questions. The joke cut both ways: against the monk and against
the courtiers.

Universal Jokes

Humour is known to be highly culture specific. However, I believe some items from *Shishuo* constitute humour that can be widely understood. They are based on human frailties and follies common to people of all races, religions and nationalities. Some present the less powerful — such as children, women and the socially inferior — snubbing the more powerful — adults, men and social superiors. These reflect universal instincts, not those culturally specific to China at any age or time. One such universal type of joke concerns the uncouth and unsophisticated — usually the laughing stock of those who consider themselves refined. In *Shishuo* I call these country bumpkin jokes, a type that Christie Davies has shown exists around the world.[36] *Shishuo* also has jokes that relate to interaction between adults and children; I have assigned these to the category of universal child-versus-adult jokes. By the same token, interaction between the sexes constitutes the category of man-versus-woman jokes; another may be termed the mavericks. In this category, the protagonists openly display irreverence, sometimes in self-defence against accusations of bizarre behaviour. The final category I identify is human foibles, which deals with the entire spectrum of human weaknesses. I will discuss these in order.

Country Bumpkin Jokes

During the Wei and Jin dynasties (265–534 CE), a privileged few connected with the emperor vied to show off fabulously extravagant lifestyles. Many stories in *Shishuo* tell of the outrageous forms of such competitions in lavishness. At the juncture of Western and Eastern Jin dynasties, around 317, there was a great population shift from north to south China because the north was occupied by militarist non-Chinese regimes. People of the Eastern Jin dynasty south of the Yangtze River enjoyed an easier life than their northern neighbours because of the milder climate and more productive land, and prided themselves on also being more cultured. Northerners who had already reached the south and who adopted this more materialistic, perhaps more refined, southern culture were familiar with southern food and drink. Those who came later appeared relatively uninitiated. The following is one of many *Shishuo* entries deriding these new arrivals, who were seen as unsophisticated members of the literati:

> 蔡司徒渡江，見彭蜞，大喜曰：「蟹有八足，加以二螯。」令烹之。既食，吐下委頓，方知非蟹。後向謝仁祖説此事，謝曰：「卿讀爾雅不熟，幾為勸學死。」

> When Cai Mo [Ts'ai Mo] crossed the Yangtze River, he saw a sand-crab, and was greatly delighted, crying out, "The edible crab has eight legs plus two claws." Whereupon he gave the order to have it boiled. But only after he had eaten it and subsequently vomited it up and been miserably sick did he realize it was not an edible crab.

> Later when he was speaking to Xie Shang [Hsieh Shang] about the incident, Xie said, "You didn't read the *Erya* thoroughly enough, and were nearly killed by your ancestor's 'Essay on exhortation to learning'."[37]

Cai Mo 蔡謨 (281–356) was a scholar and official of the Eastern Jin dynasty who came from present-day Henan province in the yellow loess region north of the Yangtze where seafood was probably seldom served. That is why, when he saw a sand crab, he remembered two lines from *Quanxue pian* 勸學篇 (Essay on exhortation to learning) by his revered ancestor Cai Yong 蔡邕 (132–92): "A crab has eight legs and two claws." Thus he mistook it to be an edible crab. However, the ancient word book *Erya*[38] says "a sand crab is like a crab but small". Although this *Shishuo* entry contains two quotations from the classics, the humour is based more on the northerner's lack of what southerners might have considered common knowledge of aquatic creatures. What is especially absurd about Cai Mo's behaviour is his bookish way of identifying the crab and his rashness in eating what he thought he had identified.

Child-Versus-Adult Jokes

For anyone wishing to conduct research on children in old Chinese texts, *Shishuo* is a rich source.[39] Almost all its children are smart aleck types, perhaps because wit was so highly valued during the Wei–Jin period and the quick tongue of a precocious child was evidently highly appreciated. This may have been a reaction to the emphasis on detailed textual study that flourished in the preceding Eastern Han dynasty

(25–220 CE). Following the earlier example about the Zhong brothers' clever speeches at court, another entry about imperial precocity illustrates the general type:

> 晉明帝數歲，坐元帝膝上。有人從長安來，元帝問洛下消息，潸然流涕。明帝問何以致泣？具以東渡意告之。因問明帝：「汝意謂長安何如日遠？」答曰：「日遠。不聞人從日邊來，居然可知。」元帝異之。明日集羣臣宴會，告以此意，更重問之。乃答曰：「日近。」元帝失色，曰：「爾何故異昨日之言邪？」答曰：「舉目見日，不見長安。」

> When the Jin Emperor Ming (Sima Shao [Ssu-ma Shao], reigned 323–25) was only a few years old, he was sitting on the knees of his father, Emperor Yuan [reigned 317–23]. There was a man present who had come from Chang'an. Emperor Yuan (Sima Rui [Ssu-ma Jui]) was asking him news of Luoyang, sobbing all the while and letting his tears flow. Emperor Ming asked, "Why does it make you cry?" Emperor Yuan then told him the whole story of the eastward crossing of the Yangtze River and took the occasion to ask Emperor Ming, "In your opinion, how far away is Chang'an compared with the sun?"

> He replied, "The sun is farther away. Since I never heard of anyone coming here from the sun, we can know it for certain."

> Emperor Yuan marvelled at him. The next day he assembled all the ministers for a banquet to report this remark, and once more he asked the same question.

> This time Emperor Ming replied, "The sun is nearer." Emperor Yuan turned pale [and asked abruptly], "But why did you change from what you said yesterday?"

> He replied, "By just lifting your eyes you can see the sun, but [even if you lift your eyes] you can't see Chang'an."[40]

Emperor Yuan was a distant member of the imperial house of Jin, and Chang'an and Luoyang had been his home. In 311, China's northern neighbours, the Xiongnu, invaded northern China, took the Jin emperor prisoner and subsequently killed him around 317, bringing to an end what was later known as Western Jin. Emperor Yuan was at that juncture the Prince of Langye and a provincial governor stationed south of the Yangtze. Being the only surviving imperial prince, he was put on the throne as the founding emperor of the Eastern Jin dynasty. Since his empire now mainly comprised territory south of the Yangtze, he naturally missed his home in the north, which is why he wept when talking to the traveller from Chang'an. While parents who have tried to show their children off to others can no doubt identify with the feelings of Emperor Yuan, they are unlikely to have offspring as gifted as the young Emperor Ming, who redeemed himself while saving face for his parent.

Man-Versus-Woman Jokes

Shishuo is the earliest Chinese text to devote a whole chapter to women (with the exception of texts devoted solely to the edification of women, such as the *Lienü zhuan* (Biographies of exemplary women).[41] Entries about women in *Shishuo* can also be found in many other chapters as well and their humour reveals a surprisingly liberal and sympathetic attitude towards women. In fact, the fall from pre-eminence of Confucianism during the Wei–Jin period brought a relaxation of constraints on women, who seem to have enjoyed more freedom in speech and behaviour, witnessed by the following:

> 王夷甫雅尚玄遠，常嫉其婦貪濁，口未嘗言「錢」字。婦欲試之，令婢以錢遶牀，不得行。夷甫晨起，見錢閣行，呼婢曰：「舉卻阿堵物。」

> Wang Yan [Wang Yen] had always esteemed the Mysterious and Remote, and, being continually vexed by the avarice of his wife, Lady Guo, and by her worldly contamination, he never let the word "cash" pass his lips. Desiring to test him, his wife had a female slave surround his bed with cash, so that he could not walk past it. When Yan awoke in the morning and saw the cash obstructing the way, he called in the slave and said, "Get these objects out of here!"[42]

Lady Guo (d. c.300),[43] being a cousin of Empress Jia, the consort of Emperor Hui of Jin (reigned 290–306), used her influence to sell government positions and hence accumulated great wealth. Even her husband, Wang Yan (256–311),[44] a leading philosopher and powerful minister in his own right, could not curb her avarice. The phrase he coined to get around mentioning stuff that he despised — "these objects" — became a classic in Chinese culture: the colloquial term *aduwu* 阿堵物 (objects, things) entered the language as a synonym for money.

Humour could be drawn from complex interpersonal relations, as the following story shows:

> 諸葛令女，庾氏婦，既寡，誓云：「不復重出！」此女性甚正彊，無有登車理。恢既許江思玄婚，乃移家近之。初，誑女云：「宜徙。」於是家人一時去，獨留女在後。比其覺，已不復得出。江郎莫來，女哭詈彌甚，積日漸歇。江虨暝入宿，恆在對牀上。後觀其意轉帖，虨乃詐厭，良久不悟，聲氣轉急。女乃呼婢云：「喚江郎覺！」江於是躍來就之曰：「我自是天下男子，厭，何預卿事而見喚邪？既爾相關，不得不與人語。」女默然而慚，情義遂篤。

Zhuge Hui [Chu-ko Hui]'s daughter, Wenbiao [Wen-piao], was the wife of Yu Hui [Yü Hui]. After she became a widow she vowed that she would never again leave her home in marriage. Now this girl's nature was extremely proper and firm, and there was no prospect of ever getting her to set foot again in a wedding carriage. But since Zhuge Hui had promised her in marriage to Jiang Bin [Chiang Pin], he moved the family to be near the Jiangs. At that time, tricking his daughter, he had announced, "It's time to move," whereupon all the members of the family left at once, leaving the daughter behind alone. When she woke up to what had happened, it was already too late for her to leave.

When Jiang Bin came that evening the girl cried and carried on at great length, but after several days she gradually subsided. Jiang Bin then came in after dark to spend the night, but still remained on the opposite bed. Later, observing that her mood was growing calmer, Bin at length feigned a nightmare, not awaking for a long while as his cries and gasps became more and more agitated. Finally the girl called for her slave girl and said, "Call to Mr. Jiang and wake him up!"

At this Jiang leaped up and came over to her, saying, "I myself am a man of the world.[45] What have my nightmares to do with you that I should be called [by you]? But since we have this mutual relationship, you can't very well avoid talking with me." The girl was silent and ashamed, and after this her feelings and attitude grew more and more affectionate.[46]

It is telling that instead of forcibly demanding his rights as a husband, Jiang Bin was patient enough to take pains to gain her acceptance gradually: he could be held up as a model for the SNAGs of the twenty-first century! This is a gentle humour that subtly conveys its moral under cover of a deception, mixing tears and laughter. Interestingly enough, the story also indicates that in fourth-century China the parents of a widow did not insist that she remain chaste but on the contrary encouraged her to marry again; in fact, many similar stories can be found in *Shishuo* as well as elsewhere.[47] The concept of chastity for widows appears to have become more pervasive over time, as in later centuries widow celibacy was not only widely expected by the husband's family, but also considered an honour to the woman's natal family, which naturally led to pressure from relatives to comply.[48]

In the two passages above, the women are certainly not portrayed as submissive but they are nevertheless outwitted. The humour is at the women's expense and their aims are belittled and negated: the men seem to have won these particular rounds in the gender wars. There are, however, many instances of men losing:

許允婦是阮衛尉女，德如妹，奇醜。交禮竟，允無復入理，家人深以為憂。會允有客至，婦令婢視之，還答曰：「是桓郎。」桓郎者，桓範也。婦云：「無憂，桓必勸入。」桓果語許云：「阮家既嫁醜女與卿，故當有意，卿宜察之。」許便回入內。既見婦，即欲出。婦料其此出，無復入理，便捉裾停之。」許因謂曰：「婦有四德，卿有其幾？」婦曰：「新婦所乏唯容爾。然士有百行，君有幾？」許云：「皆備。」婦曰：「夫百行以德為首，君好色不好德，何謂皆備？」允有慚色，遂相敬重。

Xu Yun [Hsü Yün]'s wife was the daughter of Ruan Gong [Juan Kung] and the younger sister of Ruan Kan [Juan K'an]. She was extraordinarily homely. After the marriage ceremony was over, Yun had no intention of ever entering her apartment again. The members of her family were very upset over this. It happened that Yun was having a guest come, and his wife had a female slave look to see who it was. She returned and reported, "It's Master Huan." Now "Master Huan" was Huan Fan.

The wife said, "Then there's nothing to worry about. Huan will surely urge him to come to my apartment."

As expected, Huan said to Xu, "Since the Ruan family gave you a homely daughter in marriage, they obviously did so with some purpose in mind. You would do well to look into it."

Accordingly, Xu had a change of heart and entered his wife's apartment. But the moment he saw her he immediately wanted to leave again. His wife foresaw that if he went out this time there would be no further chance of his returning, so she seized his robe in an effort to detain him. Xu took the occasion to say to his wife, "A wife should have four virtues. How many of them do you have?"

His wife answered, "Where your bride is deficient is only in her appearance. But a gentleman should have a hundred deeds. How many have you?"

"I have them all."

"Of those hundred deeds, virtue is the first. If you love sensual beauty, but don't love virtue, how can you say you have them all?"

Yun looked ashamed and thereafter held her in respect and honour.[49]

It seems Xu Yun's wife knew that Huan was a trusted friend whose sensible advice would induce her new husband to enter her chamber again. Although the most obvious source of the humour here is the predicament of the ugly woman, she is also a smart woman who ends up having the last laugh when she outsmarts a smart man.

It may be that this turning of the tables was more amusing in its time precisely because it inverted the normal power structure, but it certainly contributes to the surprisingly modern feel of the *Shishuo*. It strikes at men's frequent failure to see the obvious, when women can show more common sense. Another entry dealing with forms of address between husband and wife shows just how far women could (jokingly) push this space created for them, as reflected in recorded humour of the time. In the Wei–Jin period, women used three types of second-person pronouns.[50] The two relevant to this story are *jun* 君, an honorific used by men among equals and also the usual term used by women to address their husbands; and *qing* 卿, a term used between two male friends on informal terms with each other. It was, of course, highly irregular for a woman to address her husband thus:

王安豐婦，常卿安豐。安豐曰：「婦人卿壻，於禮為不敬，後勿復爾。」婦曰：「親卿愛卿，是以卿卿；我不卿卿，誰當卿卿？」遂恆聽之。

Wang Rong [Wang Jung]'s wife always addressed Rong with the familiar pronoun "you" [*qing*]. Rong said to her, "For a wife to address her husband as 'you' is disrespectful according to the rules of etiquette. Hereafter don't call me that again."

His wife replied, "But I'm intimate with you and I love you, so I address you as 'you'. If I didn't address you as 'you', who else would address you as 'you'?" After that he always tolerated it.[51]

Wang Rong[52] was in fact a pre-eminent minister at court, yet in this story he was not able to enforce prescribed formal etiquette on his wife. This instance in particular, together with some others, is frequently cited by scholars as a sign that gender constraints did slacken during this period.[53]

In *Shishuo*, the relationship between man and woman is open and straightforward, and a woman is rarely made the object of a sexist joke. Sexual jokes are in fact remarkably absent and the following may be the only one that approaches being risqué — and, even so, the joke is placed in the privileged mouth of the emperor:

> 元帝皇子生,普賜羣臣。殷洪喬謝曰:「皇子誕育,普天同慶。臣無勳焉,而猥頒厚賚。」中宗笑曰:「此事豈可使卿有勳邪?」
>
> When Emperor Yuan's son was born, he made presentations all around to his ministers. In expressing his thanks, Yin Xian [Yin Hsien] said, "The birth of the imperial son is cause for the whole realm to rejoice together. But since your servant [myself] earned no merit in the matter, he doesn't presume to hope for such a generous gift."
>
> Laughing, the emperor said, "In a matter of this kind how could I have let you earn any merit?"[54]

Jokes About Mavericks

Humour can also be a tool of self-defence as well as an expression of irreverence. In the time of *Shishuo*, some idea of the rights of the individual was gradually emerging and, accordingly, behaviour considered bizarre could actually be viewed as a sign of individualism. In the following passage, Liu Ling's humorous put-down of impertinent interference is in defence of his own freedom of action:

> 劉伶恆縱酒放達,或脫衣裸形在屋中,人見譏之。伶曰:「我以天地為棟宇,屋室為衣,諸君何為入我中?」
>
> On many occasions Liu Ling, under the influence of wine, would be completely free and uninhibited, sometimes taking off his clothes and sitting naked in his room. Once when some persons saw him and chided him for it, Ling retorted, "I take heaven and earth for my pillars and roof, and the rooms of my house for my pants and coat. What are you gentlemen doing in my pants?"[55]

Liu Ling (221–300) was one of the group leaning towards Daoist thinking that was later called the Seven Worthies of the Bamboo Grove, and was known for his iconoclasm and outlandish behaviour. His claim to take heaven and earth as his pillars and roof seems to derive from the Daoist idea of the integral relationship between humankind and the natural universe; it removes humanity from its small world of mundane existence in clothes, rooms and houses, and even towns and cities, to the context of the universe.[56] The *Daren xiansheng zhuan* 大人先生傳 (Biography of Master Great Man) by Ruan Ji 阮籍 (210–63), Liu Ling's friend and a fellow member of the Seven Worthies,[57] is based on exactly the same idea, which is central to Daoism.[58] A parallel combination of liberation and humour may be found in the deliberately bizarre behaviour of early Christian Holy Fools, canonized in the Byzantine and Russian Orthodox churches.[59]

On a more mundane level, lack of proper interpersonal respect within the family can also be licensed by humour. In the next item, a nephew's lack of respect, shown in his criticism of his uncle, is as elegant as it is funny:

> 衛江州在尋陽，有知舊人投之，都不料理，唯餉「王不留行」一斤。此人得餉，便命駕。李弘範聞之曰：「家舅刻薄，乃復驅使草木。」

> While Wei Zhan [Wei Chan] was stationed in Xunyang, an old friend came to him for shelter (as a refugee from the North), but he did not provide for him at all,[60] except only to give him one catty [a measure] of the herb *wang-bu-liu-xing* 王不留行. After the man had gotten his present, he immediately ordered his carriage.

> When Wei's nephew, Li Chong [Li Ch'ung], heard about it, he remarked, "My maternal uncle is so penny-pinching that he even made plants and trees do his bidding."[61]

Old friends seeking refuge expected their host to provide a lifestyle comparable to the one they had been used to, and perhaps even monetary help. Hence the phrase "did not provide for him at all" suggests that Wei Zhan was distinctly lacking in hospitality, and moreover that even the unsatisfactory level of hospitality he did provide was time-limited. The name of the herb *wang-bu-liu-xing* means literally "the king does not stop you from going", a hint that Wei did not wish to offer hospitality indefinitely.

The following story turns on one of the literati being highly sarcastic about his own class. Making fun of books, he hints that the abundant collection he possesses in his mind/stomach has not helped him in any practical way. Books were revered in traditional Chinese culture and this reverence extended to those who read books — the literati. The fourth century BCE Daoist philosopher Zhuangzi, however, was a pragmatist who believed that, unless it was accompanied by common sense, book learning was useless for the welfare of the common people. The *Shishuo* joke echoes a similar story in the *Zhuangzi*, in which a craftsman ridicules books.[62] Perhaps out of disillusionment, the present hero, He Long, also came to perceive the uselessness of books and the futile pursuits of the literati.

> 郝隆七月七日出日中仰臥。人問其故？答曰：「我曬書」。
>
> On the seventh day of the seventh month He Long [Ho Lung] went out in the sun and lay on his back. When people asked what he was doing, he replied, "I'm sunning my books."[63]

It was customary at the height of summer, on the seventh day of the seventh month, to bring one's winter bedding and clothes out into the sun to get rid of moisture accumulated during the colder months. People who owned books would, of course, take advantage of the hot weather to sun them as well. He Long, who was said to own no possessions but to have mastered a great deal of book learning, could therefore only sun the books he had learned and stored in his stomach. (Chinese people believe memory is stored in the stomach or heart, not in the brain.) The ironic humour turns on He Long laughing at himself for having nothing else worth sunning.

Jokes About Human Foibles

The corrective purposes of satire, even if used gently, certainly have a place in *Shishuo*. When faults are to be found among the great, they are fair game for comment and ridicule, as in the following examples.

> 王丞相有幸妾姓雷，頗預政事納貨。蔡公謂之「雷尚書」。
>
> Chancellor Wang Dao [Wang Tao] had a favourite concubine, surnamed Lei, who used to interfere a good deal in matters of state and would accept bribes. Cai Mo used to refer to her as "President Lei".[64]

This is a satirical reference to the chancellor giving too much power to his concubine, highlighting the human frailty and folly common to powerful men (and women) across all cultures and times.

More unusual, perhaps, is the satirical image carefully depicted, line by line, stage by stage, to build a kind of caricature of useless rage in the following entry:

> 王藍田性急。嘗食雞子，以筋刺之，不得，便大怒，舉以擲地。雞子於地圓轉未止，仍下地以屐齒蹍之，又不得，瞋甚，復於地取內口中，齧破即吐之。
>
> Wang Shu was by nature short-tempered. Once while he was attempting to eat an egg he speared it with his chopstick, but could not get hold of it. Immediately flying into a great rage, he lifted it up and hurled it to the ground. The egg rolled around on the ground and had not yet come to rest when he got down on the ground and stamped on it with the teeth of his clogs, but again failed to get hold of it. Thoroughly infuriated, he lay on the ground and seized it in his mouth. After biting it to pieces he immediately spewed it out.[65]

This type of joke, with its almost slapstick topic and image, is rare in *Shishuo*. The visual humour easily crosses cultural and linguistic boundaries, and it can be enjoyed by anyone, anywhere without the need for commentary and background knowledge. The foible is indeed universal, even if the hero's agility is not. The Western parallels that come to mind are descriptions of performances by the skilled actors of sixteenth century Italian *commedia dell-arte*, based on a mime tradition as ancient as that in China.[66]

Jokes That are Lost in Translation

It is common knowledge that explaining a joke destroys its value as humour. Some of the jokes in *Shishuo* require a great deal of explanation — and even then, readers from another culture may still not find them at all humorous. The humour of these entries can be classed as lost in translation — not merely on the grounds of language, but because they are jokes that depend upon more than superficial knowledge of an entrenched local concept. Similarly, jokes based on certain taboos simply lose their humour when conveyed to cultures without the same taboo. To transfer jokes of this kind, it is necessary first to explain the social taboo to members of the target language and also to point out which words are taboo and why. After all this explaining, is the joke worth telling or translating? The emotional force was simply not there from the beginning. There are, of course, many such jokes in *Shishuo*. In order to allow readers to judge whether such humour is effectively lost forever, here is an example.

The Chinese had a strong taboo on using someone's official name: friends and acquaintances were expected to use a person's *zi* 字 or courtesy name. Therefore, the best way to insult someone was to utter to their face words that comprised their father's name or part of it. The skill of individuals who were prepared to do this, and do it well, became a much admired source of amusement.

> 鍾毓為黃門郎，有機警，在景王坐燕飲。時陳羣子玄伯、武周子元夏同在坐，共嘲毓。景王曰：「皋繇何如人？」對曰：「古之懿士。」顧謂玄伯、元夏曰：「君子周而不比，羣而不黨。」

> Zhong Yu served as a palace attendant and possessed a quick wit. One time he was present at a banquet in the house of Prince Jing [Ching] of Qin [Ch'in] (Sima Shi [Ssu-ma Shih]). At the time Chen Qun [Ch'en Ch'ün]'s son, Tai [T'ai], and Wu Zhou [Wu Chou]'s son, Gai [Kai], were with him among the company, and were both teasing Yu.

> Prince Jing said, "What sort of man was Gao You [Kao Yu 皋繇]?"

> Yu replied, "A virtuous knight of antiquity." Then, turning around, he said to Chen Tai and Wu Gai, "A gentleman is 'all-embracing and impartial'; he 'keeps company with all men, and joins no factions'."[67]

Zhong Yu's father's name You 繇 occurs in Prince Jing's question. However, the son's reply not only incorporates Prince Jing's father's name, Yi 懿 (meaning virtuous), but also includes Chen Tai's father's name, Qun 群 (meaning keeping company with others), and even Wu Kai's father's name, Zhou 周 (meaning all-embracing). While the story may no longer unleash the loud laughter of a joke that gets away with violating a taboo, it is still possible to admire the battle of wits and to acknowledge the one-upmanship involved in teasing all three of them in one sentence.

Conclusion: The Humorous Techniques of *Shishuo*

Since *Shishuo* was not created principally as a humorous work, strictly speaking it cannot be regarded as characterized by certain techniques of humour. We can only observe that certain techniques do occur when the humour of some of its entries is analyzed.

A principal device giving rise to humour is incongruity: the contrast between the language used and the situation in which it is used. There are many examples of contrast between the solemn and weighty language of the classics and its use in mundane, even ridiculous, situations. Incongruity is also found in the verbal battles between adults and children, where children gain the upper hand and show up the immaturity and lack of clarity in their opponents' thinking. Literati in-group jokes provide the most obvious examples, but perhaps the ultimate example is the episode of the slave girl being dragged through the mire while quoting the classics to answer her female colleague's question (also quoted from the classics) about why she is being punished in this way.

Paradox also forms part of *Shishuo*'s humour, seen mostly in arguments put forward to win a debate, which fail under closer scrutiny to stand up to logic. The argument put forward by Emperor Yuan's son to justify his claim that the sun is closer than the city of Chang'an is clearly such a paradox, and it combines with the comedy of the clever child outdoing the adult to create a very funny story. Philosophically, *Shishuo* challenges logical thinking; it is even anti-logic in showing how easy it is to turn logic on its head. The humour stems from unexpected and sudden shifts in perspective, providing a surprise ending.

Although satire is often used — sometimes by the speakers of the jokes against others but also in retaliation against the speakers — the tone is not bitter or overly critical. *Shishuo* is pervaded by a gentle and detached irony, unlike the savage attacks of the Augustan satirists in the West. An excellent example of satirical rebuttal is the story of inhospitable Wei Chan being charged by his nephew with having made even plants and trees do his bidding.

Given this tone, it is not surprising that few of *Shishuo*'s jokes involve slapstick or visual jokes. The description of how Wang Shu dealt with his recalcitrant egg is a rare exception. Presumably the sensibilities of the elite audience of the book precluded this kind of humour. Sexual and scatological jokes about the body are certainly not foreign to Chinese culture: joke books about the exploits of the Ming scholar/ rascal Xu Wenchang 徐文長 (1523–93), for instance, are full of such humour.[68] Such jokes, however, are completely absent from *Shishuo* and would have been considered vulgar and not worthy of either the readers or the compilers of the work. As noted, the only faintly risqué joke — made by Emperor Yuan about Yin Xian's part in the birth of his son — is subtle and placed in the mouth of the all-powerful emperor.

Across the world, the common butt of jokes is a representative of an underclass or minority. Except for the story about new immigrants from the north and one or two others not quoted here, *Shishuo* is not guilty of such discrimination. In the ever-present competition between northerners and southerners, its episodes do not seem to favour one side or the other, as is demonstrated by the war of words between Xi Zuochi and Sun Chuo. Among the jokes about foreigners, the one about the monk Gaozuo from Central Asia portrays him as a man of superior intelligence who has outwitted his Chinese hosts. *Shishuo* does not laugh at minorities or the under-privileged, such as women, children and slaves. If anything, it laughs at the rich and powerful, the ministers, scholars and generals. This subversive power of humour is probably what Plato had in mind when he attributed to Socrates the view that the true essence of the ridiculous is ignorance in the weak who are thus unable to retaliate when ridiculed.[69]

Reflecting the society which gave birth to *Shishuo*, there is even an example of self-satirizing, a type of humour considered politically correct in today's modern world. The Wei–Jin period in which the people of these stories lived, down to the subsequent period of division when the work was compiled, was politically chaotic, with regimes changing rapidly. Because of the devastation of war and upheaval, old morality was discarded and old standards of behaviour were revised in order for people to survive. As a result, people were more open-minded and pragmatic, and this allowed humanity to shine through the shattered dogmas of old. It seems logical that *Shishuo*'s humour should be open-minded and lacking in prejudice. Even from the gender perspective, *Shishuo* is something of an equaliser. It laughs at women and belittles their efforts to be agents of change, but by the same token it also laughs at men's blocked vision, self-righteousness and weaknesses. Through its humour, we even catch glimpses of many strong women with independent minds in the educated elite.

In a similar vein, *Shishuo* reveals an irreverent attitude towards authority and a disregard of rites and rituals. Its humour allows it to ignore the traditional social order of deferring to age and to the male, and to repeatedly portray women and children as having the upper hand in arguments. Gu Kaizhi deriding the popular Luoyang scholar's chant is a typically bold critique of a trend that was said to have been adopted by prestigious scholars and prime ministers. Li Chong's sarcasm about his maternal uncle's stinginess fearlessly crosses the line of propriety that required the younger generation to show respect for their elders. Wang Rong's wife refuses to stop calling him "dear" and directly challenges the propriety governing the husband-and-wife relationship. Evidently, even the atmosphere at the court of Emperor Yuan was so relaxed that he could joke about Yin Xian's declaration that he had done nothing to deserve a gift on the birth of the imperial prince. To include such a joke in a work that, if not actually compiled by an imperial prince, was at least compiled under his patronage, also indicates the liberal ambience of the age. While they are inspired by philosophical conviction, Liu Ling's actions and justifications for going naked must take the prize for ultimate irreverence. Satirical humour like this is confrontational because it questions and critiques the status quo.

Although there are jokes in *Shishuo* that can be appreciated by everybody, most of its humour was best shared by the in-group of literati who created these jokes and for whom neither explanation nor interpretation was necessary. This group and its inheritors have kept *Shishuo* alive for more than a millennium and a half, and their members — no longer limited to Chinese-literate audiences — have spread it to other East Asian countries and now all over the world.

7

Chinese Humour as Reflected in Love-Theme Comedies of the Yuan Dynasty

Andy Shui-lung Fung and Zhan Hang-Lun

Since humour in China dates back to ancient times, it is naturally to be found in most periods and forms of Chinese art and literary texts, including scripts from classical Chinese drama. Of the latter, the most famous are the comedies from the Yuan dynasty (1279–1368). These pieces are known chiefly from surviving texts,[1] and although there is a strong performance tradition, there is little evidence about the precise circumstances of their original production. They represent an astonishing mastery of comic art that still remains popular.

In China, dramatic performances of what is usually called opera rather than drama date back more than a thousand years to at least the eighth century, and were closely associated with the imperial court. One important form is known as *zaju* 雜劇 (variety plays). In the Northern Song dynasty (960–1127), *zaju* consisted of singing, dancing, music, comic elements and acrobatic performance, and were divided into three parts: an introduction that generally commented on contemporary affairs; the main story; and comic and acrobatic acts. The content of each part was quite separate. New forms of *zaju* emerged in the Southern Song dynasty (1127–79), while the original, renamed *yuanben* 原本, continued in its original form in the north during the Jin dynasty (1115–1274). When north and south China were reunited under the Yuan dynasty, the northern form became dominant and eventually replaced southern forms.

The Yuan dynasty saw many innovations in *zaju*, including a musical structure based on combining various tunes into sets. Some tunes were derived from folk music and some from older dramatic airs. There were seven sets commonly in use at this time. Flutes, clappers and drums were used for accompaniment. A complete drama was divided into four *zhe* 折 (acts) and one *xiezi* 楔子 (prologue or interlude). Roughly, the four acts represented the commencement, development, climax and resolution of the plot. There was internal consistency of music and rhyme scheme in every *zhe* and each *zhe* was sung by either the male or female lead actor. Other characters usually had only spoken dialogue. The scripts of Yuan *zaju* consisted mainly of lyrics and spoken dialogue, with some brief directions for stage action.[2] Another innovation was greater use of vernacular language and the introduction of stock acting roles such as the female role (*dan* 旦), the male hero (*sheng* 生), the "painted-face" (*jing* 淨) and the clown (*chou* 丑). These were specialized roles played by both actors and actresses, where the specific name and social rank of the character varied from play to play (comparable roles would be those of the *commedia dell'arte* and stock characters such as the *ingénue* and the villain in Italian opera). The comic role of the *chou* is discussed below.

The subject matter of these opera plots expanded greatly to include not only stories based on history and legend but also others related to contemporary society, and in many of them comedy and humour play an important part. Readers not familiar with classical Chinese drama will nevertheless know something of comparable Western comedy, particularly the works of William Shakespeare. By drawing comparisons and distinctions with some types of comedy found in the Shakespearean canon and elsewhere, the comic techniques and humour found in this remarkable Yuan drama can be more easily understood in reasonably straightforward terms. Many comic techniques are in fact common to both these groups of plays, despite the gaps that separate them in time, geography, language and societal beliefs. Of course, there are also many differences as well as similarities.[3]

Despite China's long cultural and artistic history, it was not until the Yuan dynasty that drama reached its Golden Age, as both Shih Chung-wen and Colin Mackerras have noted in their studies of the Chinese theatre.[4] Popular ever since, the Yuan dramas are justly admired. Famous later dramatists of the early Ming dynasty, such as Li Kaixian 李開先 (1502–68) and Tang Xianzu 湯顯祖 (1550–1616), each had private collections of over a thousand scripts. Unfortunately only about 250 complete works are still extant. One may well ask how many of these scripts truly belong to the genre of comedy, since there is no clear-cut distinction between comedy and tragi-comedy in traditional Chinese drama. The best estimate is that, of the 250, no more than 30 are outright comedies. To facilitate comparison with Shakespearean comedy, discussion here is based on the following 13 love-theme comedies because, like Shakespearean comedy, these are humorous, have remained popular and are also very readable (although it needs to be borne in mind that these texts were written to be sung or declaimed).[5]

- Dai Shanfu 戴善甫, *Fengguang hao* 風光好 (Story of good scenery)
- Guan Hanqing 關漢卿, *Jinxian chi* 金線池 (The golden thread pond)
- Guan Hanqing, *Jiu fengchen* 救風塵 (Save the prostitute)
- Guan Hanqing, *Xie Tianxiang* 謝天香 (Maiden Xie Tianxiang)
- Guan Hanqing, *Yu jingtai* 玉鏡台 (Jade mirror-stand)
- Li Haogu 李好古, *Zhang sheng zhu hai* 張生煮海 (Scholar Zhang boiling up the sea)
- Shi Junbao 石君寶, *Jinqian ji* 金錢記 (The story of the coin)
- Shi Zizhang 石子章, *Zhu wu ting qin* 竹塢聽琴 (Listening to *qin* music in the bamboo hut)
- Wang Shifu 王實甫, *Xixiang ji* 西廂記 (The west chamber)
- Zhang Shouqing 張壽卿, *Hong li hua* 紅梨花 (Red pear flowers)
- Zheng Guangzu 鄭光祖, *Zhou Meixiang* 㑇梅香 (Zhou Meixiang, the scholar maidservant)
- Anon, *Fu Jinding* 符金錠 (Maiden Fu Jinding)
- Anon, *Yuanyang bei* 鴛鴦被 (Quilt with mandarin duck pattern)

Chief among these is the perennially popular *Xixiang ji* 西廂記 (The west chamber), remade as a 1927 silent film, *Romance of the western chamber* (see poster in Figure 7.1) and remaining popular today on TV and in film.

In terms of comic technique, a principal device used in all these plays (and in others that are more serious in nature) to attract and hold the attention of their audiences is verbal wit. As Rex Gibson notes, English audiences of the Elizabethan period also seem to have loved word play and punning,[6] and such intellectual wittiness has always been considered an important characteristic of European high comedy. Since Greek and Roman times, high comedy traditionally has been distinguished from more visual or low comedy largely on this basis

Figure 7.1   Film poster by anonymous artist for the Minxin Film Company (Shanghai) 1927 silent movie, *Romance of the western chamber* 西廂記, directed by Hou Yao (1900–45), based on the Yuan drama *Xixiang ji* 西廂記 by Wang Shifu 王實甫. Black and white copy of PD-ART from Wikimedia Commons, http://en.wikipedia.org/wiki/File:Romance_of_the_Western_Chamber_poster. jpg (accessed 29 January 2010).

(although in contemporary times such a distinction is less clear-cut).[7] There is a significant difference between the Chinese and European theatrical traditions in this approach to the comic, as no distinction is traditionally made between high and low in Chinese comedy. In Yuan comedy, for example, humour is expressed quite freely in the action of the plot, through characterization and through being embedded in the comic language, without concern for issues of good taste or sentiment. Despite this, these pieces were regarded as literary achievements equal in status to tragedies or other serious dramas.

The use of poetry or verse-forms is also thought to distinguish high comedy from low comedy, and some scholars of Chinese comedy maintain that comedy is bound to use a particular style of language to achieve a particular generic effect — and thus that verse is more suited to high comedy and to tragedy.[8] Samuel Taylor Coleridge (1772–1834), however, believed that individual writers could achieve true poetry in either the comic or the tragic form,[9] and that each might select their own style and adjust the ratio of prose to verse in using comic language as they saw fit. This certainly reflects the practices of the classical Chinese comedy authors, and we conclude that in neither the East nor the West are there fixed rules or limits on the use of language — or indeed on any other dramatic techniques to achieve comic effect. We would agree with Coleridge's view[10] that the only true limitations are the imagination and creativity of the writer, operating within the bounds of theatrical practicality and good artistic taste.

Comic techniques used in Yuan love-theme comedies

Irony

As a component of verbal wit, irony must be singled out for discussion. Drama uses two kinds of irony: verbal and dramatic. Setting dramatic irony aside for later discussion, verbal irony involves saying one thing but meaning another, and naturally it is an effective and much-used tool of comedy,[11] arousing the audience's interest by setting them an amusing puzzle to resolve. It can also bear a subtler interpretation, however. Abrams points out that, as an act of communication, the true meaning of verbal irony may be directly opposite to the implied meaning, or the same speaker may speak the opposite (contradict himself or herself) within a short period of time.[12] As such, an ironic utterance need not necessarily be comic. One famous example is the highly serious and nuanced scene in Shakespeare's *Julius Caesar*, where Mark Antony repeatedly calls Brutus "an honourable man" when he means quite the opposite.[13] Therefore, using irony as a reliable indicator of the comic can be dangerous. Nevertheless, it is an important tool for many comedy writers, including those of the Yuan period, who were particularly skilful in their use of verbal irony for humorous effect.

One excellent example comes from the famous comedy by Wang Shifu (1250–1307?), *Xixiang ji* (The west chamber). The plot of this comedy revolves around Scholar Zhang 張生, who is on his way to the capital to sit the national civil service examination. On the way he comes to a Buddhist monastery where he sees and falls in love with a beautiful young lady named Cui Yingying 崔鶯鶯. Yingying's mother has promised her to someone else, but by defeating some bandits Scholar Zhang gains approval to marry her. However, when Zhang departs for his examination, Yingying's mother tries to marry her off to her original suitor. Scholar Zhang returns just in time to prevent this and the two are finally married in a happy conclusion.[14] In a scene set during Zhang's absence, Yingying — a true comic heroine who would be at home in the work of Shakespeare — discovers her maid Hongniang 紅娘 bringing a love letter from Zhang. Keeping a straight face instead of rejoicing, Yingying scolds her as follows:

> 小賤人，這東西那里將來的？我是相國的小姐，誰敢將這簡帖來戲弄我！我幾曾慣看這等東西！告過夫人，打下你個小賤人下截來！
>
> You bad girl, where did you get this from? I am the daughter of the Prime Minister, how dare you bring me this rude letter and play tricks with me? If I were to tell Mama, she would break your leg![15]

Since earlier in the drama the audience has seen that Yingying is in fact in love with Scholar Zhang, they know very well that Yingying is saying one thing but meaning quite the opposite. Not surprisingly, Yingying's maid, Hongniang, is not scared at all and in response to the threat she cheekily replies: 我將這簡帖兒去夫人行出首去來 "Very well, I'll take this letter from Scholar Zhang to old Mama, and confess that it's my fault!"[16]

Immediately, of course, the situation reverses itself as it appears that Yingying and Zhang's secret love affair will be exposed, so that the original reversal is ironically compounded by the response. Yingying immediately softens, surrenders to Hongniang, and hastens to say that she was just joking. This allows Hongniang to win hands down by saying: 放手，看打下下截來！ "Hands off [the letter]; otherwise [Mama] will break your leg!"[17] This further twist, in which she plays back to her mistress the mistress's own threat, always makes the audience burst into laughter.

Comparing dramatic irony with verbal irony, the first is more embedded in the structure of events and plots. It appears when one whole scene, event or line of argument contrasts sharply with another and, like verbal irony, can be serious as well as humorous.[18] A typical dramatic — even tragic — example from Shakespeare is the sequence in *Macbeth* in which King Duncan's line about Macbeth — "He was a gentlemen on whom I built an absolute trust" — is followed immediately by Macbeth entering and starting to plot the murder of Duncan.[19] Here the ironic contrast is made visual by the sequence of actions, rather than being contained in the words spoken.

Exploiting this mechanism for comic effect is a common tool in Yuan comedy. *Jinqian ji* (The story of the coin) by Shi Junbao (1192–1276?), for example, is another comedy where the plot revolves around the conflicts between civil service careers and personal affections, involving marriage between rich and poor. In this play, Prefect Wang 王府尹 requests the scholar He Zhizhang 賀知章 to call on another scholar, Han Yi 韓翃, and on his behalf offer him a position as personal tutor to Wang's children. Zhizhang is reluctant to go: he believes he understands Han's temperament and views, since they have been good friends for many years, and he expects Han to turn down such a humble position on the spot. He therefore replies at once to the Prefect:

老相公所言之事不必去問。此人與眾不同，腹隱司馬之才，心似彌衡之傲，內心剛烈，外貌欠恭。今歲攛過卷子，早晚除授，怎肯與人做門館？

Your Honour, there is no need for me to go. This man Han Yi is no ordinary person. His extraordinary talents are as high as the famous scholar Sima, and his temperament is as proud as the scholar Mi Han. He has a strong personality and shows no respect to anyone. He just took part in the civil examination this year, and I expect him to be offered a position as a senior civil servant and to be promoted sooner or later. How could he possibly accept the humble position of family tutor?[20]

It is only after Wang begs him repeatedly that He Zhizhang reluctantly agrees to try to persuade his friend. To his surprise, Han Yi agrees at once to be Prefect Wang's family tutor. The reason, however, soon appears — it is a secret love! The dramatic irony then lies in the fact that now He Zhizhang has succeeded in his task, he unhappily feels obliged to lie to the Prefect about the process in order to conceal why consent was given so readily. In a splendidly funny scene, he ridiculously exaggerates his own skills of persuasion and oratory in order to explain how he overcame his friend's (non-existent) reluctance:

老相公，飛卿兄弟不肯做門館。小官磨了半截舌頭，才得依允。

Your Honour, my brother Feiqing [飛卿, another name for Han Yi] did not agree at first. You should understand that it was only after I disposed of half of my tongue, and my saliva ran dry, that he reluctantly agreed to be your family tutor![21]

The contradictions between the characters' expectations and the actual outcomes, and between what Zhizhang says and what the audience knows to be true, create an illogical inconsistency between cause and effect to which the audience always responds with laughter.[22] Such comic effects on stage can be produced either by inconsistent behaviour or verbal responses, inconsistency in characters or situations, or by any combinations of these. In current Western humour theory, these would be described as incongruity effects.[23]

Another equally entertaining example comes from the comedy *Zhu wu ting qin* (Listening to *qin* music in the bamboo hut). Here the female lead is a beautiful Daoist nun named Zheng Cailuan 鄭彩鸞 who has fallen in love with the scholar Qin Xiuran 秦脩然. When Prefect Liang 梁府尹 wants to use her temple to offer hospitality to a friend, at first she strongly opposes the idea. However, before long she finds out that this friend is none other than the scholar Qin, who happens to have stolen her heart — of course she changes her mind. By that stage, it is she who has to persuade Liang (who has given up his original plan) to use the temple so that she can have her chance to meet the scholar. Here is how she does it:

〔梁州尹云〕姑姑，我一徑的來借你觀中淨房一間，安排酒肴，管
　　待個客官。
〔正旦云〕相公，這的是祝壽的道院，外觀不雅，葷了鍋灶。
〔梁州尹云〕便葷了有誰知道？
〔正旦云〕做的個褻瀆麼，葷了灶不中用。
〔梁州尹〕真個不肯？
〔正旦云〕不可不可，跳出俺那七代先靈來，我也不肯。
　　…

〔正旦扯正末衣服科云〕相公在這裡坐坐不妨事。

〔梁州尹云〕這裡是祝壽的道院，外觀不雅。

〔正旦云〕有誰知道？

〔梁州尹云〕葷了你那鍋灶，做的個褻瀆麼。

〔正旦云〕外邊有一個小鍋兒哩。

Prefect Liang: Dear (Daoist) Aunt, would you let me use a clean room in your temple to prepare good food and wine in order to show hospitality to a guest?

Female lead: Your honour, this temple is meant for ceremonies such as the ritual of longevity. I'm afraid a meat dish would defile our cooking stove and our tradition of being vegetarian!

Prefect Liang: Who would know about such defilement?

Female lead: Who would bear responsibility for such defilement? None of the cooking stoves or utensils could be used afterwards!

Prefect Liang: Is it really impossible?

Female lead: No, no! I would not agree to it even if seven generations of my ancestors came out from their graves to beg me!

. . .

Female lead (pulling the Prefect's cloak): Your honour is welcome to host your friend here if you wish!

Prefect Liang: This temple is meant for ceremonies such as the ritual of longevity, it would not be appropriate!

Female lead: Who would know?

Prefect Liang: Who would bear responsibility for such defilement? None of the cooking stoves or utensils could be used afterwards!

Female lead: There is a small pot outside [that can be used]![24]

These reversals of situation and relationship (pleading and rejecting roles being exchanged between the two characters) combine with a precise reversal of the direction of the dialogue and even reuse of the same words to produce a very strong comic effect. The mechanical techniques of reversal and repetition are among the most important identified by Henri Bergson (1854–1941) in his work *Le rire* (1901), which analyses the various theatrical devices found in farcical stage-comedies of that time.[25]

Many such examples of reversals in situation and dialogue are found in other Yuan comedies. The entire plot of *Jinxian chi* (The golden thread pond) is a comedy of errors and misunderstandings between the male and female lovers and inconsistency on the part of the lovers themselves. At one point, for example, the female lead, Maiden Du Ruiniang 杜蕊娘, vows that she will never mention the name of the scholar Han Fuchen 韓輔臣 but repeatedly breaks her vow, to much laughter from the audience.[26] Another example comes from *Fengguang hao* (Story of good scenery), in which conflict arises from love affairs between lovers of different nationalities. Again, personal inconsistencies give rise to much of the comedy: Scholar Tao Gu 陶穀, for example, boasts during the day that he will not visit a brothel but at night succumbs to the temptation.[27] In the comedy *Xie Tianxiang*, the scholar Liu Yong 柳永 repeatedly tells people in the national capital that his good friend Prefect Qian 錢大尹 is trustworthy and reliable but is taken unawares when, as soon as Qian arrives in town, he takes Liu's own lover, Maiden Xie Tianxiang, as his concubine. Ironically, this is due to good intentions on Qian's part — but this motive is unknown to Liu.[28]

Repetition is also frequently used for comic effect, including repeating sentences with the same structure and repeating body movements or gestures.[29] Bergson draws an analogy between the pressure that builds from such repetitions and ironic contradictions in comedy and a steam engine — the hotter the steam, the greater the persuasiveness and the fun.[30] Although, as in Shakespeare, the few stage directions remaining in the texts of Yuan dramas do not give sufficient information to allow full and authentic reconstruction of the acting techniques used to deliver these techniques, even the bare texts of the comedies demonstrate their authors' mastery of these techniques.

Satire, Imagery and Malapropisms

As previous examples have shown, verbal irony becomes particularly amusing when characters are led to reveal their own weaknesses — often unconsciously. By contrast, when audiences see one actor deliberately and skilfully exposing the weaknesses of another, the comic effect is more satirical and mocking. While this is also enjoyable for the audience, it carries an overtone of intentional social and/or personal criticism, which is the defining characteristic of satire. In the love-theme comedies of the Yuan dynasty, the objects of such satirical mockery can be categorized as either morally bad characters or simply as *huaji* 滑稽 (laughable) people.[31]

An extreme example appears in the comedy *Jiu fengchen* (Save the prostitute) by the famous playwright Guan Hanqing (1226–1302).[32] Zhou She 周舍 is undoubtedly a bad character and a villain, being the spoilt son of a local rich and influential man. The plot revolves around how the weak and seemingly helpless prostitute Song Yinzhang 宋引章 defeats this villain with help from her brave and clever female friend, Zhao Pan'er 趙盼兒. The author makes fun of Zhou in every way, presenting him as the target of strongly satiric language and effectively establishing an image of a totally base character. He is portrayed as a glutton, constantly eating and drinking, and thus becomes the focus for the extensive food references that characterize this dramatic text. There are 19 references to wine and food, 12 to rice and 19 to actions of eating, amounting to a total of 50 textual references to food and eating. Symbolic meanings as well as comic exaggeration are embedded in these food references, the imagery of which has the effect of thoroughly mocking Zhou.

From the other characters comes milder mockery and repeated use of ironic descriptors, such as the remarks by *Jiu fengchen*'s female lead, Zhao Pan'er. In Act 1, she says of Zhou She: 那廝雖穿著幾件虼蜋皮, 人倫事曉得甚的 "Although Zhou She owns a few sets of expensive clothing, he knows nothing about being a human!"[33] In Act 2, Pan'er continues to use this very ironic tone, this time using animal imagery: 見的便似驢共狗…舔又舔不著 "He looks like a donkey or a dog . . . like a dog that cannot lick [water that is out of reach]."[34] Perhaps the playwright's harsh treatment of Zhou She is explained by the fact that during the Mongol Yuan dynasty there was widespread suffering among the people of Southern China due to shortages of food.[35]

Although Zhou She is clearly marked out as the butt of laughter and ridicule by all, a high point of laughter occurs when, in a conversation between him and a waiter in the inn, his own slip of the tongue foreshadows his eventual destiny — to end up in prison. This dialogue is worth quoting in full:

〔周舍云〕不問官妓私科子,只等有好的來你客店裡,你便來叫我。

〔小二云〕我知道。只是你腳頭亂，一時間那里尋你去?
〔周舍云〕你來粉房裡尋我。
〔小二云〕粉房裡沒有呵？
〔周舍云〕賭房裡來尋。
〔小二云〕賭房裡沒有呵？
〔周舍云〕牢房裡來尋。

Zhou She: When you see either private or public prostitutes come to the inn, inform me at once.

Waiter: I know. But your movements are hard to predict. Where can I expect to find you?

Zhou She: Look for me at the brothel!

Waiter: If you are not in the brothel?

Zhou She: Look for me at the gambling club!

Waiter: If you are not in the gambling club?

Zhou She: [In the] prison cell![36]

It is striking indeed that here the classical comedy of the Yuan dynasty prefigures modern psychoanalytic theory in its use of the slip of the tongue.[37] Another verbal technique identified from Western comedy is the malapropism. The term derives from Mrs Malaprop, a character in Richard Brinsley Sheridan's play *The rivals* (1775), a woman who continually muddled words with similar sounds to great comic effect. More technically known as catachresis, the technique in fact predates Sheridan and is sometimes called Dogberryism[38] after the parallel character in Shakespeare's *Much ado about nothing* (1598). It is frequent in Yuan comedy.

Comic misunderstanding also affects plots. In *Fu Jinding* (Maiden Fu Jinding), for example, the villain Han Song 韓松 conspires to prevent the marriage between Zhao Kuangyi 趙匡義 and the beautiful maiden Fu Jinding by kidnapping her while she is travelling to the marriage hall. The villainous plan is discovered in time, however, and Zheng En 鄭恩, a warrior and good friend to Zhao Kuangyi, takes the place of the bride in the curtained wedding sedan chair. After the villain Han Song kidnaps the person he believes to be the bride, he is appalled to discover inside the closed chair a terrifying warrior instead of a beautiful girl. The hilarious dialogue that takes place between them culminates in a belated statement of the all too obvious:

〔韓松云〕我揭開這轎簾試看咱。〔做見鄭恩科〕
〔鄭恩云〕兀那韓松，你認的我麼？我是你公公哩！
〔韓松云〕原來不是小姐，可是這個大漢。

Han Song: Let me open the curtain to see my beauty . . . [Sees Zheng En inside; surprised]

Zheng En: You evil man, Han Song! Can't you recognize me? I am your grandfather!

Han Song: Alas! My mistress has disappeared! And it's a man instead![39]

It is easy to imagine the acting out of this denouement by fine comic actors, making the most of the fact that the audience is breathlessly waiting for the springing of the trap. Bergson would describe this as "the robber robbed" type of reversal achieved by "qui-pro-quo" (this taken for that).

Verse and Classical Poetry

In the European theatre — despite the views of Coleridge — comedy traditionally has been associated with prose rather than poetry, and with the use of low-status characters such as servants, clowns or drunkards. Such uneducated figures are, of course, more likely to speak in prose, although this is not always the case and neither is the reverse — significantly, serious and tragic characters such as Iago in Shakespeare's *Othello* and Edmond in *King Lear* actually speak many lines in prose. However, most of Shakespeare's comedies are in fact written in prose — including almost 90 per cent of *The merry wives of Windsor* and over half of *Twelfth night, As you like it* and *Much ado about nothing*.[40] Yuan playwrights made great use of verse and even long poems in their comedies, creating a lively and elevated atmosphere as we shall see.

The Yuan comedies *Yu jingtai* (Jade mirror-stand) and *Hong li hua* (Red pear flowers) both have opening poems to be declaimed, which not only serve to foreshadow the plot but also establish a pleasantly indulgent and humorous atmosphere for the audience and prepare them to expect amusement. *Yu jingtai*, which is about the romantic love between the scholar Wen Qiao 溫嶠 and his lover Liu Qianying 劉倩英, starts with the following poem:

不分君恩重，能憐玉鏡台。
花從仙禁出，酒自御廚來。
設席勞京尹，題詩屬上才。
遂令魚共水，由此得和諧。

Grateful to the kindness of the emperor,

Talent has been shown in the jade mirror-stand.

Beautiful flowers here come from the royal garden,

Good wine bottles are served from the royal kitchen.

The high officer from the capital treats us to a banquet,

The talented scholar writes an excellent poem.

From now on the fish and the water

May live in harmony for ever and ever.[41]

Later, in Act 4, the scholar Wen Qiao tries hard to impress his bride-to-be, Liu Qianying, by demonstrating his superior talents in an "ink brush and poetry competition". Thus, as well as the poem declaimed at the beginning of the play, several other poems are incorporated into the dramatic action. Poetry competitions of this kind in classical Chinese love stories resemble the legendary medieval tourneys between European knights, designed to win the favour of a noble lady — except that, as here, the duel can also be fought out between the sexes. The high-flown romantic comedy created by this battle of the wits recalls the famous verbal duels between Shakespearean characters such as Beatrice and Benedict in *All's well that ends well*, or Millamant and Mirabelle in *The way of the world*, the famous Restoration comedy by William Congreve (1670–1729). These are all comedies about and for an educated elite, an audience well versed in aesthetic matters and the delights of verbal contests.

Another duel using poetry comes from the comedy *Hong li hua*, where in Act 2 the scholar Zhao Ruzhou 趙汝州 meets a beautiful lady and they engage in a poetic dialogue as follows:

〔正旦唸詩科云〕本分天然白雪香，誰知今日卻濃妝。
鞦韆院落溶溶月，羞窺紅脂睡海棠。
〔趙汝州云〕妙妙妙，小生也做一首。
〔唸詩科云〕換卻冰肌玉骨膚，丹心吐出異香來。
武陵溪畔人休説，只恐夭桃不敢開。

Leading Actress [chanting her poem]:

She is a beauty by nature, fragrant and looking like natural white snow,
Why then does she try heavy makeup and shine even brighter today.
Full moon in a flowery garden with a swing,
She's afraid to be seen and her sleeping pose looks like a rosy red begonia flower.
Zhao Yuzhou: Good, good, good! Let me write a poem to respond.
[*chanting his poem*]:
Like a beautiful lady, with icy skin and jade bones,
Her central petals are spreading exotic fragrance.
You people of Wuling River should tell no one,
Lest the peach blossom is unwilling to open.[42]

Both poems are written very correctly in accordance with the rules of classical poem composition. They are not in themselves humorous, but they lead to laughter because of Zhao's mistaken belief that he has met a ghost and not a beautiful lady. This turns the scene from romantic duel to outright comedy, which eventually produces laughter. Such very human foolishness is in ironic contrast to the formal chanting of serious poems, and once again it is easy to visualize how actors would exploit these transitions from high drama to low comedy. Like Shakespeare and Congreve,[43] the Yuan comedy playwrights saw the combining of poetry with comedy as appropriate and effective for their purposes. Despite the previously noted reservations of some Chinese scholars, good drama can and will exploit a mixture of all relevant elements, including the performance competency of the actors, to enhance its effects — whether those are comic or tragic.

Intellectual Wit

The importance of verbal duelling in Yuan comedy indicates that intellectual wit is one of its leading comic devices, involving the use of many different language skills. Driven by conscious intentionality on the part of the comic characters and comedians who use it, verbal wit is exemplified by contemporary stand-up comedians around the world. It combines intellectual word play with humorous performance skills and requires expertise in both areas. As many critics have noted,[44] writers and audiences of Elizabethan comedy loved intellectual wit, and such techniques were also well developed in Yuan comedy. Sometimes the passages could be quite transgressive, introducing a powerful note of satirical criticism into the comedy. Take, for example, the following dialogue from *Xixiang ji* where the maid Hongniang mocks the villain Zheng Heng 鄭恆 (the English translation has been rendered very freely in an attempt to capture the satirical word play):

〔紅唱〕君瑞是個肖字，這壁著個立人，你是個木寸馬戶尸巾。

〔淨唱〕木寸馬戶尸巾，你道我是個村驢屌！ （第四本，3:6）

Hongniang sings: Scholar Junrui is best described by the word "mart". To this I add a big "S" [in front]. As for you, "pid" and "pig" is the word, with "stu" in front.

Zheng Heng sings: "Pid" or "pig" together with "stu" in front. So you are saying that I am a "stupid pig"![45]

A more literal translation of the passage, which captures the scatological references, would run as follows:

Hongniang: Junrui is the character *qiao* 肖 (like, resemble) standing next to the character *ren* 人 (human). You are the characters *mu* 木 (wood), *cun* 寸 (inch), *ma* 馬 (horse), *hu* 戶 (household), *shi* 尸 (body) and *jin* 巾 (napkin)!

Zheng Heng: What? *Mu, cun, ma, hu, shi* and *jin*! You are really saying that I am *cun* 村 (village) *lu* 驢 (donkey) *diao* 屌 (penis)!

Another example comes from Act 2 of *Xie Tianxiang* where Prefect Qian, with a plot in mind, demands that the courtesan (often also called "sing-song girl")[46] Xie Tianxiang should sing the Song dynasty poet Liu Yong's famous song *Ding fengbo* 定風波 (Taming the storm). According to government regulations at the time, it was forbidden to mention in public the names of senior government officials or members of the royal family, but the first line of the song contains Qian's own name, *Ke* 可: 自春來慘綠愁紅，芳心事事可可 (Since spring, one regrets the green and feels depressed by the red; one's virtuous intentions are divided and uncertain *keke*). Qian planned this stratagem to trap Tianxiang into the forbidden action, aiming to prevent her from seeing her beloved scholar again. However, to his surprise she recognizes the trap and, while singing, carefully changes the words *keke* to *jiji* 已已

Figure 7.2 Two Peking Opera actors in a garden, Beijing, early 1930s. From *A Photographer in Old Peking*, p. 153. Photograph by Hedda Morrison, reproduced with permission.

(personal). Her demonstration of quick-wittedness on stage always pleases the audience enormously.[47] Such verbal duelling between the sexes requires parity of status for two paired actors, as in Figure 7.2, showing two young actors from the 1930s dressed in the traditional costumes of Peking Opera, a related form.

Puns, Double Entendres and Comic Relief

Puns[48] or *double entendres* are forms of intellectual wit that exploit the auditory effect of speaking and hearing. Because of this, they are particularly suitable for use in the live theatre, as opposed to texts written only for reading rather than performance. Such punning word plays are very common and very funny, because one sound in Chinese can represent many different words with entirely different meanings, giving plenty of scope for comic effects.[49] Rhetorical devices in Yuan comedies frequently play with words having either the same or slightly different sounds as well as meanings. An example drawn from *Jiu fengchen* illustrates these points. In Act 1, after a heated debate with her girlfriend Zhao Pan'er, the prostitute Song Yinzhang 宋引章 is obviously unhappy and proceeds to make fun of her friend, saying: 今日也大姐，明日也大姐，出了一包兒膿 "I call you *dajie* [elder sister] today, tomorrow, and every day. I hope you'll have your own big *dajie* [big carbuncle]!"[50]

On another occasion, the villain of the comedy, Zhou She, says to the kindly Zhao Pan'er: 請姨姨吃些茶飯波 "Auntie, please enjoy some good food and drink some tea!" And Zhao Pan'er immediately replies: 你請我？家裡餓皮臉也揭了鍋兒底，窨子裡秋月不曾見過這等食 "Are you inviting me [to a meal]? There are many hungry people around you, and you seldom help them! I'm afraid it happens less frequently than a lunar eclipse or a full moon!"[51] The eclipse was commonly believed to be caused by a giant heavenly dog (*tian gou* 天狗) biting the moon, so because Zhou She is talking about food (*shi* 食) and eating, Zhao Pan'er mocks his customary selfishness by punning about the lunar eclipse (*yue shi* 月食).[52]

Clever puns also appear frequently in the comedy *Zhu wu ting qin*. In Act 2, for example, the female lead Zheng Cailuan 鄭彩鸞 says: 將那個包待制看成做水晶塔 "You are looking down on Bao Zheng 包拯 who is about to be appointed [to a senior official position] and [you] regard him as a crystal pagoda."[53] The pagoda is a Daoist or Buddhist tower also known as *foutu* or *futu* 浮圖. *Futu* sounds very similar to *hutu* 糊塗, which means stupid or mentally confused. Here Zheng uses the pun to mock Prefect Liang. Other interesting puns occur in a dialogue between Zheng Cailuan and the Prefect in Act 2 of the same drama:

〔正旦唱〕這絃向那市面上難尋，欲要呵，則除江心裡旋打。

〔梁尹云〕老夫説絃，她説江心裡旋打，可是魚。這的呵，老夫賢愚不辨。

Cailuan: This string (*xuan* 絃) can hardly be found in the market place. If you really want it, you have to swish your net (*xuanda* 旋打) for it in the middle of the river.

Prefect Liang: I say string (*xuan*) and she replies that I have to swish my net (*xuanda*) in the middle of the river, that is referring to fish (*yu* 魚) . . . Alas [she is making a pun and mocking me for] not being able to distinguish between *xuan* [a pun for "being smart" *xian* 賢] and *yu* [a pun for "being stupid" *yu* 愚]![54]

This is usually a prompt for much laughter from the audience, since they appreciate the verbal punning as well as the joking relationship between the two characters.

Common puns found in Yuan comedy include plays on words such as *yu* 魚 (fish) and *yu* 愚 (stupid), *xuan* 絃 (string) and *xian* 賢 (smart or virtuous man), *qing* 晴 (sunny day) and *qing* 情 (love affair). In comparison, studies have shown that puns in Shakespearean comedy tend to be short words with multiple meanings, such as light, dear, lie and kind, and pairs of homonyms such as heart/hart, sun/son, cousin/cozen (the relative/to trick).

Comic relief usually refers to comic scenes inserted into a serious drama to relieve tension with laughter, but the term also describes scenes of low comedy with knock-about farce inserted into a high or witty comedy, in which easily recognisable comic stereotypes such as clowns reduce a tense atmosphere by more physical comedy. This can also be achieved by introducing a low or scatological reference or pun into a high-flown dialogue. The well-known scene with the gravediggers in *Hamlet* (Act 5, Scene 1), the doorkeeper in *Macbeth* (Act 2, Scene 3), the prominence given to the sayings of the Fool in *King Lear* or those of the bawdy old Nurse in *Romeo and Juliet*[55] are all good examples of this device. Similarly, puns as comic relief occur frequently in both serious and comic Yuan operas, including *Liangshi yinyuan* 兩世姻緣 (Marriage relationship after reincarnation), *Qujiang chi* 曲江池 (Long winding river pond) and *Baihua ting* 百花亭 (Pavilion of a hundred flowers), as well as the comedies *Zhou Meixiang* 綢梅香 and *Yuanyang bei* 鴛鴦被. Like many of the Shakespearean examples mentioned, these pieces actually belong to the genre of tragicomedy rather than to pure comedy. As already noted, the comedy of Yuan drama, like that of the Elizabethan stage, was not a "pure" genre along the lines of classical Western theory. It was — and remains — a highly successful "mixed" genre, employing a wide and effective variety of comic techniques across the entire spectrum of low to high comedy.

Conclusion

The techniques used by the authors of the Yuan comedies are very similar to those of Western comedy, naturally with some variations and differences in approach. Like Shakespeare, these men of genius had no hesitation is combining poetry with prose, but they also used many whole poems as well as excerpts from poems, literary allusions and quotations, all to great comic effect. The examples discussed above show that Yuan comedy playwrights were highly skilled in techniques such as verbal irony, dramatic irony, satirical comment, association of imagery with character, slips of the tongue, intellectual wit, puns and *double entendres*, and even scatological references. These techniques are certainly not unique to China. Their application in Yuan comedy remains insufficiently studied.

It is significant that the task of establishing a happy, humorous atmosphere in a Yuan romantic comedy tends to be evenly distributed between the characters, including both the leading roles and all the supporting ranks, as well as both male and female roles. Indeed, one could justifiably argue that many female characters in the Yuan comedies are simply better and more attractive people than their male counterparts, and that to a certain extent they exhibit the spirit of feminism even in that early and war-torn age. Comic relief, or broader comedy, is not confined to lower-class characters — although, as in Elizabethan comedy, the *chou* (clown) is common and significant. In the anonymous *Yuanyang bei*, for example, the Daoist nun is played as a *chou* role and her character is crucial to the deceptions and mistakes upon which the plot turns.

When the *chou* is found in a comedy with a court setting or as someone who serves in the retinue of nobility or the emperor, the role may function as a court jester or like a Shakespearean fool. One example occurs in Scene 2 of *Han gong qiu* 漢宮秋 (Autumn in the Han palace) by Ma Zhiyuan 馬致遠 (1250?–1324), where the *chou* plays an entertaining character called Chang Shi 常侍.[56] Ironic and witty professional jesters had been a feature of imperial court life in China from very early times, and were especially noted during the Han and Tang dynasties,[57] but Yuan comedies with contemporary settings reflected the customs of the Mongol government of the time, which did not include court jesters.

Since the jester-figure can be regarded as the ancestor of the *chou*, their relationship deserves more study than it has so far received.[58]

Just as classical European comedies such as the works of Molière and Congreve were multifunctional, providing social critique as well as entertainment, so their Chinese counterparts had outstanding educational value as well as being highly entertaining. These comedies are in fact "edutainments" — both enjoyable and educational, embodying subtle illustrations of themes relating to Confucianism and Daoism.[59] Contemporary audiences undoubtedly appreciated the topicality of the plots, which explored and reflected new views of life as well as the new language skills developed by the playwrights of these love-theme comedies. Readers of the time could both enjoy the plays at the theatre and read or review the texts at home in their leisure hours. During the Yuan dynasty, when many ordinary Chinese suffered under Mongol rule and endured both material hardship and political suppression, these playwrights provided enjoyment. They also explored social problems such as the roles and duties of females in society, the rise of new commercial forces and the fate of the Han Chinese imperial family, as well as more eternal themes such as the unpredictability of personal fame and glory.[60] While we do not know for certain how far contemporary audiences extended beyond the educated class, the popularity of the *zaju* both as drama and reading material continued without a break, so that they continued to reach a wide public and still do today. In fact the advent of television and video has brought them a whole new audience, and contemporary productions of leading comedies such as *Xixiang ji* 西廂記 (based on the opera of the same name, already cited) are even available on YouTube. Whether reading these scripts or, for the more fortunate, witnessing them in performance, readers and audiences alike cannot but admire the optimism and positive attitude displayed by their inspiring lead characters in the face of hardship and difficulty of all kinds. As Coleridge observed, comedy at its best can achieve the heights of poetry: it is perhaps this above all which justifies their comparison with Shakespearean comedy.

8

How Humour Humanizes a Confucian Paragon:
The Case of Xue Baochai in *Honglou meng*

Weihe Xu

If one were to poll people on any Chinese street as to which is *the* greatest Chinese novel of all times, the chances are most would say *Honglou meng* 紅樓夢, or *Shitou ji* 石頭記 (as it was originally titled, hereafter *HLM*), known in English as *The Dream of the red chamber* or *The Story of the stone*.[1] This work is an eighteenth-century 120-chapter novel by Cao Xueqin 曹雪芹 (1715–63/64) and Gao E 高鶚 (1738?–1815?) that first circulated in hand-transcriptions among Cao's relatives and friends (see Figure 8.1 for a page from the earliest such extant edition, the 1754 *Jiaxu* edition).[2] Should anyone unfamiliar with the novel wonder about its claimed greatness, most Chinese would be happy to help by comparing it with Shakespeare's plays, on the assumption that these are among the *greatest* of world literature. The plays and *HLM* certainly share one critical similarity: both have inspired massive branches of scholarship, Shakespeare studies (known in Chinese as *Shaxue* 莎學) and *HLM* studies (*Hongxue* 紅學, sometimes humorously referred to in English as "Redology").

Serious scholarship implies the worthiness of its subject. The importance, richness and profundity of *HLM* is suggested by another analogy the Chinese love to make: the novel is an encyclopaedia of traditional Chinese society and culture, thanks to its insightful depiction of an aristocratic family in late imperial China (thirteenth to nineteenth centuries), its vivid portrayal of hundreds of distinctive characters and its minute accounts of their lives, sometimes traversing multiple worlds: the mythical, the realistic and the idyllic (such as the gorgeous Prospect Garden [*Daguan yuan* 大觀園], where the novel's hero dwells with his flower-like maiden cousins and their maids). In a nutshell, the plot of *HLM* delineates the gradual and irreversible disintegration of the Jia clan — a magnificent and powerful family in the capital with intimate imperial connections (one of its members is a much-beloved imperial concubine). Concomitant with the clan's epic collapse is the tragic unravelling of a love triangle between three star-crossed cousins, the novel's hero Jia Baoyu 賈寶玉 and heroines Lin Daiyu 林黛玉 and Xue Baochai 薛寶釵.

The discussion below concerns only Xue Baochai, focusing in particular on her humour, a *blinder* spot, so to speak, since *HLM*'s humour at large is a blind spot in the ever-expanding Redology.[3] Such "humour blindness" is baffling, for what encyclopaedia is there without an entry on humour — a supposedly universal human trait and an integral aspect of human culture? As many people would say that absence of humour would make an encyclopaedia incomplete and life insufferable, I would say that "humourless criticism" has impeded full appreciation or enjoyment of *HLM*'s complexity and beauty by keeping us from many of its amusing nuances or subtleties. The critical reception of Baochai is a case in point.

Ever since the novel's first printed edition appeared in 1791, Baochai has had haters, admirers and sympathisers. Her haters prevailed for 200 years until the late 1960s, when more and more readers came to favour or sympathize with her. The difference between her detractors and supporters could not be starker, as the former demonize and the latter apotheosize her. Thus she becomes either a fiend incarnate, an extraordinary thief of virtue (*xiangyuan zhi you* 鄉願之尤) seen as even more abominable than evil (*geng shen yu xiete ye* 更甚於邪慝也),[4] or "a saint" embodying "ideal womanhood . . . generated and endorsed by Confucian teachings", which deserves to be called perfect (*kan cheng wanmei* 堪稱完美).[5] However, this "language of perfection" tends to exalt her beyond humanity into divinity, as an adoring apologist claims that the novelist meant to apotheosize her so that she represented the loftiest conduct that transcends both worldliness and vulgarity (*chaofan tuosu* 超凡脫俗).[6]

Between these two extremes lies a middle position, which anchors her squarely in the human realm: she is neither a monster nor a demigoddess, but a far superior and yet still flawed human being[7] — a complex character with both longcomings (*changchu* 長處) and shortcomings (*duanchu* 短處).[8] This re-visioning of Baochai reflects the rise of humanistic criticism, a growing trend since the late 1970s.[9]

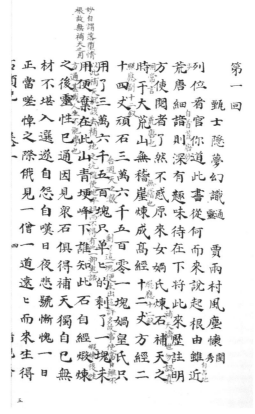

Figure 8.1　Annotated first page of the earliest extant edition (known as the Jiaxu [1754] edition) of *Honglou meng* by Cao Xueqin.　Black and white copy of facsimile in *Qianlong Jiaxu Zhiyanzhai chongping* Shitou ji, 1961, *juan* 1, p. 4. Every effort has been made to locate any holder of copyright.

Despite their differences, however, the three views share some striking similarities.　For instance, Baochai's demonizers and apotheosizers both believe that the novelist portrayed her as a *perfect* maiden, although the former hold that her perfection is meant to be deceptive, whereas the latter insist that it is genuine. Nevertheless, both reduce her to a flat character who is either utterly evil or utterly good — that is, either a devil or a saint. As we will see, such *dehumanizing* readings could not be further from the reality of the novel, to which only the humanistic criticism comes close. But all three are equally humour blind.

Such endemic oversight has led to either the claim that there are "only slight infusions" of humour in *HLM*,[10] or the complaint that "we are scarcely allowed to enter into [Baochai's] inner world to get a glimpse of her secret joys or sorrows".[11] However, I contend that her humour, so artfully deployed by the novelist, not only offers precisely such an entrance or insight into her private self but also subtly subverts her public image of perfection and (re)humanizes her.[12] I will show that the novelist could not have intended to portray her as either a perfect hypocrite or a perfect paragon, but intended to show her as a fledgling maiden who is striving to become a perfect Confucian gentlewoman (*shunü* 淑女). Although in the public eye she may appear to have succeeded in her goal, privately — as a flesh-and-blood young woman — she is caught in a perennial tug-of-war between her instincts, desires, emotional impulses and subconscious thoughts, and her keen sense of Confucian propriety resulting from her education — in other words, between her nature and her nurture or, in Freudian terminology, her id and her superego. The latter does not always succeed in guarding the former so that it slips out from time to time in a slip of the tongue, or bubbles to the surface in jokes. Such resurfacings of nature in humour often surprise us by disclosing sides of her personality that she, answering to her superego, takes pains to censor or conceal. These failures in her private struggle constitute the "curves" that prevent her character from being flattened by her ostensible image as a perfect maiden, rendering her rounder and more human.

Xue Baochai's Prenatal Imperfections and Postnatal Education

Being human means above all being imperfect, as in an old Chinese proverb: "no person is perfect" (*ren wu wanren* 人無完人). In other words, imperfection is a hallmark of humanity. Besides, in accordance with another old Chinese belief, human nature is irreducible, although modifiable, and is bound to manifest itself in one way or another.[13] These two assumptions are fundamental to the humanistic critique (and mine) of Baochai. Most importantly, they are consistent with the world-view or, more precisely, the human-view (*renguan* 人觀) that underpins *HLM*'s approach to characterization.

In Chapter 2, through the mouth of a character (Jia Yucun 賈雨村), the novelist gives an eloquent and elaborate account of human genesis from three kinds of *qi* 氣 (ether, energy or influence) — that is, *zhengqi* 正氣 (good ether), *xieqi* 邪氣 (evil ether) and a mixture of the two.[14] These moralized ethereal influences give birth to three kinds of people: (1) the exceptionally good (*daren* 大仁), such as those sage emperors and thinkers (for instance, Confucius) who bring order to the world; (2) the exceptionally evil (*da'e* 大惡), such as the most hateful villains (Hitler would be an anachronistic Western example) who plunge the world into chaos; and (3) the rest of the human masses (*dazhong* 大眾), the myriad combinations of the good and evil ethers. Among this last and morally ambiguous group of humans live many uncommon creatures who

> are incapable of becoming either the greatly good or greatly bad; but . . . [who are] superior to all the rest in sharpness and intelligence and inferior to all the rest in perversity, wrongheadedness and eccentricity. Born into a rich or noble household, they are likely to become great lovers or the occasion of great love in others . . . (*SS* 1:78–9; *HLMBS* 1:20)

The original Chinese terms for "great lovers or the occasion of great love in others" are *qingchi* 情癡 (literally, romantic idiots or anyone obsessed with their love) and *qingzhong* 情種 (literally, romantic seed or anyone prone to fall in love easily and/or repeatedly). Since both connote perversity, wrongheadedness and eccentricity,[15] it seems more concise to render them into English as "romantic eccentrics".

According to this human-view, Xue Baochai cannot be either a sage or a villain, and so must be a member of this romantic sub-group of the third "human kind". She was indeed born into an immensely wealthy family (we are told in fact it is one of the four wealthiest families in Nanjing, a former capital of imperial China). She was also born a romantic eccentric, belonging to the same batch of lovesick souls (*yi gan fengliu yuanjia* 一干風流冤家) as her cousins Jia Baoyu and Lin Daiyu. Their romantic nature is revealed at the beginning of the novel by a supernatural Buddhist monk on his way to have these "amorous wretches" incarnated in human form (*SS* 1: 52; *HLMBS* 1: 7). As we will see, however, Baochai turns out to be a rather stunted romantic eccentric because her predisposition to the romantic mode is severely chilled, although not cured, by her upbringing, which counteracts but does not eradicate her amatory nature. Thus the novel's human-view dictates that she is meant to be *flawed*, both pre- and post-natally.

It is therefore no coincidence that since birth she has suffered from *redu* 熱毒 (literally, noxious internal heat), "a congenital tendency to over-heatedness" or a tendency to physical, temperamental or emotive excess. Being a disease (*bing* 病) from the womb (*cong dai li dailai de* 從胎裏帶來的) (*SS* 7: 167–8; *HLMBS* 7: 70–1), this pathological over-heatedness is an *innate* blemish on her humanity. It also symbolizes her inveterate romantic predisposition and her potential romantic eccentricity. These underlying tendencies are confirmed by Baochai herself when she confides in Daiyu that she used to be a naughty girl, crazy about romantic literature and avidly reading it behind the adults' backs. Only after their "beatings and lectures and burning of books" did she finally stop (*SS* 42: 333; *HLMBS* 42: 448).

Just as her natural disposition is ineradicable but controllable through discipline, so her over-heatedness is incurable but manageable through medicine, which temporarily relieves its overt symptoms of coughing and wheezing (*chuansou* 喘嗽). Made from various white flowers of all seasons mixed with rain, dew and snow, this finicky remedy is aptly called "Cold fragrance pills" (*lengxiangwan* 冷香丸). (*SS* 7: 168–9; *HLMBS* 7: 71–2). As such, the remedy takes on a symbolic significance, corresponding to Baochai's Confucian — or, more precisely, Neo-Confucian — discipline of conforming to the Rites (*li* 禮).[16] Thus, just as the pills cool her prenatal over-heatedness, her education chills her inborn amatory impulses, turning her into a reformed former romantic or a born-again Neo-Confucian.

Baochai comes from a refined and highly cultivated family of Confucian scholars. Despite her gender, she has apparently received from her late father a fine Confucian education. The novel takes almost every opportunity to portray her as a maiden-scholar who is erudite in traditional Chinese arts and thought, be they Buddhist, Daoist, Confucian or Neo-Confucian. There are details in the novel to suggest, for example, that Baochai is highly conversant with the works of Zhu Xi 朱熹 (1130–1202), the arch-Neo-Confucian philosopher whose exegeses of the Confucian classics were a staple of late imperial Chinese curriculum, and she cites him easily and aptly in conversation.[17] Her educational success is also reflected in her family's response to an imperial call that "daughters of hereditary officials and distinguished families . . . have their names sent in to the Ministry for selection to be study-companions" of princesses (*SS* 4: 118–19; *HLMBS* 4: 42). One of the reasons that Baochai's family moved from Nanjing to the capital and lodged with the Jia family was so that she could await this selection, evidencing her family's confidence in her qualifications. The titles of the job, *cairen* 才人 (literally, talented person) or *zanshan* 贊善 (literally, aid of virtue),[18] make clear its two basic prerequisites: education and decorum, commonly termed *zhi shu da li* 知書達禮 (knowing the Confucian classics and following the Rites).[19] Baochai's family believes that she meets both criteria, being steeped in the classics and, as I will show, always trying to conduct herself in accordance with the Rites.

The Rites, as explained elsewhere in this book,[20] were regarded as the supreme embodiment of human refinement and civility. They constituted the ultimate norms of propriety and were the best cultivator of virtue in pursuit of the highest of Confucian virtues, *ren* 仁 (humaneness). Thus, learning and practising them were the other staples of traditional Chinese education, which aimed not only to impart book knowledge but also to foster proper conduct. A goal of Confucian self-discipline was to keep one's desires and emotions within the bounds of the Rites, and thereby well away from any impropriety or immorality. This classical position was later radicalized by Neo-Confucians (under the influence of Daoism and Buddhism) into something even more ascetic, urging that desires — especially of the romantic kind — be annihilated (*mie* 滅). As a result, in late imperial China with Neo-Confucianism reigning supreme as state ideology, absence of amatory feelings or behaviour became a laudable womanly virtue.

Baochai's cultivation of this virtue and her internalization of its underlying stoic ethics and aesthetics are patent not only in her friendly lectures to other girls about women's proprieties and responsibilities,[21] but also in her poem on the white crab-flower, which professes: "For beauty in plain whiteness best appears" (*Dan ji shi zhi hua geng yan* 淡極始知花更艷: *SS* 37: 223; *HLMBS* 37: 388). Her conscientious strivings are borne out by what critics observe to be the two tactics of her strategy for propriety, *cang* 藏 (to conceal) and *lou* 露 (to reveal): she is eager to reveal her virtuousness to others, and at the same time she tries hard to conceal anything in and about her that the Rites would censure.[22] The foremost of such improprieties is, of course, her romantic nature, and therefore not only has she long since given up reading romantic literature; she also jealously guards against any expression of her amatory feelings. For instance, during her visit to Jia Baoyu after he has been savagely beaten by his father in punishment:

> Baochai was relieved to see him with his eyes open and talking again. She shook her head sadly.
>
> "If you had listened to what one said, this would never have happened. Everyone is so upset now. It isn't Grandmother and Lady Wang, you know. Even —"
>
> She *checked herself* abruptly (*you mang yan zhu* 又忙嚥住), regretting that she had allowed her feelings to run away with her, and lowered her head, blushing. (*SS* 34: 156; *HLMBS* 34: 350, my italics)[23]

This constant inhibition of natural desire and passion creates an austere aura about Baochai which, if depicted in colour and sensation, would be white and cold, the two prominent characteristics of snow *xue* 雪 — an important symbol of Baochai since her last name, Xue 薛, puns on it.[24] She is not only likened to a cold, snow-white beauty (*SS* 65: 292; *HLMBS* 65: 735); her abode is also described as a *xuedong* 雪洞 (snow cave), since it is stark and bare of ornaments. Moreover, she is often associated with other cold and/or white things such as the famous "Cold fragrance pills", the plain white crab-flower and the charming but apparently passionless (*wuqing* 無情) peony (*SS* 63: 224–9; *HLMBS* 63: 698–701). In these ways, the novelist suggests the lengths to which Baochai has gone in practising Neo-Confucian stoicism. Yet she may have gone a bit too far, so Grandmother Jia 賈母, the widowed matriarch of the clan, admonishes her for having made her boudoir look too austere and self-effacing to be natural for a young girl (*SS* 40: 295, 296; *HLMBS* 40: 428, 429).

The earliest and most authoritative of traditional commentators, Zhiyanzhai 脂硯齋 (Red ink-stone studio), refers to Baochai as *zhishu shili nüfuzi* 知書識禮女夫子 (a female Confucius who knows the classics and the Rites).[25] This epithet denotes a paragon of decorum with a perfect ability to stay within the bounds of the Rites, anticipating her later reception as such an exemplar. But Zhiyanzhai's full comment actually points out that she is *not always* so — in other words, she does not always behave like a straitlaced female Confucius since her self-control is not always that perfect.[26] Her innate humanity is represented visually in an early illustration of the heroine catching butterflies, shown in Figure 8.2. This well-known episode has been variously interpreted — for instance, as representing Baochai's ambition to catch (and replace) the heroine Daiyu in the affections of the novel's hero, Baoyu, but also as a manifestation of her playful nature as a young girl momentarily freed from her sense of lady-like propriety.

Figure 8.2   Baochai catching butterflies. Black and white copy of a print by Gai Qi 改琦 (1774–1827) in *Honglou meng tu yong*, 2004, *juan* 1 (unpaginated, originally published 1879). Reproduced with kind permission of the Beijing National Library.

Indeed, as is suggested by her mixed nature and associated symbols which contain both positive and negative aspects, she is not intended to be a paragon of propriety *all* the time. As we see below, the novel portrays her not just as a young *lady* but also as a young *girl*, who succumbs to her nature — if only sometimes and unwittingly — against the influence of her nurture. In other words, she is designed (predestined) to not always be so successful in repressing her raw self as she is in her visit to Baoyu above. If her image as an ascetic paragon dehumanizes her, then these passionate slippages naturalize and normalize her, making her more like the rest of us who are flawed and often unable to bridle our improper feelings, thoughts or actions. What is particularly significant is that such outbreaks of her nature against nurture often occur under cover of her humour.

Humorous (Re)Humanization of Baochai

In Chapter 42, Baochai gives a comparative analysis of a lampoon her cousin Daiyu makes of Granny Liu, a greedy family acquaintance visiting from the countryside, as "Old mother locust" (*SS* 42: 334–5; *HLMBS* 42: 449). This critique illustrates the keenness of Baochai's own sense of humour, which is confirmed by acclaim from her audience that she "excelled as a commentator no less than Daiyu and Xifeng, in their different ways, as wits".[27] The compliment seems doubly sincere, since they also witnessed earlier a spectacular display of her satirical wit at a crab-eating party. Towards the end of that party, Baoyu suggested they compose poems on eating crabs. For a laugh (*qu xiaor ba* 取笑兒罷), Baochai offered the following verse, which bowled over her audience:

> "桂靄桐陰坐舉觴，長安涎口盼重陽。
> 眼前道路無經緯，皮裏春秋空黑黃。"
> 看到這裏，眾人不禁叫絕。寶玉道："寫得痛快，我的詩也該燒了。"又看底下道：
> "酒未敵腥還用菊，性防積冷定須薑。
> 於今落釜成何益，月浦空餘禾黍香。"
> 眾人看畢，都說："這是食螃蟹絕唱。這些小題目原要寓大意，纔算是大才。只是諷刺世人太毒了些。"

(*HLMBS* 38: 408–9)

> "With wine cups in hand, as the autumn day ends,
> And with watering mouths, we await our small friends.
> A straightforward breed you are certainly not,
> And the goodness inside you has all gone to pot —"

There were cries of admiration at this point.

"That's a very neat bit of invective!" said Baoyu. "I can see I shall have to burn *my* poem now!"

They read on.

> "For your cold humours, ginger; to cut out your smell
> We've got wine and chrysanthemum petals as well.
> As you hiss in your pot, crabs, d'ye look back with pain
> On that calm moonlit cove and the fields of fat grain?"

When they had finished reading, all agreed that this was the definitive poem on the subject of eating crabs.

"It's the sign of a real talent," they said, "to be able to see a deeper, allegorical meaning in a frivolous subject — though the social satire *is* [a little too harsh]!" (*SS* 38: 257–8, my translation in brackets)

Calling it social satire (*fengci shiren* 諷刺世人), the party clearly read the poem as an allegory deriding lawless, callous and unscrupulous people who are as crooked, cold-blooded and (morally) smelly as sideways-scuttling crabs and whose treachery is as futile and self-destructive as the goodness inside the crabs cooked and eaten. Clever as it is, the poem might seem wittier still if also read (as some traditional commentators have done) as a *personal satire* vituperating Baoyu and Daiyu.[28] But before elucidating such a reading, I note that the poem not only testifies to the creative potency and artistic sophistication of Baochai's humour; it also betrays an aspect of her personality that she may wish to keep to herself when in a less playful and more sober frame of mind — that is, her dispositional over-heatedness, which her audience intuits when they comment that her satire is *tai du le xie* 太毒了些 (a little too venomous).

Even though poetic, such a joking outburst of moral fury mars her image as a *gentle* woman. It clashes not just with the general Confucian principle of moderation but also with the Rites that require a virtuous woman to be gentle and sedate, constant and quiet, chaste and orderly, not to utter vicious words, and to shun jest and laughter.[29] Baochai herself repeatedly invokes these womanly precepts when admonishing the other girls, telling Daiyu, for example:

> As an old saying goes, "Lack of talent is a virtue for women". The most important of all is for us to be chaste and quiet. Our work (weaving, embroidery, and sewing) comes next. As for writing poetry, it is a mere boudoir diversion. One can have it, and one can do without it. Girls from families like ours do not need a reputation for literary talent.[30]

From this orthodox perspective, flaunting one's allegorical invectives, even as a poetic joke at a private gathering, is a far cry from being ladylike.

Baochai would be still more unladylike, harsh — even vicious — and the poem thus much funnier if we read it as her covert lampoon of Baoyu and Daiyu being as unruly or deviant as live crabs and as futile as cooked ones. For their thinly veiled love and dreams of a marital future together violate the decorum that disenfranchises men and women from expressing love and choosing their marriage partners, prescribing instead segregation of the sexes and conferring on their parents the prerogative of arranging marriages.[31] Otherwise, courtships and matrimonies would be scandalous and "despised by parents and countrymen" (*fumu guoren jie jian zhi* 父母國人皆賤之).[32] Such consequences are evoked in the novel by the horror of Baoyu's maid Aroma (Xiren 襲人) after overhearing her master deliriously pledging his heart to Daiyu. Aghast at the likelihood of an ugly scandal developing, Aroma wonders how she might arrange matters to prevent it (*SS* 32: 135; *HLMBS* 32: 339).[33] Quite conceivably, the good girl Baochai would scorn such wayward goings-on, knowing they will lead nowhere despite the lovers' burning passion and tearful pledges of fidelity, all just as vain as the lifelessness of the cooked crabs. This poetic conceit is quite prophetic, for Baoyu and Daiyu are never able to become husband and wife, thanks to their elders' fateful arrangements that tear them apart forever.

The likelihood that Baochai applies the conceit this way is increased by two phrases she uses to describe Baoyu, Daiyu and the crabs: *meile jingwei* 沒了經緯 (deviant) and *pili chunqiu* 皮裏春秋 (with concealed criticism). In Chapter 32, Baochai complains to Aroma about Baoyu: "*Ta rujin shuohua yuefa meile jingwei* 他如今説話越發沒了經緯" (lately he lacks even more decorum in his speeches) (*HLMBS* 32: 339). Originally meaning vertical and horizontal lines in weaving, *jing* 經 and *wei* 緯 later came to denote north–south and east–west bound paths, respectively. As a set phrase, *jingwei* can be a metaphor for pattern, order, rule, propriety, and so on. Then, absence of *jingwei* (*wu jingwei* 無經緯) means being deviant, lawless, unscrupulous, improper, and so on. It is in both its literal and figurative senses that Baochai uses *jingwei* to poeticize the crabs: *Yanqian daolu wu jingwei* 眼前道路無經緯 (The paths before you that you follow are all patternless). Such parallelism insinuates that this is how Baoyu also behaves.

The second phrase appears in the following line — *Pili chunqiu kong heihuang* 皮裏春秋空黑黃 (In vain are all the springs and autumns, the black and yellow goodies, under your shells) — which forms a couplet with the preceding line. The term *pili chunqiu* is a metaphor for unvoiced appraisal,[34] derived from the style of *The spring and autumn annals* (*Chunqiu* 春秋), a history of the State of Lu (722–481 BCE) allegedly edited by Confucius. It is held that the book's terse descriptions contain the Master's praise or criticism of recorded events and personages, a method called *chunqiu bifa* 春秋筆法 (the rhetoric of hidden judgments). It is no coincidence that, four chapters later, Baochai says this is the method Daiyu uses when she lampoons Granny Liu as "Old mother locust".

However, the contexts of these *pili chunqiu* references imbue the term with unmistakable negativity. As one critic asserts, it connotes a crafty or scheming mind (*xinji guishen* 心機詭深) intending manipulation, deception or a wicked kind of wit.[35] Yet at the outset Daiyu is introduced as an extraordinarily intelligent girl with many chambers in her heart (*xinqiao* 心竅) (*SS* 3: 103; *HLMBS* 3: 32). According to ancient Chinese belief, these chambers, or eyes in the heart (*xinyan* 心眼), are the source of intelligence, enabling one to see with the mind's eye. So the more *xinqiao* or *xinyan* one has, the smarter one is. By contrast, an obtuse person is often said to lack such eyes (*queshao xinyan* 缺/少心眼), or not to have opened up the chambers in his heart (*xin bu kai qiao* 心不開竅). If *xinqiao* is a positive or at least a neutral word, *xinyan* often denotes a calculating or scheming mind (*xinji* 心計). In *HLM*, Daiyu is portrayed as making others think she has too many eyes in her heart (*xinyan tai duo* 心眼太多), (that is, is over-sensitive or even paranoid) or has small heart-eyes (*xiao xinyan* 小心眼) (is petty-minded or intolerant), which make her prone to unfounded doubts, unnecessary misgivings and cutting sarcasm. As one character observes, "Miss Lin likes to say mean things to others, and she is also narrow-minded" (*Lin guniang zuili you ai kebo ren, xinli you xi* 林姑娘嘴裏又愛刻薄人, 心裏又細) (*SS* 27: 28; *HLMBS* 27: 277; my translation).

Hence the couplet in question indirectly calls Baoyu and Daiyu a pair of bad crabs — an unruly one coupled with a crafty one. Baochai thus appears to be engaging in the rhetoric of hidden judgements and abusive humour with relish and vengeance. For, seen in the larger context of the preceding chapters, her poem can also be read as retaliation for earlier impertinence by Baoyu and Daiyu. In Chapter 30, the three had engaged in a brawl of sarcasms, a scene I will analyse later. Suffice it for now to say that after a flash of outrage over a botched and offensive witticism by Baoyu about her plumpness, Baochai restrains herself from launching more stinging repartee, partly because of her sense of propriety and partly for fear of embarrassing Baoyu too much. It seems she has neither forgotten nor forgiven his impropriety; thus in Chapter 32 she complains to Aroma that Baoyu is getting ruder and ruder in his speech (*mei le jingwei*).

Nor does Baochai forget or forgive Daiyu's derision at the end of Chapter 34. Deeply hurt by her brother Xue Pan's remark that she has taken Baoyu's side because she harbours special feelings for him, Baochai weeps for a whole night. Next morning, unfortunately, the first person she meets is Daiyu. Seeing Baochai unusually dispirited and with clear signs on her face of having been crying, Daiyu thinks she has secretly been grieving for Baoyu because of the thrashing he received. The thought amuses Daiyu:

> 黛玉⋯⋯便在後面笑道："姐姐也自保重些兒。就是哭出兩缸眼淚來，也醫不好棒瘡。" (*HLMBS* 34: 360)
>
> "Don't make yourself ill, coz," she called out, almost gleefully . . . "Even a cistern-full of tears won't heal the smart of a beating!" (*SS* 34: 172)

Baochai pretends not to have heard Daiyu and goes away. Although she is able to ignore Daiyu's unprovoked sarcasm for the moment, it seems to be difficult for her to forget it, for Daiyu's innuendo has rubbed salt into the wound inflicted earlier by her brother's insult. Presumably the resulting pain makes both more memorable.

The poems by Baoyu and Daiyu in Chapter 38 on eating crabs may have recalled these offences by eulogizing the crabs' tasty fat and meatiness in spite of their cold nature.[36] Their mock praise may have been completely innocent, free from any malice towards Baochai.[37] Yet her memory of their insolence, as well as her nature, conceivably makes her so sensitive that she takes their words as making fun once again of *her* plumpness and coldness (apparent austerity). Thus she counter-attacks with her own poem, tooth for tooth. For example, in referring to the crabs as *wuchang gongzi* 無腸公子 (gutless princes), Baoyu may well be deprecating himself as witless. Extending his self-disparagement in her own poem, Baochai implies that he is worse than witless: he is rule-less. Similarly, where Daiyu praises the appetising goodies inside the crabs, Baochai insinuates that they are just as ineffectual as Daiyu's own over-crafty wit is in ridiculing and judging others.

Thus with one poem Baochai kills two kinds of crabs: she mocks not only immoral people in the outside world but also two impertinent persons inside the family. In so doing, she vents her spleen and takes her revenge. (The poetry contest between the three is hence a sequel to their earlier sarcastic brawl in Chapter 30, and it is small wonder that both scenes star only the three of them.) The poem thus also allows glimpses into some dark corners of Baochai's character — those latent and not completely tamed emotions. Disarmed by the convivial merriment, which is enhanced by playful versifying on the peculiar creatures they are eating, her superego lets down its guard, so that some otherwise censored tendencies seep out: over-harshness, intolerance and vindictiveness — all normally checked because they contravene the cardinal Confucian virtue of *ren* 仁.

Although not all Baochai's symptoms of dispositional over-heatedness are as dire as these, some are equally unbecoming to a "female Confucius". Her contribution to another poetry contest on willow catkins — a kind of playful thematic revolution — is an example. After critiquing the other entries as conventionally pessimistic, she prefaces her own with this claim:

寶釵笑道：". . . 我想柳絮原是一件輕薄無根無絆的東西，然依我的主意，偏要把他說好了，纔不落套。所以我謅了一首，未必合你們的意思。. . ."

"白玉堂前春解舞，東風捲得均勻。"

湘雲先笑道："好一個'東風捲得均勻'。這一句就出衆人之上了。"

又看底下道：

"蜂團蝶陣亂紛紛，幾曾隨逝水，豈必委芳塵。

萬縷千絲終不改，任他隨聚隨分。

韶華休笑本無根，好風頻借力，送我上青雲。"

衆人拍案叫絕，都說："果然翻得好氣力，自然是這首爲尊 . . ."
(*HLMBS* 70: 787)

Baochai said, smilingly: "Willow floss is a light and airy thing. It seems to me that the best way to avoid the clichés that this subject invites is to [make it desirable to be light and airy]. That is the principle on which I have tried to compose my poem; but you may not think I have succeeded . . ."

"In mazy dances over the marble forecourt,
Wind-whorled, into trim fluff-balls forming —"

"Bravo!" said Xiangyun. "'Wind-whorled, into trim fluff-balls forming': that line is better than anything the rest of us have written."

They read on.

"Like fluttering moths or silent white bees swarming:
Not for us a tomb in the running waters,
Or the earth's embalming.
The filaments whence we are formed remain unchanging,
No matter what separates or unifies.
Do not, earth-child, our rootlessness despise:
When the strong wind comes he will whirl us upwards
Into the skies."

They thumped the table enthusiastically.

"Undoubtedly this poem is the best . . ." (*SS* 70: 387–8)

This happy, optimistic and uplifting poem certainly accomplishes what it sets out to do, rendering lightness and rootlessness as praiseworthy qualities that enable willow floss to defy gravity and fly high. The humour lies in Baochai's deliberately topsy-turvy yet delightfully logical *re*-presentation of a conventional theme with delicate beauty. Her rebellious, inverting humour seems to open a channel for some personal undercurrents to gush up, which are palpable not only in the poem's dynamic imagery of whirling winds and soaring, dancing catkins but also in its sonorous notes of complacent triumph, aloofness and defiance. As many have noted, the poem acts as her inner monologue or self-portrait.[38] Such externalization of her inner self may be completely unwitting, as it is usually repressed by her apparent modesty (*qian* 謙), a requisite virtue for women to ensure their (inherent) status as humble and weak (*bei ruo* 卑弱).[39]

The greatest of several immodesties betrayed here involves male political ambitions. The possibility that Baochai may harbour such thoughts is suggested by the poem's concluding image of willow floss borne on vernal gales and ascending into the azure sky. Most critics take the azure sky (*qingyun* 青雲) as alluding only to the position of Baoyu's wife, the future matriarch of the clan.[40] Such a reading is certainly valid, but inaccurate and utterly unflattering, as it renders Baochai a mere pretender to domestic power. Nor does it do justice to the image's rich implications. *Qingyun* (literally, black cloud) is often a figure of speech for great ambition for high position in government. In fact, the poem's last two lines: *haofeng pin jie li, song wo shang qingyun* 好風頻借力，送我上青雲 (frequent strong winds lend me power / and send me up to the black clouds) echo *ping bu qingyun* 平步青雲 (to walk with ease amidst black clouds) and *chunfeng deyi* 春風得意 (spring breeze, a sense of fulfilment), two common metaphors for feelings of joy and satisfaction resulting from rapid promotion in officialdom. Hence the lines may be taken as alluding to Baochai's wish to be selected as a study-companion of imperial princesses — the azure sky with herself (uprooted from her native place) as the rootless willow floss and the imperial summons as the vernal gales.

Since the post is decreed by the emperor, such an aspiration would not count as immodest unless Baochai desired something more, such as potential *political* impact from the appointment. That she is at least aware of this possibility can be deduced from her articulation of the purposes of reading books: these are, she tells Daiyu, to understand the principles of things (*ming li* 明理); to assist the state to govern the people (*fu guo zhi min* 輔國治民); and, as she urges Baoyu, to establish oneself and make a name for one's family (*li shen yang ming* 立身揚名). Here, as she is keenly aware, she is essentially echoing the

Confucian objectives of learning *for men*. Yet she regrets that few men have achieved these goals. So it seems not too far-fetched to say that, consciously or subconsciously, she may wish that she *were* a man so that she could go out and accomplish them. Since she *is* a woman, being a princessly study-companion will be her best chance to directly serve the state, through her influence on the princesses and, through them, on their men who are most likely part of the polity.

According to the Rites, of course, it is improper for women to meddle in state affairs, as governance is strictly men's responsibility, while women's lies squarely *within* the threshold of home. Evidently, Baochai fully understands this division of social responsibilities. Yet her behaviour suggests that having a strong sense of propriety does not mean that one never has improper desires or aspirations, nor does it guarantee that one can always suppress them. They may drift out, as here, when the excitement of poetic inspiration loosens the tie on the bag so that the cat of a latent political ambition slips out. Such over-ambition marks another symptom of Baochai's dispositional over-heatedness. And once again it is disclosed to readers through the mediation of humour.

Unquestionably, a major component of this over-heatedness is her inborn romantic ardour. Often suppressed, this natural energy can partly be released by her humour. In Chapter 25, for instance, Daiyu feels great relief on hearing that Baoyu has begun to recover from his illness (caused this time by a curse):

> "Bless His Holy Name!" Daiyu murmured fervently.
>
> Baochai laughed, but said nothing. The others were mystified.
>
> "Why do you laugh, Cousin Bao?" Xichun asked her.
>
> "I was thinking how busy He of the Holy Name must be," Baochai said. "Apart from working for the salvation of all sentient beings, He has to protect the sick and hasten their recovery. [Now that they are recovering, He will turn to take care of Miss Lin's marriage.] What a lot He has to keep Him busy! Don't you find the thought rather amusing (*kexiao* 可笑)?"
>
> Daiyu affected scorn (*cui le yi kou* 啐了一口), but was blushing hotly.
>
> "You are all horrid. Instead of following good examples, you all imitate [Xifeng] and make nasty, cheap jokes (*pin zui e she* 貧嘴惡舌) all the time."

She raised the portière and went out. (*SS* 25: 506; *HLMBS* 25: 261–2; my translation in square brackets)

"Nasty, cheap jokes" refers to Xifeng's riposte to Daiyu several days previously about accepting some Siam tea Xifeng had given her: "You know the rule: drink the family's tea, the family's bride-to-be." By alluding to this age-old engagement rite, Xifeng evoked the idea of a union between Baoyu and Daiyu (*SS* 25: 499; *HLMBS* 25: 257). (This *joking* proposal of marriage may well have been intended to signify that they were not meant to be husband and wife after all.) At this moment, only Baochai remembers Xifeng's quip and brings it up teasingly to accuse Daiyu of thinking ahead about matrimony with Baoyu.

As usual, Baochai's humour reveals more about what is in *her* mind than in anybody else's. We cannot tell for sure whether Daiyu is thinking about marrying Baoyu, but Baochai's joke proves that *she* is thinking about it. It suggests that she may have been thinking about it ever since Xifeng made the joke, and perhaps even about her own union with Baoyu — who, as we will see later, has long attracted her attention. In fact, her joke reflects the preoccupation of every adolescent girl in *HLM*: marriage. The more marriageable the girls become, the more anxious they get. This is because marriage is *the* peg on which hangs their future happiness, yet they have little say in this event (commonly called *zhongshen dashi* 終身大事, the great event that will affect the rest of one's life), since everything has to be decided by their parents (and is thus often dictated by parental whim). This time-honoured protocol makes it embarrassing for a girl even to hear mention of a possible husband, let alone talk about such things herself, which would be insufferably uncouth. This is borne out by Daiyu's offended feelings described above, and by blushes or giggles among the girls whenever such taboo subjects come up in chit-chat.

But humour — especially about *another* person's marriage — helps alleviate their mounting marriage anxiety since the talk can readily be dismissed as a mere joke. Many boudoir jests in *HLM* therefore revolve around another person's marriage. Baochai's jests are no exception, as we have just seen; and on other occasions she also kids Daiyu and other girls about their marital prospects. She too suffers from marriage anxiety. This is natural and understandable, because marriage is logically her back-up plan should Plan A for becoming a princessly study-companion fall through. For pre-modern Chinese women, the prospect of happy matrimony all-importantly depended on whether they could marry Mr. Right. For many girls in *HLM*, he is Baoyu; as Xifeng says to Daiyu, "Good looks, good family, good income. There are no snags that I can see. It's a perfect match." (*SS* 25: 499; *HLMBS* 25: 257) He also has a kind heart and a deep respect for women — in fact, he *worships* them, especially beautiful girls whom he regards as the most superior of human beings. At the novel's outset, he is declared to be a kind and understanding friend of women by virtue of his unique "lust of the mind" (*yiyin* 意淫), a kind of altruistic, egalitarian and polygamist-like love and considerateness.[41] Such an empathetic ladies' man naturally causes secret wishes to burgeon in the minds of many girls around him,[42] including Baochai. This is attested to by her very first joke with Baoyu, where once again humour reveals the underlying emotional truth.

This occurs during the homecoming of Baoyu's elder sister, Yuanchun 元春, an imperial concubine. To test their progress in learning, she asks her siblings and cousins to write verses on the magnificent Prospect Garden specially constructed for her visit. While Baoyu is still working on his, Baochai stealthily suggests that he change a particular image in one poem to avoid contradicting his sister. Under pressure, Baoyu cannot think of a suitable alternative poetic allusion. Before supplying him with one, Baochai shakes her head, clicks her tongue and says with a mocking smile:

> Tut, tut, tut! If this is what you are like tonight, Heaven knows what you'll be like in a few years' time when you come to take the Palace Examination. Probably you'll find you have forgotten even the *Child's first primer of rhyming names* . . . (*SS* 18: 368; *HLMBS* 17, 18: 182)

Significantly, *only* Baochai notices the inappropriateness in Baoyu's text. Such exceptionally close attention points to a hidden attraction (which is also borne out by her frequent visits to him).[43]

Equally significant is Baochai's reference to the palace examination, which betrays her wish to shape Baoyu into Mr. Right by prodding him to prepare himself diligently for adulthood. In imperial China, passing this examination (the last level of the civil service examinations) signified momentous success in one's career because it guaranteed a job in the government and opportunities for fortune and/or fame. Since wealth and status were regarded as necessary conditions for a good life, such success was most desirable in a future husband. To Baochai's dismay, studying for the examinations is the last thing that Baoyu wants to do, and he uses every excuse to shun it; moreover, he despises those who do it, calling them "career worms" (ludu 祿蠹).[44] Because of this enormous snag (as Xifeng would call it), he is not quite as perfect a Mr. Right as he might have been, which is why everyone (except Daiyu) tries to persuade him to devote himself to study. Baochai does this through jest as above, and by giving him humorous pennames for their poetry club such as Wushimang 無事忙 (Mr Much ado about nothing) and Fuguixianren 富貴閒人 (Rich and honourable idler) (*HLMBS* 37: 385, 386; cf. *SS* 37: 218). Clearly, both dig at him for idling with girls, trying to serve and please them instead of doing something that matters for his future career.

Many readers hold that Baochai's interest in Baoyu is devoid of true feeling, and is purely motivated by selfish desires, vanity or lust for power. I believe this is inaccurate. Her near slip of the tongue, mentioned above, shows genuine care for him and her acceptance of the marriage eventually imposed on them strongly bespeaks her love for him, since by then he has lost nearly all his appeal as an ideal husband. The disappearance of his talisman jade (a symbol of his soul) ravished away his intelligence, reducing him to a mere good-looking, automaton-like idiot, and any quick recovery seems out of sight. Their wedding is hastily arranged as a kind of shock therapy, a last attempt to turn his luck, by pretending to him that he is marrying Daiyu. Baochai's cooperation in this deception is as selfish in relation to Daiyu as it is selfless in relation to Baoyu, since marrying him under these circumstances amounts to sacrificing any normal marital life, and thus evinces a profound love. People may say that her consent springs more from obedience to her elders than from love for Baoyu, but cannot it spring from both? Her wholehearted devotion to taking care of him after their marriage (by delaying their conjugal consummation, for example, until it might help his recovery as a kind of sex therapy) makes her love even more manifest. Furthermore, in retrospect it was already evident in her jealousy of Daiyu, her arch-rival.

Given that jealousy is an attendant passion of love, the more amatory people are, the more susceptible they are to jealousy and the more difficulty they have in suppressing it. Yet in traditional and polygamous China, it had to be surmounted in order to maintain familial harmony among wives, and its absence was celebrated as a virtue. To prevent and deter it, the Rites not only stipulated hierarchy, privileges, even sleeping arrangements between a husband and his wives, but also listed wifely jealousy as a main justification for a husband to divorce his wife.[45]

Noted for her generous and tolerant disposition, Baochai appears to be free from jealousy. However, a closer look reveals that her conscientious self-discipline has not entirely immunized her from this deleterious emotion; nor is she always successful in completely suppressing it, as is evidenced by her envious humour. While jealousy and envy share two essential passions, craving and resentment, they differ in that a jealous person guards what they have (or what they think they have), so will be resentfully suspicious of the influence of a rival, whereas an envious person resents others for having what they lack and desire.[46] In Chapter 27, for instance, Baoyu and Tanchun 探春, his half-sister by one of his father's concubines, briefly step away from Baochai and Daiyu to discuss some private matters. After Daiyu has also left, the narrator says:

> There was an amused interruption at this point from Baochai, who was still standing where they (Baoyu and Tanchun) had left her a few minutes before:
>
> "Do finish your talking and come back soon! It's easy to see that you two are brother and sister. As soon as you see each other, you get into a huddle and start talking about family secrets. Would it *really* be such a disaster if anything you are saying were to be overheard?" (SS 27: 37; HLMBS 27: 282)

In these teasing words we can detect a desire to be included in this secret-sharing closeness between Tanchun and Baoyu, something Baochai perhaps subconsciously wishes to possess between herself and him.

If in this case she is only wishful, she sounds truly discontented when she sees the magnificent rain cape made from mallard-head feathers that Grandmother Jia has given to a newcomer Xue Baoqin 薛寶琴, Baochai's paternal cousin. With a laugh, Baochai remarks:

> To each a different fortune meted — that's certainly a true saying.
> I never dreamt that she would be coming here — much less that
> when she did, Lady Jia would immediately fall for her like this! (*SS*
> 49: 475; *HLMBS* 49: 525)

As if to aggravate her displeasure at the fond and special treatment that Baoqin receives from the old lady (which Baochai has not, despite all her efforts to please her), a message comes from the matriarch telling Baochai not to be "too strict with Miss Qin; she's still only little and should be allowed to have her own way . . . if there's anything Miss Qin wants, she shouldn't be afraid to ask for it." Baochai's reaction is depicted thus:

> Afterwards she nudged Baoqin playfully.
> "*I* don't know! Some people have all the luck. You'd better leave us, hadn't you, before we start maltreating you? It beats me. What have *you* got that *I* haven't got?" (*SS* 49: 475; *HLMBS* 49: 526)

Her resentment is unmistakable.

Like two sides of a coin, Baochai's envy can become jealousy with a flip of circumstances, particularly when Baoyu and Daiyu are involved. One occasion makes this manifest with a momentary eruption of Baochai's emotive over-heatedness that blasts to smithereens its feeble, joking cover. In Chapter 30, after the stormiest and most scandalous of their fights, Baoyu and Daiyu make up and are dragged off by Xifeng to Grandmother Jia to demonstrate their reconciliation. Baochai happens to be present. Evidently not too thrilled about it all, she is further displeased when Baoyu apologizes to her for his inability to attend Xue Pan's birthday party, giving the excuse that he is unwell. This is a flagrant lie, for everyone knows he has been busy begging Daiyu's forgiveness. Baochai's displeasure is voiced in her response that apologies are unnecessary since they are cousins who see each other all the time, otherwise it would surely be rather unfriendly (*SS* 30: 97; *HLMBS* 30: 310). This first reflection of her discontent is only a distant rumble that quickly becomes a deafening thunderclap when she tells Baoyu why she herself is not at the birthday party watching the opera: "I can't stand the heat . . . I did watch a couple of acts of something, but it was so hot that I couldn't stay any longer. Unfortunately none of the guests showed any sign of going, *so I had to pretend I was ill in order to get away.*" (my italics) Exposed, an acutely embarrassed Baoyu scrambles to change the subject. With a stupid laugh, he blurts out:

> "No wonder they compare you to Yang Guifei, cousin. You are well covered like her, and they always say plump people fear the heat."
>
> The colour flew into Baochai's face. An angry retort was on her lips, but she could hardly make it in company. Yet reflection only made her angrier. Eventually, after a scornful sniff or two, she said:
>
> "I may be like Yang Guifei in some respects. [Unfortunately, I don't have a brother or a cousin who is capable] of becoming a prime minister." (*SS* 30: 97–8; *HLMBS* 30: 317; my translation in square brackets)

Ouch! Here the malice of Baochai's retaliatory sarcasm comes out in full force, cutting Baoyu to the quick.

What is so offensive about Baoyu's comparison that it ignites Baochai's wrath in spite of her efforts to restrain it? Historically, Yang Guifei 楊貴妃 (719–56) was the most beloved concubine of the Tang Xuanzong Emperor 玄宗 (685–762). In literature and popular culture, she is not only noted for her voluptuous beauty that makes her one of the four great Chinese beauties but she is also notorious for her liaison with An Lushan 安祿山 (d. 757), a border general (of Iranian and Turkish descent) who led the rebellion (755–63) that began the demise of the Tang empire. Thus her name connotes infidelity, lechery and treason, even in a joking comparison about her type of beauty.

Baochai may also well remember that Baoyu sometimes compares Daiyu to Xi Shi 西施 (b. 506 BCE), the foremost of the four great Chinese beauties and the embodiment of the delicate type of female beauty (as opposed to the plump type represented by Yang Guifei). As the legend goes, Xi Shi sacrificed both her beauty and her body in order to revenge her country, the State of Yue, by seducing its conqueror, the King of Wu. Her successful scheme of beauty enabled Yue eventually to topple Wu, so that her name often evokes not only beauty but patriotic heroism as well. Quite conceivably, Baochai would resent Baoyu comparing Daiyu to Xi Shi as illustrating his bias towards, and heartless treatment of, herself, and such thoughts further inflame her anger over being likened to Yang Guifei and urge an incisive response.

Her bitterly sarcastic repartee virtually calls Baoyu good for nothing. By prime minister, she refers to Yang Guozhong 楊國忠 (d. 756), Yang

Guifei's infamous cousin who became a high-ranking court official and eventually prime minister, thanks to the emperor's surpassing love for his cousin. His venality and corrupt administration provided a major excuse for An Lushan's rebellion, contributing to the decline of the Tang. On the surface, Baochai negates Baoyu's comparison of her to Yang Guifei by claiming that she has no Yang Guozhong-like brother or cousin, but underneath she insinuates her lack of a brother or a cousin as *capable*, albeit wickedly, as Yang Guozhong, because both Xue Pan and Baoyu are useless — the former due to his wildness, the latter because of his repugnance for serious study and an official career. Consequently, Baoyu will not make the level of even a petty official, let alone prime minister, although his own elder sister is a beloved imperial concubine.

At this juncture, a maid provides Baochai's jealous anger with a further outlet, so she fires another salvo at Baoyu and Daiyu:

> It happened that just at that moment a very young maid called Prettikins jokingly accused Baochai of having hidden a fan she was looking for.
>
> "I *know* Miss Bao's hidden it," she said. "Come on, Miss! Please let me have it."
>
> "You be careful," said Baochai, pointing at the girl angrily and speaking with unwonted stridency. "When did you last see *me* playing games of this sort with anyone? If there are other young ladies who are in the habit of *romping about* with you, you had better ask *them*."
>
> Prettikins fled. (*SS* 30: 98; *HLMBS* 30: 731)

Baochai's stinging accusation of impropriety on the part of Daiyu (and thus between her and Baoyu) is oblique but palpable. And the narrator carefully suggests that the innuendo results from Baochai detecting Daiyu's gloat over Baoyu's offensive comparison:

> Baoyu's rudeness to Baochai had given Daiyu secret satisfaction. When Prettikins came in looking for her fan, she had been on the point of adding some facetiousness of her own at Baochai's expense; but Baochai's brief explosion caused her to drop the prepared witticism and ask instead what play the two acts were from that Baochai said she had just been watching.
>
> Baochai had observed the smirk on Daiyu's face and knew very well that Baoyu's rudeness must have pleased her. [Now on hearing Daiyu's question, she replied, smilingly:]

> "The play I saw was *Li Kui abuses Song Jiang and afterwards has to say he is sorry*."
>
> Baoyu laughed.
>
> "What a mouthful! Surely, with all your learning, cousin, you must know the proper name of that play? It's called *The abject apology*."
>
> "*The abject apology*?" said Baochai. "Well, no doubt you clever people know all there is to know about abject apology. I'm afraid it's something I wouldn't know about."
>
> Her words touched Baoyu and Daiyu on a sensitive spot, and by the time she had finished, they were both blushing hotly with embarrassment. (*SS* 30: 98–9; *HLMBS* 30: 317; my translation in brackets)

The effect of Baochai's verbal bombardment is noticed by Xifeng who, having guessed what is going on among the trio, jocosely compares their hot and bothered expressions to those resulting from eating raw ginger. At any rate, the whole episode highlights Baochai's imperfection in managing not only jealousy but anger (*qi* 氣), one of the four vices that popular morality admonishes a decent person to shun.[47]

Although she briefly loses her temper, Baochai quickly recovers her self-control. How she checks herself is equally character-revealing, demonstrating both her proper side and her care for Baoyu. The narrator tells us that, "Baochai was about to add something, but seeing the abject look on Baoyu's face, she laughed and held her tongue." Certainly propriety requires one to know when to stop and it is praiseworthy that Baochai can do so even amid her seething jealousy. But it seems that what truly enables her to do so are her feelings for Baoyu, which allow her to notice his misery and hold fire.

However, ceasefire neither makes her forget about their offences nor pacifies her rage, since shortly afterwards we see her enjoying a jealous dig at Baoyu by Daiyu over his praise of Xiangyun. As Wang Meng points out, the sight of her adversaries fighting one another naturally gives her satisfaction.[48] And she still recalls the insults after a considerable lapse of time, as her crab-eating poem attests; even after Baochai and Daiyu reach a mutual understanding,[49] Baochai's jealousy continues to surface in bantering with Daiyu about her prospective marriage. Interestingly, these jokes are never about Daiyu marrying Baoyu but always about *someone else*, including Xue Pan, the worthless playboy.[50] It seems that, subconsciously, Baochai still wishes to remove Daiyu from Baoyu by imagining her sent elsewhere.

While Baochai preserves her sense of humour throughout the novel, its expression diminishes as the disintegration of the Jias gathers pace in the last 50 chapters. Also, the more she internalizes the norms of propriety, the fewer inner improprieties she reveals via humour. In fact, her later humour becomes increasingly Confucian in terms of its didactic and practical usage, a feature suggested by her reference to the Spring–Autumn method in analysing Daiyu's lampoon of Granny Liu. As I argue elsewhere,[51] the Confucian view of proper humour is that it should be instructive and useful in resolving issues in life, and this is indeed the direction the novel shows her taking. However, increased appropriateness of her humour does not mean that she becomes perfect; rather, it signifies that her flaws are less often manifested in humour.

Conclusion by Extrapolation

Baochai's early humour betrays the full gamut of her inner and repressed tendencies such as over-harshness, rebelliousness, masculine ambition, envy, jealousy, anger, malice, vengeance and gloating. Although all of these are natural human emotions, from the Confucian perspective they are improper — even harmful — and therefore to be inhibited. Their existence in Baochai thus belies her perceived image as flawless and effectively (re)humanizes her as a conscientious but flawed young woman who still has some inner "demons" to subdue. Given the novel's overall view of humanity, it is unlikely that the author/s intended Baochai to be either a downright villain or a perfect paragon; there is no discernable authorial attempt either to demonize or apotheosize her. Rather, considerable efforts are made to prevent her nurture from overwhelming her nature. It is as if, having conceived of her as a mixed-ether person who has made long strides in becoming a "female Confucius", the novelist then tried to keep her from becoming perfect because perfection would violate her predetermined make-up as a human being (of which one integral ingredient is imperfection). As we have seen, any dehumanizing effect from her scrupulous observance of the Rites is mitigated by her humour, which allows repeated outbreaks from her not yet properly cultivated self.

Such characterization seems to embody a kind of humanism subscribing to both classical Confucian and late-Ming and early-Qing liberal human-views. Fundamental assumptions shared by these two outlooks include that humans are flawed; that human nature (typified by its most primeval parts, desire and emotion) is ineradicable but cultivable; and that human nurture, best represented by human culture, is a necessary part of humanity, which is itself a synthesis of nature and culture. The fullest humanity lies then in a perfect balance between those two; any deficiency or excess will result in less humanity. Seldom achieved, such a perfect balance remains an ideal, while imbalance is a common reality and a source of much human imperfection. Baochai's over-cultivation, as I have shown, would make her too cold to be natural for a young girl and thereby less like a normal or real human being.

Neo-Confucianism, as noted earlier, radicalized classical Confucianism by advocating elimination of human desire in order to recover the *tianli* 天理 (heavenly principle), which meant making human nature conform to the Rites as the earthly embodiment of *tianli*, the finest and highest form of human culture and the full measure of humanity. The ascetic nature of such cultural humanism incurred a backlash from liberal-minded literati in late Ming and early Qing (roughly sixteenth to early eighteenth centuries). The liberal conception of humanity (as an over-correction) tugged them towards the other extreme or natural humanism, emphasizing *zhen* 真 (the true), *ziran* 自然 (the natural) and *qing* 情 (the emotive) to counter the perceived falsehood, artificiality and inhumanity of cultural humanism. The liberal argument boils down to a tautology: what is true is natural, and vice versa. Then, what could be more natural than things spontaneously flowing from human nature such as sexual desire and romantic passion? And what could be more real than human imperfection that is predetermined by the mixed bag of human nature? In other words, a true human being is by nature flawed and amatory. The ethical and aesthetic implication of the natural–true tautology is that the natural and true is also good and beautiful. In part, this explains the flourishing of romanticism, eroticism and realism in late Ming and early Qing literature: passions and flaws make characters more appealing as they look more human and life-like.

Our novelist is evidently a liberal humanist and realist to the extent that he refuses to allow cultural policing totally to triumph over human nature by rendering it completely submissive to external artificial control. He is also too fine an artist to portray Baochai as a robotic embodiment of propriety or a simplistic character. However, his aesthetics are not as extreme as outright liberal naturalism or Neo-Confucian culturalism. They lie closer to the classical Confucian human-view, but are infused with a measure of modernity as are his conception of mixed-ether humanity, his aesthetics of imperfection and his realism in characterization. All these in fact anticipate the modern theory of round fictional characters: those who cannot be defined by a single idea or quality, who are three-dimensional, mutable and often surprise readers with hidden facets or fresh extensions of their personalities. As such, they are more like real, living and changing human beings. By contrast, flat characters are defined by a single idea or quality and are thus two-dimensional and immutable, usually a type or a caricature.[52] Seen from this point of view, the continuing popularity of the novel and its lively characters such as Baochai is not surprising.

Moreover, the author's use of humour calls to mind the Freudian theory of jokes (even though this may not be the most highly regarded of theories on humour nowadays). For Freud, jokes often provide insights into the human unconscious, as do dreams or slips of the tongue, because they represent moments when the superego may be duped into slackening its normal censorship by the trickery of "dream-work" and "joke-work", so that natural and potentially antisocial impulses such as sexuality, hostility, blasphemy and enjoyment of absurdity can express themselves. In the case of jokes, this is done safely with the ready excuse that "it's only a joke".[53] As we have seen, Baochai repeatedly displays such instinctive behaviour to vent herself or to hurt others emotionally. The finesse with which our novelist employs humour in this Freudian fashion reflects not only his unflinching fictional realism and humanism but also a deep intuitive insight into the human psyche. Such perspicacity also partly explains what is so great about this eighteenth-century novel: it has the eternal appeal of any classic and its humour rings as true to us today as it has always done.

9

Contextualizing Lin Yutang's Essay "On Humour": Introduction and Translation

Joseph C. Sample

The *Lunyu banyuekan* 論語半月刊 (Analects Fortnightly) first appeared in 1932 in Shanghai with the stated aim of promoting humour, and its instant success resulted in the following year being declared "The Year of Humour" in literary circles. The highly charged political climate of the time is discussed in detail by Qian Suoqiao in Chapter 10 of this volume, together with an account of the aims and objectives of the journal's chief editor, Lin Yutang 林語堂. In response to the barrage of criticism as well as excitement stirred up by his ideas about humour and his magazines, Lin published "Lun youmo" 論幽默 (On humour) in *Lunyu banyuekan* in two sections, on 16 January and 16 February 1934.[1] Of the many books, essays and articles that he wrote, Lin considered this text to be one of his best.

Admittedly, when analysed as a literary work, *Lun youmo* is subject to the criticism that it is too general and overly selective in its treatment of several thousand years of Chinese literature, and also to the socio-historical critique that Lin's overall argument about the importance of humour was somewhat irrelevant, considering the chaotic political and cultural atmosphere in which the text was written. When reading it, we must keep in mind that, in addition to definitions and explanations, we also find interpretation — of a country, a people, its past, present and, perhaps most importantly, its future. We find as well one man's genuine pride about and admiration of China, intermixed with his growing sense of fear and concern. Lin never claimed that the troubles and tragedies of society could be banished by a few moments of hilarity. Instead, he simply advocated a less acerbic type of humour — one that appealed to an individual's inherent sense of the comical — as an antidote to the mockery, bitterness and indignation that had become so prevalent at all levels of Chinese society.

Figure 9.1   Lin Yutang with his wife, Lin Liao Tsuifeng, in China in the 1940s. Photograph courtesy of Hsiang Ju Lin (their daughter).

Lun youmo is situated between discourses, a mixture of old and new Chinese and Western thought and tradition. In this regard, the essay is useful both to people interested primarily in studies of world literatures but who may not be familiar with individuals such as the Eastern Jin dynasty poet Tao Qian 陶潛 (365–427 CE), and those immersed in social, historical and political research on China who may not be fully aware of the role Lin Yutang played in defining "revolutionary" literature. Lin clearly placed his literary work within what he believed to be the Daoist philosophical tradition, as opposed to Confucianism — which, rightly or wrongly, he credited with many of the faults and failings of contemporary society. Whether this assumption was justified may be gauged to some extent by two other chapters in this book, Chapter 4 by Weihe Xu on the place of humour in Confucianism and Chapter 5 by Shirley Chan on humour in the *Liezi*, a key Daoist text.

As far as humour theory is concerned, Lin preferred above other past writers and thinkers on this subject the English man of letters George Meredith (1828–1909), who delivered his famous "Essay on comedy and the uses of the Comic Spirit" as a lecture at the London Institution on 1 February 1877,[2] and later illustrated his theories with a deservedly popular novel, *The egoist* (1879).[3] Lin elevated the idea of humour to the level of Meredith's famous Comic Spirit because he was trying to reinterpret Chinese culture *vis-à-vis* Western modernity. At the time when he was writing, there was no generally accepted Chinese word (or concept) for humour — although, as he describes, there were terms for closely related concepts and feelings such as satire (*fengci* 諷刺) and the laughable (*huaji* 滑稽). Lin proposed *youmo,* not only as an important neologism but also as a specialized and novel concept, following Meredith's views, of good-tempered humour and laughter. In fact, he offers it as a kind of transcendent or mediated position between tragedy and comedy that extends beyond the realm of literature. It is, he feels, the mark of a civilized nation.

Figure 9.2   Lin Yutang and family — wife Lin Liao Tsuifeng, their son Richard Ming Lai and daughters Taiyi Lin Lai and Hsiang Ju Lin — on the occasion of his eightieth birthday, celebrated in 1975 in Hong Kong. Photograph courtesy of Hsiang Ju Lin.

In translating this work, I have included notes for most of the Chinese and Western literary works and authors mentioned in the text. Notes also proved necessary because Lin occasionally refers to texts without mentioning any titles, such as in the opening section where he discusses "the ancient collection of three hundred anonymously written poems", but does not state that he means the *Shijing* 詩經 (Book of poetry). Beyond this, I have added other kinds of notes since the original text does not contain any bibliographic or in-text citations, and I also have added quotation marks around terms or entire phrases that have unique counterparts in English or special meanings in Chinese. For example, early in the text Lin mentions the "nine schools and one hundred philosophies", which is actually a combination of two separate Chinese terms, and later in the same passage he describes people who saw through the "principles of love and its manifestation in conduct". If I feel that such quoted material has a significant generic or historical implication, this is explained in notes; otherwise, I assume that readers can understand the meaning of the quoted material from the context of the given passage. For those interested in understanding more of Lin Yutang's thought, his significance and his background, this chapter should be read in conjunction with that by Qian Suoqiao, which is fully referenced to other studies and biographical accounts of this remarkable figure, and his writings and times.

"On humour"

by Lin Yutang

> One excellent test of the civilization of a country . . . I take to be the flourishing of the Comic idea and Comedy; and the test of true Comedy is that it shall awaken thoughtful laughter.
>
> — George Meredith, "Essay on comedy"[4]

Part I

Humour (*youmo* 幽默) is a part of life; therefore, when a culture develops to a certain extent, humorous literature will inevitably appear. With the development of intelligence those who have sufficient ability to cope with all kinds of issues will produce works of humour. In some cases humour emerges when those who are intelligent begin to be suspicious of human wisdom and begin to see human stupidity, self-contradiction, stubborn bias and self-importance. The Persian astronomer and poet Omar Khayyam was of this sort.[5] In the ancient collection of three hundred anonymously written poems, a humorous attitude appears in the poem where the author was feeling the emptiness of life and singing:

> You have carriages and horses
> But you will not drive them.
> You will drop off in death,
> And another person will enjoy them.[6]

The words of the woman in the "Odes of Zheng" (*Zheng feng* 鄭風) who said, "Are there no men other than you who admire me?" also contain the idea and beauty of humour, which, as a reflective and unhurried manner, enables a person to be unrattled by sentimentalism and adversity.[7] When the top intellectuals appeared, such as Zhuangzi, humorous ideas and essays developed from their intellectual abilities to analyse political issues and convince emperors of their views and solutions. Zhuangzi, therefore, can be considered the father of Chinese humour. The Grand Historian claimed that the origin of Zhuangzi's *huaji* 滑稽 (the concept of the laughable) could be traced back to Laozi, with which we cannot disagree.[8] In the Warring States period, individuals who discussed political topics, such as Gui Guzi and Chunyu Kun, also possessed the ability to argue ludicrously.[9] At this time China's cultural and spiritual life was truly energetic as the "nine schools and one hundred philosophies" gradually emerged like a courtyard filling with the brightness of spring as strange and fantastic flowers burst forth with their unique scents and colours. In this free and open atmosphere, self-reflection and expressiveness appeared and individuals' thoughts walked separate paths as they thoroughly studied, probed and traced ideas to their very roots. If these ideas were sufficiently different, they would develop them, discovering their own paths. It was in this atmosphere that an "earnest" group and a "detached" group of thinkers were formed. Those who were willing to sacrifice their own lives for justice, such as Mozi, the literati who strove to become government officials, or people like Confucius, are all examples from the earnest group. Those who would not pluck out one of their own hairs to benefit others, such as Yang Zhu, or those who resorted to obscurantism in seeing through the "principles of love and its manifestation in conduct", such as Zhuangzi and Laozi, were all members of the detached group.[10] With the detached group, humour naturally appeared as their comments were uninhibited, their writing strokes sharp and their essays profound, promising and unconstrained by finer points of etiquette. Those who worked tirelessly, according to the detached group, were only laughable. The Confucians, who paid close attention to such conventions as the thickness of the wood on the inside and the outside of coffins and who insisted on mourning for a prescribed period of time after a family member's death, could not keep out Zhuangzi's boisterous laughter. Consequently, in the history of Chinese thought, Confucianism and Daoism became two major ideologies, representing an orthodox faction and a humorist faction. Later, because the Confucians advocated a hierarchical relationship between the emperor and his subjects, and because the emperors and Confucian scholars and sovereign leaders' interests were shared, and they thus cooperated, the Confucian faction was able to suppress competing ideologies and to build a dominant position, which in turn paved the way for future Chinese pedants. Humour, however, is a way of looking at and criticizing human life, and it cannot be fully suppressed or destroyed despite the pressure of the ruler's orthodox teachings. Furthermore, the fountainhead of Daoist thought is broad, and the spirit of Laozi's and Zhuangzi's articles did not disappear even after so many dynasties of literary orthodoxy. Therefore, although philosophies after the mid-ancient period seemed inspired only by the Confucians' orthodox teachings, in reality Confucianism and Daoism were two separate forces at work.[11] The Chinese people who were in power believed in Confucianism, and those who were not in power followed Daoism as they wandered in the woods, consigning themselves to nature, producing artwork related to nature and cultivating their personal character and affections. Chinese literatures, with the exception of the emperor's court literature, all benefited from the humour of the Daoist philosophy. The court literature was not "real" literature in the sense that it was only used to manage affairs. Truly expressive Chinese literature, such as rhythmically chanted poetry, touches our souls most deeply and returns us to nature, and this type of literature belonged entirely to the humorous and liberal

Daoists. If China did not have this Daoist literature — if it only had the humourless Confucian orthodox precepts — then Chinese poetry would be so dull, and the Chinese people's souls so depressed.

Laozi and Zhuangzi were unquestionably of the detached faction, as seen in Zhuangzi's "The happiness of fish" (*Yu zhi le* 魚之樂), "Dreaming of a butterfly" (*Hudie zhi meng* 蝴蝶之夢), "Discourse on swords" (*Shuo jian zhi yu* 説劍之喻) and "The frog in the well and the sea turtle" (*Wa bie zhi yu* 蛙鱉之語), all of which are humorous. Laozi said [to Confucius]:

> The men of whom you speak are dead, and their bones have already mouldered to dust. Only their words alone are still extant. I observe that the good merchant hides his treasures deeply as if he were poor, and the noble man of great virtue appears stupid. Put away your proud air and your many desires, your affection and exaggerated plans. All this is of no use to you. That is what I have to tell you, and that is all.[12]

It does not matter whether or not the Warring States period historian Sima Qian transmitted these facts correctly, because the strong scent of [Laozi's] contemptuous air makes it difficult for people to accept. Although we read Laozi's and Zhuangzi's writings to see how to conduct ourselves, we always come away feeling that they had too much sarcasm and too little affection. In terms of profoundness and depth, however, their "looking askance at the ways of the world" is assuredly an expression of the true "comic spirit". Laozi had a wry smile, and Zhuangzi's smile was unrestrained. The sound of Laozi's laughter was sharp, and the sound of Zhuangzi's laughter was boisterous. The detached group could have become cynical and disgusted with the world, but by arriving at cynicism and disgust, they would have lost an essential element of true humour. Qu Yuan and Jia Yi had very little humour for just this reason.[13] What is called *youmo*, then, is gentle and sincere, unbiased, and at the same time concerned with the destiny of humankind. This is what the West calls humour. Alert and trenchant satire is called *yuti* 鬱剔 (wit).[14] In retrospect, Confucius himself was gentle yet stern, reverent yet content. There was nothing that he desired and nothing that was necessary for him, as his ambiguous attitude towards right and wrong was approaching a genuinely humorous attitude.

The contrast between Confucius's humour and the Confucians' humourlessness is a most obvious fact. What I glean from Confucius is not his deference and solicitude, but his faith in leisurely living. Pedants adopt his deference and solicitude, but not his faith. What I love most is his humour during his time of failure, such as the Confucius who asked, "Am I a gourd that can tolerate hanging on the wall and go without food for days?" Not the young, arrogant and successful Confucius who had Shao Zhengmao killed. Pedants all love the Confucius who had Shao Zhengmao killed, not the humorous Confucius who agreed with Dian.[15] Even after Confucius died, Mencius was able to be very humorous, and his story "The boy who secretly climbed over a wall of his employer to meet with the employer's daughter" is something that even today's scholars would disdain telling.[16] The parable "The man from the State of Qi, his wife, and his concubine" is also quite satiric.[17] Mencius, however, is closer to wit, not humour, because his works have more reasoning and less feeling and, over time, all the Confucian scholars became more depraved and are now not deserving of discussion. Although the famous talent Han Fei did produce unique essays with intricate explanations, these are only examples of a college professor's style of humour in that they were calculated and lacking in spontaneity.[18] Finally, Dongfang Shuo and Mei Gao were the forebears of Chinese *huaji*, which is also not true humour.[19] After the Zhengshi reign period of the Cao Wei period [240–290 CE], Wang Bi and He Yan founded Spiritualism, and Daoism regained strength, which, when combined with the continued leadership of the Seven Sages of the Bamboo Grove, thoroughly cleansed pedanticism and started a neo-Daoist movement.[20]

In this atmosphere, the Daoists' way of thinking accommodated the people's desire for self-expression, and the philosophy of the Zhou dynasty's Qin State excitedly changed like the flowers and trees turning from their glorious bloom at the height of summer to the seasoned depths of early autumn, emerging with an attitude of indifference to worldly gain and self-satisfaction.[21] This philosophical movement resulted in the cultivation of the mature humour of the great poet Tao Qian at the end of the Jin dynasty.[22] Tao Qian's "Reproving my sons" (*Ze zi* 責子) has an artistic, well-versed sense of humour. His nonchalant attitude and self-contentedness are not the same as the unrestrained style of Zhuangzi, yet neither does he have Qu Yuan's grief and indignation. Tao Qian and Qu Yuan both had talents that were under-appreciated, but Tao Qian's "The return" (*Gui qu lai ci* 歸去來辭) does not have the sorrowful tone of Qu Yuan's "Divination" (*Bu ju* 卜居) or "The old fisherman" (*Yu fu* 漁父). Tao Qian and Zhuangzi similarly advocated the "recovery of our original nature", yet [Tao's] attitude towards admonishing social conventions does not have Zhuangzi's vigilant manner. Tao would not compromise his integrity just to earn a small salary in a dead-end job, but he pitied those who sacrificed their ideals in order to make a living. Zhuangzi, however, criticized those seeking official rank and pay as cattle confined to their pens and swine waiting to be slaughtered. Therefore, when Zhuangzi's indignant and boisterous laugh filtered down through the ages to Tao Qian, it merely turned into a mild smile. The reason that I say this is not that I want to put down Zhuangzi and praise Tao, it is only that I want to present the many different kinds of Chinese humour. Whereas Zhuangzi was the best at the humour of arguing and debating, Tao was the forebear of the humour of poeticizing self-satisfaction. Zhuangzi's is probably the humour of the *yang* and Tao Qian's is the humour of the *yin*. This difference originated in their differences in temperament and disposition. Today, the Chinese people do not understand humour's meaning, thinking that all humour should be satiric, and so this is why I have tried to provide examples of "leisurely" humour.

After Zhuangzi, the humour of arguing and debating was not to be seen because bold and unconstrained thinking was always suppressed by the orthodox views of the imperial powers. For 2000 years, everybody expressed views that coincided with the beliefs of the ancient sages and the literati merely performed ritual acrobatics at the Confucian temples. Thus the so-called uninhibited nature of Neo-Confucians' great works were actually rather routine and minor tricks, and their so-called intellectual superiority was just the same.[23] Throughout this time the court literati came to despise those who expressed novel ideas or whose conversations transcended their accepted opinions, accusing such individuals of being deceitful or rebelling against the Way and in some cases blaming them for overthrowing the country. According to Fan Ning, the crimes of the Spiritualists Wang Bi and He Yan exceeded those of China's [legendary tyrant] Jie Gui as the literati felt that, because of these independent thinkers, virtue was obscured, elegance was taken prisoner, morality broke down and the central China plains were lost.[24] Wang favoured "pure conversations" (*qingtan* 清談), but after these were blamed as one of the omens for the perishing of the Jin dynasty, would anyone afterward dare to make detached statements? For 2000 years, the talented cherished "dreams of the literati" assisting the ruler in governing the empire and leading as dukes in governing the country and collecting taxes. Who among them would dare to write essays expressing their grief and indignation, let alone in their free time write works of satire — or even more so dare to be humorous? The literati always talked about virtue and morality. They tried to fool people by cheating themselves at the same time. They knew clearly that they lied to each other frequently, but they would not allow others to expose their hypocrisy. The propaganda of today's politicians and the fighting factions has been just like the literati maintaining their serious expressions, only now warlords are actually destroying the country and the state's high officials are the ones causing harm to our national cause. Reading this propaganda makes almost everyone yearn for Emperors Tang and Wu and the halcyon days of Yao and Shun.[25] When listening to the speeches of the government officials who extort money and the military men who traffic narcotics, it sounds as though they make Confucius and Duke Zhou ashamed and embarrass Xunzi and Mencius.[26] They could not even see who [it was that] Mencius ridiculed in his story of the wife crying in the courtyard when her husband returned home.[27] How would they spend their free time appreciating the humour of Mencius?

Humour, after all, is a part of life. We do not always understand the reasons for tears and laughter, but just because the court literati excluded such things from their own lives does not mean that they were successful in causing them to die out. Thus, in literary works, one cannot see the humour derived from discussing political topics, and one definitely can see relaxed humour or "humour to cheer one's heart" in various poems. As for the men of letters' occasional comical *huaji* essays, such as "Farewell to poverty" (*Song qiong wen* 送窮文) by Han Yu and "Drive out the cats" (*Zhu mao wen* 逐貓文) by Li Yu, these were only amusements.[28] The literati simply cannot write true works of humour. In fact, it is only among the writers of the school of

Self-Expression that we find some very humorous literature, such as Ding An's "individualist talks", Zhonglang's "persistence discussions" and Zi Cai's "conversations about temptations".[29] Additionally, outside the realm of traditional literature the literati all read "Rustic words of a man from Eastern Qi" (*Qidong yeyu* 齊東野語)[30] and the novels about low-ranking officials, every one of which had humorous elements. And was humour present in the works of the Song dynasty storytellers, the operas of the Yuan dynasty, the legends of the Ming dynasty and the novels of the Qing dynasty? For example, the characters in *Water margin* (*Shuihu zhuan* 水滸傳), Li Kui 李逵 and Lu Zhishen 魯智深 can at one moment make you cry or laugh — or cry and laugh — and then the next moment you are at a loss as to whether to laugh or cry.[31] This surpasses satiric criticism and reaches a condition of sympathetic humour. In *Journey to the west* (*Xiyouji* 西游記),[32] the monkey, the novice monk and Zhu Ba Jie, in addition to making us cheerful, definitely give us a feeling of enthusiastic sympathy, which is an essential element of humour. In *The scholars* (*Rulin waishi* 儒林外史),[33] almost every chapter presents a human sentiment of one truly familiar with the ways of the world and, in addition to humour, provides a mixture of satire as well. *Romance of the mirrored flowers* (*Jinghua yuan* 鏡花緣)[34] is about women and the sovereign world, and Yu Gu in *Travels of Lao Can* (*Lao Can youji* 老殘遊記)[35] also has many enlightening discussions on people's wisdom, which are not easily found in orthodox literature. To find China's truly humorous literature, one should look in the dramas, legends, novels and ditties, just as one should look in the dramas, legends, novels and ditties for the best Chinese poetry.

Part II

Orthodox Chinese literature did not allow for humorous expression, so the Chinese people did not understand the nature of humour and its function. People often adopted a scornful attitude towards humour, and Confucian moralists even went so far as to assume an attitude of hatred or fear, because they believed that once a humorous writing style spread, life would lose its seriousness and orthodoxy would be overturned by sophistry. This orthodoxy is similar to the Confucian moralists' seeing women as being dangerous, exposing their incomprehension of the function of sex in human life; or it is similar to their looking at the novel as the "minor way" of petty officials, exposing their incomprehension of imaginative literature.[36] As I have said repeatedly, humour is a part of human life. The Confucians were able to exclude humour from their memorial tablets, rhymed inscriptional verses and reports to the emperors, but they were not able to exclude humour from the lives of the people. Life will forever be filled with humour, just as life will always be filled with sadness, sexual desire and imagination — even the lives of those Confucian scholars who composed essays of utmost Confucian orthodoxy. Didn't they also laugh and joke when they talked among friends? The only difference is that their essays lacked the enrichment of humour. Look again in Zhu Xi's "Memoirs of illustrious ministers" to see all what literary men dared not write in books — but from time to time they did say things that were very rich in humour. Let us examine a few examples:

> [Entry for Zhao Pu] Taizu wanted to put Fu Yanqing in charge of the army.[37] The king of Han often pleaded that because Yanqing's fame and position were already great it was not proper to give him any more military power. The emperor, not listening to his advice, issued a proclamation. The king of Han, grabbing the proclamation, asked for an audience with the emperor. The emperor asked, "Why are you suspicious [of Fu Yanqing]? I have treated him with such kindness, how could he turn against me?" The king replied, "Your Honour, how is it that you were able to turn against Emperor Shi Zong?" The Emperor fell silent and the proclamation was discontinued.[38]

This has insight into human emotion and is the best kind of humour.

> The Empress Dowager Zhao Xian was intelligent and wise and had managed and decided the great affairs of the state. When she fell seriously ill, Taizu served her medicine, never leaving her side. The empress dowager asked him, "Do you know why you are given all under the sky?" The emperor said: "This is all a blessing that my ancestors and you extended to me." The empress said laughing, "Not really. It's merely because the Chai clan had a child running the empire."[39]

Everything Taizu said was the language of an orthodox Confucian "putting on appearances". Yet the empress dowager was able to obliterate Taizu's "meritorious founding of the dynasty", telling him that his rule over the empire was the result of the Chai clan's misfortune of having a child become emperor. These words and this kind of insight are really similar to George Bernard Shaw telling us of Napoleon's explanation of one of his great military victories — that it was entirely accomplished by his horse finding a shallow spot to cross a river.[40] Is not the best humour that which exposes the truth?

In terms of defining humour, there are the analyses of Plato, Immanuel Kant, Thomas Hobbes, Henri Bergson and Sigmund Freud. Bergson fails to grasp the essence of humour, and Freud's definition is too specialized. My favourite discussion of humour is still the English novelist George Meredith's "Essay on comedy". He describes the Comic Spirit in a paragraph that is very difficult to translate [into Chinese]; nevertheless, I propose the following sketchy translation.[41]

> If you believe that our civilization is founded in common-sense (and it is the first condition of sanity to believe it), you will, when contemplating men, discern a Spirit overhead . . . It has the sage's brows, and the sunny malice of a faun lurks at the corners of the half-closed lips drawn in an idle wariness of half tension. That slim feasting smile, shaped like the long-bow, was once a big satyr's laugh, that flung up the brows like a fortress lifted by gunpowder. The laugh will come again, but it will be of the order of the smile, finely tempered, showing sunlight of the mind, mental richness rather than noisy enormity. Its common aspect is one of unsolicitous observation, as if surveying a full field and having leisure to dart on its chosen morsels, without any fluttering eagerness. Men's future upon earth does not attract it; their honesty and shapeliness in the present does; and whenever they wax out of proportion, overblown, affected, pretentious, bombastical, hypo-critical, pedantic, fantastically delicate; whenever it sees them self-deceived or hood-winked, given to run riot in idolatries, drifting into vanities, congregating in absurdities, planning shortsightedly, plotting dementedly; whenever they are at variance with their professions, and violate the unwritten but perceptible laws binding them in consideration one to another; whenever they offend sound reason, fair justice; are false in humility or mined with conceit, individually, or in the bulk — the Spirit overhead will look humanely malign and cast an oblique light on them followed by volleys of silvery laughter.[42] That is the Comic Spirit.[43]

The sound of this kind of laughter is genial and soft, and it starts with the soul's intuitive comprehension. Ridicule is selfish; but humour is sympathetic. Therefore, humour and vilification are not the same because vilification itself is lacking the intuitive comprehension of reason and is not able to be introspective. The emotions associated with humour are remote and detached, so humour produces laughter but not anger. Yet humour also is grounded in understanding and is able to infiltrate idealized concepts. Meredith said it well when he stated that perceiving the Comic Spirit enables us to experience the pleasure of shared sympathy. Those who vilify are desperate, their words are fiery and they only fear that observers will not sympathise with them. Humorists know that anyone with reason will sympathise with them, and because they all share the same feelings, the humorists will not resort to fiery language or wish to beat their opponents down. Everything they laugh at is their opponents' foolishness, so they only have to point that out. Clear-minded people will agree with this. Only those who do not understand humour need to be ridiculed.

Meredith's essay also makes many distinctions between humour and satire:

> You may estimate your capacity for Comic perception by being able to detect the ridicule of them you love, without loving them less: and more by being able to see yourself somewhat ridiculous in dear eyes, and accepting the correction their image of you proposes . . .
>
> If you detect the ridicule, and your kindliness is chilled by it, you are slipping into the grasp of Satire.
>
> If instead of falling foul of the ridiculous person with a satiric rod, to make him writhe and shriek aloud, you prefer to sting him under a semi-caress, by which he shall in his anguish be rendered dubious whether indeed anything has hurt him, you are an engine of Irony.
>
> If you laugh all around him, tumble him, roll him about, deal him a smack and drop a tear on him, own his likeness to you and yours to your neighbour, spare him as little as you shun, pity him as much as you expose, it is a spirit of Humour that is moving you.[44]

All that Meredith discusses about the essence of humour is revealing, yet I would still like to add a few sentences about the Chinese people's misunderstanding of humour. The influence of Chinese orthodoxy is so great that it leads most Chinese people to think that humour is the same as "wisecracking satire".[45] When writing, people traditionally had to show concern for social conditions and hence they could only satirize affairs of the day. These satirical comments were then turned into essays.[46] Although humour and satire are close, humour does not have satire's directed purpose. All satire has a tendency to be vicious, but by removing the acridity and creating a more diluted mood satire can become humour. If you seek to write something humorous, however, you must first be emotionally detached from a situation and bring along a sense of Buddhist benevolence. Anger then will not flourish in your essay, and readers will get a sense of your indifference. Humour, after all, is a dispassionate, distant observer, which is why our laughter often brings tears and our tears bring laughter. Humorous essays are light, natural, unlike *yuti* essays, which dazzle, surprise, disrupt and defeat. Nor are humorous essays similar to witty essays, which start with a cunning, clever argument. A humorous essay is somewhere between smooth and courteous and vigorous and unrestrained. It is natural, careless about details and without ornamentation. When reading humorous essays, you cannot point out which sentences make you laugh, you can only read and allow the humour to awaken your spirit and comfort your heart. This is because humour is natural while wit is artificial. Humour is objective; *jijing* 機警 [literally, alert; sharp-witted; vigilant] is subjective. Humour is watered down; wit and satire are sharp and cutting. A transcendent understanding of worldly affairs gives one a "heart filled with happiness" and allows one to write in a relaxed style. Humour will appear automatically in articles that do not compromise with shameful, disgraceful and moralistic Confucian standards, beg for praise from the scholar-bureaucrats or curry the common people's favour.

Part III

There are broad and narrow definitions of humour. In Western usage, the general definition of humour encompasses everything that makes people laugh, including even dirty jokes. (What are called humour magazines in the West publish mostly coarse jokes, and the literary style of these magazines is not very sophisticated. Magazines such as the French-language *Sourire* and the English-language *Ballyhoo*, for example, are simply "intolerable to the eye".) In precise definitions, humour is distinguished from wit, satire and ridicule, and although these all contain elements of laughter — bitter laughter, boisterous laughter, light laughter, giggling laughter — they are still all different. Laughter also contains every kind of purpose and attitude: some kinds of laughter are severe, some are gentle, some are spiteful, some are sympathetic, some are "a few words that induce a smile", some are "based on one's outlook on life", and some are thoughtful and committed. The best humour is naturally that which simultaneously expresses a clever brilliance and abundant wisdom, such as the kind that Meredith said belongs in the "smile of the meeting of the hearts" category. Among every kind of style, this is the richest emotionally. Nevertheless, humour and its related styles all make people laugh just the same, so the nature of laughter and the techniques of humour are surely worth discussing.

Theories on laughter can be traced back to Aristotle and Plato. Kant's theory by and large corresponds to Aristotle's. This theory is called a "reaction to one's expectations", which occurs when one is feeling tense but then someone says something that eases the tension and thereupon the brain receives a feeling of levity and produces laughter. Kant said "laughter is an affection arising from the sudden transformation of a strained expectation into nothing".[47] Both wit and the precise definitions of humour can be explained in this way. Freud's *Wit and its relation to the unconscious* has a good example:

> In his distress a needy man borrowed twenty-five dollars from a wealthy acquaintance. The same day he was discovered by his creditor in a restaurant eating a dish of salmon with mayonnaise. The creditor reproached him in these words: "You borrow money from me and then order salmon with mayonnaise. Is that what you needed the money for?" "I don't understand you," responded the debtor. "When I don't have money I can't eat salmon with mayonnaise. When I have money I mustn't eat it. Well then, when shall I ever eat salmon with mayonnaise?"[48]

The rich friend asked a question in a state of misdoubt. We are all sympathetic with the needy man, and we thought he must be embarrassed until we hear his answer — the tension then suddenly dissipates. This is an example of our nerves producing laughter. There is another way of stating this. When laughing, we observe other people in embarrassing or unfortunate situations, or when they do something clumsy or foolish, it makes us feel that we are better than they are. Therefore, we laugh. If we see someone fall down, but we ourselves stand stable, we laugh. When you notice someone busy chasing fame and fortune, but you yourself are free from worldly desires, you can again laugh. But, if you know of an official who, like you, works in the capital and used to have the same rank as you, but has just obtained an advanced position and higher social status, you may feel jealous and therefore you do not laugh. If you see someone caught under a collapsed house and you will soon be affected, you cannot laugh because you will feel panic. Thus the origin of laughter is seeing through life's disgrace and misfortune where we are not involved, allowing our psyches to receive a kind of cheerful feeling. People read essays that admonish others for this same reason. When a person tells of a previous embarrassing experience, observers oftentimes cannot help but laugh. Naturally, those who are being laughed at may not be too pleased, and so their embarrassment might transform into humiliation and anger. The more that humour uses general references to humankind, the more it attains an element of sympathy because a listener will believe that he is not the target of the laughter, and even if it is directed at his social class, he may not be included among those referred to. The person being laughed at also does not feel that it is necessary that others chastise his personal characteristics or his social status. For example, when *Analects Fortnightly* scolds an official who works in the capital, the official is still able to read it and laugh. When we chide professors who "earn salaries by reviewing old things", they are able to endure this with a clear conscious because it is not at all threatening.[49] The more a two-sided argument involves specific individuals, such as the disagreements between Wang Jingwei and Wu Zhihui, the less humorous it is, since personal distress and ruthlessness are too easily added.[50] Otherwise, generally and indiscriminately satirizing society and people's lives has an emotional appeal that is naturally deeper and thus closer to the essence of humour.

The reaction to the unexpected is an element of every essay. (Related [to this], puns are the most superficial form of humour yet their natural, quick-witted elements are truly fine. There is an art form to the sudden change in meaning due to a word's double meaning.) Such reactions are sometimes the results of an individual's ne'er-do-well attitude (see the previous joke) or because the people in the joke are rather thickheaded. Other reactions, however, are due to understanding the principle or reasons for something, and thus being able to see through human relationships. This type of unexpected reaction must begin with a clear, alert mind, for there is not a specific sequence that leads to the understanding, making it similar to Lady Gongsun wielding a sword: you will never know which movement she will take next because there is no set routine.[51] Those who are humorous are naturally quick-witted. For example, one time during a speech by [British Prime Minister] Lloyd George, a feminist activist stood up and said, "If you were my husband I would certainly poison you." George responded, "If I were your husband, I would certainly eat poison."[52] This is an instance of needing to act according to the circumstances. The story of the unattractive woman meeting with King Xuan of the State of Qi and of his taking her as a royal concubine is truly a little mischievous and is also a kind of humour.[53] Of course, one must be cautious because being mischievous and saying or doing unreasonable things can change a person's opinion and incur dislike. Good humour all begins with common sense. It unexpectedly appears and depends on people speaking their minds. When talking, people generally combine propriety with falsehood, and listening to them does not feel strange until someone righteously speaks the truth, which then causes everybody to laugh noisily. This brings to mind Freud's explanation that when inhibitions are suddenly released, like a horse released from its reins, our souls are naturally relaxed, enabling us to laugh. For this reason, humour can easily become obscene because obscene talk can also be used to relax inhibitions. In the appropriate environment, obscene talk is good and healthy for the psyche. According to my experience, when college professors and accomplished scholars get together to have a *tête-à-tête*, they always joke about their sex lives. So what is called obscene and improper is purely a matter of society's social customs. In some places you can discuss certain things that in other places you cannot. Social interaction in England's middle class can leave a speaker tongue-tied when compared with the social interaction of the aristocracy. Generally, high and low classes are very open, and it is only the educated middle class that has many limitations. The English may approve of things that the French do not approve of. Or maybe the Chinese do not approve of things [of which] the English approve. The time period also makes a difference, as seventeenth-century England had many words that people would not dare to use. Shakespeare's time was also like this; yet this does not mean that people's minds today are necessarily purer than those of the people of Shakespeare's time because discussing sex actually has the benefit of adding subtlety to one's conversations. In a well-known Chinese example, Chunyu Kun 淳于髡 told King Wei of the State of Qi that if he [Chunyu] drank one cask of wine he could become drunk, and if he drank ten casks of wine he could become drunk.[54] King Wei responded, "If you drink one cask and you are already drunk, how is it that you are even able to drink ten?" Chunyu Kun replied that when he was in the presence of the emperor, drinking only one or two casks would make him drunk; if he was sitting in mixed company, holding hands without being reprimanded and staring [at a female partner] without inhibition, her earrings falling to the front and hairpins to the rear, he could then drink eight casks. And:

> When the sun sets and the wine is gone,
> We gather the cups and press close together.
> Men and women share a mat,
> Slippers and stockings mingled,
> Cups and plates in disarray,
> Candles in the hall extinguished,
> The host asks me to stay and sends off the other guests,
> The collar of my silk coat is unfastened,
> There is a faint aroma of incense.
> At this time I am happiest and can drink ten casks of wine.

Although this poem cannot be called salacious, the story itself is about the loss of inhibitions, and thus its humorous element could quite easily become obscene. In another example, when the emperor accused Zhang Chang of painting his wife's eyebrows, Zhang argued, "Isn't there much more between couples?"[55] This can also be considered humorous because it makes a reasonable argument disregarding the social taboos.

This type of explanation is close to *huaji*, and here are several other examples as further evidence. The famous German, Hermann Graf von Keyserling, invited writers from different countries to contribute articles to *The book of marriage*. George Bernard Shaw was asked to write his opinion on marriage, but instead wrote a letter stating, "No man dare write the truth about marriage while his wife lives." The book contains many long, thoughtful and meaningful arguments, and Keyserling added that sentence into the introduction.[56] In an example from China, according to legend someone once asked a Daoist about the secrets of living a long life. The Daoist said that if you can control your desire, do nothing extraordinary, eat simple meals, live with nature, keep away from delicacies and stay away from women, then you can live thousands of years. Someone then questioned what was the benefit of living a long life if it was so uninteresting? He would prefer a premature death. Such a response is quite reasonable. In the West there is a similar story. There once was a teacher who liked to drink. When he drank, he always got drunk. Therefore he had no students and was very poor. A person once kindly suggested to him, "You are so knowledgeable. Should you quit drinking, then you would surely have many students, right?" The teacher responded, "The reason I teach is so I can drink. If I stop drinking, why should I have students?"

From the previous jokes we clearly know the origin and disposition of our laughter, but these jokes are all quick-witted responses, which takes us back to wit and *huaji* because the laughter-producing principles in these examples are all the same. Composing a humorous sketch, then, is different from writing an aphorism or an epigram because the humour cannot be forced. Nowadays, in Western countries there are many humorous essays and just about every popular magazine has one or two humorous columns. These columns are light-hearted and they often use slang in commenting on current events, allowing the humour to enter deeply into the readers' hearts and minds, as seen, for example, in the works of Will Rogers.[57] Some essayists use writing styles that are really no different from the styles in popular magazine columns, such as Stephen Peacock's literary sketches, G. K. Chesterton's long commentaries and discussions on life or George Bernard Shaw's promotion of "isms".[58] Most of these essayists have lively writing styles and use a refreshing, natural approach as the dominant aspect of their writing. Their writing is not the same as a Chinese comedic drama because the humour is not meant to be absurd. Their essays do not have the tone of a Confucian moralist, and the essays are not clownish either. The writing in these essays combines sobriety with humour, casually discussing society and life. Reading these types of essays does not make one feel pretentious or give one a reason to feel repelled. On the other hand, they can talk professionally when it comes to serious affairs. Because of fewer constraints, humorous essays allow for genuine feelings of joy, anger, sorrow and delight to be expressed. In short, in Western literature the humorous essay is by and large the most ingenious type of literary essay. Every person who writes humorous essays, in addition to having a lively writing style, must first possess a unique understanding that comes from observing life. Just as one can have a humorous attitude or a humorous outlook on life, those who write works of humour develop a certain style and express a mood which, regardless of the situation, enables them to put a pen to paper and produce interesting observations. Related to this is the common Chinese belief that to study poetry one needs to roam the landscape, observe people's lives and cultivate one's soul, not just study the four tones in classical Chinese or lecture on the technical problems of "wasp's waists" and "crane's knees".[59]

Consequently, we know that you cannot write humorous articles unless you have a profound understanding of life and a reflective outlook on life, and unless you are able to say reasonable things. Any country's culture, lifestyle, literature or thought needs to be enriched by humour. If a people do not have this enrichment of humour, their culture will become more hypocritical with each passing day, their lives will be closer and closer to cheating, their thought pedantic and outdated, their literature increasingly withered and their spirit increasingly obstinate and ultra-conservative. One situation will lead to the other and a false life and literature will emerge, resulting in a surface that speaks with fervour and indignation but a heart that is decrepit, outdated and mouldy, providing only 50 per cent warmth and sincerity and half a lifetime of numbness. It will also produce a state of mind that is temperamentally unpredictable, susceptible to sentimentality, morbidly sensitive, hysterical, megalomaniacal and wildly depressed. If *Analects Fortnightly* is able to summon the warring politicians to cut down on their fighting, swindling and deceitful propaganda, then our accomplishments will not be insignificant.[60]

10

Discovering Humour in Modern China:
The Launching of the *Analects Fortnightly* Journal and the "Year of Humour" (1933)

Qian Suoqiao

One of the most important phenomena in the Chinese cultural scene of the 1930s was the introduction of *youmo* 幽默 (humour) by Lin Yutang 林語堂, who founded the Analects School of writers (*Lunyu pai* 論語派). The launching of the journal *Analects Fortnightly* (*Lunyu banyuekan* 論語半月刊, hereafter referred to as *Lunyu* 論語 or *Analects*), in 1932 to introduce and promote humour in Chinese culture was so successful that humour suddenly became the talk of the town — or, in Lu Xun's words, "Bang! Everybody everywhere is suddenly talking about *youmo* and writing *xiaopin* 小品 ("little-taste", or short and familiar) essays."[1] In addition to *Analects*, a number of other journals appeared with the same objective of promoting humour and laughter, including *Yijing* 易經, edited by Jian Youwen 簡又文 (1896–1978), and *Tanfeng* 談風, edited by Hai Ge 海戈. Lin Yutang also launched two more journals, *Renjianshi* 人間世 (This human world) and *Yuzhou feng* 宇宙風 (Cosmic wind), successively. The year 1933 was consequently referred to as the "Year of Humour", and Lin Yutang was hailed as Master of Humour (*youmo dashi* 幽默大師), which further consolidated his position as a leading essayist in modern China.[2] Indeed, the introduction and translation of humour constitute a significant (cross-)cultural discourse in the formation of Chinese cultural modernity.[3] What has been little noted, however, is that the discourse of humour in modern Chinese literature and culture was very much a bilingual practice of cross-cultural translation. I will discuss the biographical and literary practices of Lin Yutang to reveal the nature and significance of the humour discourse in modern Chinese literature and culture.

"The Little Critic"

In September 1927, Lin Yutang arrived in Shanghai. His time there, until he left for the United States on 1 August 1936, was his most formative period. Later, Lin would recall that "after six months of service I got tired of the revolutionists, and from 1927 on I devoted myself solely to authorship exclusively."[4] However, that did not seem to be a very accurate hindsight. The watershed event in Lin's literary career was in fact when he became the weekly columnist for the column "The little critic" in the journal *The China Critic* in 1930, and it was not until September 1932, when he assumed editorship for the journal *Analects*, that he can be said to have devoted himself exclusively to literary writing. The period from 1927 to 1930 was, however, an important transitional stage, both intellectually and materially.

To sketch out the historical background, by the end of 1927 most of the colonial treaties imposed on China by the West had been abolished, and China was again unified under a central Nationalist (Kuomintang/KMT) government, even though it would take President Chiang Kai-shek another couple of years to fight and/or buy out all the warlord factions. China seemed to be on the path to modernity. The Great Revolution, or Northern Expedition, was basically over. Yet for most progressive intellectuals the revolution had come to a bitter end, due to the split between the Nationalists and the Communists and the ensuing terror caused by a massive purge of Communist Party members. For progressive intellectuals like Lin Yutang, it was not that so much that they supported the radical tactics employed by the Communists during the revolution to push for class warfare, but that the revolution represented spiritual idealism for a young China, while the crackdown on the Communists who were allied with the Nationalists in the revolution killed that very idealism. As Lin put it:

> Our imagination was fired, our enthusiasm was kindled; thousands of young men have fled from home and school from the outermost provinces to join the Nationalist forces, they have toiled and they have sweated, and thousands have gladly laid down their lives on the altar of Nationalism that their dream of a regenerated and redeemed China might come true. But, alas! Icarus soared too near the sun, the wax of his wings melted, and he fell back upon the earth. The war has ended — so has all idealism.[5]

The paradox of the Great Revolution of 1927 lies in the fact that it was the Communist youth who supplied much of the spiritual idealism and dynamism for the movement. Once the revolution was victorious, conservative Nationalists, afraid of Communist infiltration within the KMT, turned around and purged their comrades-in-arms and bloodily suppressed the radical elements in the revolution. While the Communist armed forces had a setback, both militarily and politically, the idealist spirit could hardly be suppressed. Rather, it surged back in a more radical form. In his "The little critic" column of 11 September 1930, Lin Yutang offered an account of what had happened to the Chinese intellectual scene in the last couple of years after the revolution:

> Anybody who visits the new book shops on Foochow Road [in Shanghai] will see that over 70 per cent of the new books on the market have to do with Russia, Karl Marx, and names ending in a *-ov*, or a *-lev*. A list of the literary works of Russian authors which have been translated in the last two years would put to shame any professor of modern Russian literature in Harvard or Columbia . . . For Russia has conquered Young China and claimed her as her own. People who imagine that the ideas and ideology of the students of today are those which precipitated the May 30th Affair in 1919, or those that made possible the Nationalist Revolution in 1927 are sadly mistaken. Young China has gone red in the last three years *after* the nationalist revolution.[6]

The signal event for the victory of this red surge was the winning over of Lu Xun 鲁迅 (1881–1936) as head of the League of Left-Wing Writers established in Shanghai in 1930.[7] As one of the leaders of the literary revolution of 1917, Lu Xun had exerted tremendous influence on the intellectual youth, and had always been at the forefront of progressive young China. But that did not mean that Lu Xun was ideologically pro-Communist. In the face of suppression and darkness, Lu Xun's favourite strategy was to feign death. During the heyday of white terror in Guangzhou in 1927, Lu Xun was invited to give a lecture at a government-backed college, and a refusal would have been taken as blatant non-cooperation with the Nationalist revolutionary government. So Lu Xun

> gave a most dazzlingly amazing lecture on the state of literature in the third century CE, in which he unravelled the story of how some scholars had to affect a fit of drunkenness for two months in

order to avoid political complications. The audience was amused, admired his originality and brilliant interpretation throughout, and of course failed to see the point.[8]

However, such a pretend-death attitude was no longer satisfactory to the revolutionary youth who believed the Nationalist revolutionists had hijacked and betrayed the revolutionary idealistic spirit, and they turned to Soviet Russia for spiritual guidance. The renewed banner was revolutionary literature, or proletariat literature, as opposed to the new literature of the literary revolution of 1917. Quite understandably, Lu Xun became the very target of revolutionary literature and was condemned as an old hand lagging behind the new progressive tide of proletariat revolution. In fact, Lu Xun was also translating Russian literary theory himself while fighting against the young radical theorists of proletariat literature. However, when the Left League was established in 1930, Lu Xun was successfully won over, under the directive of the Chinese Communist Party, to lead the alliance. In Lin's words:

> Chow Tso-jen 周作人 [Zhou Zuoren], Ch'ien Hsün-tung 錢玄同 [Qian Xuantong], Yu Tah-fu 郁達夫 [Yu Dafu] and others of the Yu-ssu 語絲 [yusi, thread of words] school were too much individualists to join the throng. Lu Hsün [Lu Xun] fought, resisted the tide for a year, and then went over to the enemy camp. In about a year's time, the revolution in literature was so far successful that no formidable out-and-out opponent was left on the field.[9]

It is interesting to note that when it came to commenting on the Russian cast of young China, Lin Yutang took a neutral stance, as he was merely "to record a fact, not to pass a judgment",[10] even though his tone was one of sympathetic understanding. But clearly he counted himself as belonging to the group of Zhou Zuoren and Yu Dafu — too much individualists to join the new tide. That is not to say that Lin Yutang did not go through a soul-searching process after the Nationalist revolution was over. He called himself a wanderer in the wilderness, a lone traveller walking his own walk, observing the world through his own eyes, and "it is precisely in such lonely wandering that it fits to know thyself and know the universe and the meaning of life."[11] Through such independent wandering and searching, Lin Yutang eventually emerged to lead a literary and cultural movement of humour, which became a formidable alternative to the Leftist dominance in modern Chinese literature and culture. In examining this transitional period, two aspects of Lin's life and works need to be noted: the fact that Lin achieved financial independence through the very successful compilation of English textbooks and the translation of the Crocean theory of the art of expression into Chinese (see below).[12]

In the newly established Nanjing government, Cai Yuanpei 蔡元培 (1868–1940), the former chancellor of Peking University, re-emerged as the intellectual leader, serving as minister of education and president of Academia Sinica (*Zhongyang yanjiuyuan* 中央研究院), founded in 1928. Soon after Lin Yutang arrived in Shanghai, he was appointed by Cai as a member of Academia Sinica and made its English editor-in-chief. He continued to pursue his philological studies, publishing a number of papers in linguistics in both English and Chinese, while the job at Academia Sinica paid a monthly salary of 300 *yuan* — similar to that of a university professor, a rather high standard at that time. It should be noted that Lin thus belonged to the Western-educated professional class; unlike most young urban writers who found themselves without a profession in the new social order and dependent on meagre royalties from their literary writings, he was financially secure.

Moreover, Lin Yutang was able to turn his philological expertise into significant commercial success. As a professor of English and a linguist, he had always wanted to write a textbook for learning English. He negotiated a book contract with Kaiming Bookstore and compiled the *Kaiming English Book*, which became so successful that another major publisher tried to commission a rival textbook by an inexperienced fresh graduate, who apparently plagiarized parts of Lin's *Kaiming English Book*. The case was taken to court and fought over in Shanghai's newspapers with claims and counter-claims from both publishers. Eventually, the censorship committee of the Ministry of Education voted to confirm the existence of plagiarism in the rival text and banned its publication. Ironically, newspaper publicity over the trial greatly enhanced sales of the textbook.[13] According to a long-term editor of Kaiming Bookstore, Lin's *Kaiming English Book* was compiled with great linguistic expertise and accompanied by lively and appropriate literary texts, plus drawings by the famous artist Feng Zikai, so that it became the bookstore's best-selling book.[14] Indeed, millions of Chinese started to learn English from Lin's textbook, and it brought him substantial financial gain, earning him the sobriquet "king of royalties" in Shanghai's literary and cultural world.

Lin's financial success from compiling the English textbook owed much to his Western training and background, from his college years at St John's in Shanghai to graduate study in America and Germany, which set him further apart again from many writers making ends meet with miniscule royalties. Intellectually, Lin was also differentiating himself from the mainstream Russian craze for proletariat literature. Apart from continuing to contribute Chinese essays to the journal *Yu-ssu*, as noted, Lin devoted himself to translating the Crocean theory of aesthetics into Chinese, which resulted in the publication of *Xinde wenping* 新的文評 (New criticism) in 1930, a collection of translated essays related to the theory of expression.[15] This was a significant move, given the overwhelming attention being given elsewhere to translating Russian works. By introducing and translating this theory, Lin claimed to be wandering off on his own path in the wilderness, and holding on to the belief that literature ought to be an individual expression of one's own distinct personality. In this respect, he was very much going against the current trend, which regarded literature as a propaganda tool for revolutionary goals. When later combined with his introduction of the concept of humour, Lin's theory of expression as the defining element for literary discourse would constitute, and remains, a major alternative to the Leftist utilitarian notion of literature as an ideological propaganda tool.

In 1928, an English-language weekly, *The China Critic*, was launched by a group of Western-trained Chinese professionals. This was the first English-language journal produced exclusively by Chinese. According to Durham S. F. Chen, one of the founders of the journal, the publication of *The China Critic* was occasioned by the Jinan Incident of 3 May 1928, when Cai Gongshi 蔡公時 (Tsai Kung-shih, 1881–1928), Special Commissioner of Foreign Affairs, was brutally assassinated by the Japanese. The English weekly was launched specifically "to present the Chinese point of view on current affairs".[16] Its founding members included Chen Qinren 陳欽仁 (Ch'en Ch'in-jen), a Missouri-trained journalist; Zhu Shaoping 朱少屏 (Chu Shao-p'ing, 1882–1942), the energetic secretary of the Shanghai YMCA; Gui Zhongshu 桂中樞 (Kwei Chung-shu), a brilliant journalist and practising lawyer; and Liu Dajun 劉大鈞 (D. K. Lieu), a distinguished economist. The editorial board membership changed somewhat over time, but some of the more well-known members included Quan Zenggu 全增嘏 (T. K. Chuan, 1903–84), a Western-trained philosopher; Pan Guangdan 潘光旦 (Quentin Pan, 1899–1967), a distinguished eugenicist who oversaw the book review column; and Lin Yu 林幽, Lin Yutang's younger brother, who was responsible for the Overseas Chinese column. Lin Yutang was associated with the group early on, as he started contributing in 1928, but he did not become a columnist for the weekly until 3 July 1930 when he started "The little critic" column

> which immediately caught on with the reading public. The weekly pieces Dr. Lin wrote and published in this column were all light essays on any imaginable subject. They were so delightful and entertaining that they were eagerly devoured as soon as a copy of the weekly came to hand.[17]

Though members of *The China Critic* group were professionals from different fields, their common ground was their Western training and educational background — and, of course, their English proficiency. In a sense, the weekly appearance of *The China Critic* signalled the coming of age of a new generation of Western-trained, English-proficient, professional Chinese intellectuals. Given his educational background, Lin Yutang epitomized the emergence of this English-speaking class. Some of the members of *The China Critic* group — particularly Quan Zenggu, Pan Guangdan and Lin Yu — would also become core members of the *Lunyu* group. Moreover, the literature of humour later promoted in *Lunyu* had its origin in fact in Lin's "The little critic" column.

Lin's first column piece attempted to define what he meant by the title "The little critic." By giving the column this name, he deliberately tried to shun the big issues or serious topics that usually dominated newspaper headlines, such as the London Naval Conference or the progress of Nationalism in China. In reporting such serious topics, one had to wear a tie ("dog-collar" in Lin's words), tighten oneself up and be respectful. Moreover, one had to be constantly alert to the whims of the censors:

> The thing has gone so far now that they have put a few censors to see that the few natural human barks issuing from the dog-collar should neither be so loud as to disturb the extremely sensitive nerves of the censors' masters, nor take place when all villadom and officialdom are getting ready to go to bed.[18]

As a result, the serious big papers in China "have lost even the capacity to pronounce a 'damn' as humanity ought to pronounce it".[19] By contrast, the "little critic" would leave serious issues to the big newspapers, and free himself from the dog-collar. Instead, he would concentrate on commenting on things familiar to him in his own manner. And if he were to feel like barking, he would bark:

> We do not mean to say that we are going to bark louder, but let us bark humanly. After all, a man can be quite a human being when he takes off his dog-collar and his stiff shirt, and comes home sprawling on the hearth-rug with a pipe in his hand. In this unbuttoned mood shall we speak.[20]

When later he collected his "The little critic" essays in a book, Lin acknowledged that his column writings had basically followed the principle he set out in the initial statement, but said that the above statement had a grave error: the official "we" ought to be replaced by the personal "I".[21] That was a very important correction. It is precisely through the personal I/eye that "The little critic" is able to present to us a panoramic view of Chinese life in transition to modernity in the 1930s. Later, in his memoirs, Lin himself attributed his later success to this style:

> It all started with my writing in the "Little Critic". I had established myself as an independent critic, neither a Kuomintang man, nor for Chiang Kai-shek, and at times a merciless critic. I had dared to say when cautious critics refrained for the sake of pacifying everybody. At the same time, I had been developing a style, the secret of which is [to] take your reader into confidence, a style you feel like talking to an old friend in your unbuttoned words.[22]

From May 1931 to May 1932, Quan Zenggu became the alternate columnist for "The little critic", as Lin Yutang participated in the annual conference of the Cultural Cooperation Committee of the League of Nations held in Switzerland as a delegate from Academia Sinica, and subsequently stayed on in Europe for a year.[23] When he came back in the summer of 1932, there had been a significant change in the political climate due to the increasing encroachment of the Japanese invasion of China. When the Japanese Army invaded Manchuria on 18 September 1931, it stirred massive and unprecedented patriotic fervour among the Chinese public, and national salvation became the dominant preoccupation of the public media. It was in such a stifling sociopolitical climate that the humour magazine *Analects* was born from informal salon gatherings at the house of Shao Xunmei 邵洵美 (Sinmay Zao 1906–68).

Shao was a Romantic poet and a well-known Shanghai dandy from an aristocratic family background.[24] He owned the *Shidai* 時代 (Times) publishing company (which later published the *Analects*) and was a gentlemanly host of numerous cultural salons at his home. Frustrated by the stifling cultural climate, a group of friends, including Lin Yutang, Quan Zenggu, Pan Guangdan, Li Qingya 李青崖 (1886–1969), Shao Xunmei and Zhang Kebiao 章克標 (1900–2007), gathered at Shao's house and thought up the idea of launching a humour magazine, and Lin Yutang was chosen to be its chief editor. Besides his Shanghai friends, some of them associated with *The China Critic*, Lin Yutang invited many of his Beijing friends associated with the journal *Yu-ssu*, including Zhou Zuoren, Sun Fuyuan and Yu Dafu, to be core contributors to *Analects* (the chosen title); hence the formation of the Analects School of writers in modern Chinese literature. Actually, the term merely refers to a loose group of independent and liberal-minded men of letters around the journal *Analects*, not really to a school of thought.

In the editorial afterword of the inaugural issue of *Analects*, Lin Yutang explained the meaning of the journal title as follows:

> Everybody knows *Analects* is one of the Confucian classics, so apparently our journal is a fake. But we did not mean to make a forgery of the Confucian classic, that's not what we meant.

Rather, in a humorous sleight of hand, *lunyu* 論語 was taken literally to mean commentary (*lun* 論) and discourse (*yu* 語). In other words, *Analects* was launched simply to serve as a platform for a group of friends' freestyle commentary and salon-style discourses and conversations on various personal, social and cultural topics. However, they did share a similarity in style. Just as the Confucian classic was a random collection of Confucius's sayings, the humour journal was also going to be a free forum of opinions and discourses by a group of friends who did not belong to any particular political organization and did not follow any particular ideological direction. Furthermore, as Lin explained, in the Confucian classification of canonical works, the

Figure 10.1 Cover page of the first issue of *Lunyu banyuekan* (Analects Fortnightly), published by the Shidai (Times) Publishing House, Shanghai, 1932. Unknown artist; publisher ceased to exist during the Sino-Japanese War. Every effort has been made to locate any holder of copyright. From a copy held by the Widener Library, Harvard University.

Annals of Spring and Autumn (Chunqiu 春秋) was supposed to be much more important than the *Lunyu* because it was an orthodox moral history. Likewise, contemporary critics writing in the humour journal merely attempted to offer random thoughts and comments without any intention of proposing orthodox moral standards for society.[25]

If the title of the journal was a humorous take on the Confucian classic, the "Ten commandments of the Analects School colleagues" that appeared in consecutive issues of the journal, beginning with the first, seem to reflect a biblical inspiration, at least in terms of their name and format. In translation (see Figure 10.2 for original), they read:

1 We do not oppose the revolution.

2 We do not criticize those whom we do not think much of, but we do criticize those whom we love and esteem (such as our beloved motherland, contemporary militarists, hopeful writers, and not-yet-hopeless revolutionists).

3 We do not curse people outright. (Try to have humour without discursive violence. There is no need to call a national thief Father, nor is there any need to call him Son-of-a-bitch.)

4 We do not take money from others, nor do we speak for others. (We shall not do any paid propaganda for any party, but we might, if we like, do free propaganda, or even counter-propaganda.)

5 We do not follow any fashionable trend, and shall not follow any powers that be. (We refuse to be fans of Chinese opera stars, movie stars, society stars, literary and arts stars, political stars, or stars of any other kind.)

6 We do not flatter each other and we oppose overbearing affectedness. (Avoid using flattering terms such as "poet," "scholar" or "my friend Dr. Hu Shi".)

7 We do not compose stuffy verses and we do not publish erotic lyrics.

8 We do not pretend to uphold public justice and righteousness. Rather, we only try to express frank and honest opinions of our own.

9 We do not attempt to get rid of bad habits (such as smoking, tea drinking, enjoying plum blossoms or reading). We do not advise anyone to quit smoking.

10 We do not say our own writing is no good.[26]

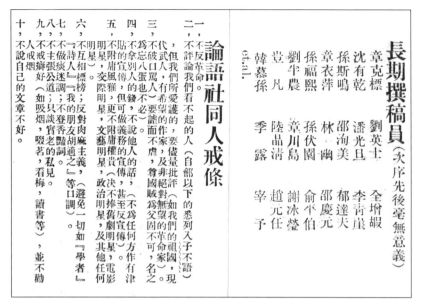

Figure 10.2 Part of the inside cover of the first issue of *Lunyu banyuekan* (Analects Fortnightly), 1932, showing the "Ten commandments" of the journal and the names of the editorial committee. Note the list's Westernizing conclusion, set in Chinese print order: "et al." The publisher, Shidai Publishing House, Shanghai, ceased to exist during the Sino-Japanese War; every effort has been made to locate any holder of copyright. From a copy held by the Widener Library, Harvard University.

Humour as Social Critique

Unexpectedly, the journal immediately became popular, especially among urban youth and on college campuses. It was said that if the Ministry of Education wanted to make an announcement, it could just run an ad in *Analects* and the message would be spread to all students.[27] The success of the journal owed much to the particular kind of cross-cultural interpretation of humour that Lin Yutang proposed and put into practice, both in the English-language "The little critic" column and the Chinese-language *Analects* magazine. As detailed in the full translation of the essay by Joseph Sample, reproduced in Chapter 9 of this volume, Lin's "Essay on humour" (*Lun youmo* 論幽默), a typical treatise from the *Analects*, incorporates Meredith's notion of the "Comic Spirit" into Chinese Confucian and Daoist notions of tolerance and detachment to invoke a cross-cultural notion of *youmo*. To Lin, *youmo* embodies the comic spirit and is supposed to contain a level of significance higher than the normal use of humour in Western literature, as "most of the humour magazines in the West such as *Punch* and *Life* are prone to lowly and vulgar jokes".[28] When Meredith's notion of the comic spirit is thus incorporated into the Chinese cultural tradition, *youmo* is seen as that which reveals "a mellow and detached *daguan* 達觀 disposition", and conveys "a certain philosophy of life and a critique of life".[29] In other words, Lin says, only when you become a cool and detached observer will you achieve a sympathetic and reasonable understanding of life so that you can laugh at its ironies with tolerance. In this "Essay on humour", Lin attributes the Chinese comic spirit largely to Daoist cultural philosophy and further differentiates two kinds of *youmo*: the masculine kind, or humour of sociocultural discourses (*yilun zongheng zhi youmo* 議論縱橫之幽默); and the feminine kind, or humour of poetic self-leisure (*shihua zishi zhi youmo* 詩化自適之幽默).[30]

While Lin employs these two terms in his essay to discuss humour in Chinese cultural tradition, his own literary practices during this period comprise two similar categories of humour writing: humour of social critique and humour of self-release — the former is more socially or outwardly oriented, while the latter is more self- or inwardly oriented.

On 13 March 1930, the newly constituted Nationalist (KMT) government in Nanjing prepared to welcome the official visit of Crown Prince Frederik of Denmark. Nanjing officials regarded the slum area along the main highway, with hundreds of shabby huts inhabited by poor migrants from rural areas, as a disgusting sight that would cause the government to lose face in front of the Western royal visitor. So on a rainy night, with no warning to the inhabitants and no alternative shelter offered, the huts were torn down and the inhabitants were driven out by force. Reports of the action appeared in *The China Times* newspaper in Shanghai, but were so categorically denied by the government that *The China Times* had to issue a statement of apology. However, as the Chinese saying goes, "fire cannot be wrapped up by paper", and photographs taken at the scene of the demolished huts and tents were published, to the great embarrassment of officials. Lin Yutang exposed this incident in the English-language *The China Critic*:

> Unless two plus two makes five in China, we must believe either that the Mayor's publicity office is carrying the special art of diplomats a little too far, or else *The China Times* staff correspondent has succeeded in taking spiritist pictures. Being no believer in spiritism, I am inclined to believe that it is the photographs that do not lie.[31]

To Lin Yutang, it was a joke that government officials would attempt to cover up and lie in the face of pictorial evidence. The humorous critic was, however, walking a tightrope and constantly testing the limits of government censorship. The publication of Lin's exposé enraged the Nanjing authorities so much that: "K. P. Chu, the manager of *The China critic*, immediately took the night train [to Nanjing], apologized and promised to behave like a good citizen for the good of the country."[32]

For Lin Yutang, the promotion of humour in early 1930s China was primarily a means of engaging in sociopolitical critique, or what George Kao calls the "humour of protest".[33] On the occasion of the arrest of Chen Duxiu 陳獨秀 (1879–1942), former Chinese Communist Party secretary and renowned intellectual leader of the New Culture Movement, Madam Sun Yat-sen published a statement in the 3 November 1932 issue of *The China Critic*, calling for the formation of a general committee for the protection of civil rights in China in defence of all political prisoners and victims of the terror imposed by the Nationalist regime. Lin immediately echoed that call in his "The little critic" column essay, "For a civic liberty union", published in the same issue of *The China Critic*. "Madam Sun's cry for justice sounds very much like a voice in the wilderness, and in the end I am afraid the wilderness will drown the voice," wrote Lin.[34] Since the establishment of the new Nationalist government, the call of Hu Shi 胡適 (1891–1962) for civil rights protection had been the only dissident voice, through his series of essays published in the *Crescent Moon Monthly* (Xinyue 新月), but eventually Hu's voice was silenced under threat and he himself had to move from Shanghai to Beijing. In response to Madam Sun's call for the establishment of a civic liberties union, Lin Yutang's humorous suggestion was that the current Minister of Justice of the Nanjing government, Lo Wengan (Lo Wen-kan 羅文幹 1888–1941), should head the organization, because this Lo Wengan had proposed the same ideas for the protection of civil liberties when he was Minister of Finance in the previous Beijing (Peking) government, and had been put in jail for eight months for insisting on due legal procedures. Lin expanded on this theme, republishing the 1924 proposals to pin Lo down and force him to make good his words.

Of course, Lo did not participate in the China League for Civil Rights, which was proposed by Madam Sun Yat-sen and subsequently set up in Shanghai on 30 December 1932. Madam Sun served as the chair and the members of its central executive committee included Cai Yuanpei, Yang Quan 楊銓 (1893–1933), Lin Yutang, Zou Taofen 鄒韜奮 (1895–1944) and Hu Yuzhi 胡愈之 (1896–1986), as well as the American activist Harold Isaacs, who arrived in Shanghai in December 1930, "a twenty-year-old tyro journalist in search of experience and definition",[35] as he later described himself. After serving as a reporter for the American-owned *Shanghai Evening Post & Mercury*, Isaacs launched his own weekly journal, *China Forum*, promoting Leftist literature despite government censorship. Another American activist, the feminist revolutionary Agnes Smedley, was also involved in the activities of the China League for Civil Rights. According to Smedley, Lin Yutang was the most vocal liberal intellectual, after Hu Shi, to advocate protection of civil rights and the rule of law, particularly through his "The little critic" columns. She wrote: "In the scholastic hierarchy Dr. Lin Yu-tang occupied a place about half-way between Dr. Hu Shih [Hu Shi] and the revolutionary Lu Hsün [Lu Xun]."[36] Within the China League for Civil Rights, it was Lin, Isaacs and Smedley who were responsible for publications and correspondence in English.[37]

The China League for Civil Rights was a unique alliance of liberal intellectuals like Hu Shi, Lin Yutang and Yang Quan on the one hand and Leftist-revolutionary intellectuals like Madam Sun, Lu Xun, Harold Isaacs and Agnes Smedley on the other. However, while they were united in promoting the protection of civil rights for the people and the culture of the rule of law under the Nationalist government, their emphases in action were different. For liberal intellectuals, protection of civil rights was intended not as a revolutionary act to overthrow the existing republic, but rather as a fundamental principle for a democratic republican government. For Leftist intellectuals like Madam Sun and Lu Xun, the Nationalist government had betrayed the revolution and turned to suppressing the Communists, who were continuing to pursue revolutionary aims. The government defended its violation of civil rights as necessary to suppress Communist insurgency, real or imagined. In one campaign, the league protested against the secret arrest and death from torture of the journalist Liu Yusheng by the governor of Jiangsu province, General Gu Zhutong 顧 祝同 (Ku Chu-t'ung). Liu had exposed opium traffic and other corrupt practices condoned by Gu, so the governor accused Liu of being a Communist. Thus calls for the protection of civil rights in 1930s China would always risk the danger of being labelled a political defence for the Communist revolution, whether it was justifiable or not.

In a lecture for the China League for Civil Rights delivered at the Chinese YMCA in Shanghai on 4 March 1933, Lin Yutang presented an animalistic–humanistic rationale for freedom of speech. He noted that the problem with this concept derived from the faculty of speech itself, since "only human beings have articulate language, while the cries of animals serve only as the signals for immediate instructive needs, like the cries of pain, hunger, fear, satisfaction".[38] Aesop's fables were libels on the animal kingdom because they made animals mimic human speech. If a fox were to see a bunch of grapes hanging high above it, it would leave them. It was the human who forced the fox to say the grapes were sour. Speech was thus a defining human faculty, he said. Lin came to his point:

> Bernard Shaw has rightly said that the only kind of liberty worth having is the liberty of the oppressed to squeal when hurt and the liberty to remove the condition which hurt them. The kind of liberty we need in present-day China is exactly this liberty to squeal when hurt, and not the liberty to talk.[39]

In other words, it was really the "animalistic right" for which people were fighting. Lin pointed out that there was in fact no absolute notion of freedom of speech. For instance, people would be bound to offend their neighbours if they really voiced what they thought of them. In the social context of China, freedom of speech for the people meant a limit on the freedom of action for officials, who naturally would take freedom of speech as a nuisance and guard their liberty to muzzle the press. These two kinds of liberties were diametrically opposed:

> The militarists would like to condemn people to death in secret
> tribunals, but the League demands open trials. The officials would
> like to kidnap their opponents and make them disappear from the
> surface of the earth, but the League wants to send public telegrams,
> demanding to know their whereabouts. The League will become a
> greater and greater nuisance in proportion as it is able to carry out
> its program.[40]

In the political context of 1933 China, the league proved to be more
than a nuisance. In the spring of 1933, the Leftist writer Ding Ling
丁玲 (pseudonym of Jiang Bingzhi 蔣冰之, 1904–86) was kidnapped
by a secret KMT clique known as the Blue Shirts (*lan yi she* 藍衣社).
Yang Quan, the secretary of the league, took up Ding Ling's case with
the government and appealed to the public to take action against
her abduction. He was assassinated on the steps of the government-
sponsored research institute where he worked, the Academia Sinica,
on 18 June 1933. Lin Yutang received threats that he would be the
next target.[41] As a consequence, the China League for Civil Rights was
dissolved. The government's brutal and indiscriminate suppression
of dissidence merely hardened the confrontational nature of the
conflict between the Nationalist and the Communist revolutionaries.
Caught in such a war, liberal intellectuals were often accused of being
Communists and also became victims of the terror. In this respect, Lin
Yutang's humorous discourse of social critique was actually a means of
constantly testing the limits of freedom of speech under the Nationalist
government engaged in civil war with the Communist revolutionaries.
It was this type of humour that allowed Lin to carve out such a space
for social critique.

In his "The little critic" column on 23 October 1930, Lin Yutang took
to task Hu Hanmin 胡漢民 (1879–1936), chairman of the Legislative
Yuan of the Nationalist government. Hu had stated that not a single
official had been guilty of abuse of power since the establishment of the
Nanking government. Lin commented that it took a lot of courage to
make such a statement. He said he would have put it more modestly:

> "not a single official had been put into prison since the
> establishment of the Nanking Government". There I should be on
> a completely safe ground. The ground is so safe that any coward
> would be willing to make the statement.[42]

Lin then went on to echo a recent speech by Chiang Kai-shek that called for the establishment of a clean and irreproachable government. That would have been a noble call, Lin said, but added that "it would, however, be more to the point if Mr. Chiang had said that we want 'More Prisons for Politicians'".[43] Here, Lin Yutang was not so much reproaching Generalissimo Chiang as using candid humour to make explicit the hollowness of the politician's words. Lin was not joking in this case. To him, the Confucian tradition of entrusting government to scholar-officials was the root-cause of contemporary political sickness. The solution lay in a legal concept of government that assumed all politicians were potential thieves and so built prisons ready for them.

Lin Yutang had a lot to say on Chinese political sickness. In one of his most entertaining political satires, entitled "On political sickness", he noted that politicians' claims of being sick constituted a phenomenon unique to China. Their sicknesses would bewilder resident foreign correspondents, who would conclude that there was no end to the diseases plaguing government officials:

> Among the more fashionable diseases which every retiring official takes care to announce in his circular telegram, I may mention softened brain and hardened liver, ulcerated stomach and outraged spleen, flat chest and high blood pressure, weak heart and shattered nerves, diabetes, Bright's disease, beri-beri, rheumatism, insomnia, arteria sclerosis pile, fistula, chronic dysentery, chronic constipation, loss of appetite, disgust with politics, an exaggerated desire (which is a form of fixation) to wear the peasant's cotton gown, longing for mammy, life weariness, melancholia, *impuissance* (by inference), etc. But of course, diabetes beats them all.[44]

For one thing, Lin explained, the officials' diseases were good excuses and powerful bargaining tools. An official could use his alleged disease to blackmail others so that if, say, the Minister of Finance did not get what he wanted for his budget, he could threaten sick leave because of his weak heart. This would be a face-saving way of retiring with the real intention of getting advancement. On the other hand, Lin suggested that some officials' diseases, especially digestive disorders, were very real, as "all of them overeat and . . . all their mental energy that should have been devoted to the affairs of the nation has been consumed in digesting shark's fins and birds' nests and stewed pig's foot".[45] So Lin charged: "As far as I can see, there is no hope for China, unless some sensible minister is willing to start a general diet reform and incur social calumny by giving his official guests only four-course dinners."[46]

Besides the Chinese social establishment, the foreign community in Shanghai was not immune to Lin Yutang's humour of social critique. The city in the 1930s was a semi-colonial society where a substantial foreign community resided in the International Settlement or the French Concession, where they enjoyed the protection of extraterritoriality. Foreigners in China took this special status for granted, including even progressive-minded "friends of China". Helen Foster Snow, for instance, was appalled when she was told that being pro-Chinese might mean giving up extraterritoriality. To her mind, "no foreigner could live here without that". As she explained:

> . . . under extraterritoriality, people living abroad enjoy freedom from the jurisdiction of the country in which they reside, and are responsible only to the laws and courts of their native country. Because of extraterritoriality and "gunboat diplomacy", foreigners were sacrosanct in China; foreign women were strictly sacrosanct. No Chinese ever touched a foreign woman — it was taboo.[47]

In "An open letter to an American friend", Lin Yutang imagined that he was writing to an American friend who had a nephew engaged in an egg-products business in Shanghai. Lin tried to assure him that a peaceful American should not be concerned about the possibility of the abolition of extraterritoriality, since this related only to the criminal code. As a law-abiding businessman, his nephew would not land in gaol. When the US State Department insisted on the privilege of extraterritoriality, they were actually "taking an insurance policy for some of its nationals who are 'bad risks' (technically speaking), by making all of you, ninety-eight per cent of whom are 'good risks', decent people, pay the premium".[48] Lin argued that such an insurance policy was unnecessary:

> Why, I have travelled in your esteemed country, the United States of America, and have even dared to reside in New York without finding out first what the American code says about the difference between pilfering, burglary, and robbery and what are the legal punishments for assault on women.[49]

If his American friend insisted that extraterritoriality was a modern convenience, Lin told him that such convenience was only enjoyed by two kinds of people: Chinese government officials and American nationals. Rather than insist on such a privilege, Lin advised that his friend's nephew should learn some basic Chinese phrases such as *duibuqi* 對不起 (pardon me) or *nihao* 你好 (hello), which would offer great convenience. The advice to the foreigner thus carried a sting in the tail and turned into a snipe against colonially minded white supremacists at home and abroad who failed to exhibit even basic courtesies.

Humour as Release of Self

In the literary and cultural world of 1930s Shanghai, Bernard Shaw's one-day visit on 17 February 1933 was a big event. The year 1933 was hailed as the "Year of Humour", due to the promotion of *youmo* by Lin Yutang and his journals, and the visit by one of the masters of humour in the Western literary world was certainly a high point of the year. Bernard Shaw was received by Madam Sun and the China League for Civil Rights. Hundreds of reporters waited at the harbour to greet the famed playwright and satirist — but in vain, as he avoided the media and was secretly escorted to meet Cai Yuanpei at the Academia Sinica. Madam Sun held a luncheon at her residence attended by Cai Yuanpei, Lu Xun, Lin Yutang, Harold Isaacs and Agnes Smedley. The next day, a picture that later became famous appeared in all major newspapers showing Bernard Shaw, Madam Sun, Cai Yuanpei, Lu Xun, Lin Yutang, Harold Isaacs and Agnes Smedley gathered in Madam Sun's garden.[50] In fact, the Shanghai newspapers and journals consumed every possible bit of information concerning Shaw's brief visit. Lin's *Analects* journal devoted a special issue to it on 1 March 1933. At the luncheon, due to his fluency in English, Lin Yutang engaged in extensive conversation with Shaw. The talk focused on two biographies of Bernard Shaw, one by Archibald Henderson and one by Frank Harris.[51] Lin Yutang commented that Henderson's account was rather dry while Harris's seemed much livelier. Shaw's reply was frank:

> Well, that may be true. But Harris was an impossible man. He was so poor that he had to write a biography to make ends meet.

> Originally he wanted to write a biography of Jesus Christ but the publisher would have none of it, so he wrote a biography of Bernard Shaw. Yet he didn't really know my life and got many facts wrong. And just as he was about to finish, he died unfortunately and left the draft to me. I had to spend the whole damn three months to edit and correct the facts he got wrong, but left his opinions intact . . . Some of my friends wrote to me to protest the sarcastic remarks in the book and told me that Harris should not have said those things and I should not have published them. Well, those passages were in fact written by myself.[52]

To Lin Yutang, Shaw's complete frankness and his ability to laugh at himself revealed the best kind of comic spirit. He believed that the secret of humour was to be natural and to be oneself, to face oneself in the mirror and to tear down hypocritical disguise. The ability to laugh at oneself came from a kind of broad-mindedness that took a detached attitude towards one's own imperfections. From his comments on Shaw and from a series of essays that Lin wrote about himself — discourses about his life experience and his practices in an emerging modern urban milieu — one can glean a sense of what he called the other type of humour besides social critique: the "feminine" kind or the "humour of poetic self-leisure".

A new urban middle class emerged in 1930s Shanghai, paralleling the modernization drive of the KMT government, despite ongoing civil war and the threat of Japanese aggression. In his own life and in his bilingual essays, Lin Yutang fashioned an urban lifestyle for himself that epitomized a new modern sensibility and included a sense of humour. According to Bernardine Szold Fritz, Lin was known as one of the few Chinese writers who could support himself from his writing, long before his *My country and my people* became a bestseller in the United States.[53] Every Friday, Lin went to dinner with colleagues from *The China Critic*, and then a dozen or so would go to the dance halls, to drink beer or tea and to look at the pretty girls. Sometimes they would invite girls to their table and chat with them about their family background and their life as dance hostesses in metropolitan Shanghai. After a couple of hours of night-life diversion, Lin would go home to work for several more hours. After all, Y. T. was a true family man with three lovely daughters and a supportive, educated wife.

For most of his early time in Shanghai, the Lin family occupied a house at 42 Edinburgh Road in the International Settlement, but on 18 September 1932 — on the first anniversary of the Japanese occupation of Northeast China — Lin wrote in his "The little critic" column that he had to move to a flat. He confessed that on such a national day of indignation, he should not be writing about such a trivial topic, but since the government had already decided, on behalf of the people, to fight the Communists before dealing with the Japanese and had demanded that the public shut up about national affairs, he might as well write about why he had to move to a flat. He said he was forced to do it because his neighbour had bought a radio and obliged the Lins to listen to *his* favourite radio music, such as Jeanette MacDonald's "March of the Grenadiers" and "Suzhou crooning", which he tuned in to endlessly whenever he felt like it. "Under such circumstances," Lin wrote, "an Englishman would go to his neighbor and say 'You stop that, or I shall write to the police. A Chinese gentleman with any culture at all would prepare to adapt himself to the environment and seek the peace of his soul by ignoring the existence of his nerves."[54] But as an "English educated Chinese", Lin could do neither, so he put a "To let" sign in front of his house and moved into a flat.

Living in an apartment was not Lin's idea of a decent human lifestyle. To his mind, modern civilization could not be called real civilization "until it can make it possible for every man to have a few yards of soil which he can call his own, where he can plant peas and tomatoes, and where his children can catch crickets and get comfortably dirty".[55] The only thing that made his move acceptable to him was that the apartment window looked over a wilderness of grand old trees and green meadows. By 3 August 1933, however, we learn that the Lins had moved back to their house, "living like a human being again". He could smell the soil again, have frogs and toads and even a harmless little green snake in the garden, and enjoy cicadas singing in the poplar trees. Living in a house kept him close to nature, which he reckoned was the most natural way of living. After all, what necessity was there to go to summer resorts if not to get away from the city and go back to nature and re-experience this? "Few people realize that it is the lizards and snakes that make your summer resorts and outings so memorable."[56] When spring came, the garden was full of life. The willow trees turned green and flowers were blooming everywhere. In his delightful essay, "Spring in my garden", Lin describes how every animal — human animal and real animal — was caught up in spring fever. All his servants — his "boy", the cook, the cook's wife Huangma — tried to find excuses to get away from daily drudgery. Even the father pigeon flew from the nest, leaving the mother pigeon and the eggs behind.[57]

To live in a house so as to feel close to nature was one way of keeping one's natural self, or at least of being reminded of one's animal self. But to be natural was not an easy task for anyone living in 1930s China, as the social and cultural pressures for conformity could be overwhelming. For a Western-educated returnee, inability to fit in with the social mores of traditional Chinese culture (even though it was rapidly modernizing) could be a serious impediment to a cross-cultural life. He would have to become a Chinese gentleman again. But what *was* a Chinese gentleman? In "How I became respectable", Lin Yutang offers the rather sarcastic definition that a Chinese gentleman must possess three things:

> (1) a serious desire to lie or conceal one's feelings by one's words, (2) the ability to lie like a gentleman, and (3) the mental calm shown by taking both your own lie and that of your fellow-men's with a sense of humour.[58]

Clearly, to become a Chinese gentleman, one needed to understand the Chinese sense of humour. After several lessons in life, Lin explained, he was quite able to conform strictly to this code. For example, when asked by a foreign friend about President Chiang Kai-shek's recent baptism, Lin's reply was: "Why, it is a fine thing. Another soul saved!"[59]

Precisely because of the social and cultural push for conformity, Lin Yutang insisted that humour should be part of literature just as it was part of life, but it seemed impossible for him to convince the Chinese public of this at the time:

> For according to the old tradition, no one except a clown would condescend to crack a joke in public, and editors and statesmen regard it as shocking and not permissible in good form to relieve their serious discourses on the salvation of the country with a line of humour.[60]

Such puritanical constraint made people rigid and hypocritical. Instead of producing middle-school critics who talked as if they were 40, Lin pointed to the importance of keeping the heart of a child — for instance, by enjoying Mickey Mouse cartoons. Lin proclaimed that those who had lost the capacity to enjoy Mickey Mouse were probably incapable of any imagination and fantasy. Free from the limitations of time and space, animated cartoons gave full rein to the human imagination in a way that surpassed other forms of art:

> There we are carried back into the dream world of our childhood in which nothing is impossible. The cartoons, therefore, achieve for us a liberation of the human spirit and transfer us into a magic world so long as that picture lasts.[61]

Similarly, Lin proclaimed that crying during movies was normal human behaviour and nothing to be ashamed of:

> Because I often cry at movies, I always like a person sitting next to me silently blowing his or her nose or leaving the theatre with a shining streak over his face. I am inclined to think that he is a better man for that.[62]

Of course, if a man cried too often he would be called a sentimental idiot, but to restrain emotions over a powerful piece of work of art merely made people slaves to conventionality, contrary to human nature. There were tears in life — tears of sorrow and tears of delight. Some cried at a sentimental story, some cried over reunion or departing. "But let him cry whoever feels like crying, for we were animals before we became reasoning beings, and the shedding of a tear, whether of forgiveness or of pity or of sheer delight at beauty, will do him a lot of good."[63]

In following one's heart and expressing one's feelings naturally, Lin's words also reflected his own personality. In her biographical sketch, written shortly after the publication of Lin's bestseller *My people and my country* in 1935, Fritz tells us that "above all things, Y. T. is a poet".[64] What Fritz meant was that Lin's personality was quite poetic, in the sense that it defied conventionality and was devoid of pompousness. One of Lin's favourite diversions was to fly kites with his children, and he loved thinking up games and playing with novel gadgets. Once the Lins invited some foreign friends to a fancy restaurant for a dinner that included 24 dishes. The family had put a lot of time and effort into planning this banquet. At the dinner, however, one guest wore a kind of trick ring purchased from a folk-craft shop in Beijing. Lin noticed this, took hold of it and was completely fascinated by it. He totally lost himself in trying to solve the puzzles of the ring, and became quite oblivious to the feast. On another occasion, according to Fritz, she went on an outing to Hangzhou with the Lins. They drove down from Shanghai and Lin led them to the tomb of a concubine famous in Chinese history. Throughout the trip, Lin was ecstatic about the scenery and cursed the stupidity of living in the city of Shanghai. After they arrived in Hangzhou, they planned to drive along the Qiantang River on a road newly built through the mountains. When they got on the hilly road next morning, everybody was excited to see the spectacular view, but Lin was somehow totally consumed in reading a novel. He had started reading it the previous night and couldn't stop until he found out what happened in the end. And when he did finish reading and raised his head to see the view, the scenery had already become quite ordinary.

In fashioning for himself a poetic lifestyle with appreciation of a sense of humour, Lin Yutang did not see Chinese culture as totally negative, even though he was sharply critical of its conformity and conventionality. In fact, he was rather keen on drawing out the modern and poetic elements of Chinese culture to contribute to a poetic lifestyle of humour. From the humorous perspective — the modern perspective of a Western-educated cross-cultural intellectual — certain Chinese cultural traits could assume surprisingly competitive advantages over Western cultural norms. As Lin explained, for instance, the age-old Chinese custom of clasping one's own hands in greeting was superior to the Western custom of shaking hands. Just for hygienic reasons, hand-shaking did not make sense when all kinds of germ-saturated stuff, like coins and paper money, passed through one's hands. And different kinds of hand-shaking made people vulnerable to different kinds of pressure. "You may have the YMCA type of shaking hands: the man pats you on the shoulder with one hand and gives you a violent shake with the other until all your joints are ready to burst within you."[65] And one might also have those furtive and retiring handshakes that suggested one's opponent was very much afraid of one, which also negated the whole purpose of greeting. Even though everyone knew that the Western custom of hand-shaking had been passed down from the barbaric days of Europe, Lin admitted helplessly that the custom was gaining ground worldwide while the age-old Chinese custom of shaking one's own hands was fast disappearing. On another note, Lin also saw the calisthenic value of kowtowing. As he explained, unlike Western physical exercises, Chinese hygiene involved bodily movements of moderation designed to conserve energy and to achieve ultimate harmony between mind and body. Like such gestures as *jingzuo* 靜坐 (sitting still or meditation), *duo fangbu* 踱方步 (walking in a series of rounded and continuous movements), *fuxiu* 拂袖 (the movement of jerking one's sleeves before leaving), or *daqian* 打千 (the Manchu ladies' greeting gesture of bending one knee), the Chinese etiquette of kowtowing connoted the highest and most unique art of Chinese culture:

> Make three kowtows and raise yourself again to the erect posture as far as the upper part of the body is concerned. The act of raising and bending one's body gives a wonderful, beneficial exercise to the abdominal muscles and helps better than any massage to dissolve excessive fat around the belly. If done to careful timing, it encourages deep breathing and stimulates the blood circulation.[66]

In one of his celebrated bilingual essays, "The lost mandarin", Lin lamented the disappearance of the mandarin class in China, as "a mandarin was a real polished gentleman" — "His voice was deep and resonant, his bearing poised and calm, his language was an art, and his personality was a combination of scholarship, suavity, rascality and high breeding."[67] The Manchu dynasty might have been corrupt, but the mandarin class was the product of Chinese cultural refinement. Mandarin speech was a work of art, but it was the entire ambience:

> the personality of the speaker, the furniture of the room, the atmosphere of decorum, the tone of his voice, and perfect accent and refined phraseology, the round silken fan, the mandarin moustache and the *makua* — all united to give that harmonious artistic effect.[68]

The mandarin was a scholar-official who was well versed in classical literature, philosophy and history. And if he was corrupt, at least he was corrupt in an elegant fashion. By contrast, a contemporary Republican official might very well be a graduate of Oberlin (the liberal arts college Oberlin College, Ohio), who "can only lie and lie in the most uncouth, impudent, incompetent and immoral fashion".[69]

Fritz provides an anecdote that demonstrates Lin's sense of artistic appreciation. At an evening gathering at a friend's home (most probably at Shao Xunmei's house), a young foreign couple who had just arrived in Shanghai wanted to try smoking opium — a common desire for many newly arrived Westerners to experience the coveted high fancifully promised through opium smoking. The host gladly offered the opportunity, and lay down on the left side of the opium couch while the young foreign woman lay down on the right side facing him. As the guests were watching them inhaling the smoke, Lin slipped away to the wall and suddenly turned off the electric lights. In Fritz's words:

> That was the poet again. The difference was something unbelievable, for instantly the whole scene became unreal, mysterious, glamorous. The small flame threw a pale fan of light toward the two faces, lighting them from below so that the whites of their eyes gleamed and the color of their skin became like opalescent wax, and when they turned their eyes downward, they resembled angels in reverie, but when they opened their eyes and looked from side to side or out in the room where the rest of us sat or stood in quiet groups, they seemed like young satyrs.[70]

As soon as they finished the pipes and the lights were turned on again, the spell was over. Then the host asked whether anyone else would like to try. Everyone turned to Lin Yutang to urge him to try. They had seen him smoking cigars but no one had seen him in the spell-like atmosphere of opium smoking:

> Laughing and backing off, his arms out at right angles, his hands raised in protest, Y. T. refused.
>
> "I'm a parson's son," he said, "I simply couldn't."
>
> There was a chorus of protest. "Go on, this once. You ought to try it once, everybody else does."
>
> "No," he said, this time quite seriously. "I love to watch it. I find it a fascinating spectacle to watch, but I watch this with the same feeling of horror that people say you get watching a snake. I'm

sure it has to do with my early Christian training. Although the Christianity has gone, the moral training remains, and I know that I would be physically unable to put an opium pipe to my lips."

"But you couldn't get a habit from trying it once," said our host.

"Yes, but no one would have the habit if he hadn't tried it once. Go ahead, don't mind me," he broke off, laughing again. "My black cigar habit is just as bad as your opium habit, I'm sure. But the Bible didn't prejudice me against cigars!"[71]

As the biographical and literary practices of Lin Yutang demonstrate, the flowering of the *youmo* phenomenon in the 1930s Chinese cultural scene was an East–West cross-cultural product that emerged from the particular socio-historical milieu of modern China. Designed to get away from the stifling environment of partisan politics that treated literature as a mere tool of propaganda, the introduction of humour opened up an alternative space for social critique and for a search for self and identity in an emerging modern life. Despite the twists and turns of cultural politics in modern China, the fact that *youmo* has now become a permanent modern Chinese word and a generally acknowledged cultural term attests to its relevance and endurance.

Notes

Chapter 1

1. Lin Yutang, "On humour", trans. Joseph C. Sample.
2. Jeremy Goldkorn, "Stifled laughter: How the Communist Party killed Chinese humor".
3. See Joseph Sample's discussion of Lin Yutang's distinction between *huaji* and *youmo* in Chapter 9; also Chao Chih Liao, "Humor versus *huaji*". The term *huaji* is no longer in common use in spoken Chinese with its original meaning.
4. Shakespeare, *Hamlet*, II, ii, 90.
5. Samuel Johnson, *A dictionary of the English language*, Vol. 2, p. 1412.
6. Mark Twain, *Mark Twain's notebooks and journals*, Vol. 3, Notebook 24 (April–August 1885), p. 164.
7. George Meredith, *An essay on comedy and the uses of the comic spirit*, p. 8.
8. Henri Bergson, *Le rire*.
9. Meredith, *An essay on comedy*, pp. 61–2.
10. Also referred to in English as the Kuomintang (KMT) or Guomindang.
11. Scholarly studies by Xue-liang Ding, Christopher C. Rea, Diran John Sohigian and others of the impact of politics on contemporary humour in China will hopefully form part of a companion volume to the present. For online comment, see note 2 above.
12. See, for instance, George Kao, *Chinese wit and humor*, pp. xviii–xxiii; Chao-chih Liao, "Humor versus *huaji*".
13. Discussed in Lily Xiao Hong Lee's chapter.
14. As Weihe Xu points out in his chapter on Confucianism and humour.
15. For detailed discussion and background, see Qian Suoqiao's chapter.
16. M. H. Spielmann, *The history of "Punch"*, pp. 99–100.
17. See translation and commentary by Joseph. C. Sample.
18. See Marina Davila Ross, Michael Owren and Elke Zimmermann, "Reconstructing the evolution of laughter in great apes and humans"; Barbara Wild et al., "Neural correlates of laughter and humour: Review

article"; and Jaak Panksepp and Jeff Burgdorf, "'Laughing' rats and the evolutionary antecedents of human joy?"

19. John Haldon, "Humour and the everyday in Byzantium", p. 60. For an English translation, see *The philogelos, or, laughter-lover*, also discussed in the chapter by Lily Xiao Hong Lee.

20. See, for instance, Jon Kowallis, trans., *Wit and humor from Old Cathay*; George Kao, *Chinese wit and humor*.

21. See Marjolein 't Hart, "Humour and Social Protest: An Introduction".

22. See Marjorie K. M. Chan, "Cantonese opera and the growth and spread of vernacular written Cantonese in the twentieth century". Her study of humour in 1950s and 60s Cantopop songs may form part of a companion volume to the present.

23. Chao-Chih Liao, *Taiwanese perceptions of humor* ; Chao-Chih Liao and Goh Abe, "A comparison of Taiwanese and Japanese appreciation of English jokes"; Hsu Chih-Chun 徐芝君, Hsueh-Chih Chen 陳學志 and Fa-Chung Chiu 邱發忠, "Qianwan bie xiao, buran nide taidu hui cong kan xiaohua zhong xielou: bianyi lei youmogan zhinengdu tiaozheng lilun de yanzheng" 千萬別笑，不然您的態度會從看笑話中洩露：貶抑類幽默感知能度調整理論的驗證 (Don't laugh, or your attitude will be revealed from reading jokes: Adjustment theory of disparagement humour appreciation); and Chen Hsueh-Chih 陳學志, Shu-Ling Cho 卓淑玲 and Hwei-Der Lai 賴惠德, *Jiejue wenti fahui chuangyi de ci hao fangfa jiushi faxian qi zhong de youmo* 解決問題發揮創意的次好方法就是發現其中的幽默：幽默中的創意與創意中的幽默 (Finding the embedded humor in creative problems is the second best way to solve them: Humorous creativity and creative humor).

24. Joel Martinsen, "Joke advertising", *Danwei*, 28 December 2008, http://www.danwei.org/blogs/joke_advertising.php (accessed 4 June 2009).

25. See, for instance, Kate Burridge, *Weeds in the garden of words: Further observations on the tangled history of the English language*, pp. 28–9.

26. Heiyō Nagashima, "*Sha-re*: A widely accepted form of Japanese wordplay".

27. C. T. Hsia, "The Chinese sense of humor", 30–6. Originally composed for a cultural familiarization manual in 1953, the essay remained unpublished until 1978; it is also available online.

28. Hsia, "The Chinese sense of humor".

29. C. Davies, *Ethnic humour around the world: A comparative analysis*; and C. Davies, *Jokes and their relation to society*.

30. C. Davies, "The dog that didn't bark in the night: A new sociological approach to the cross-cultural study of humor".

31. Henry W. Wells, *Traditional Chinese humor: A study in art and literature*, pp. 227–8.

32. Wells, *Traditional Chinese humor*, p. 227.

33. For example, René T. Proyer, Willibald Ruch and Guo-Hai Chen, "Positive psychology and the fear of being laughed at: Gelotophobia and its relations to orientations to happiness and life satisfaction in Austria, China, and Switzerland"; Guo-Hai Chen, "Validating the Orientations to Happiness Scale in a Chinese sample of university students "; Guo-Hai Chen and Rod A. Martin, "A comparison of humor styles, coping humor, and mental health between Chinese and Canadian university students"; and Chen Guo-Hai 陳國海, "Guonei jiaoxue youmo yanjiu shuping 國內教學幽默研究述評 (A literature review of humour research in teaching in mainland China)". Further significant work by several of these researchers is forthcoming.

34. Tiquia's translation. For more detail about the *Han shu*, see note 34.

35. *Qi* is variously translated as air, breath or energy flow, but in this book the original Chinese word — now widely used in TCM — is retained.

36. For a description of this approach in Zen Buddhism, see Conrad Hyers, *Zen and the comic spirit*.

37. In Sima Qian, *Shiji*, *juan* 126; for an English translation, see Sima Qian, *Records of the Grand Historian of China: Qin dynasty*.

38. Ban Gu, *Han shu*, pp. 2841–76. The name *You* may not be a surname but may simply mean "humorist" or "jester". Although Ban Gu 班固 (32–92 CE) is credited with authorship of this great work, it was started by his father and completed in 111 CE by his sister, Ban Zhao 班昭, after Ban Gu himself had been sentenced to prison.

39. Ban, *Han shu*, pp. 2841–76; Kowallis, *Wit and humor from Old Cathay*, p. 6.

40. Noted by Beatrice Otto in *Fools are everywhere: The court jester around the world*, pp. xx and 280. The role of the court jester is discussed in the chapters by Weihe Xu and by Andy Shui-lung Fung and Zhan Hang-Lun.

41. Kowallis observed that recorded stories of *huaji* do not prove that China had a tradition of valuing humour in its own right: "None of this is humor for humor's sake, since it all serves to prove a point." Kowallis, p. 7.

42. Lu Hsün, *Zhongguo xiaoshuo shi lüe*, pp. 206–7.

43. Translated by Kowallis, *Wit and humor in Old Cathay*, p. 7. For tables of jokes about sub-groups and by country, see Davies, *Jokes and their relation to society*, pp. 2–3, 108, 188 and 201.

44. See Richard Mather, trans., *Shih-shou hsin-yü: A new account of tales of the world*.

45. See Vibeke Børdahl and Jette Ross, *Chinese storytellers: Life and art in the Yangzhou tradition*. A short video of a performance of one style of *shuo gu* is available at: http://v.youku.com/v_show/id_XMTU5Mjk3MTA0.html (accessed 23 March 2011).

46. For an in-depth account of this time, see chapter 10.

47. See for example, articles by John Lent and Xu Ying in *International Journal of Comic Art*; Bi Keguan 畢克官 and Huang Yuanlin 黄远林, *Zhongguo manhua shi* 中國漫畫史 (History of Chinese cartoons); Chang-tai Hung, "The fuming image: Cartoons and public opinion in Late Republican China, 1945-1949"; and Christoph Harbsmeier, *The cartoonist Feng Zikai: Social realism with a Buddhist face*. See also and Diran John Sohigian, "Contagion of laughter: The rise of the humor phenomenon in Shanghai in the 1930s".

48. See chapters 9 and 10 for Lin Yutang's views. A study by Diran John Sohigian of Bergson's influence will hopefully form part of a companion volume to the present.

49. See Kong Shuyu, "*Big Shot from Beijing*: Feng Xiaogang's *He Sui Pian* and contemporary Chinese commercial film"; and Zhu Ying, "Feng Xiaogang and Chinese New Year Films". For more recent developments in comic film, see articles in the special issue (vol. 20, no. 2, 2008) of *Modern Chinese literature and culture* on "Comic visions of modern China", edited by Christopher G. Rea and Nicolai Volland.

50. Barak Kushner, "Laughter as materiel: The mobilization of comedy in Japan's fifteen-year war".

51. A study is forthcoming by Christopher C. Rea, hopefully to form part of a companion volume to the present.

52. For documentation of this phenomenon, see Jing Wang, *Brand new China: Advertising, media, and commercial culture*; Charles S. Gulas and Marc G. Weinberger, *Humor in advertising: A comprehensive analysis*; and Heather J. Crawford, Gary D. Gregory, James C. Munch and Charles S. Gulas. "Humorous appeals in advertising: Comparing the United States, Australia and the People's Republic of China".

53. http://www.chinese-tools.com/china/crazy/2008-10-15-joke-exhibition-garden.html (accessed 5 June 2009).

54. Hsia, *The Chinese sense of humor*, p. 26.

55. Kao, *Chinese wit and humor*, p. 250.

56. Kowallis, *Wit and humor from Old Cathay*, pp. 99–100.

57. Personal communications.

58. Personal communication.

59. The *San zi jing* was probably written in the thirteenth century. It is usually attributed to Wang Yinglin 王應麟 (1223–1296).

60. Personal communication.

61. Wang Xiaofeng, "Kuaile yu youmo".

62. See Weihe Xu's chapter on Confucius and humour, note 73, for derivation of the name.

63. Caiyun mantianfei 彩雲漫天飛 (pen name), *Dayou shi* 打油詩.

64. English translations of some classic "one-handed" or solo *xiangsheng* can be found in Zhang Shouchen, *Traditional comic tales*.

65. Colin Mackerras, *The performing arts in contemporary China*, pp. 102–4.

66. See, for example, Alisa Freedman, "Street nonsense: Ryūtanji Yū and the fascination with interwar Tokyo absurdity", and Kyōko Ōmori, "Narrating the detective: *Nansensu*, silent film *benshi* performances and Tokugawa Musei's absurdist detective fiction", in *Japan forum*'s special issue on urban nonsense.

67. See studies cited in notes 47 and 50.

68. See the critical review by Maya Kovskaya in *NY Arts*.

69. European garden follies, in spite of their name, were not generally humorous in intent, but rather intended to inculcate a sense of tragic nostalgia for the past. Interestingly, early European follies often took the form of mock Chinese temples.

70. See, for example, Christie Davies, "Humour and protest: Jokes under Communism"; Emil Draitser, ed., *Forbidden laughter: Soviet underground jokes*; and Lisunia A. Romanienko, "Carnival laughter and the disarming of the opponent: Antagonism, absurdity and the avant-garde: Dismantling Soviet oppression through the use of theatrical devices by Poland's 'Orange' solidarity movement". Compare studies of jokes under the Nazi regime such as F. K. Hillenbrand, *Underground humour in Nazi Germany 1933–1945*.

71. Hsia, *The Chinese sense of humor*, p. 35.

72. See, for example, John Morreall, "Humor in the Holocaust: Its critical, cohesive, and coping functions".

73. For an early version of Xue-liang Ding's study, published in *The Financial Times* (Chinese language edition on 10 March 2010), see: http://www. chinareform.net/2010/0116/7793.html (accessed 21 April 2011). Like other significant work referred to in notes 11 and 2, the full study will hopefully form part of a companion volume to the present.

74. Personal communication.

75. Personal communication.

76. Quoted in Richard Solomon, *Chinese negotiating behaviour: Pursuing interests through 'old friends'*, pp. 88–9.

77. Dangerous jokes in the West are more likely to be ones made at the expense of suffering "victim" groups and they incur social disapproval rather than political reprisal (with the exception of humour infringing legal limits, such as copyright law, defamation or matters of public security such as joking about bombs on planes when at the airport, etc.). There are nevertheless some highly sensitive ones that, at least before the advent of the internet, circulated only by word of mouth, such as the series of dirty "Royal Family" jokes.

78. Wang Xiaobo, *Wenming yu fanfeng* 文明與反諷 (Civilization and satire) in *Wang Xiaobo wenji*, Vol. 4, pp. 356–9.

79.   See Deng's speech, "Hold high the banner of Mao Zedong Thought and adhere to the principle of seeking truth from facts", *People's Daily*, 16 September 1978: http://english.peopledaily.com.cn/dengxp/vol2/text/b1220.html (accessed 1 April 2009).

Chapter 2

1.   Robert M. Stelmack and Anastasios Stalikas, "Galen and the humour theory of temperament", p. 255.

2.   Willibald Ruch, "Forward and overview: A new look at an old concept", p. 7. Ruch relies on *Europäische Schlüsselwörter,* ed. Wolfgang Schmidt-Hidding, Band 1: *Humor und Witz.*

3.   The first edition of *Punch magazine* was published on Saturday, 17 July 1841, printed by Joseph Last of Fleet Street.

4.   William D. Howarth, "English humour and French comique? The cases of Anouilh and Ayckbourn", pp. 72–82.

5.   For an account of the five elements theory, see Joseph Needham, *Science and civilisation in China*, Vol. 2, pp. 243–68; and for a visual representation, "Nature according to the five elements", Figure 3.1, in Chapter 3. Āyurvedic medicine, possibly the original source of both the Chinese and Western theories, includes *tridoṣa-vidyā*, the "doctrine of the three humours"; see "The Science of the humours", from Vāgbhaṭa's *Heart of medicine*, in Dominik Wujastyk, trans. and ed., *The roots of Āyurveda: Selections from Sanskrit medical writings*, pp. 230–6.

6.   Galen was a prominent Greek physician, surgeon and philosopher whose most famous surviving works include *On the natural faculties* and *On temperaments*; see Peter Brain, *Galen*, pp. 1–5. Another influential figure was Isadore of Seville (d. 636CE), whose contributions to the theory are particularly reflected in four Old English (Anglo-Saxon) texts on medicine; see Lois Ayoub, "Old English *wæta* and the medical Theory of the Humours", pp. 332–46.

7.   Willibald Ruch, "Foreword and overview: A new look at an old concept", pp. 7–8.

8.   *Traité du Ris, Contenant son essence, ses causes et mervelheus effais, etc., item La Cause morale du Ris de Democrite, expliquee et temoignée par Hippocras (traduite de Grec en Fransais par J. Guichard). Plus, un Dialogue sur la Cacographie Francaise, avec des annotations sur l'orthographie de M. Joubert (par C. de Beauchatel)* (Treatise on Laughter, Containing its essence, causes and marvellous effects etc; includes Democritus' work, "The Moral cause of Laughter", explicated and evidenced by Hippocratus [translated from the Greek into French by J. Guichard]. Plus, "A Dialogue on French bad handwriting with annotations on orthography by Monsieur Joubert" [by C. de Beauchatel]). Paris: [A. l'Angelier], 1579. Translated by G. de Rocher as Joubert's *Treatise on laughter*.

9. Gutenberg texts respectively at http://www.gutenberg.org/ebooks/3694 and http://hollowaypages.com/jonson1692out.htm (both accessed 7 March 2011).

10. Quotations are from Arikha's website at http://www.passionsandtempers. com (accessed 28 October 2010), where she offers readers an opportunity to diagnose their own "humoural personality" with an online questionnaire.

11. Willis is credited with identifying the eleventh cranial nerve (accessory nerve) and in 1666 published his work on this and other discoveries, *Cerebri anatome, cui accessit nervorum descriptio et usus*, 1664 and 1681.

12. William F. Bynum, "Every man in his humour" stresses the importance of this message.

13. See, for instance, Karli K. Watson, Benjamin J. Matthews and John A. Allman, "Brain activation during sight gags and language-dependent humor", pp. 314–24; and Vinod Goel and Raymond J. Dolan, "Social regulation of affective experience of humor", pp. 1574–80. Both studies used fMRI.

14. Robert M. Stelmack and Anastasios Stalikas, "Galen and the humour theory of temperament", p. 255.

15. Psychiatric diagnoses are categorized by the *Diagnostic and Statistical Manual of Mental Disorders*, now in its fourth edition (the DSM-IV). Published by the American Psychiatric Association, the manual covers all mental health disorders for both children and adults.

16. Giovannantonio Forabosco, "The ill side of humor: Pathological conditions and sense of humor", pp. 271–92.

17. For a valuable recent summary, see Rod A. Martin, *The psychology of humor: An integrative approach*, pp. 331–3.

18. Reviewed by Martin, *The psychology of humor*, pp. 275–6, 305–7 and 331–3.

19. See, for example, a review of findings in Steven J. Kirsh, "Cartoon violence and aggression in youth", pp. 547–57.

Chapter 3

1. The "endogenous heart" embraces the physical heart and its animating forces, which generate emotions. For a full discussion of the term, see below and note 24.

2. See Graeme Tobyn, *Culpepers's medicine: A practice of Western holistic medicine*, p. 62; also Yanhua Zhang, *Transforming emotions with Chinese medicine: An ethnographic account from contemporary China*, p. 69.

3. *New Oxford American dictionary*, sv *qi*. Another valuable definition of *qi* is "an expression of the natural order of life" (see Elisabeth Rochat de la Vallee, *A study of qi*, pp. 4–9). The author terms it "an expression of the natural yin and yang order of life".

4.   Pioneered by Martin Seligman of the Positive Psychology Center at the University of Pennsylvania in, for example, Martin E. P. Seligman, *Authentic happiness: Using the new positive psychology to realize your potential for lasting fulfilment* and Christopher Peterson and Martin E. P. Seligman, *Character strengths and virtues.*

5.   Chen Xinwang, *Han Ying chengyu, chanyu, changyong cihui huibian*, p. 24.

6.   John DeFrancis, *ABC Chinese–English dictionary*, p. 679.

7.   The *bagua* (literally, eight symbols) are eight trigrams used in Daoist cosmology. Each symbol has three lines, either "broken", thus *yin*, or "unbroken", *yang*. The trigrams relate to the five elements. *The book of changes* comprises 64 pairs of trigrams with six lines in each (the hexagrams) and commentary on them. Note that *qi* is also variously spelt chi, chhi, ki or khi, depending on the romanization system used. I have standardized it as *qi*.

8.   Translation by Yosida Mitukuni, "The Chinese concept of nature", p. 77.

9.   Neo-Confucianism as formulated by Zhu Xi 朱熹 (1130–1200) saw the world as based on *dao*, expressed through both principle (*li*) and *qi* (understood as the material embodiment of the *dao*). See Wing-tsit Chan, *A sourcebook of Chinese philosophy.*

10.   On-Cho Ng, "Toward an interpretation of Ch'ing ontology", pp. 36–7.

11.   Feng Yu-Lan [Feng Youlan], *A Short history of Chinese philosophy*, p. 653.

12.   Zhejiang Provincial TCM Research Office, Wen yi lun *pingzhu*, p. 213.

13.   Cf. Derk Bodde's translation of *hua* as "evolutionary operations" (processes) in the passage quoted above.

14.   Roth's translation in Harold D. Roth, *Original Tao: Inward training (nei yeh) and the foundations of Taoist mysticism*, p. 73.

15.   Zhejiang Provincial TCM Research Office, Wen yi lun *pingzhu*, pp. 164–5.

16.   A. C. Graham refers to these *wu xing* as "five walkings", *Two Chinese philosophers, Ch'eng Ming-tao and Ch'eng Yi-ch'uan*, p. 35.

17.   Zhao Fen, *Zhongyi jichu lilun xiangjie*, pp. 14–16.

18.   The original text reads *tian ren tong qi ye* 天人同气也, Chen Dingsan and Jiang Ersun, *Yixue tanyuan*, p. 16.

19.   Translation by A. C. Graham, *Disputers of the Tao*, p. 486.

20.   G. W. Leibniz, *Discourse on the natural theology of the Chinese*, p. 9.

21.   Joseph Needham, *Clerks and craftsmen in China and the West*, p. 342.

22.   Zhang, *Transforming emotions with Chinese medicine*, p. 74.

23.   Ma Zhongxue, *Zhongguo yixue zhenfa da quan*, p. 378.

24.   Classical TCM practitioner Chen Dingsan (1875–1960) explained how the exogenous five elements translate into the human endogenous five elements, becoming endogenous organ systems in "Tian ren he yi" 天人合一 (The oneness of nature and humanity), in Chen and Jiang, *Yixue tanyuan*, pp. 1–2. See also "Ren bing da qi wuxing er sheng zangfu", in Peng Ziyi, *Yuan yundong de gu zhongyixue*, pp. 8–10.

25. Yasuo Yuasa, *The body: Self-cultivation and Ki-energy*, p. 111. Note variant spelling of *qi* in this text.

26. Nathan Sivin, *Medicine, philosophy and religion in ancient China: Researchers and reflections*, pp. 1–2 (characters added).

27. Helen Verran, "Foreword", in Rey Tiquia, *Traditional Chinese Medicine: A guide to its practice*, p. vii; see also pp. 1–10.

28. The definition of acu-tracts as "the pathways of *qi* transformations originating from the visceral and hollow organs" (Tang zong hai rong chuan, *Yijing jingyi*, p. 66) is used by the author in "Traditional Chinese Medicine as an Australian tradition of health care", pp. 96, 269–75.

29. Tiquia, *Traditional Chinese Medicine,* pp. 142–3.

30. Yang Yifang, *Yang Yongxuan zhongyi zhenjiu jing yan xuan*, p. 28.

31. Yang, *Yang Yongxuan zhongyi zhenjiu jing yan xuan*, p. 29.

32. Needham, *Clerks and craftsmen in China and the West*, p. 365.

Chapter 4

1. The significance of the Rites is discussed below.

2. *Rujia* (lit. the school of scholars) is another term for Confucianism.

3. For studies of this term, see Timoteus Pokora, "The etymology of *ku-chi*" and Timoteus Pokora, "Ironical critics at ancient Chinese courts (*Shih chi*, 126)"; also Jiang Liangfu, "Huaji kao", which the author follows in translating the term.

4. For a survey of pre-Qin Chinese humour, see Zheng Kai, *XianQin youmo wenxue*.

5. Liu Xie, *Wenxin diaolong quanyi,* ed. Long Bikun (hereafter *WXDL*), pp. 167–77.

6. See the prefaces to *Xiaofu* 笑府, *Guangxiaofu* 廣笑府 and *Gujin xiao* 古今 笑, in *Zhongguo lidai xiaohua jicheng*, Vol. 1, p. 498 and pp. 542–3; and Vol. 2, pp. 1–3 and 712–13, respectively.

7. *Xing zi ming chu* 性自命出 (hereafter *XZMC*), one of the recently excavated bamboo writings (inscribed on bamboo strips, c. 300 BCE) from Guodian; in Li Tianhong, *Guodian zhujian xing zi ming chu yanjiu,* p. 135.

8. *Yucong er* 語叢二, in Jiang Guanghui, ed., *Guodian Chujian yanjiu* (hereafter *GCYJ*), pp. 29–30.

9. For varying length lists, see "Zhongyong" 中庸, in *Liji* p. 370; "Tian Zifang" 田子方, in *Zhuangzi quanyi*, p. 364; "Wen Wang guanren di qishi'er" 文王官人第七十二, in Huang Huaixin, ed., *Da Dai Li ji huijiao jizhu*, Vol. 2, p. 1117; "Tianlun pian" 天論篇 and "Zhengming pian" 正 名篇, in *Xunzi*, pp. 170, 232, 235; and "Liyun" 禮運, in *Liji*, p. 164. All quotations of these and other sources are from editions listed in the Bibliography and, unless otherwise stated, translations from Chinese texts are my own.

10. *GCYJ*, p. 29.

11. Li, *Guodian zhujian xing zi ming chu yanjiu*, p. 178. Cf. *Xingqing lun* 性情論, in *Shanghai bowuguan Zhanguo Chuzhushu (1)* (hereafter *SBZC*), pp. 270–1; and *Zhuangzi quanyi*, pp. 52, 364.

12. See respectively, Wang Bing, "Chongguang buzhu Huangdi neijing suwen", *juan* 2, p. 5a; Li Fang, "Renshi bu sanshi'er", in *Taiping yulan*, *juan* 391, p. 1b; and Lu Ji, *Wen fu*, p. 115 (where Owen translates "When thought fares through joy, there will surely be laughter").

13. Such etymology reflects traditional Chinese concepts or perceptions of things. See, for instance, *WXDL*, p. 169; Cao Chen, *Shehua lu Shehua lu*, p. 98.

14. See *GCYJ*, pp. 16, 31, 33–4, 59–60, 75–6, 84. The *Liji* is the traditional source for early Confucian thought, which includes not just Confucius's thinking but that of his disciples, their students such as Zi Si and later pre-Qin Confucians such as Mencius and Xunzi. *Liji's* reliability derives from its inclusion of writings by some of Confucius's contemporary followers. Its depth and scope is such that it has always been read as one of the core Confucian classics (numbered variably as five, six, nine or thirteen). Its encyclopaedia-like nature makes the *Liji* more useful for studying Confucian concepts of human life and proper conduct than, say, *Lunyu* (*The analects*), which lacks such breadth.

15. *Lunyu baihua jinyi*, p. 38.

16. Liu Xiang, *Xinxu Shuoyuan*, p. 147.

17. *Xunzi*, pp. 232–3; Huang, *Da Dai Liji huijiao jizhu*, Vol. 2, pp. 60–1.

18. *Zhongyong*, in *Liji*, p. 370; and Li, *Guodian zhujian xing zi ming chu yanjiu*, p. 176.

19. *XZMC*, pp. 134, 144.

20. Michael Puett, "The ethics of responding properly", in Halvor Eifring, ed., *Love and emotions in traditional Chinese literature*, p. 46.

21. *Mengzi baihua jinyi*, 6A.2.

22. Li, *Guodian zhujian xing zi ming chu yanjiu*, pp. 135–97. Cf. *Xingqing lun*, in *SBZC*, pp. 220–80.

23. Ban Gu, *Baihu tong*, Vol. 2, *juan* 3B; for the full etymology of *zhong* see Chen Kehua, *Rujia zhongyong zhi dao yanjiu*, pp. 4–42; cf. Ta hsüeh *and* Chung yung (The highest order of cultivation *and* On the practice of the mean), trans. Andrew Plaks, pp. 23, 108.

24. See *Zhongyong*, in *Liji*, p. 378; and discussion in Chapter 3 of this volume, by Rey Tiquia.

25. Li, *Guodian zhujian xing zi ming chu yanjiu*, p. 133. Cf. *Xingqing lun*, in *SBZC*, pp. 293–314.

26. *Liji*, p. 370, and "Ta hsüeh" *and* "Chung yung", p. 25.

27. "Ta hsüeh" *and* "Chung yung", p. 25 (an interpretative translation by Plaks).

28. For glosses of this term, see *The analects of Confucius*, pp. 34–8; and "Ta hsüeh" *and* "Chung yung", p. 109.

29. The *Shijing* (Book of songs) comprises 305 poems or songs, some possibly dating from 1000 BCE. It forms part of the Confucian *wu jing* 五經 (Five classics), was quoted by Confucius himself and studied by generations of Confucian scholars as an aid to understanding aspects of human society.

30. *Liji zhushu (shang),* p. 13.

31. Liu, *Xinxu Shuoyuan*, p. 137. Cf. *Lunyu baihua jinyi,* 17.23.

32. Weihe Xu, "The Confucian politics of appearance — and its impact on Chinese humor", p. 26.

33. See Christoph Harbsmeier, "*Confucius ridens*: Humor in the *Analects*", pp. 133–4.

34. On the day of a *daxiang* ceremony, mourners can take off mourning clothes and put away walking sticks, so that three years' mourning is "often interpreted as meaning into the third year" rather than three entire years: *The analects of Confucius*, p. 214, 5n; also *Liji zhushu (shang)*, pp. 71, 72, 73.

35. Zi Gong was the style name of Duanmu Ci 端木賜, one of Confucius's disciples (see reference below).

36. See *Liji zhushu (xia)*, pp. 482–3.

37. *Maoshi zhushu (xia)*, p. 84; *Lunyu baihua jinyi*, 1.15; *Erya zhushu*, p. 39; and the *Daxue* 大學 chapter in *Liji zhushu (xia)*, pp. 631–2.

38. *Maoshi zhushu*, p. 84.

39. Both comments from *Maoshi zhushu*, p. 84.

40. Inferable from a dialogue between Confucius and Zi Gong (*Lunyu baihua jinyi*, 1.15).

41. See Qian Zhongshu, *Guanzhui bian*, Vol. 1, pp. 91–2; Liu Zongyuan, "Yu Yang Huizhi shu" 與楊誨之書, and "Du Han Yu 'Mao Ying zhuan' hou ti" 讀韓愈毛穎傳後題, in his *Liu Hedong ji*, Vol. 3, pp. 115–16 and Vol. 4, p. 113. See also *Gudian xiqu meixue ziliao ji*, p. 35.

42. Pu Songling, "Ying Ning" 嬰寧, in *Liaozhai zhi yi*, p. 155.

43. See Xu, "The Confucian politics of appearance", pp. 514–27.

44. *The analects (Lun yü)*, trans. D. C. Lau, p. 101; cf. *Lunyu baihua jinyi*, 10.4. Given the length of this passage, the parallel Chinese text is omitted. Some suggest this chapter originally described the private and public conduct of the ideal gentleman, only later associated with the historical Confucius (for example, *Analects of Confucius*, pp. 13, 1n, 55; also E. Bruce Brooks and A. Taeko Brooks, *The original analects: Sayings of Confucius and his successors*, pp. 59, 65, 67). Whichever the case, it certainly reflects a Confucian ideal of public deportment.

45. See Sima Qian 司馬遷, *Kongzi shijia di shiqi* 孔子世家第十七, p. 1915. There are several slightly differing versions of this story, five in *Kongzi jiayu shuzheng* 孔子家語疏證, pp. 2–4.

46.   See Zheng, *XianQin youmo wenxue*, pp. 128–39.

47.   For two slightly differing lists of types of admonition and remonstration, see Liu, *Xinxu Shuoyuan*, p. 72; and *Kongzi jiayu shuzheng* p. 27. Since *juejian* and *fengjian* are indirect admonitions, the two terms are often interchangeable (see *Maoshi zhushu*, pp. 12, 14).

48.   For the lives of some historical court jesters, see Sima, *Shiji*, Vol. 10, *juan* 126, pp. 3179–203. For discussion of their performances and license, see Feng Yuanjun, "Guyou jie" 古優解, "Hanfu yu guyou" 漢賦與古優 and "Guyou jie buzheng" 古優解補正, in *Feng Yuanjun gudian wenxue wenji*, pp. 3–77, 78–94, 95–123; Beatrice K. Otto, *Fools are everywhere: The court jester around the world*, pp. 105–6.

49.   *Erya zhushu*, p. 37.

50.   See *Shijing quanyi*, p. 409; *Jinguwen Shangshu quanyi*, pp. 23, 33, 52; *Lunyu baihua jinyi*, 16.10; and *Liji*, p. 328.

51.   Here, Confucius is described as gentle but strict (*wen er li* 溫而厲).

52.   According to Waley, *ren* originally denoted "men of a tribe". He sees *ren* as "the display of human qualities at their highest" and gives an etymological relationship between it and gentleness (*Analects of Confucius*, pp. 27, 28).

53.   Harbsmeier, "*Confucius ridens*", pp. 157, 158. Other important studies of Confucius's humour include Lin Yutang, "Lun Kongzi de youmo", pp. 22–7; and Zheng, *XianQin youmo wenxue*, pp. 114–27. See Chapters 9 and 10 of this volume, by Joseph Sample and Qian Suoqiao respectively, for Lin's views about humour.

54.   Liu, *Xinyu Shuoyuan*, p. 160. Cf. *Kongzi jiayu*, p. 21. Given the length of this passage, I omit the parallel Chinese text.

55.   Brooks and Brooks, *The original analects*, p. 158.

56.   As does Harbsmeier, "*Confucius ridens*", p. 137.

57.   *Kongzi shijia di shiqi*, pp. 1921–2. For an earlier version, see Han Ying, *Hanshi waizhuanjuan*, 9, pp. 9b–10b. Later versions appear for instance in Wang Chong "Guxiang di shiyi" 骨相第十一, in *Lun heng*, *juan* 3, p. 88; Ban, *Baihu tong*, Vol. 2, *juan* 3B, p. 217; and *Kongzi jiayu*, p. 61. Harbsmeier, "*Confucius ridens*", pp. 148–9, argues that *sangjia zhi gou* is a perfectly standard phrase meaning "a homeless (*sàngjia* 喪家) dog", but that Confucius jokingly misconstrues it as meaning "the dog in a house of mourning".

58.   See Rod A. Martin et al., "Individual differences in uses of humor and their relation to psychological well-being: Development of the humor styles questionnaire".

59.   Cf. Aristotle, *Nicomachean ethics*, Book 2, 1109a.

60.   Harbsmeier, "*Confucius ridens*", p. 149.

61.   For conjecture about this, see Brooks and Brooks, *The original analects*, p. 164.

62. See discussion above.

63. See, for instance, poems no. 30 and 254 in *Shijing quanyi*, pp. 38, 399; "Shigu di yi" 釋詁第一, and "Shixun di san" 釋訓第三, in *Erya zhushu*, pp. 8, 39; Xu Shen 許慎, *Shuowen jiezi* 說文解字, p. 35; and *WXDL*, p. 167.

64. Chen Gaomo 陳皋謨, "Ban'an xiaozheng" 半庵笑政, in *Zhongguo lidai xiaohua jicheng*, Vol. 3, p. 86. Interestingly, Shakespeare uses a similar metaphor for insidious treachery: "There's daggers in men's smiles" (*Macbeth* Act II).

65. Chapter 6 of this volume, by Lily Xiao Hong Lee, discusses one of these collections, the *Shishuo xinyu* 世說新語 (A new account of tales of the world).

66. In *Gudian xiqu meixue ziliao ji*, p. 35.

67. *Zhongguo lidai xiaohua jicheng*, Vol. 2, p. 453.

68. *Zhongguo lidai xiaohua jicheng*, Vol. 3, p. 87.

69. Li Yu, p. 306.

70. Li, *Xianqing ouji*, p. 308.

71. *Zhongguo lidai xiaohua jicheng*, Vol. 2, p. 453.

72. Li, *Xianqing ouji*, p. 306.

73. Wang Jide, *Wang Jide qulü*, pp. 148–9. See also Chapter 7 of this volume on comic style in Yuan drama, by Andy Shui-lung Fung and Zhan Hanglun. This quotation includes reference to Zhang Dayou 張打油 who, as tradition has it, lived during the Tang dynasty (618–907) and was so noted for his doggerel that the genre was named after him. Doggerel verses are discussed in Chapter 1 of this volume.

74. Yang Xiong, "Yangzi fayan wuzi", p. 1b.

75. Ge Hong, *Baopuzi*, pp. 239–45.

76. Wm Theodore de Bary et al., *Self and society in Ming thought*, p. 3.

77. See Pi-Ching Hsu, *Beyond eroticism: A historian's reading of humor in Feng Menglong's Child's folly*, pp. 143–54.

78. Although many were not dwarves, the two were closely associated in common perception — see, for example, Han Fei 非 (280–233 BCE), "Nan san", p. 168; Sima, *Shiji*, Vol. 10, *juan* 126, p. 3202; and Feng, *Feng Yuanjun gudian wenxue wenji*, pp. 44–6. Cf. Timoteus Pokora, "Ironical critics", p. 61. For connections with Yuan period stage comedy, see Chapter 7 of this volume.

79. Ban Gu, "Jia Zou Mei Lu zhuan" 賈鄒枚路傳, in Ban Gu, *Han shu*, Vol. 8, *juan* 51.

80. Sima, *Shiji*, Vol. 10, pp. 3197–203. These *huaji* biographies are also discussed in Chapter 1 of this volume.

81. *Zhongguo lidai xiaohua ji*, Vol. 1, p. 388.

82. *Zhongguo lidai xiaohua ji*, Vol. 2, p. 2.

83. Li, *Xianqing ouji*, p. 307.

84. *Zhongguo lidai xiaohua ji*, Vol. 3, pp. 129–30.

85.   *Zhongguo lidai xiaohua ji*, Vol. 3, p. 129.

86.   Li, *Xianqing ouji*, pp. 305–6. Cf. Wang, *Wang Jide qulü*, p. 165.

87.   *Zhongguo lidai xiaohua jicheng*, Vol. 4, p. 738.

88.   *Zhongguo lidai xiaohua jicheng*, Vol. 1, p. 250.

89.   See, for instance, Plato, *The republic*, Book 10.606; Aristotle, *Parts of animals*, Book 3, Ch. 10; also Mary A. Grant, *The ancient rhetorical theories of the laughable: The Greek rhetoricians and Cicero*, pp. 13–17.

90.   Karl Jaspers, *The origin and goal of history*, pp. 1–21, 51–77.

91.   See Chapter 1 of this volume for more on internet humour.

Chapter 5

1.   Christoph Harbsmeier, "Humor in ancient Chinese philosophy".

2.   See below and note 6 for a discussion of the meaning of *huaji*.

3.   See Chapters 9 and 10 of this volume for detailed discussion.

4.   Michelle C. Sun, "Humor literature as a lens to Chinese identity".

5.   Cf. Chapter 1 of this volume.

6.   For example, Lin Yutang distinguishes *youmo* from *huaji*, claiming that the former can be both serious and sobering, yet funny 亦莊亦諧, and also that its essence is "sympathy towards the happenings in the world" 悲天憫人. *Huaji*, on the other hand, is "low class ridicule or jest" 低級的笑談. See Chen Ninggui, *Lin Yutang youmo jinju*, p. 15.

7.   It is probably for this reason that some Sinologists argue there was no need to borrow or create the term *youmo* because of the existence of the word *huaji* in Chinese tradition. See also Chao-chih Liao, "Humor versus *huaji*".

8.   Sima Qian, "Huaji liezhuan", in *Shiji*, no. 66, *juan* 126.

9.   Sima, *Huaji liezhuan*, no. 66, *juan* 4.

10.   Also see Lionel Giles, trans., *Taoist teaching from the Book of Lieh-Tzŭ*, p. 13.

11.   The *Shiji* mentions Zhuang Zhou (the proper name of Zhuangzi) as one who attacked Confucian social conventions by being a humorist 鄙儒小拘，如莊周等，又滑稽亂俗. See Sima Qian, *Mengzi Xun Jing liezhuan* 孟子荀卿列傳 (Collective biographies of Mengzi and Xunzi), in *Shiji*, Vol. 7, p. 2348.

12.   Zhuangzi, *Basic writings/Chuang Tzu*, trans. Burton Watson, p. 1. On the other hand, Kirkland argues that there is no historic evidence for the existence of Zhuang Zhou at all: see Russell Kirkland, *Taoism: The enduring tradition*, pp. 33–4.

13.   See Zhuangzi, "Xiaoyao you" 逍遙遊：夫列子禦風而行，冷然善也，旬有五日而後反，彼於致福者，未數數然也. For a discussion of Liezi appearing in the *Zhuangzi*, see Xiao Dengfu, *Liezi tanwei*, pp. 140–3.

14.   Zhuangzi, *Basic writings*, p. 26.

15.   A. C. Graham, *The Book of Lieh-tzu*, p. 1.

16.   Graham, *Book of Lieh-tzu*, pp. 3–13.

17. For convenience, the term "recasting" is employed to refer to the literary device of putting a particular figure's ideas or characters into another figure's position.

18. Yang Bojun, *Liezi jishi, juan* 1, "Tianrui" pian 天瑞篇, pp. 15–16.

19. Graham, *Book of Lieh-tzu*, "Heaven's gifts", p. 26. Graham's translation is modified here, and throughout his translations are adopted with similar modifications, particularly where *pinyin* is used for proper names.

20. 子曰：汝奚不曰：其為人也，發憤忘食，樂以忘憂，不知老之將至。See "Shuer" pian 述而篇 in the *Lunyu* 論語 (Analects). It is also said that Confucius set his mind on learning from the age of fifteen (子曰：吾十有五而志于學): see "Weizheng" pian 為政篇 in the *Lunyu*.

21. Graham, *Book of Lieh-tzu*, "The Yellow Emperor", p. 52; Yang, *Liezi* jishi, *juan* 7, "Yang Zhu" pian 楊朱篇, pp. 49–50.

22. Graham, *Book of Lieh-tzu*, "Yang Zhu", pp. 148–9; Yang, *Liezi jishi, juan* 7, "Yang Zhu" pian, pp. 49–50.

23. Graham, *Book of Lieh-tzu*, "Yang Zhu", pp. 153–4.

24. *Lie Yukou* 列禦寇, in *Zhuangzi*, in Cao Chuji, *Zhuangzi qianzhu*, p. 489.

25. *Qiu shui* 秋水, in *Zhuangzi*, in Cao, *Zhuangzi qianzhu*, p. 231.

26. Yang Bojun, *Liezi jishi, juan* 2, "Huangdi" pian 黃帝篇, p. 24. See also Graham, *Book of Lieh-tzu*, "The Yellow Emperor", p. 33.

27. Graham, *Book of Lieh-tzu*, p. 35.

28. Graham, *Book of Lieh-tzu*, "Heaven's gifts", pp. 30–1; Yang, *Liezi jishi, juan* 1, "Tianrui" pian, pp. 21–2.

29. Graham, *Book of Lieh-tzu*, pp. 55–6; Yang, *Liezi jishi, juan* 2, "Huangdi" pian, pp. 52–3. See also Graham, *Book of Lieh-tzu*, "The Yellow Emperor", p. 33.

30. Graham, *Book of Lieh-tzu*, p. 38; Yang, *Liezi jishi, juan* 2, "Huangdi" pian, p. 52.

31. Graham, *Book of Lieh-tzu*, "The Yellow Emperor", pp. 39; Yang, *Liezi jishi, juan* 2, "Huangdi" pian, pp. 52–3.

32. Graham, *Book of Lieh-tzu*, "King Ming of Zhou", p. 68; Yang, *Liezi jishi, juan* 3, "Zhou Muwang" pian 周穆王篇, pp. 65–6.

33. Graham, *Book of Lieh-tzu*, pp. 38–9, 44; Yang, *Liezi jishi, juan* 2, "Huangdi" pian, p. 24.

34. While there is no systematic discussion of human emotions (*qing* 情) in the Confucian classic texts, recently discovered texts attributed to the Confucian school suggest that human emotions are human attributes that enable us to respond to external stimuli. Following that conceptualization, music and rituals need to be employed to cultivate proper human feelings. A detailed discussion can be found in Shirley Chan, "Human nature and moral cultivation in the Guodian 郭店 text of the *Xing Zi Ming Chu* 性自命出 (Nature derives from mandate)". See also Chapter 8 of this volume, by Weihe Xu, on Confucian thought and "proper emotions".

35.   Graham, *Book of Lieh-tzu*, "King Mu of Zhou", p. 73; Yang, *Liezi jishi, juan* 3, "Zhou Muwang" pian, p. 70.

36.   This can be seen in both the *Lunyu* and the *Mengzi*. Confucius's disciple Zengzi comments, "A scholar must be strong and resolute, for his burden is heavy, and his journey is long. His burden is humanity: is this not heavy? His journey ends only with death: is this not long?" (曾子曰：士不可以不弘毅，任重而道遠。仁以為己任，不亦重乎？死而後已，不亦遠乎?) See "Taibo" pian 泰伯篇 in the *Lunyu* (Confucius, *The Analects of Confucius*, p. 36). Also Mencius says that "to be above the power of riches and honours to make dissipated, of poverty and mean condition to make swerve from principle, and of power and force to make bend — these characteristics constitute the great man" (富貴不能淫，貧賤不能移，威武不能屈。此之謂大丈夫) (see Mengzi, "Tengwen Gong II", in James Legge, *The Chinese classics*, Vol. 1, p. 265).

37.   Graham, *Book of Lieh-tzu*, "Explaining conjunctions", p. 161; note modified translation; Yang, *Liezi jishi, juan* 8, "Shuofu" pian 説符篇, p. 155.

38.   In the General Theory of Verbal Humour (GTVH) developed by Victor Raskin and Salvatore Attardo, this is part of what is termed "knowledge resources" (KRs) — see, for example, Salvatore Attardo, *Linguistic theories of humor*, pp. 222–9.

39.   Harbsmeier, "Humor in ancient Chinese philosophy", p. 308.

40.   Lu Xun, *The true story of Ah Q*, trans. Yang Hsien-yi and Gladys Yang. Chinese studies of humor, wit and satire in the works of modern writers such as Lu Xun, Lao She and Qian Zhongshu are too numerous to list. The author is grateful to Christopher Rea for pointing out that studies and commentary on *Ah Q*, for instance, have been anthologized in a volume of nearly 700 pages: Peng Xiaoling and Han Aili, eds, *Ah Q qishi nian*.

41.   Tsai, *Liezi shuo: yu feng er xing de zhesi*.

42.   See Ben Davis, "Guy Smiley"; and the artist's own web-gallery at http://www.yueminjun.com/en/biography/bio09.html (accessed 11 February 2010).

Chapter 6

1.   Quotations in this chapter are from Richard Mather's definitive English translation, *Shih-shuo hsin-yü: A new account of tales of the world*, in which he used Wade–Giles romanization, here changed to pinyin. In some cases, Mather's translation is changed slightly to highlight the humour and some passages not related to the humour have been omitted. Of the many versions of the Chinese text, references here are to the standard text: Yu Jiaxi, ed., *Shishuo xinyu jianshu*. The Chinese text is also available from Project Gutenberg at http://www.gutenberg.org/etext/24047 (accessed 10 January 2010).

2.   *Hou Han shu*, 78.2513.

3.   Shimizu Shigeru, "Kami no hatsumei to Kokan no gakufu".

4.   *Han shu yiwenzhi* 漢書藝文志 (The bibliographic chapter of the history of Han), in *Han shu*, *juan* 30, p. 1745. The original reads 如或一言可采，此亦 芻蕘狂夫之議也 "If there is one thing that is worth adopting, it would be like the words of a grass cutter and a madman." The implication is that if they were correct, a ruler should heed the words of even a grass cutter or a madman.

5.   These ideas are shared by others, such as Yang Yong, Shishuo xinyu *jiaojian*, p. iii; Mather, *Shishuo*, p. xiv; and Zong Baihua, "Lun *Shishuo xinyu* he Jin ren de mei".

6.   Fan Ziye, "Shishuo xinyu xin tan"; Mather, *Shishuo*, p. xxvii.

7.   Lily Hsiao Hung Lee, "A study of *Shih-shuo hsin-yü*", pp. 47–51.

8.   A copy dating to the Liu–Song dynasty is recorded in Wang Zao's *Shishuo xulu*, included in the Maeda edition. See version of complete text and commentaries published by Zhonghua shuju, Beijing, in 1962. Liu Jun's commentary is in all standard texts of *Shishuo*.

9.   A discussion of the *Shishuo* text is in Yang Yong, "*Shishuo xinyu*: shuming, juanzhi, banben kao"; Mather, *Shishuo*, pp. xxvii–xxix; Lee, "A study of *Shih-shuo hsin-yü*", pp. 118–28.

10.   Qian Nanxiu, "*Daitō seigo*: An alien analogue of the *Shih-shuo hsin-yü*".

11.   Kim Jang-hwan and Lily Xiao Hong Lee, "The circulation and study of the *Shishuo xinyu* in Korea".

12.   This nexus is explored by Shirley Chan in Chapter 5 of this volume, on identifying Daoist humour in the *Liezi*.

13.   Lee, "A study of *Shih-shuo hsin-yü*", Ch. 1.

14.   For a more detailed life of Liu Yiqing see Lee, "A study of *Shih-shuo hsin-yü*", pp. 8–16.

15.   Lu Xun, *Zhongguo xiaoshuo shilüe*, p. 44.

16.   Lee, "A study of *Shih-shuo hsin-yü*", n. 14.

17.   The author is indebted to Jessica Milner Davis for information on this and other examples from Western cultures.

18.   Jan Bremmer, "Jokes, jokers and jokebooks in Ancient Greek culture", in *A cultural history of humour*, ed. Jan Bremmer and Herman Roodenburg, pp. 16–18.

19.   Derek Brewer, "Prose jest-books mainly in the sixteenth to eighteenth centuries in England", in *A cultural history of humour*, p. 97.

20.   Brewer, "Prose jest-books", p. 90.

21.   Lu Xun, *Gu xiaoshuo gouchen*, pp. 53–9.

22.   For his biography and those of other characters cited in *Shishuo*, see "Biographical notes", in Mather, *Shishuo*, pp. 488–611 (names arranged alphabetically by Wade–Giles romanization). For convenience, square brackets provide Wade–Giles romanization here where it differs from *pinyin* romanization.

23. *Shishuo*, II, 56; Yu, Shishuo xinyu *jianshu*, p. 116; Mather, *Shishuo*, pp. 7–58.

24. This is a reworking of a quotation from Kong Anguo's commentary to the *Shijing* (dating from the second half of the second century BCE), which alludes to chaff being first winnowed before being tossed out. Here, Wang Tanzhi is comparing Fan Qi to the chaff to be tossed out first while Fan Qi is comparing Wang to sand and gravel, which are left behind.

25. *Shishuo*, XXV, 46; Yu, Shishuo xinyu *jianshu*, p. 811; Mather, *Shishuo*, p. 419.

26. *Shishuo,* II, 11; Yu, Shishuo xinyu *jianshu*, p. 71; Mather, *Shishuo*, p. 34.

27. *Shishuo*, XXV, 41; Yu, Shishuo xinyu *jianshu*, p. 809; Mather, *Shishuo*, p. 417.

28. *Book of songs* 詩經, 178; Xiaoya 小雅, Caiqi 采芑. Since there are very many editions of the classic *Book of songs*, no page reference is given here or in any subsequent endnote. Here, no. 178 refers to the number of the poem; it may also be identified by the section (in this case Xiaoya) and the title of the poem (Caiqi).

29. *Book of songs*, 177; Xiaoya, Liuyue 六月.

30. *Shishuo,* IV, 3; Yu, Shishuo xinyu *jianshu*, p. 193; Mather, *Shishuo*, p. 94.

31. *Book of songs*, 36; Weifeng 衛風, Shiwei 式微.

32. *Book of songs*, 26; Weifeng, Bozhou 柏舟.

33. *Shishuo,* XXVI, 26; Yu, Shishuo xinyu *jianshu*, p. 843; Mather, *Shishuo*, p. 439.

34. See J. Michael Farmer, "Jia Nan-feng, Empress of Emperor Hui of Jin", in Lily Xiao Hong Lee and A. D. Stefanowska, eds, *Biographical Dictionary of Chinese Women: Antiquity through Sui 1600 BCE–618 CE*, pp. 302–7.

35. *Shishuo,* II, 39; Yu, Shishuo xinyu *jianshu*, p. 100; Mather, *Shishuo*, p. 50.

36. For accounts of various countries' standing joke-types and groups, see Christie Davies, *Ethnic humour around the world: A comparative analysis,* and *The mirth of nations*.

37. *Shishuo*, XXXIV, 3; Yu, Shishuo xinyu *jianshu*, p. 911; Mather, *Shishuo*, p. 480.

38. The *Erya* 爾雅 is regarded as China's oldest dictionary, probably compiled in the third century BCE.

39. An example is Richard B. Mather, "Filial paragons and spoiled brats: A glimpse of medieval Chinese children in the *Shishuo xinyu*".

40. *Shishuo*, XII, 3; Yu, Shishuo xinyu *jianshu*, p. 90; Mather, *Shishuo*, p. 298.

41. *Lienü zhuan* 列女傳 is usually attributed to the Han dynasty scholar Liu Xiang 劉向 (79–8 BCE).

42. *Shishuo*, X, 9; Yu, Shishuo xinyu *jianshu*, pp. 557–8; Mather, *Shishuo*, p. 281.

43. Lady Guo's given name is not recorded. Some details about her can be found in *Jin shu, juan* 43, pp. 1237–9, *juan* 53, p. 1459. See also Lee and Stefanowska, eds, *Biographical dictionary of Chinese women*, pp. 293–5.

44. See *Jin shu, juan* 43, pp. 1235–9.

45. In the sense of "man of affairs" or "person of elevated social status".

46. *Shishuo*, XXVII, 10; Yu, Shishuo xinyu *jianshu*, p. 858; Mather, *Shishuo*, p. 446.

47. For example, *Shishuo*, XIX, 29, where a widow's brothers wish to bring her back to her natal home, but she refuses to go because of her love for her husband; *Shishuo*, XVII, 8 is even more surprising because a father readily agrees to his daughter-in-law's remarriage after his son dies.

48. For additional discussion, see Lily Xiao Hong Lee, *The virtue of yin: Studies on Chinese women*; and Dorothy Ko, JaHyun Kim Haboush and Joan Piggott, *Women and Confucian cultures in premodern China, Korea, and Japan*.

49. *Shishuo*, XIX, 6; Yu, Shishuo xinyu *jianshu*, pp. 671–2; Mather, *Shishuo*, p. 343.

50. Lily Xiao Hong Lee, "Language and self-estimation: The case of Wei–Jin women", 156.

51. *Shishuo*, XXXV, 6; Yu, Shishuo xinyu *jianshu*, p. 922; Mather, *Shishuo*, p. 488.

52. Wang Rong (234–305) in his youth was a junior member of the Seven Worthies of the Bamboo Grove 竹林七賢, who preferred philosophical debate to public service (see Liu Ling episode below); he later collaborated with the Jin regime and ultimately attained the position of grand mentor 太傅.

53. For example, Shimokawa Chieko, "*Sesetu shingo* ni mirareru joseikan"; Qian Nanxiu, *Spirit and self in medieval China: The Shih-shuo hsin-yü and its legacy*, 141; and Lee, "Language and self-estimation", 156 and 158.

54. *Shishuo*, XXV, 11; Yu, Shishuo xinyu *jianshu*, p. 791; Mather, *Shishuo*, p. 407.

55. *Shishuo*, XXIII, 6; Yu, Shishuo xinyu *jianshu*, p. 732; Mather, *Shishuo*, p. 374.

56. In *Zhuangzi*, Chapter 2, "Qiwu", the author repeatedly raises humans to the level of heaven and earth: see *Zhuangzi jishi*, "Qiwu" 齊物, pp. 13 and 16; Lao-tzu, Chuang-tzu and James Legge, *The Tao tê ching: The writings of Chuang-tzû. The Thâi-shang tractate of actions and their retributions*, pp. 236–7.

57. Ruan Ji, "Daren xiansheng zhuan", in Chen Bojun, ed., *Ruan Ji ji jiaozhu*, pp. 161–93, esp. 161–6; see also Donald Holzman, *Poetry and politics: The life and works of Juan Chi, A.D. 210–283*, pp. 185–266. Livia Kohn, *Early Chinese mysticism: philosophy and soteriology in the Daoist tradition*, p. 101, describes Master Great Man as an eternal and universal being, beyond the rules and patterns of the world.

58.	See discussion in Chapter 5 of this volume, by Shirley Chan.

59.	See Sergey A. Ivanov, *Holy fools in Byzantium and beyond*.

60.	Mather translates this as "he provided no entertainment for him whatsoever".

61.	*Shishuo*, XXIX, 6; Yu, Shishuo xinyu *jianshu*, pp. 874–5; Mather, *Shishuo*, pp. 456–7.

62.	Zhuangzi, *Zhuangzi jishi*, pp. 217–18; Lao-tzu, Chuang-tzu and James Legge, *The Tao tê ching*, pp. 391–2.

63.	*Shishuo*, XXV, 31; Yu, Shishuo xinyu *jianshu*, p. 803; Mather, *Shishuo*, p. 413.

64.	*Shishuo*, XXXV, 7; Yu, Shishuo xinyu *jianshu*, p. 923; Mather, *Shishuo*, p. 488.

65.	*Shishuo*, XXXI, 2; Yu, Shishuo xinyu *jianshu*, p. 886; Mather, *Shishuo*, p. 465.

66.	For discussion of jesters and clowns, see Chapters 1, 7 and 8 of this volume, by Jocelyn Chey, Andy Shui-lung Fung and Zhan Hanglun, and Weihe Xu respectively.

67.	*Shishuo*, XXV, 3; Yu, Shishuo xinyu *jianshu*, pp. 780–1; Mather, *Shishuo*, p. 401.

68.	Original name Xu Wei 徐渭. These stories enjoyed a revival in the 1920s when they were introduced into popular culture by Zhou Zuoren. There are many collections, mainly concerned with Xu's wit and larrikinism. See Chang-tai Hung, *Going to the people: Chinese intellectuals and folk literature*, pp. 84–9.

69.	Plato, *Philebus*, 49b.

Chapter 7

1.	Yuan dramas available in English translation include Josephine Huang Hung, ed., *Classical Chinese plays*; Liu Jung-En, ed. and trans., *Six Yuan plays*; Adolphe Clarence Scott, ed., *Traditional Chinese plays*; William Dolby, ed. and trans., *Eight Chinese plays from the thirteenth century to the present*, and *Yuan dynasty variety plays: Yuan zaju yingyi xuanji*.

2.	For further information, see William Dolby, "Yuan drama", pp. 32–59.

3.	The authors are indebted to the editors of this volume, Jessica Milner Davis and Jocelyn Chey, for their expert advice, especially in referencing topics concerning the wider study of humour.

4.	Shih Chung-wen, *The golden age of Chinese drama: Yuan tsa-chu*, pp. 1–5; Colin Mackerras, *Chinese drama: A historical survey*, p. 51.

5.	The most popular selection today of Yuan drama is *Yuanqu xuan*, edited by Zang Maoxun in 1615 and 1616. The principal edition of the Yuan dramas used for referencing in this chapter is that edited by Zang Maoxun, and included in a new (1995) edition of the great Qing dynasty encyclopaedia published as *Xuxiu Siku quanshu*. Vols. 1760–1762 include texts of 100 Yuan dramas. Another 60 texts are contained in a supplement to this: Sui Shusen, ed., *Yuanqu xuan waibian*. Unless otherwise stated, all English translations here are by the authors.

6. Rex Gibson, *Teaching Shakespeare*, p. 81.

7. See, for example, M. H. Abrams, *A glossary of literary terms*, p. 27: high comedy is that which elicits "thoughtful laughter from spectators who remain emotionally detached from the action at the spectacle of folly, pretentiousness, and incongruity in human behavior". Low comedy "makes little or no intellectual appeal, undertakes to arouse laughter by jokes, or 'gags' and by slapstick humor or boisterous or clownish physical activity".

8. See, for instance, Chen Fangying, "*Handan ji* de xiju qingdiao", and Wang Zhiyong, "*Handan ji* de xiju yishi duhou" (discussed throughout both articles).

9. Cited in L. J. Potts, *Comedy*, p. 79.

10. Potts, *Comedy*, p. 87.

11. For example, Potts, *Comedy*, p. 77.

12. For examples, see Abrams, *A glossary*, p. 89, where he also defines verbal irony as "a statement in which the implicit meaning intended by the speaker differs from that which he ostensibly asserts".

13. Act 3, Sc. 2, ll. 82, 87, 94, 99 and 125, 127, 151, 212, and 214. Citations are from Peter Alexander, ed., *The complete works of William Shakespeare*.

14. Many studies deal with aspects of Yingying, the leading comic character in *Xixiang ji* — for example, Yan Changke, "*Xixiang ji* de xiju tese", and Zhang Shuxiang, "*Xixiang ji* de xiju chengfen".

15. *Xixiang ji*, Vol. 3, Act 2, Song 3, in Sui Shusen, *Yuanqu xuan waibian*, p. 289.

16. *Xixiang ji*, Vol. 3, Act 2, Song 3, in Sui, *Yuanqu xuan waibian*, p. 290.

17. *Xixiang ji*, Vol. 3, Act 2, Song 3, in Sui, *Yuanqu xuan waibian*, p. 290.

18. Abrams, *A glossary*, p. 89; Gibson, *Teaching Shakespeare*, p. 78.

19. *Macbeth*, Act 1, Sc. 4, l. 13 (Alexander, *The complete works*, p. 1054).

20. *Jinqian ji*, Act 2, Song 7, in Zang, *Yuanqu xuan*, Vol. 1760, p. 301b.

21. Zang, *Yuanqu xuan*, Act 2, Song 7 *houbai* 後白, Vol. 1760, p. 302a.

22. The traditional literary theory of "inconsistency" (better known in humour studies as "incongruity theory") identifies one important source of the comic. For this and other established theories of comedy, see Allardyce Nicoll, *The theory of drama*, a classic work much relied on in China since its 1985 translation by Xu Shihu under the title *Xi'Ou xiju lilun*; pp. 252–4 deal with inconsistency theory.

23. Paul Lewis, *Comic effects: Interdisciplinary approaches to humor in literature*, pp. 72–3.

24. *Zhu wu ting qin*, Act 3, Song 4 *houbai*, in Zang, *Yuanqu xuan*, Vol. 1762, pp. 363a–b.

25. Henri Bergson, *Laughter: An essay on the meaning of the comic,* trans. Cloudesley Brereton and Fred Rothwell, pp. 22–4 and 47–8.

26. *Jinxian chi,* in Zang, *Yuanqu xuan,* Vol. 1762, pp. 177b–8b.

27. *Fengguang hao,* in Zang, *Yuanqu xuan,* Vol. 1761, pp. 123a–4a.

28. *Xie Tianxiang,* in Zang, *Yuanqu xuan,* Vol. 1760, pp. 420a, 421b, 422a, 423a.

29. For discussion of impromptu gags and examples of stage effects in Chinese comedy, see Xu Jinbang, *Yuan zaju gailun,* pp. 245–60.

30. Barrett H. Clark, *European theories of the drama,* p. 392.

31. The connotations of the term *huaji* are discussed in Chapter 4 of this volume, by Weihe Xu, and Chapter 1, by Jocelyn Chey. For discussion of the purposes of satire, see Charles A. Knight, *The literature of satire,* pp. 1–8.

32. Zhang Li in *"The good person of Sichuan* and the Chinese cultural tradition", pp. 133–56, claims this play provided the inspiration for Berthold Brecht's drama from 1940, *Der gute Mensch von Sezuan* (*The good person of Sichuan*).

33. Guan Hanqing, *Jiu fengchen,* Act 1, Song 9, in Zang, *Yuanqu xuan,* Vol. 1760, p. 472b.

34. Guan, *Jiu fengchen,* Act 2, Song 10, in Zang, *Yuanqu xuan,* Vol. 1760, p. 474b.

35. Cyril Birch notes the significance of food imagery in classical Chinese drama in "Tragedy and melodrama in early *ch'uan-ch'i* plays: 'Lute song' and 'Thorn hairpin' compared" (translated by Lai Ruihe as "Zaoqi quanqi zhong de beiju yu naoju: 'Pipa ji' yu 'Jingchai ji' bijiao), pp. 237–40 and throughout. In *Jiu fengchen,* food imagery serves at least two purposes: realist portrayal of the daily life of people of lower social classes; and comic effect by making fun of "the bad guys". More examples and discussion of imagery of dining and food are found in Wang Shouzhi, *Yuan zaju xiju yishu,* pp. 152–3.

36. Guan Hanqing, *Jiu fengchen,* Act 3, Song 1, in Zang, *Yuanqu xuan,* Vol. 1760, p. 475a.

37. Identified and discussed by Sigmund Freud in Chapter 5, "Slips of the tongue", in *The psychopathology of everyday life,* pp. 53–102. This influential 1901 book was translated into Chinese by Lin Keming 林克明 in 1987 as *Richang shenghuo de xinli fenxi.*

38. Gibson, *Teaching Shakespeare,* p. 71.

39. *Fu Jinding, Xiezi* 楔子 (Opening act), dialogue before Song 1, in Sui, *Yuanqu xuan waibian,* p. 996.

40. Gibson, *Teaching Shakespeare,* p. 71.

41. *Yu Jingtai,* Act 4, Song 11, in Zang, *Yuanqu xuan,* Vol. 1760, p. 375b.

42. *Hong li hua,* Act 2, poem following Song 5, in, Zang, *Yuanqu xuan,* Vol. 1762, p. 5a.

43. Among many other critics, Potts, *Comedy*, p. 81, regards the use of poetry as one of four leading characteristics of Shakespearean comedy.

44. Potts, *Comedy*; Gibson, *Teaching Shakespeare*, p. 81; see also more recent criticism such as Penny Gay, *The Cambridge introduction to Shakespeare's comedies*, pp. 63–66, 97, amongst others.

45. Wang Shifu, *Xixiang ji*, Book 4, Act 3, Song 6, in Sui, *Yuanqu xuan waibian*, p. 317.

46. Various terms were applied to these highly trained entertainers, such as *ge ji* 歌妓 (singing female entertainer or singing courtesan), *ge ji* 歌姬 (singing beauty) and *ou zhe* 謳者 (singer). The role of sing-song girls developed a particular social significance in the late Qing period, as attested by the 1892 fictional masterpiece by Han Bangqing 漢邦卿 (1856–1894), *Haishang hua liezhuan* 海上花列傳 (Sing-song girls of Shanghai, also known as *Flowers of Shanghai*), translated by Eileen Chang under the title *The sing-song girls of Shanghai*.

47. *Xie Tianxiang*, in Zang, *Yuanqu xuan*, Vol. 1760, pp. 425b–6b.

48. Abrams, *A glossary*, p. 149, defines pun (homophonic pun) as "a play on words that are either identical in sound (homonyms) or similar in sound, but are sharply diverse in meaning".

49. For more on puns in Chinese drama, see Wang Jisi, "Yuan zaju zhong de xieyin shuangguanyu", and on puns in Chinese language generally Chapter 1 in this volume by Jocelyn Chey.

50. *Jiu Fengchen*, Act 1, dialogue after Song 7, in Zang, *Yuanqu xuan*, Vol. 1760, p. 472b.

51. *Jiu Fengchen*, dialogue after Song 13, in Zang, *Yuanqu xuan*, Vol. 1760, p. 473b.

52. This point is discussed by K. C. Leung, "*Chiu feng-chen* 《救風塵》: Anatomy of a thirteenth-century Chinese comedy", pp. 80–5.

53. *Zhu wu ting qin*, Act 2, dialogue after Song 9, in Zang, *Yuanqu xuan*, Vol. 1762, p. 361a. Bao Zheng (999–1062) was a much-praised official who served during the reign of Emperor Renzong of the Northern Song dynasty and is still invoked today as the symbol of justice. Both the English word pagoda and the Chinese word *futu* are probably derived from the Persian *butkada* (shrine for an idol).

54. *Zhu wu ting qin*, Act 2, Song 5, in Zang, *Yuanqu xuan*, Vol. 1762, pp. 360a–b.

55. See Abrams, *A glossary*, p. 28.

56. The text of *Han gong qiu* can be found under its full title, *Po you meng gu yan Han gong qiu zaju* 破幽夢孤雁漢宮秋雜劇 (*Zaju* drama "The solitary wild goose breaks the secluded dreams of autumn in the Han palace"), in Zang, *Yuanqu xuan*, Vol. 1760, pp. 282–93.

57. See Timoteus Pokora, "Ironical critics at ancient Chinese courts (*Shih chi*, 126)", pp. 49–64, discussing the licence granted to witty jesters at

imperial courts in ancient China to "speak the truth" and Chapter 4 in this volume, by Weihe Xu. The earliest records from the first century CE almost certainly predate comparable Western examples (e.g. from Byzantine and early mediaeval courts): see Beatrice K. Otto, *Fools are everywhere: The court jester around the world*, pp. 105–6, 280.

58. Ashley Thorpe, *The role of the* chou *("clown") in traditional Chinese drama: Comedy, criticism and cosmology on the Chinese stage*, focuses on the role of the jester in ritual admonition (especially pp. 15–24). Taking an anthropological perspective, it compares China with several other cultures.

59. For the Daoist approach to the use of humour in teaching, see Chapter 5 in this volume, by Shirley Chan.

60. For a discussion of these themes, see Andy Shui-lung Fung, *Yuandai aiqing xiju zhuti fenxi* (a summary version is in *Yuanqu baike dacidian*).

61. The online blurb for the 2004 production, directed by Yueh Feng 岳楓, starring Ivy Ling Po and Li Ching, reads: "a beloved on-screen couple even though both are female — Ling Po is renowned for playing male Cantonese opera roles. While visiting a temple, a young scholar is enchanted by the daughter of an important family. When rebels threaten to abduct the girl, the scholar with the assistance of a clever maid, try [sic] to save her. In addition, the young maid help [sic] bring together the young couple in spite of her family's objections." Available at http://www.56.com/u22/v_MjQzNDYxNzk.html (accessed 12 February 2010).

Chapter 8

1. This analysis is based on these editions of the novel: Cao Xueqin, *Honglou meng bashi hui jiaoben* 紅樓夢八十回校本 (ed. Yu Pingbo 愈平伯, hereafter *HLMBS*); Cao Xueqin, *The Story of the stone*, Vols 1, 2 and 3, trans. David Hawkes and John Minford; and Cao Xueqin, *The Story of the stone*, Vols 4 and 5, trans. John Minford (both hereafter *SS*). When necessary, the author uses his own translation, particularly when these others privilege the flavour of the original over precision.

2. Tradition has it that Gao E authored the novel's last 40 chapters, but this view has recently been challenged: see Du Zhijun 杜志軍, "Xin shiqi Hongxue sanshinian: 1978–2008" 新時期紅學三十年: 1978–2008 (Thirty years of Redology in the new era: 1978–2008).

3. Only recently have students of *Honglou meng* seemed to rediscover its humour. For two of the latest studies, see He Xinmin, "Yishu hua za lüye chou — *Honglou meng* de xiju tese yu xiju jingshen"; and Dong Yaping, "Qianxi Lin Daiyu de youmo".

4. Zhu Yixuan, Honglou meng *ziliao huibian*, pp. 703, 723. *Xiangyuan* refers to people whom Confucius had condemned as thieves of virtue (*de zhi zei* 德之賊) because, as Mencius later explained, they pretended to be

virtuous in order to please the public, just as eunuchs played up to their lord. But by appearing to be what they were not (*si er fei* 似而非), they confounded the semblance of virtue with virtue itself. See *Lunyu baihua jinyi*, 17.13, p. 178; and *Mengzi baihua jinyi*, 7B.37, p. 15. For more examples of vilification of Baochai, see Yisu, *Honglou meng juan*, pp. 51, 193, 195, 211, 234, 228, 229, 232, 304, 423, 476 and 778; Zhu, *Honglou meng ziliao huibian*, pp. 639, 703, 723, 778, 789 and 792; Sun Ailing, "Daguanyuan zhong wenrou de 'li' jian"; and Zou Zizhen, "*Honglou meng* de si dui yishu bianzhengfa".

5.   C. T. Hsia, *The classical Chinese novel*, p. 289; Jing Wang, *The story of stone: Intertextuality, ancient Chinese stone lore, and the stone symbolism of* Dream of the red chamber, Water margin, *and* The Journey to the West, p. 126; and Cao Xueqin and Gao E, *Honglou meng*, Vol. 1, p. 465, Vol. 2, p. 895.

6.   Yang Luosheng, "Manshuo Xue Baochai de leng".

7.   Zhang Wenzhen, "Lun Xue Baochai de 'su'".

8.   Li Xifan, "*Honglou meng* yu Ming Qing renwen sixiang"; and Li Xifan and Li Meng, "Ketan tingjide' — Xue Baochai lun". Interestingly, Li Xifan used to be the most famous of modern Baochai haters. See Li Xifan and Lan Ling, "*Honglou meng* zhong liangge duili de dianxing — Lin Daiyu he Xue Baochai", pp. 218–27.

9.   For a discussion of this trend, see Sun Weike, "Hongxue zhong renwu pingjia de fangfalun pingxi".

10.   Henry W. Wells, *Traditional Chinese humor: A study in art and literature*, p. 168.

11.   Wang, *The story of stone*, p. 126.

12.   Wang, *The story of stone*, p. 126. Ironically, Jing Wang's discussion shows she is not completely blind to Baochai's wit.

13.   For a discussion of this belief, see Chapter 4 in this volume, on the classical Confucian concepts of emotion and proper humour.

14.   For detailed discussion of the nature and significance of *qi* in human character and behaviour, including the use of humour, Chapter 3 in this volume, by Rey Tiquia.

15.   For their Chinese definitions, see also *Hanyu da cidian*, pp. 4315, 4316.

16.   Neo-Confucianism is a late, enriched, but puritanical school of Confucianism which arose in the eleventh century and dominated the next 800 years of Chinese thought.

17.   See, for instance, *SS* 56: 68; and *HLMBS* 56: 610, where she cites an essay by Zhu Xi from his collected writings published in the Qing dynasty. Although his authorship of this piece is now generally discredited, its mention evinces Baochai's familiarity with this collection.

18.   See Chen Zhao, *Honglou meng xiaokao*, pp. 101–2.

19.   This phrase is used in the novel to describe another girl, Xing Xiuyan 邢岫煙, see *HLMBS* 57: 632; cf. *SS* 57: 106.

20. Here, and for other aspects of this discussion, see Chapter 4 in this volume.

21. See *SS* 37: 235; 42: 333 and *HLMBS* 37: 396; 42: 448.

22. Bai Lingjie, "Guanyu Baochai de cang yu lou"; and Wang Yuchun, "Xue Baochai de shuangchong xingge yu duzhe de shuangchong pingjia chidu".

23. In quoting from published translations, some orthographical details such as hyphenations in characters' names have been standardized for consistency.

24. Baochai's last name 薛 and "snow" 雪 are homophones with different tones, where *Xue* (family name) is first tone and *xue* (snow) third tone. Since homophones abound in Chinese, punning is a common form of Chinese humour.

25. See Zhu, Honglou meng *ziliao huibian*, p. 406. Zhiyanzhai is known for both his evidently close relationship with Cao Xueqin and his inside information about the conception of *Honglou meng*. Perhaps originally referring to one person, the name is commonly used to designate a group of such relatives/friends as commentators.

26. Zhu, Honglou meng *ziliao huibian*, p. 406.

27. *SS* 42: 35; *HLMBS* 42: 449. Xifeng is Wang Xifeng 王熙鳳, a maternal cousin of Baoyu's and the wife of Jia Lian 賈璉, his paternal cousin. She is noted for her lively sense of humour.

28. See Yisu, Honglou meng *juan*, p. 185; and Zhu, Honglou meng *ziliao huibian*, p. 575.

29. Ban Zhao 班昭 (c.40–c.120), "Women's precepts", pp. 99, 100.

30. *HLMBS* 64: 716, my translation.

31. See *Liji* 禮記, pp. 19, 20, 203 and 206; and *Mengzi baihua jinyi*, 3B.3, p. 130.

32. *Mengzi baihua jinyi*, 3B.3.

33. Aroma is Baoyu's primary maid, and as such has a sexual relationship with him.

34. See *Hanyu da cidian*, p. 4946.

35. Cai Yijiang, Honglou meng *shi ci qu fu pingzhu*, p. 212.

36. The Chinese believe that the cold nature of crabs can be harmful to health if consumed improperly.

37. Intentional abuse of Baochai would be the last thing on Baoyu's mind, since he is always gentle and considerate to the girls. But we cannot be so sure of Daiyu's intentions, considering her wit and craftiness.

38. Sun Xun, Honglou meng *jianshang cidian*, p. 182.

39. Ban, "Women's precepts", p. 98.

40. Baoyu is the heir of the clan. See Cai, Honglou meng *shi ci qu fu pingzhu*, pp. 298–300.

41. *SS* 5: 146; *HLMBS* 5: 57. For a discussion of the origin, humour and significance of the term *yiyin* (the lust of mind), see Weihe Xu, "Lun *Honglou meng* zhong 'yiyin' yici de chuchu jiqi youmo yu yiyi".

42. Maids such as Aroma make it clear they would happily be his concubine.

43. Baochai used to visit Baoyu without apparent concern. However, in Chapter 28 the narrator informs us that, having become aware of a possible match between them, Baochai is deliberately choosing decorum and beginning to distance herself, usually needing an excuse to visit. In Chapter 36, however, she violates this by simply wanting to have a chat with Baoyu and "help him to dispel the sleepiness of the early afternoon". This visit results in a "touching domestic scene" infused with romantic, even erotic insinuations (*SS* 36: 202–3; *HLMBS* 36: 378).

44. Hawkes' translation, *SS* 19: 391; *HLMBS* 19: 194.

45. See Huang Huaixin, ed., *Da Dai Liji huijiao jizhu*, Vol. 2, p. 1388; Liu Xiang, "Gu *Lienü zhuan*", *juan* 2, pp. 43–4; and [née] Zheng, *Nü xiao jing*, p. 14.

46. *Webster's new world dictionary of the American language*.

47. The other three vices are alcoholism (*jiu* 酒), lechery (*se* 色) and greed for wealth (*cai* 財).

48. See commentary by Wang Meng in Cao and Gao, *Honglou meng*, p. 453.

49. *SS* 42: 33–34; *HLMBS* 42: 448–9.

50. *SS* 45: 398; 57: 111–12; *HLMBS* 45: 482; 57: 635.

51. See Chapter 4 in this volume.

52. See E. M. Forster, "Flat and round characters".

53. See Sigmund Freud, *Jokes and their relation to the unconscious*, Chs 2, 3 and 6.

Chapter 9

1. Part I was published in the 16 January 1934 issue; Parts II and III in the 16 February 1934 issue. The source-text for this translation is *Lun youmo* 論幽默, in *Lun youmo – Lin Yutang youmo wenxuan* 論幽默－林語堂幽默文選 (On humour — The collection of Lin Yutang's humorous writings), vol. 1, pp. 1–14. Original complex Chinese text ©1994 Linking Publishing Company. Translated with permission. Variations from the 1934 text are noted. Annotations by Joseph C. Sample.

2. First published in April 1877 in *The New Quarterly Magazine* (published by Ward Lock and Tyler, London between 1873 and 1880). The London Institution, founded in 1806, was an early provider of scientific education for the general public.

3. Republished in 1963, available online from Project Gutenberg.

4. George Meredith, *An Essay on comedy and the uses of the Comic Spirit*, p. 88. Where Lin Yutang directly translates Meredith's text, the English passage quoted is inserted, using this roughly contemporaneous edition,

including Meredith's liberal use of capitalization and indicating any omissions with square brackets, as here. For comparison, the Chinese text reads: 我想一國文化的極好的衡量，是看他喜劇及俳調之發達，而真正的喜劇標準，是看他能否引起含蓄思想的笑。麥蒂烈斯《劇論》.

5. Omar Khayyam (1051?–1123?): Persian poet, astronomer, philosopher and mathematician.

6. From the *Shijing* 詩經 (Book of poetry), p. 69.

7. *Shijing,* p. 53.

8. The Grand Historian is Sima Qian 司馬遷 (c.145–80 BCE). Zhuangzi 莊子 and Laozi 老子 were leading Daoist philosophers; for more on Daoist attitudes to humour and laughter, see Chapter 5 in this volume by Shirley Chan.

9. Gui Guzi 鬼谷子 (fourth century BCE) was from the powerful state of Chu, which existed from 740 to 330 BCE. Chunyu Kun 淳于髡 (fourth century BCE) was reputedly very learned and a clever *huaji* wit. An idler and hanger-on at the house of his father-in-law, he became a favourite of King Wei of Qi (357–320 BCE) and even a member of a famous academic academy. See David R. Knechtges, "Wit, humor, and satire in early Chinese literature (to A.D. 220)".

10. Yang Zhu 楊朱 (fourth century BCE) was a philosopher from the state of Wei who expounded egoism as opposed to the philosophy of universal love of Mozi 墨子 (or 墨翟) (468–376 BCE).

11. The mid-ancient or medieval period generally refers to the Qin 秦 (221–207 BCE) and Han 汉 (206 BCE–220 CE) dynasties.

12. "Laozi Hanfeizi zhuan" 老子韓非列傳 (Biographies of Laozi and Han Fei Zi), in Sima Qian, *Shiji* 史記 (Records of the Grand Historian), no. 3, *juan* 63.

13. Qu Yuan 屈原 (343–290? BCE) was a patriotic scholar and minister in the southern Chu kingdom. Jia Yi 賈誼 (200–168 BCE) was a writer and political commentator of the Han dynasty.

14. *Yuti* is a transliteration that Lin uses for "wit".

15. Confucius was opposed to murder; however, when he served as a minister of justice in 496 BCE, another minister, Shao Zhengmao 少正卯, caused the government to plunge into disorder and was therefore executed on Confucius's order. See Sima Qian's account of Confucius's family history (*Kongzi shijia di shiqi* 孔子世家) in *Shiji*, no. 7, *juan* 47. A story from the *Xianjin* 先進 section of *Lunyu* 論語 (The analects, *juan* 26) reports Confucius asking his disciples their aspirations. When Zeng Dian 曾點 shared his ideal life (bathing in the river with his friends, then singing while walking home after drying himself on the grass on the hills), Confucius commented, "I agree with Dian".

16. This is from *Mengzi* (The book of Mencius), p. 338.

17.	Given another reference later to the parable, here is a brief explanation. In this story, a proud man tells his wife and his concubine that he spends all day with his wealthy and well-known friends, eating and drinking heartily. One day the wife and the concubine secretly follow him and discover that he goes to a nearby cemetery and begs for scraps from other people's sacrificial food offerings. When the man returns home that evening as complacent as ever, his wife and his concubine are sitting outside crying. The term *qiren* 齊人 (person from Qi) is now used to refer to a beggar. See the memoirs of Zhu Xi, *Zhuzi quanshu*, vol. 12, p. 301.

18.	Han Fei 韓非 (c. 280–233 BCE) was one of the philosophers who founded the Legalist School.

19.	Mei Gao 枚皋 (b. 153 BCE) and Dongfang Shuo 東方朔 (c.161–87 BCE) A well-known story about Dongfang says that he once secretly drank the emperor's wine that was thought to make one immortal. When he was discovered, very drunk, the emperor ordered his execution. Dongfang Shuo quickly pointed out that if he were executed, this would prove that the wine was fake, causing great embarrassment for the emperor. The emperor spared Dongfang's life. See William H. Nienhauser, *The Indiana companion to traditional Chinese literature*, pp. 618–19.

20.	The witticisms and jests of Wang Bi 王弼 (226–249) and He Yan 何晏 (190–249) were collected in the Han-dynasty compilation *Shishuo xinyu* 世説新語 (A new account of tales of the world). See Chapter 6 in this volume, by Lily Xiao Hong Lee, for detailed discussion.

21.	Refers to the feudal state of Qin (879–221 BCE) in the Zhou dynasty (c. 1100–256 BCE), which later unified the whole country under the Qin dynasty (221–207 BCE).

22.	Tao Qian 陶潛 (365–427), also known as Tao Yuanming 陶淵明, briefly held several government positions but resigned them when he realized it was merely for economic reasons: this he considered equivalent to enslaving himself to his mouth and stomach. Ashamed at having compromised his principles, he died poor but apparently content. See Nienhauser, *The Indiana companion*, pp. 766–8.

23.	Neo-Confucianism generally refers to a school of reason during the Song dynasty (900–1200), devoted to a rational study of the natural sciences and of the Chinese classics. See Chapter 4 in this volume, by Weihe Xu, for a discussion of the implications of these attitudes for humour.

24.	Jie 桀 (personal name Gui 紂) was the last king of the Xia dynasty, which collapsed c.1600 BCE. Fan Ning 范寧 (339–401) was a magistrate who attached great weight to Confucianism and was opposed to the Spiritualism of Wang Bi and He Yan.

25.	The emperors Tang 湯 and Wu 武 were founders of the Shang 商 (1783–1123 BCE) and Zhou 周 (1100–256 BCE) dynasties, respectively. Yao 堯 (2357–2255 BCE) and Shun 舜 (around 2200 BCE) were two of the most celebrated sage kings in ancient China. Their reigns were known for peace and order.

26.   The Duke of Zhou (d. 1204 BCE) was credited by Confucians with establishing a number of rituals. Xunzi 荀子 (312?–230? BCE), a contemporary and rival of Mencius, represented another important development of Confucius' teaching with emphasis on scholarship and rituals.

27.   This story is from "The man from the State of Qi, his wife, and his concubine". See also note 18.

28.   Han Yu (768–824), *Han Yu quanji*; Li Yu (1610–1680), *Li Yu quanji*.

29.   Lin writes about the School of Self-Expression (*xingling pai* 性靈派) in his *The importance of living*, pp. 389–92. The members of this school demanded that writers express only their own thoughts and feelings. Thus they opposed imitation of the ancients and the moderns and any literary technique with strict rules. The writers Ding An 定盦 (1792–1841), Yuan Zhonglang 袁中郎 (1568–1610) and Zi Cai 子才 (1716–1798) are better known by the names Gong Zizhen 龔自珍, Yuan Hongdao 袁宏道 and Yuan Mei 袁枚, respectively. Yuan Hongdao was one of the founding brothers of the School of Self-Expression. See Diran J. Sohigian, "The life and times of Lin Yutang", for a discussion of these writers and their influence on Lin's writings.

30.   By Zhou Mi 周密 (1232–98).

31.   Leading characters in the novel by Shi Nai'an 施耐庵 (1296–1372).

32.   By Wu Cheng'en 吳承恩 (1505–80).

33.   By Wu Jingzi 吳敬梓 (1701–54).

34.   By Li Ruzhen 李汝珍 (1763–1830).

35.   By Liu E 劉鶚 (1857–1909).

36.   Inferior studies and employment were known as *xiaodao* 小道 and included such occupations as husbandry, divining and medicine.

37.   Excerpted from the entry on Zhao Pu 趙普 (922–992) in "Ba chao mingchen yanxing lu" 八朝名臣言行錄 (The words and deeds of famous ministers of eight dynasties), in Zhu Xi, *Zhuzi quanshu*, Vol. 12. Zhao helped the king of Han to recruit and enlist soldiers. The king of Han was a posthumous title; Taizu 太祖 is a title given to a dynasty's founding emperor.

38.   Emperor Shi Zong 世宗 was the ruler from whom Taizu wrested power. He served during the Jin dynasty (1115–1234) from 1161 to 1189.

39.   The Chai clan 柴氏 was the previous dynasty's ruling family.

40.   George Bernard Shaw, The man of destiny: *and* How he lied to her husband: *Two plays*, p. 75. Actually, a lieutenant made this remark.

41.   Given the difficulties confronting Lin in translating this piece of rather purple prose, his Chinese text is appended. It is, as Lin acknowledged, necessarily somewhat sketchy, but captures the essence of Meredith's original:

假使你相信文化是基於明理，你就在靜觀人類之時，窺見在上有一種神靈，耿耿的鑒察的一切…他有聖賢的頭額，嘴唇從容不緊不鬆的半開著，兩個唇邊，藏著林神的諧謔。那像弓形的稱心享樂的微笑，在古時是林神響亮的狂笑，撲地叫眉毛倒豎起來。那個笑聲會再來的，但是這回已屬於荒爾微笑一類的，是和緩恰當的，所表示的是心靈的光輝與智慧的豐富，而不是胡盧笑鬧。常時的態度，是一種開逸的觀察，好像飽觀一場，等著擇肥而噬，而心裡卻不著急。人類之將來，不是他所注意的;他所注意是人類目前之老實與形樣之整齊。無論何時人類失了體態，誇張，矯揉，自大，放誕，虛偽，炫飾，纖弱過甚；無論何時何地他看見人類懵懂自欺，淫侈奢欲，崇拜偶像，作出荒謬事情，眼光如豆的經營，如癡如狂的計較，無論何時人類言行不符，或倨傲不遜，屈人揚己，或執迷不悟，強詞奪理，或夜郎自大惺惺作態，無論是個人或是團體；這在上之神就出溫柔的謔意，斜覰他們，跟著是一陣如明珠落玉盤的笑聲。這就是俳調之神 (The Comic Spirit)。

42. This phrase, "volleys of silvery laughter", offers a good example of Lin's success in meeting the translational challenge: he pleasingly renders it as "a laugh like pearls falling into a jade platter".

43. Meredith, *An essay on comedy*, pp. 88–90.

44. Meredith, *An essay on comedy*, pp. 78–80.

45. "Wisecracking satire" (俏皮諷刺) is a combination of *qiaopi* 俏皮 (a wisecrack; a jibe; a clever remark) and *fengci* 諷刺 (to mock; to satirize; sarcasm; irony).

46. Lin implies here that those who supported only writing socially critical commentaries were motivated by desires similar to those of orthodox Confucian scholars. Traditionally, scholars were critical in commenting on current events in relation to the metaphysical Way. Such commentaries became essays, but their inherent personal involvement, as with the leftist writers, prevented them from being detached or introspective.

47. Immanuel Kant, *Kant's Critique of judgement*, p. 223.

48. Sigmund Freud, *Wit and its relation to the unconscious*, p. 61.

49. To earn salaries by reviewing old things (*wen gu er zhi xin* 溫故而支薪) is a clever play on words. It is taken from the phrase "to learn new things by reviewing old things" (*wen gu er zhi xin* 溫故而知新). The phrases "to learn new things" (*zhi xin* 知新) and "to earn a salary" (*zhi xin* 支薪) sound the same in Chinese.

50. Wang Jingwei 汪精衛 (1883–1944) was a prominent politician who established a pro-Japan government in Nanjing during the Sino-Japanese War (1937–45). Wu Zhihui 吳稚暉 (1865–1953) was a former anarchist, elder statesman and founding member of the Nationalist (KMT) Party. In 1938, Wang Jingwei went into hiding in Hanoi, Vietnam, where he composed a poem called "Luoye ci" 落葉辭 (Poem about the fallen leaves), in which he expressed pessimism about the war. He sent the poem to high-ranking KMT officials in Chongqing, and Wu Zhihui also

received a copy. Wu wrote a poem in reply using the same rhyme schemes vehemently denouncing Wang's pessimistic views. This evoked strong repercussions in literary circles and was referred to as the "poem that swept away the fallen leaves of Wang". Wang died before the Japanese were defeated, and consequently avoided the ignominy of being tried and convicted as a traitor and war criminal. Despite many worthwhile achievements before his defection, Wang is generally regarded as a traitor and held in contempt by most Chinese. The sentence referring to the Wang–Wu debate appears in the 1934 version of Lin's essay but is omitted from some published versions including the source-text.

51.   Gongsun 公孫 was the family name of a legendary woman who performed a dance called the *jianqi* 劍器; it is perhaps best known because of a poem by Du Fu 杜甫 (712–770) titled "The ballad on seeing a pupil of the Lady Gongsun dance the sword mime". The dance combined flowing rhythms with vigorous attacking movements.

52.   Lloyd George (1863–1945), British Prime Minister from 1916 to 1922.

53.   King Xuan 齊宣王 (d. 301 BCE) ruled the State of Qi (?–320 BCE) during the Warring States period. Wu Yan 無鹽 was the place where an unattractive but moralistic woman confronted the king, telling him he was wasteful and corrupt. The king was so moved by her honesty that he made her his wife. The term *wu yan* 無鹽 is now synonymous with one who is unattractive.

54.   King Wei 齊威王 was known for leading an indolent and dissipated life. This story is found in *Huaji liezhuan* 滑稽列傳 (Collective biographies of the *huaji*-ists), in Sima Qian, *Shiji*, Vol. 10, *juan* 126, or *Liezhuan* 列傳 (Biographies), *juan* 66.

55.   Zhang Chang 張敞 (d. 48 BCE) was an official of the Han dynasty who was known chiefly for painting his wife's eyebrows. The phrase "Zhang Chang paints his wife's eyebrows" is now a phrase used to refer to marital bliss.

56.   Hermann, Graf von Keyserling (1880–1946) arranged and edited *The book of marriage* in German (1925) and in English (1926). Keyserling reports (p. iii) that Shaw continued, "Unless, that is, he hates her, like Strindberg, and I don't. I shall read the volume with interest knowing that it will chiefly consist of evasion; but I will not contribute to it."

57.   Will Rogers (1879–1935) was one of the last of the so-called cracker-barrel philosophers, a tradition of American humour that includes Ben Franklin, Abraham Lincoln and Mark Twain.

58.   George Bernard Shaw (1856–1950) caused a stir on a trip to Hong Kong when he told a group of students, "Should you not be a Red revolutionary before the age of twenty, you will end up a hopeless fossil by fifty, but should you be a Red revolutionary by twenty, you may be all right by forty." Lu Xun criticized Shaw, noting that "Becoming famous by

'promoting "isms" is the trend among today's scholars", and adding that Shaw "promoted Communism by sitting in an easy chair with smiling complacency. Gaining fame by isms is like displaying a sheep's head yet selling dog meat to cheat buyers. What a deception!" See Florence Chien, "Lu Xun's six essays in defense of Bernard Shaw", p. 63.

59. Wasp's waists (*feng yao* 蜂腰) and crane's knees (*he xi* 鶴膝) are errors in versification, two of the eight standard faults in writing Chinese poetry.

60. This final sentence appears in the 1934 text of Lin's essay but is omitted from some published versions, including the source-text.

Chapter 10

1.   Lu Xun, "Yi si er xing" (Think before you do), in *Lu Xun quanji*, Vol. 5, p. 499. Translations from Chinese to English in this chapter are the author's, unless otherwise noted.

2.   For a more theoretical discussion of the humour phenomenon in modern Chinese literature and culture, see Diran John Sohigian, "Contagion of laughter: The rise of the humor phenomenon in Shanghai in the 1930s"; and Qian Suoqiao, "Translating 'humor' Into Chinese culture". This chapter builds upon available biographical sources on Lin Yutang, such as Sohigian's 1991 dissertation "The life and times of Lin Yutang" (the first biographical study on the life and times of Lin Yutang); Lin Taiyi, *Lin Yutang zhuan*; and Wan Pingjin, *Lin Yutang pingzhuan*. It also utilizes new source materials hitherto neglected, particularly Lin's bilingual and English essays written during his Shanghai years.

3.   As the author has noted elsewhere (Qian, "Translating 'humor'", 293, n. 4), Lin Yutang was not the first to attempt to translate the word humour into Chinese, but was the first to translate it as *youmo* 幽默, which became the current usage and a cross-cultural event. Wang Guowei, for instance, translated humour as *oumuya* 歐穆亞 in 1906. See also Christopher G. Rea, "A history of laughter: Comic culture in early twentieth-century China".

4.   Lin Yutang, *Memoirs of an octogenarian*, pp. 64–5.

5.   Lin Yutang, preface to *Letters of a Chinese Amazon and war-time essays*, pp. v–vi.

6.   Lin Yutang, "The little critic", *The China Critic*, 11 September 1930, 874.

7.   The issue of the collaboration between Lu Xun and the Chinese Communist Party still awaits serious critical reflection, as it is little touched upon even in more recent biographical studies on Lu Xun — see, for instance, Wang Xiaoming, *Lu Xun zhuan*.

8.   Lin Yutang, "Lusin [Lu Xun]", *The China Critic* (6 December 1928), 548.

9.   Lin, "The little critic", *The China Critic*, 11 September 1930, 874.

10. Lin, "The Little critic", *The China Critic*, 11 September 1930, 874.

11. Lin Yutang, *xu* (preface) to *Dahuang ji*, p. 2.

12. See Benedetto Croce, *The essence of aesthetic*. Lin Yutang introduced the Crocean aesthetic theory by way of American interpreters such as J. E. Spingarn. Sohigian ("The life and times", pp. 240–8) outlines Lin's translation of Spingarn's essay on criticism and its importance in the development of Lin's literary theory. In *Liberal cosmopolitan: Lin Yutang and alternative Chinese modernity* (forthcoming), the author discusses in detail Lin's cross-cultural aesthetics of integrating the Crocean theory and Chinese *xingling* 性靈 school of thought.

13. For a detailed account of the case, see Zhang Kebiao, "Lin Yutang zai Shanghai".

14. Tang Xiguang 唐錫光, *Wo yu Kaiming* 我與開明 (Kaiming Bookstore and me), quoted in Wan Pingjin, *Lin Yutang pingzhuan*, p. 116.

15. Lin Yutang, *Xinde wenping*.

16. Durham S. F. Chen, "Dr. Lin as I know him: Some random recollections".

17. Chen, "Dr. Lin as I know him", 256.

18. Lin Yutang, "The little critic", *The China Critic* (3 July 1930), 636.

19. Lin, "The little critic", *The China Critic* (3 July 1930), 636.

20. Lin, "The little critic", *The China Critic* (3 July 1930), 636.

21. Lin Yutang, preface to *The little critic: Essays, satires and sketches on China (First series: 1930–1932)*, p. iv.

22. Lin, *Memoirs*, p. 69.

23. Little is known about Lin's year-long sojourn in Europe, mostly in England. According to his elder daughter, he was working on his invention of a Chinese typewriter, but without success. See Lin Taiyi, *Lin Yutang zhuan*, pp. 64–6.

24. One of the romantic aspects of Shao's lifestyle was his well-known affair with the American writer Emily Hahn, who lived openly in Shao's house together with his family. For a more detailed study, see Leo Ou-fan Lee, *Shanghai modern: The flowering of a new urban culture in China, 1930–1945*.

25. Lin Yutang, *Bianji houji*.

26. Lin Yutang, "Lunyu she tongren jietiao". Compare the author's translation with that in George Kao, ed. *Chinese wit and humor*, p. 268.

27. Lin, *Memoirs*, p. 58.

28. Lin, "Lun youmo", 522. For a complete English version of this three-part essay, see the translation by Joseph C. Sample in Chapter 9 of this volume.

29. Lin, "Lun youmo", 434. For detailed discussion of Lin's appropriation of Meredith's notion, see Qian Suoqiao, *Liberal cosmopolitan: Lin Yutang and middling Chinese modernity*, pp. 127–159.

30. Lin, "Lun youmo", 436. The author's translation differs slightly from that given by Sample: "the humour of arguing and debating" and "the humour of poeticizing self-satisfaction", in order to highlight the "socio-cultural" vs. "self" differentiation.

31. Lin Yutang, "The Danish crown prince incident and official publicity", *The China Critic* (27 March 1930), 293.

32. Lin, *Memoirs*, p. 70.

33. Kao, *Chinese wit and humor*, p. 267.

34. Lin Yutang, "For a Civic Liberty Union", *The China Critic* (3 November 1932), 1157.

35. Harold R. Isaacs, *Re-encounters in China: Notes of a journey in a time capsule*, p. 4.

36. Agnes Smedley, *Battle hymn of China*, p. 111.

37. For membership of the League, see Sohigian, "The life and times", pp. 414–15.

38. Lin Yutang, "On freedom of speech", *The China Critic* (9 March 1933), 164.

39. Lin, "On freedom of speech", *The China Critic* (9 March 1933), 164–5.

40. Lin, "On freedom of speech", *The China Critic* (9 March 1933), 165.

41. See Helen Foster Snow, *My China years*, p. 137.

42. Lin Yutang, "The little critic", *The China Critic* (23 October 1930), 1020–1. This piece was later titled "More prisons for politicians" when included in his *The little critic* book.

43. Lin, "The little critic", *The China Critic* (23 October 1930), 1021.

44. Lin Yutang, "On political sickness", *The China Critic* (16 June 1932).

45. Lin, "On political sickness", *The China Critic* (16 June 1932), 601.

46. Lin, "On political sickness", *The China Critic* (16 June 1932), 601.

47. Snow, *My China years*, p. 65.

48. Lin Yutang, "An open letter to an American friend", *The China critic* IV (26 February 1931), 203.

49. Lin, "An open letter to an American friend", *The China Critic* IV (26 February 1931), 204.

50. Under Mao Zedong, the figures of Lin Yutang and Harold Isaacs were airbrushed out. Sohigian's doctoral dissertation reproduces this remarkable pair of images ("The life and times", p. 676).

51. See Archibald Henderson, *Contemporary immortals*; and Frank Harris, *Frank Harris on Bernard Shaw: An unauthorized biography based on firsthand information, with a postscript by Mr. Shaw.*

52. Lin Yutang, *Shui hu shui hu yangyang ying hu.*

53. Bernardine Szold Fritz, "Lin Yutang". Lin Yutang acknowledged Bernardine Szold Fritz as one of his friends who "nagged" him into writing *My country and my people* (p. xiv).

54. Lin Yutang, "I moved into a flat", *The China Critic* (22 September 1932).

55. Lin, "I moved into a flat", *The China Critic* (22 September 1932), 992.

56. Lin Yutang, "The necessity of summer resorts", *The China Critic* (3 August 1933).

57. Lin Yutang, "Spring in my garden", *The China Critic* (10 May 1934).

58.   Lin Yutang, "How I became respectable", in *The little critic*, p. 295.

59.   Lin, "How I became respectable", in *The little critic*, p. 295. Chiang's conversion to Christianity was a political move to gain support from the Western-educated class in China.

60.   Lin Yutang, "On Mickey Mouse", *The China Critic* (19 September 1935), 278.

61.   Lin, "On Mickey Mouse", *The China Critic* (19 September 1935), 279.

62.   Lin Yutang, "On crying at movies", *The China Critic* (14 November 1935), 158.

63.   Lin, "On crying at movies", *The China Critic* (14 November 1935), 159.

64.   Fritz, "Lin Yutang".

65.   Lin Yutang, "On shaking hands", *The China Critic* (22 August 1935), 181.

66.   Lin Yutang, "On the calisthenic value of kowtowing", *The China Critic* (12 December 1935), 254.

67.   Lin Yutang, "The lost mandarin", in *The little critic*, p. 288.

68.   Lin, "The lost mandarin", in *The little critic*, p. 290. A *makua* or *magua* 馬褂 is a Mandarin-style jacket worn over a gown.

69.   Lin, "The lost mandarin", in *The little critic*, p. 290.

70.   Fritz, "Lin Yutang".

71.   Fritz, "Lin Yutang".

Bibliography

Abrams, Meyer H. *A glossary of literary terms.* New York: Holt, Rinehart and Winston, 1981.

Alexander, Peter, ed. *The complete works of William Shakespeare.* Glasgow: HarperCollins, 1994.

Arikha, Noga. *Passions and tempers: A history of the humours.* New York: Harper Perennial, 2008.

Aristotle. *Nicomachean ethics.* In *The complete works of Aristotle: the revised Oxford translation,* ed. Jonathan Barnes, Vol. 2: 1729–1867. Princeton, NJ: Princeton University Press, 1984.

——. *Parts of animals.* In *The complete works of Aristotle: The revised Oxford translation,* ed. Jonathan Barnes, Vol. 1: 994–1086. Princeton, NJ: Princeton University Press, 1984.

Attardo, Salvatore. *Humorous texts: A semantic and pragmatic analysis.* Berlin: Mouton de Gruyter, 2001.

Ayoub, Lois. Old English *wæta* and the medical theory of the humours. *The Journal of English and Germanic Philology,* 94 (3) (1995): 332–46.

Bai Lingjie 白靈階. Guanyü Baochai de cang yu lou 關於寶釵的藏與露 (About what Baochai conceals and reveals). *Honglou meng xuekan* 紅樓夢學刊, 1 (2007): 123–36.

Ban Gu 班固. *Baihu tong* 白虎通 (Discourses in the White Tiger Hall). Beijing: Zhonghua shuju, 1985.

——. *Han shu* 漢書 (Book of Han). 12 vols. Beijing: Zhonghua shuju, 1962 (1975 reprint).

Ban Zhao 班昭. Women's precepts (*Nüjie* 女誡). Trans. R. H. van Gulik, in *Sexual life in ancient China: A preliminary survey of Chinese sex and society from ca. 1500 B.C. till 1644 A.D.,* 88–103. Leiden: Brill, 1974.

Bergson, Henri. *Laughter: An essay on the meaning of the comic.* Trans. Cloudesley Brereton and Fred Rothwell. Mineola, NY: Dover, 2005.

——. *Le rire: Essai sur la signification du comique.* Paris: Alcan, 1900.

Bi Keguan 畢克官 and Huang Yuanlin 黃遠林. *Zhongguo manhua shi* 中國漫畫史 (History of Chinese cartoons). Beijing: Wenhua yishu chubanshe, 1986.

Børdahl, Vibeke and Jette Ross. *Chinese storytellers: Life and art in the Yangzhou tradition*. Boston MA: Cheng & Tsui, 2002.

Birch, Cyril. Tragedy and melodrama in early *ch'uan-ch'i* plays: "Lute song" and "Thorn hairpin" compared. *Bulletin of the School of Oriental & African Studies*, 36 (2) (1973): 228–47.

The book of songs: The ancient Chinese classic of poetry. Trans. Arthur Waley, ed. Joseph R. Allen. New York: Grove Press, 1996.

Brain, Peter. *Galen*. Cambridge: Cambridge University Press, 1986.

Bremmer, Jan and Herman Roodenburg, eds. *A cultural history of humour from antiquity to the present day*. Cambridge: Polity Press, 1997.

Brooks, E. Bruce and A. Brooks. Taeko. *The original analects: Sayings of Confucius and his successors*. New York: Columbia University Press, 1998.

Burridge, Kate. *Weeds in the garden of words: Further observations on the tangled history of the English language*. Cambridge: Cambridge University Press, 2004.

Bynum, William F. Every man in his humour. *Times Literary Supplement*, 17 August 2007.

Cai Yijiang 蔡義江. Honglou meng *shi ci qu fu pingzhu* 紅樓夢詩詞曲賦評註 (Annotated *shi, ci, qu* and *fu* poems in *Dream of the red chamber*). Beijing: Beijing chubanshe, 1979.

Caiyun mantianfei 彩雲漫天飛 (pen name). *Dayou shi* 打油詩. http://q.163.com/dayoushi/blog/hbbd_yy/81685728200943004647277/#81685728200943004647277 (accessed 3 June 2009).

Cao Chen 曹臣. *Shehua lu* 舌華錄 (Flowers of the tongue recorded). Hefei: Huangshan shushe, 1999.

Cao Chuji 曹礎基. *Zhuangzi qianzhu* 莊子淺注 (Zhuangzi with brief annotations). Beijing: Zhonghua shuju, 1982.

Cao Xueqin 曹雪芹. Honglou meng *bashi hui jiaoben* 紅樓夢八十回校本 (*Dream of the red chamber* in 80 chapters, edited version). Ed. Yu Pingbo 俞平伯. Hong Kong: Zhonghua shuju, 1974.

——. *Qianlong Jiaxu Zhiyanzhai chongping* Shitou ji 乾隆甲戌脂硯齋重評石頭記 (Qianlong Jiaxu edition of *The Story of the Stone* annotated by Zhiyanzhai). 2 vols. Taipei: Taiwan shangwu yinshuguan, 1961.

——. *The story of the stone*. Vols. 1, 2, 3. Trans. David Hawkes and John Minford. New York: Penguin, 1973, 1977, 1980.

——. *The story of the stone*. Vols. 4, 5. Trans. John Minford. Bloomington, IN: Indiana University Press, 1982, 1987.

Cao Xueqin and Gao E 高鶚. *Honglou meng* 紅樓夢 (Dream of the red chamber). 3 vols. Ed. and annot. Feng Tongyi 馮統一, comm. Wang Meng 王蒙. Guilin: Lijiang chubanshe, 1994.

Chan, Marjorie K. M. Cantonese opera and the growth and spread of vernacular written Cantonese in the twentieth century. In *Proceedings of the seventeenth North American Conference on Chinese Linguistics (NACCL-17).*

Ed. Qian Gao. 1–18. Graduate Students in Linguistics (GSIL) Publications, University of Southern California, Los Angeles, 2005.

Chan, Shirley. Human nature and moral cultivation in the Guodian 郭店 text of the *Xing Zi Ming Chu* 性自命出 (Nature derives from mandate). *Dao: A Journal of Comparative Philosophy*, 8 (4) (2009): 361–82.

Chan, Wing-tsit. *A sourcebook of Chinese philosophy*. Princeton, NJ: Princeton University Press, 1963.

Chang, Eileen. *The sing-song girls of Shanghai*. New York: Columbia University Press, 2005.

Chen Bojun 陳伯君, ed. *Ruan Ji ji jiaozhu* 阮籍集校注 (Textual editing and commentary of Ruan Ji's collection). Beijing: Zhonghua shuju, 1987.

Chen Dingsan 陳鼎三 and Jiang Ersun 江爾孫. *Yixue tanyuan* 醫學探源 (Exploring the origins of medicine). Sichuan: Kexue jishu chubanshe, 1986.

Chen, Durham S. F. 陳石孚. Dr. Lin as I know him: Some random recollections. *Huagang xuebao* 華崗學報, 9 (1973): 257–8.

Chen Fangying 陳芳英. *Handan ji* de xiju qingdiao 《邯鄲記》的喜劇情調 (The tone of comedy in the *Story of Handan*). *Zhongwai wenxue* 中外文學, 13 (1) (1986): 48–69.

Chen Guo-Hai 陳國海. Guonei jiaoxue youmo yanjiu shuping 國內教學幽默研究述評 (A literature review of humour research in teaching in mainland China). *Gaodeng jiaoyu yanjiu xuebao* 高等教育研究學報 (Journal of Higher Education Research), 30 (2) (2007): 88–91.

Chen, Guo-Hai. Validating the Orientations to Happiness Scale in a Chinese sample of university students. *Social Indicators Research*, 99 (3) (2010): 431–442.

Chen, Guo-Hai and Rod A. Martin. A comparison of humor styles, coping humor, and mental health between Chinese and Canadian university students. *Humor: International Journal of Humor Research*, 20 (3) (2007): 215–234.

Chen Hsueh-Chih 陳學志, Shu-Ling Cho 卓淑玲 and Hwei-Der Lai 賴惠德. Jiejue wenti fahui chuangyi de cihao fangfa jiushi faxian qizhong de youmo 解決問題發揮創意的次好方法就是發現其中的幽默：幽默中的創意與創意中的幽默 (Finding the embedded humour in creative problems is the second best way to solve them: Humorous creativity and creative humour). *Yinyong xinli yanjiu* 應用心理研究, 26 (2005): 95–115.

Chen Kehua 陳科華. *Rujia zhongyong zhi dao yanjiu* 儒家中庸之道研究 (A study of the Confucian way of the Mean). Guilin: Guangxi shifan daxue chubanshe, 2000.

Chen Ninggui 陳寧貴, ed. *Lin Yutang youmo jinju* 林語堂幽默金句 (Golden words from Lin Yutang's humour). Taipei: Dehua chubanshe, 1982.

Chen Xinwang 陳訢望. *Han Ying chengyu, chanyu, changyong cihui huibian* 漢英成語,讒語,常用詞語彙編 (A collection of Chinese idioms, proverbs and phrases with English translations). Beijing: Zhishi chubanshe, 1984.

Chen Zhao 陳詔. *Honglou meng xiaokao* 紅樓夢小考 (A small textual criticism of *Dream of the red chamber*). Shanghai: Shanghai shudian chubanshe, 1999.

Chien, Florence. Lu Xun's six essays in defense of Bernard Shaw. *The Annual of Bernard Shaw Studies*, 12 (1992): 57–78.

Clark, Barrett H. *European theories of the drama*. Rev. ed. by Henry Popkin. New York: Crown, 1965.

Confucius. *The analects (Lun yü)*. Trans. D. C. Lau. Harmondsworth: Penguin, 1979.

———. *The analects of Confucius*. Trans. Arthur Waley. London: George Allen & Unwin, 1949.

———. *Confucius Sinarum philosophus . . .* [A translation of the *Ta Hsüeh*, the *Chung Yung* and the *Lun Yü*. With a commentary and map]. 3 vols. Ed. and trans. Prospero Intorcetta, Christian Herdtrich and Francis Rougemont. Paris: printed by André Cramoisy, sold by Daniel Horthemels, 1687.

Crawford, Heather J., Gary D. Gregory, James M. Munch and Charles S. Gulas. Humorous appeals in advertising: Comparing the United States, Australia and the People's Republic of China. *Journal of business research* (in press).

Croce, Benedetto. *The essence of aesthetic*. Trans. Douglas Ainslie. London: Heinemann, 1921.

Davies, Christie. The dog that didn't bark in the night: A new sociological approach to the cross-cultural study of humor. In *The sense of humor*, ed. Willibald Ruch. 293–306. Berlin: Mouton de Gruyter, 1998.

———. *Ethnic humour around the world: A comparative analysis*. Bloomington, IN: Indiana University Press, 1990.

———. Humour and protest: Jokes under Communism. In *Humour and social protest* (*International Review of Social History*, supplement 15), ed. Marjolein 't Hart and Dennis Bos. 291–303. Cambridge, UK: Press Syndicate of the University of Cambridge, 2007.

———. *Jokes and their relation to society*. Berlin: Mouton de Gruyter, 1998.

———. *The mirth of nations*. New Brunswick, NJ: Transaction, 2002.

Davila Ross, Marina, Michael J. Owren and Elke Zimmermann. Reconstructing the evolution of laughter in great apes and humans. *Current Biology*, 19 (13) (2009): 1106–11.

Davis, Ben. Guy Smiley. *Artnet*. http://www.artnet.com/magazineus/reviews/davis/davis11-12-07.asp (accessed 10 February 2010).

de Bary, Wm Theodore and the Conference on Ming Thought. *Self and society in Ming thought*. New York: Columbia University Press, 1970.

de Crespigny, Rafe. *A biographical dictionary of Later Han to the Three Kingdoms (23–220 AD)*. Leiden: Brill, 2007.

DeFrancis, John. *ABC Chinese–English dictionary*. Honolulu: University of Hawaii Press, 1996.

Dolby William. Yuan drama. In *Chinese theater from its origins to the present day*, ed. Colin Mackerras. 32–59. Honolulu: University of Hawaii Press, 1983.

Dolby, William, ed. and trans. *Eight Chinese plays from the thirteenth century to the present*. New York: Columbia University Press, 1978.

——. *Yuan dynasty variety plays* (Yuan zaju yingyi xuanji): *Chinese dramas of the first golden age of Chinese theatre*. Edinburgh: Carreg, 2003.

Dong Yaping 董亞萍. Qianxi Lin Daiyu de youmo 淺析林黛玉的幽默 (Preliminary analysis of Lin Daiyu's humour). *Honglou meng xuekan* 紅樓夢學刊, 3 (2008): 302–3.

Draitser, Emil, ed. *Forbidden laughter: Soviet underground jokes*. Bilingual edition. Los Angeles, CA: Almanac, 1980.

Du Zhijun 杜志軍. Xin shiqi Hongxue sanshinian: 1978–2008 新時期紅學三十年: 1978–2008 (Thirty years of redology in the new era: 1978-2008). *Honglou meng xuekan* 紅樓夢學刊, 2 (2008): 10–11.

Eifring, Halvor, ed. *Love and emotions in traditional Chinese literature*. Leiden: Brill, 2003.

Erya zhushu 爾雅註疏 (Notes and commentaries on *Towards correctness*). In *Sibu beiyao* 四部備要, vol. 12. Shanghai: Zhonghua shuju, 1936.

Fan Ziye 範子燁. Shishuo xinyu xin tan 世說新語新探 (A new probe into *Shishuo xinyu*). *Xuexi yu tansuo* 學習與探索, 99 (1995): 118–24.

Feng Yuanjun 馮沅君. *Feng Yuanjun gudian wenxue wenji* 馮沅君古典文學文集 (Collected essays by Feng Yuanjun on classical literature). Jinan: Shandong renmin chubanshe, 1980.

Feng Yu-Lan [Feng Youlan]. *A short history of Chinese philosophy*. Ed. and trans. Derk Bodde. New York: Macmillan, 1973.

Forabosco, Giovannantonio. The ill side of humor: Pathological conditions and sense of humor. In *The Sense of humor: Explorations of a personality characteristic*, ed. Willibald Ruch, 271–92. Berlin: Mouton de Gruyter, 1998.

Forster, E. M. Flat and round characters. In *Essentials of the theory of fiction*, ed. Michael Hoffman and Patrick Murphy, 40–7. Durham, NC: Duke University Press, 1988.

Freedman, Alisa. Street nonsense: Ryūtanji Yū and the fascination with interwar Tokyo absurdity. *Japan Forum*, special issue on "Urban nonsense", 21 (1) (2009): 11–33.

Freud, Sigmund. *Jokes and their relation to the unconscious*. Trans. James Strachey. New York: Norton, 1960.

——. *The psychopathology of everyday life*. Trans. Anthea Bell. London: Penguin, 2003.

——. *Richang shenghuo de xinli fenxi* 日常生活的心理分析 (The psychopathology of everyday life). Trans. Lin Keming 林克明. Taipei: Zhiwen chubanshe, 1987.

——. *Wit and its relation to the unconscious*. Trans. A. A. Brill. New York: Moffat, Yard, 1916.

Fritz, Bernardine Szold. Lin Yutang, an unpublished biographical sketch of Lin Yutang. The John Day Company archive, Princeton University, Box 123, Folder 54.

Fung, Andy Shui-lung 馮瑞龍. Yuandai aiqing xiju zhuti fenxi 元代愛情喜劇主題分析 (An analysis of the themes of love-theme comedy of the Yuan dynasty). *Zhongwai wenxue* 中外文學, 18 (7) (1989): 101–16.

——. Yuandai aiqing xiju zhuti fenxi 元代愛情喜劇主題分析 (An analysis of the themes of love-theme comedy of the Yuan dynasty). In *Yuanqu baike dacidian* 元曲百科大辭典 (Encyclopedia dictionary of Yuan drama). 1116–17. Beijing: Xueyuan chubanshe, 1991.

Gai Qi 改琦. *Honglou meng tu yong* 紅樓夢圖咏 (Illustrations for and poems on the *Dream of the red chamber*). Originally published in 4 *juan*, 1879. Republished in 2 vols. Beijing: Beijing tushuguan chubanshe, 2004.

Gay, Penny. *The Cambridge introduction to Shakespeare's comedies*. Cambridge: Cambridge University Press, 2008.

Gibson, Rex. *Teaching Shakespeare*. Cambridge: Cambridge University Press, 1998.

Giles, Lionel, trans. *Taoist teaching from the Book of Lieh-Tzü with introduction and notes by Lionel Giles* (The wisdom of the East series), 2nd ed. (original ed. 1912). London: John Murray, 1947.

Ge Hong 葛洪. *Baopuzi* 抱樸子 (The master who embraces simplicity). Shanghai: Shanghai guji chubanshe, 1990.

Goel, Vinod and Raymond J. Dolan. Social regulation of affective experience of humor. *Journal of Cognitive Neuroscience*, 19 (9) (2007): 1574–80.

Goldkorn, Jeremy. Stifled laughter: How the Communist Party killed Chinese humor. *Danwei* (16 November 2004). http://www.danwei.org/tv/stifled_laughter_how_the_commu.php (accessed 18 January 2010).

——. The text message as satire. *Danwei* (2 May 2008). http://www.danwei.org/mobile_phone_and_wireless/dirty_rivulets_of_the_mainstre.php (accessed 4 June 2009).

Graham, A. C. *The Book of Lieh-tzu* (The wisdom of the East series). London: John Murray, 1960.

——. *Disputers of the Tao*. Chicago: Open Court, 1989.

——. *The two Chinese philosophers Ch'eng Ming-tao and Ch'eng Yi-ch'uan*. London: Lund Humphries, 1958.

Grant, Mary A. *The ancient rhetorical theories of the laughable: The Greek rhetoricians and Cicero*. Madison, WI: University of Wisconsin Press, 1924.

Gudian xiqu meixue ziliao ji 古典戲曲美學資料集 (Collected materials concerning the aesthetics of classical operas). Ed. Wei Fei 隗芾 and Wu Yuhua 吳毓華. Beijing: Wenhua yishu chubanshe, 1992.

Gulas, Charles S. and Marc G. Weinberger. *Humor in advertising: A comprehensive analysis.* Armonk, NY: M. E. Sharpe, 2006.

Haldon, John. Humour and the everyday in Byzantium. In *Humour, history and politics in late antiquity and the early Middle Ages,* ed. Guy Halsall, 48–73. Cambridge: Cambridge University Press, 2002.

Han Fei 韓非. Nan san 難三 (Refutations part three). In *Han Feizi xuan* 韓非子選, 165–79. Shanghai: Shanghai renmin chubanshe, 1974.

Han Ying 韓嬰. *Hanshi waizhuan* 韓詩外傳 (Han's outer remarks concluding with lines from *Book of Songs*). 2 vols. Shanghai: Shangwu yinshuguan, (?)1922.

Han Yu 韓愈. *Han Yu quanji* 韓愈全集 (Works of Han Yu). Beijing: Renmin chubanshe, 2001.

Hanyu da cidian 漢語大詞典 (Large dictionary of the Chinese language). Ed. *Hanyu da cidian* bianji weiyuanhui 漢語大詞典編輯委員會. Shanghai: *Hanyu da cidian* chubanshe, 2002.

Harbsmeier, Christoph. *Confucius ridens*: Humor in the *Analects. Harvard Journal of Asiatic Studies,* 50 (1) (1990): 133–4.

——. Humor in ancient Chinese philosophy. *Philosophy East and West,* special issue on "Philosophy and humor", 39 (3) (1989) 289–310.

——. *The cartoonist Feng Zikai: Social realism with a Buddhist face.* Instituttet for sammenlignende kulturforskning. Serie B, No. 67. Oslo: Universitetsforlaget, 1984.

Hsu Chih-Chun 徐芝君, Hsueh-Chih Chen 陳學志 and Fa-Chung Chiu 邱發忠. Qianwan bie xiao, buran nide taidu hui cong kan xiaohua zhong xielou: bianyi lei youmogan zhinengdu tiaozheng lilun de yanzheng 千萬別笑，不然您的態度會從看笑話中洩露：貶抑類幽默感知能度調整理論的驗證 (Don't laugh, or your attitude will be revealed from reading jokes: Adjustment theory of disparagement humour appreciation). *Yinyong xinli yanjiu,* 26 (2005): 143–165.

Harris, Frank. *Frank Harris on Bernard Shaw: An unauthorized biography based on firsthand information, with a postscript by Mr. Shaw.* London: Victor Gollancz, 1931.

Henderson, Archibald. *Contemporary immortals.* New York: Appleton, 1930.

He Xinmin 賀信民. Yishu hua za lüye chou — Honglou meng de xiju tese yü xiju jingshen 一樹花雜綠葉稠 — 紅樓夢的喜劇特色與喜劇精神 (Blossoms amid foliage green and dense — the comedic features and spirit of *Dream of the red chamber*). *Honglou meng xuekan* 紅樓夢學刊, 2 (2006): 191–205.

Hillenbrand, F. K. *Underground humour in Nazi Germany 1933–1945.* London: Routledge, 1995.

Holzman, Donald. *Poetry and politics: The life and works of Juan Chi, A.D. 210–283.* Cambridge: Cambridge University Press, 1976.

Hou Han shu 後漢書 (History of Later Han). Beijing: Zhonghua shuju, 1965.

Howarth, William D. English humour and French comique? The cases of Anouilh and Ayckbourn. *New Comparison*, 3 (1987): 72–82.

Hsia, C. T. The Chinese sense of humor. *Renditions*, 9 (1978): 30–84. http://www.renditions.org/renditions/magazine/09.html (accessed 3 June 2009).

——. *The classical Chinese novel*. New York: Columbia University Press, 1968.

Hsu, Pi-Ching. *Beyond eroticism: A historian's reading of humor in Feng Menglong's Child's folly*. Lanham, MD: University Press of America, 2006.

Huang Huaixin 黃懷信, ed. *Da Dai Li ji huijiao jizhu* 大戴禮記彙校集注 (Collated Elder Dai's Book of Rites with collected annotations). 2 vols. Xi'an: Sanqin chubanshe, 2005.

Hung, Chang-tai. *Going to the people: Chinese intellectuals and folk literature*. Cambridge, MA: Harvard University Press, 1985.

——. The fuming image: Cartoons and public opinion in Late Republican China, 1945-1949. *Comparative Studies in Society and History*, 36 (1) (1994): 122–145.

Hung, Josephine Huang, ed. *Classical Chinese plays*. 2nd ed. London: Vision Press, 1972.

Hyers, Conrad. *Zen and the comic spirit*. London: John Knox, 1975.

Isaacs, Harold R. *Re-encounters in China: Notes of a journey in a time capsule*. Armonk, NY: M. E. Sharpe, 1985.

Ivanov, Sergey A. *Holy fools in Byzantium and beyond*. Trans. Simon Franklin. Oxford: Oxford University Press, 2006.

Jaspers, Karl. *The origin and goal of history*. Trans. Michael Bullock. New Haven, NH: Yale University Press, 1953.

Jiang Guanghui 姜廣輝, ed. *Guodian Chujian yanjiu* 郭店楚簡研究 (Studies of the Chu bamboo slips from Guodian). Shenyang: Liaoning jiaoyu chubanshe, 1999.

Jiang Liangfu 姜亮夫. Huaji kao 滑稽考 (Study of *huaji*). *Sixiang zhanxian* 思想戰線, 2 (1980): 71–3, 80.

Jinguwen Shangshu quanyi 今古文尚書全譯 (Complete translation of the modern and ancient texts of archaic documents). Ed. Jiang Hao 江灝, Qian Zongwu 錢宗武 and Zhou Pingjun 周秉鈞. Guiyang: Guizhou renmin chubanshe, 1990.

Jin shu 晉書 (History of Jin). Beijing: Zhonghua shuju, 1974.

Johnson, Samuel. *A dictionary of the English language*. London, 1755. http://www.archive.org/details/dictionaryofengl01johnuoft.

Joubert, Laurent. *Treatise on laughter*. Trans. Gregory D. de Rocher. (Original pub. 1579.) Tuscaloosa, AL: University of Alabama Press, 1980.

Kant, Immanuel. *Kant's Critique of judgement*. Trans. J. H. Bernard. London: Macmillan, 1914.

Kao, George, ed. *Chinese wit and humor*. New York: Coward-McCann, 1946.

Keyserling, Hermann Graf von. *The book of marriage: A new interpretation by twenty-four leaders of contemporary thought*. New York: Harcourt, Brace, 1927.

Kim Jang-hwan and Lily Xiao Hong Lee. The circulation and study of the *Shishuo xinyu* in Korea. *Early Medieval China,* 12 (2006): 31–67.

Kirkland, Russell. *Taoism: The enduring tradition.* New York: Routledge, 2004.

Kirsh, Steven J. Cartoon violence and aggression in youth. *Aggression and Violent Behavior,* 11 (6) (2006): 547–57.

Knechtges, David R. Wit, humor, and satire in early Chinese literature (to A.D. 220). *Monumenta Serica,* 29 (1971): 79–98.

Knight, Charles A. *The literature of satire.* Cambridge: Cambridge University Press, 2004.

Ko, Dorothy, JaHyun Kim Haboush and Joan Piggott. *Women and Confucian cultures in premodern China, Korea, and Japan.* Berkeley, CA: University of California Press, 2003.

Kohn, Livia. *Early Chinese mysticism: Philosophy and soteriology in the Daoist tradition.* Princeton, NJ: Princeton University Press, 1992.

Kong Shuyu. *Big Shot from Beijing*: Feng Xiaogang's *He Sui Pian* and contemporary Chinese commercial film. *Asian Cinema,* 15 (1) (2003): 175–187.

Kongzi jiayu 孔子家語 (Sayings of Confucius and his disciples). Annot. Wang Su 王肅. Shanghai: Shanghai guji chubanshe, 1990.

Kongzi jiayu shuzheng 孔子家語疏證 (Sayings of Confucius and his disciples with commentaries). Comp. Chen Shike 陳士珂. In *Congshu jicheng chubian* 叢書集成初編. Ed. Wang Yunwu 王雲五. 506–9. Shanghai: Shangwu yinshuguan, 1959.

Kovskaya, Maya. Han Bing: Chinese performance art engaging life on the margins. *NY Arts* (November–December 2005). http://www.nyartsmagazine.com/index.php?option=com_content&task=view&id=3495&Itemid=701 (accessed 9 June 2009).

Kowallis, Jon Eugene von, trans. *Wit and humor from Old Cathay.* Beijing: Panda, 1986.

Kushner, Barak. Laughter as materiel: The mobilization of comedy in Japan's fifteen-year war. *The International History Review,* 26 (2) (2004): 300–330.

Lai Ruihe 賴瑞和. Zaoqi quanqi zhong de beiju yu naoju: "Pipa ji" yu "Jinchai ji" bijiao 早期傳奇中的悲劇與鬧劇:《琵琶記》與《荊釵記》比較 (Comparison of 'The story of a pipa' and 'The story of a hairpin': Tragedy and melodrama in early *quanqi* drama). *Zhongwai wenxue* 中外文學, 8 (10) (1980): 154–81.

Lao-tzu, Chuang-tzu and James Legge. *The Tao tê ching: The writings of Chuang-tzû. The Thâi-shang tractate of actions and their retributions.* 1969. Taipei: Ch'eng-wen, 1976.

Lee, Leo Ou-fan. *Shanghai modern: The flowering of a new urban culture in China. 1930–1945.* Cambridge, MA: Harvard University Press, 1999.

Lee, Lily Hsiao Hung. A study of *Shih-shuo hsin-yü*. Ph.D. thesis, University of Sydney, 1982.

Lee, Lily Xiao Hong 李蕭虹. *Shishuo xinyu zhengti yanjiu* 世說新語整體研究 (A comprehensive study of *Shishuo xinyu*). Shanghai: Shanghai guji chubanshe, 2011.

——. Language and self-estimation: The case of Wei–Jin women. *Journal of the Oriental Society of Australia*, 25/26 (1993–94): 150–64.

——. *The virtue of yin: Studies on Chinese women.* Sydney: Wild Peony, 1994.

Lee, Lily Xiao Hong and A. D. Stefanowska, eds. *Biographical dictionary of Chinese women: Antiquity through Sui 1600 BCE–618 CE.* Armonk, NY: M. E. Sharpe, 2007.

Legge, James. *The Chinese classics.* 5 vols. Taipei: SMC Publishing, 1994.

Leibniz, G. W. *Discourse on the natural theology of the Chinese.* Trans. Henry Rosemont Jr. and Daniel J. Cook. Honolulu: University Press of Hawaii, 1977.

Leung, K. C. *Chiu feng-chen* 《救風塵》: Anatomy of a thirteenth-century Chinese comedy. *Chinese Culture*, 24 (4) (1983): 77–87.

Lewis, Paul. *Comic effects: Interdisciplinary approaches to humor in literature.* Albany, NY: State University of New York Press, 1989.

Liao, Chao-chih. Humor versus *huaji*. *Journal of Language and Linguistics*, 2 (1) (2003): 25–46. www.jllonline.co.uk/journal/2_1/chao-chih2_1.html (accessed 9 February 2010).

——. *Taiwanese perceptions of humor.* Taipei: Crane, 1998.

Liao, Chao-Chih and Goh Abe. A comparison of Taiwanese and Japanese appreciation of English jokes. *Feng Chia Journal of Humanities and Social Sciences,* 3 (2001): 181–206.

Li Fang 李昉. Renshi bu sanshi'er 人事部三十二 (Human affairs, section 32). In "Taiping yulan" 太平禦覽. In *Sibu congkan* 四部叢刊, vol. 44. Shanghai: Shanghai shudian, 1985.

Liji 禮記 (The book of rites). Ed. Zhang Wenxiu 張文修. Beijing: Beijing Yanshan chubanshe, 1995.

Liji zhushu (shang) 禮記註疏 (上) (Book of rites with annotations and commentaries, vol. 1). In *Sibu beiyao* 四部備要, vol. 6. Shanghai: Zhonghua shuju, 1936.

Liji zhushu (xia) 禮記註疏 (下) (Book of rites with annotations and commentaries, vol. 2). In *Sibu beiyao* 四部備要, vol. 7. Shanghai: Zhonghua shuju, 1936.

Lin Taiyi 林太乙. *Lin Yutang zhuan* 林語堂傳 (Biography of Lin Yutang). Taipei: Lianjing, 1989 (also Tianjin: Zhongguo xiju chubanshe, 1994).

Lin Yutang 林語堂. Bianji houji 編輯後記 (Editorial afterword). *Lunyu banyuekan* 論語半月刊 (Analects Fortnightly), 1 (16 September 1932): 46.

——. *Dahuang ji* 大荒集 (The great wilderness). Shanghai: Shenghuo shudian, 1934.

——. Lun Kongzi de youmo 論孔子的幽默 (On Confucius's humour). In *Lin Yutang mingzhu quanji* 林語堂名著全集, 16. Changchun: Dongbei shifan daxue chubanshe, 1994.

———. Lun youmo 論幽默 (On humour). *Lunyu banyuekan* 論語半月刊 (Analects Fortnightly), 33 (16 January 1934): 434–8 (Part 1); and 35 (16 February 1934): 522–5 (Parts 2 and 3).

———. Lun youmo 論幽默 (On humour). In *Lun youmo – Lin Yutang youmo wenxuan* 論幽默 — 林語堂幽默文選 (*On humour — The collection of Lin Yutang's humorous writings*), 1: 1–14. Taipei: Linking Publishing Co., 1994.

———. Lunyu she tongren jietiao 論語社同仁戒條 (Ten commandments of the *Analects* School colleagues). *Lunyu banyuekan* 論語半月刊 (Analects fortnightly), 1 (16 September 1932), inside cover.

———. Shui hu shui hu yangyang ying hu 水乎水乎洋洋盈乎 (Coming afar from the ocean). *Lunyu banyuekan* 論語半月刊 (Analects fortnightly) (1 March 1933): 404.

———. *Xin de wenping* 新的文評 (New criticism). Shanghai: Beixin shuju, 1930.

Lin Yutang. *The China critic*. Lusin [Lu Xun] (6 December 1928): 547–8; The Danish Crown Prince incident and official publicity (27 March 1930): 293–6; The little critic (3 July 1930): 636–7; The little critic (11 September 1930): 874–5; The little critic (23 October 1930): 1020–2; An open letter to an American friend, IV (26 February 1931): 203–5; On political sickness (16 June 1932): 600–1; I moved into a flat (22 September 1932): 991–2; For a civic liberty union (3 November 1932): 1157–8; On freedom of speech (9 March 1933): 164–5; The necessity of summer resorts (3 August 1933): 766–7; Spring in my garden (10 May 1934): 448–50; On shaking hands (22 August 1935): 180–1; On Mickey Mouse (19 September 1935): 278–80; On crying at movies (14 November 1935): 158–9; On the calisthenic value of kowtowing (12 December 1935): 253–4.

———. *The importance of living*. New York: William Morrow, 1996.

———. *Letters of a Chinese Amazon and war-time essays*. Shanghai: Commercial Press, 1930.

———. *The little critic: Essays, satires and sketches on China (First series: 1930–1932)*. Shanghai: Commercial Press, 1935.

———. *Memoirs of an octogenarian*. Taipei: Mei Ya, 1975.

———. *My country and my people*. New York: John Day, 1935.

Li Ruzhen 李汝珍. *Jinghua yuan* 鏡花緣 (Romance of mirrored flowers). Shanghai: Shanghai guji chubanshe, 2007.

Li Tianhong 李天虹. *Guodian zhujian xing zi ming chu yanjiu* 郭店竹簡性自命出研究 (A study of the Guodian bamboo-slip text, "Human nature comes from the decree of Heaven"). Wuhan: Hubei jiaoyu chubanshe, 2003.

Liu E 劉鶚. *Lao Can youji* 老殘遊記 (The travels of Lao Can). Jinan: Jilu shushe, 1982.

Liu, Jung-En, ed. and trans. *Six Yuan plays*. Harmondsworth: Penguin, 1972.

Liu Xiang 劉向. Gu *lienü zhuan* 古烈女傳 (Ancient biographies of virtuous women). In *Congshu jicheng jianbian* 叢書集成簡編, vols. 814–15, 1–256. Taipei: Taiwan shangwu yinshuguan, 1966.

——. *Xinxu Shuoyuan* 新序説苑 (New compilation of argumentations and stories). Shanghai: Shanghai guji chubanshe, 1990.

Liu Xie 劉勰. *Wenxin diaolong quanyi* 文心雕龍全譯 (Complete translation of The literary mind and the carving of dragons). Ed. Long Bikun 龍必錕. Guiyang: Guizhou renmin chubanshe, 1992.

Liu Yiqing 劉義慶. *Shishuo xinyu* 世說新語 (A new account of tales of the world). Beijing: Zhonghua shuju, 1962.

Liu Zongyuan 柳宗元. *Liu Hedong ji* 柳河東集 (Collected works of Liu Hedong). 5 vols. Taipei: Taiwan shangwu yishuguan, 1965.

Li Xifan 李希凡. *Honglou meng* yü Ming Qing renwen sixiang 紅樓夢與明清人文思想 (*Dream of the red chamber* and Ming/Qing humanist ideology). *Honglou meng xuekan* 紅樓夢學刊, 1 (2004): 121–5.

Li Xifan 李希凡 and Lan Ling 藍翎. *Honglou meng* zhong liangge duili de dianxing — Lin Daiyu he Xue Baochai 紅樓夢中兩個對立的典型 — 林黛玉和薛寶釵 (Two opposite heroines in *Dream of the red chamber* — Lin Daiyu and Xue Baochai). In *Honglou meng pinglun ji* 紅樓夢評論集, 218–27. Beijing: Renmin wenxue chubanshe, 1973.

Li Xifan 李希凡 and Li Meng 李萌. "Ketan tingjide" — Xue Baochai lun "可嘆停機德" — 薛寶釵論 ("Alas for the paragon of female virtue" — a discussion of Xue Baochai). *Honglou meng xuekan* 紅樓夢學刊, 2 (2005): 203–29.

Li Yu 李漁. *Li Yu quanji* 李漁全集 (Works of Li Yu). Hangzhou: Zhejiang guji chubanshe, 1992.

——. *Xianqing ouji* 閑情偶寄 (A random deposit of idle thoughts). Ed. Zhang Ping 張萍. Xi'an: San Qin chubanshe, 1999.

Lu Ji 陸機. *Wen fu* 文賦 (The poetic exposition on literature). In *Readings in Chinese literary thought*, trans. and comment Stephen Owen, 87–179. Cambridge: Harvard University Press, 1992.

Lu Xun 魯迅. *Gu xiaoshuo gouchen* 古小說鈎沉 (Fragments culled from old fiction). Beijing: Renmin wenxue chubanshe, 1951.

——. *Lu Xun quanji* 魯迅全集 (The complete works of Lu Xun). 18 vols. Beijing: Renmin wenxue chubanshe, 2005.

——. *Zhongguo xiaoshuo shilüe* 中國小說史略 (Brief history of Chinese fiction). Hong Kong: Sanlian shudian, 1958; Beijing: Renmin wenxue chubanshe, 1972.

Lu Xun [Hsün]. *The true story of Ah Q*. Trans. Yang Hsien-yi and Gladys Yang. Peking: Foreign Languages Press, 1972.

Lunyu baihua jinyi 論語白話今譯 (Modern Chinese translation of the Analects). Ed. Gou Chengyi 勾承益 and Li Yadong 李亞東. Beijing: Zhongguo shudian, 1992.

Ma Zhongxue 馬仲學. *Zhongguo yixue zhenfa da quan* 中國醫學診法大全 (A complete collection of Chinese medicine examination methodology). Shandong: Jinan shi kexue jishu chubanshe, 1991.

Mackerras, Colin. *Chinese drama: A historical survey*. Beijing: New World Press, 1990.

——. *The performing arts in contemporary China*. London: Routledge, 2004.

Maoshi zhushu (xia) 毛詩註疏 (下) (Mao edition of the *Book of songs* with annotations and commentaries, vol. 2). In *Sibu beiyao* 四部備要, vol. 3. Shanghai: Zhonghua shuju, 1936.

Martin, Rod A. *The psychology of humor: An integrative approach*. Amsterdam: Academic Press, 2007.

Martin, Rod A. et al. Individual differences in uses of humor and their relation to psychological well-being: Development of the humor styles questionnaire. *Journal of Research in Personality*, 37 (1) (2003): 48–75.

Martinsen, Joel. Joke advertising. *Danwei* (28 December 2008). http://www.danwei.org/blogs/joke_advertising.php (accessed 4 June 2009).

Mather, Richard B. Filial paragons and spoiled brats: A glimpse of medieval Chinese children in the *Shishuo xinyu*. In *Chinese views of childhood*, ed. Anne Behnke Kinney. 111–26. Honolulu: University of Hawaii Press, 1995.

——. *Shih-shou hsin-yü: A new account of tales of the world*. Minneapolis, MN: University of Minnesota Press, 1976.

McAleavy, Henry, trans. *The Chinese bigamy of Mr. David Winterlea*. London: Allen & Unwin, 1961.

Mencius 孟子. *Mengzi* 孟子 (The book of Mencius). In Zhu Xi 朱熹, *Sishu zhangjuji zhu* 四書章句集註. Beijing: Zhonghua shuju, 1983.

Mengzi baihua jinyi 孟子白話今譯 (Modern Chinese translation of the *Book of Mencius*). Ed. Li Shuang 李雙. Beijing: Zhongguo shudian, 1992.

Meredith, George. *The egoist*. Ed. Angus Wilson. New York: New American Library (Signet Books), 1963. http://www.gutenberg.org/etext/1684.

——. *An essay on comedy and the uses of the comic spirit*. London: Constable, 1927.

Mitukuni, Yosida. The Chinese concept of nature. In *Chinese Science: Explorations of an ancient tradition*, ed. Joseph Needham, Shigeru Nakayama and Nathan Sivin. 71–89. Cambridge MA: MIT Press, 1973.

Morreall, John. Humor in the Holocaust: Its critical, cohesive, and coping functions. In *Hearing the voices: Teaching the Holocaust to future generations*, Proceedings of the 1997 Annual scholars' conference on the Holocaust and the Churches, ed. Michael Hayse et al. 103–12. Merion Station, PA: Merion International, 1999. Holocaust Teacher Resource Center: http://www.holocaust-trc.org/holocaust_humor.htm (accessed 9 June 2009).

Morrison, Hedda. *A photographer in Old Peking*. Oxford: Oxford University Press, 1985.

Nagashima, Heiyō. *Sha-re*: A widely accepted form of Japanese wordplay. In *Understanding humor in Japan*, ed. J. M. Davis. 75–6. Detroit, MI: Wayne State University Press, 2008.

Needham, Joseph. *Clerks and craftsmen in China and the West*. Cambridge: Cambridge University Press, 1970.

——. *Science and civilisation in China. Vol. 2: The history of scientific thought.* Cambridge: Cambridge University Press, 1956.

New Oxford American dictionary (electronic resource). Ed. Erin McKean. New York: Oxford University Press, 2005.

Ng, On-Cho. Toward an interpretation of Ch'ing ontology. In *Cosmology, ontology and human efficacy: Essays in Chinese thought,* ed. Richard J. Smith and W. Y Kwok. 35–57. Honolulu: University of Hawaii Press, 1993.

Nicoll, Allardyce. *The theory of drama.* London: Harrap, 1931.

——. *Xi'Ou xiju lilun* 西歐戲劇理論 (The theory of European drama). Trans. Xu Shihu 徐士瑚. Beijing: Zhongguo xiju chubanshe, 1985.

Nienhauser, William H. *The Indiana companion to traditional Chinese literature.* Bloomington, IN: Indiana University Press, 1986.

Ōmori Kyōko. Narrating the detective: *Nansensu,* silent film *benshi* performances and Tokugawa Musei's absurdist detective fiction. *Japan Forum,* special issue on "Urban Nonsense", 21 (1) (2009): 75–93.

Otto, Beatrice K. *Fools are everywhere: The court jester around the world.* Chicago: University of Chicago Press, 2001.

Panksepp, Jaak and Jeff Burgdorf. "Laughing" rats and the evolutionary antecedents of human joy? *Physiology & Behavior,* 79 (2003): 533–47.

Peng Xiaoling 彭小苓 and Han Aili 韓藹麗, eds. *Ah Q qishi nian* 阿Q七十年 (Seventy years of Ah Q). Beijing: Beijing shiyue wenyi chubanshe, 1993.

Peng Ziyi 彭子益. *Yuan yundong de gu zhongyixue* 圓運動的古中醫學 (Ancient Chinese medicine's concept of cyclical motion). Beijing: Zhongguo zhongyiyao chubanshe, 2007.

Peterson, Christopher and Martin E. P. Seligman. *Character strengths and virtues.* Oxford: Oxford University Press, 2004.

The philogelos or laughter-lover. Trans. B. Baldwin (from A. Theirfelder, ed., Munich, 1968). Amsterdam: J. C. Gieben, 1983.

Plato. *Philebus.* Trans. Robin A. H. Waterfield. Harmondsworth: Penguin, 1982.

——. *The Republic.* In *Great books of the Western world,* trans. Benjamin Jowett. Vol. 7: 295–441. Chicago: Encyclopaedia Britannica, 1955.

Pokora, Timoteus. The etymology of *ku-chi. Zeitschrift der Deutschen morgenländischen Gesellschaft,* 122 (1972): 149–72.

——. Ironical critics at ancient Chinese courts (*Shih chi,* 126). *Oriens Extremus,* 20 (1973): 49–64.

Potts, L. J. *Comedy.* London: Hutchinson, 1966.

Proyer, René T., Willibald Ruch and Guo-Hai Chen. Positive psychology and the fear of being laughed at: Gelotophobia and its relations to orientations to happiness and life satisfaction in Austria, China, and Switzerland. *Humor: International journal of humor research,* in press.

Pu Songling 蒲松齡. *Liaozhai zhi yi* 聊齋志異. (Strange tales from the chitchat studio). Ed. Zhu Qikai 朱其鎧. 3 vols. Beijing: Renmin wenxue chubanshe, 1983.

Qian Nanxiu. *Daitō seigo*: An alien analogue of the *Shishuo xinyu*. *Early medieval China*, 4 (1998): 49–82.

——. *Spirit and self in medieval China: The Shih-shuo hsin-yü and its legacy*. Honolulu: University of Hawaii Press, 2001.

Qian Suoqiao. *Liberal cosmopolitan: Lin Yutang and middling Chinese modernity*. Leiden / Boston MA: Brill, 2011.

——. Translating "humor" into Chinese culture. *Humor: International Journal of Humor Research*, 20 (3) (2007): 277–96.

Qian Zhongshu 錢鍾書. *Guanzhui bian* 管錐編 (A collection of limited views). 5 vols. Beijing: Zhonghua shuju, 1996.

Raskin, Victor. *Semantic mechanisms of humor*. Dortrecht: Reidel, 1985.

Rea, Christopher G. and Nicolai Volland. Comic visions of modern China: Introduction. *Modern Chinese Literature and Culture*, 20 (2) (2008): 5–20.

Rea, Christopher G. A history of laughter: Comic culture in early twentieth-century China. Ph.D. dissertation. Columbia University, 2008. http://www.proquest.com, publication no. AAT 3317601 (accessed 24 November 2009).

Rochat de la Vallee, Elisabeth. *A study of* qi. Biddles/Kings Lynn, Norfolk: Monkey Press, 2006.

Romanienko, Lisunia A. Carnival laughter and the disarming of the opponent: Antagonism, absurdity and the avant-garde: Dismantling Soviet oppression through the use of theatrical devices by Poland's "orange" solidarity movement. In *Humour and social protest* (International Review of Social History, supplement 15), ed. Marjolein 't Hart and Dennis Bos. 113–52. Cambridge, UK: Press Syndicate of the University of Cambridge.

Roth, Harold D. *Original Tao: Inward training* (nei yeh) *and the foundations of Taoist mysticism*. New York: Columbia University Press, 1999.

Ruch, Willibald. Foreword and overview: A new look at an old concept. In Willibald Ruch, ed., *The sense of humor: Explorations of a personality characteristic*. 3–14. Berlin: Mouton de Gruyter, 1998.

Schmidt-Hidding, Wolfgang, ed. *Europäische Schlüsselwörter. Band 1: Humor und Witz*. München: Huber, 1963.

Scott, Adolphe Clarence, ed. *Traditional Chinese plays*. Madison, WI: University of Wisconsin Press, 1975.

Seligman, Martin E. P. *Authentic happiness: Using the new positive psychology to realize your potential for lasting fulfilment*. London: Nicholas Brealey, 2002.

——. *Learned optimism*. New York: Knopf, 1991.

Shanghai bowuguan cang Zhanguo Chuzhushu (1) 上海博物館藏戰國楚竹書 (1) (Warring States Chu bamboo books archived in the Shanghai Museum; 1). Ed. Ma Chengyuan 馬承源. Shanghai: Shanghai guji chubanshe, 2001.

Shaw, George Bernard. The man of destiny *and* How he lied to her husband: *Two plays*. New York: Dodd, Mead, 1897.

Shi Nai'an 施耐庵. *Shuihu zhuan* 水滸傳 (Water margin). Beijing: Renmin chubanshe, 2006.

Shih, Chung-wen. *The golden age of Chinese drama: Yuan tsa-chu*. Princeton, NJ: Princeton University Press, 1976.

Shijing 詩經 (Book of songs). In Zhu Xi 朱熹, *Shiji zhuan* 詩集傳, *juan* 6. Shanghai: Shanghai guji chubanshe, 1980.

Shijing quanyi 詩經全譯 (Complete translation of the *Book of songs*). Ed. Yuan Yu'an 袁愈荌 and Tang Moyao 唐莫堯. Guiyang: Guizhou renmin chubanshe, 1993.

Shimizu Shigeru 清水茂. Kami no hatsumei to Kokan no gakufu 紙の發明と后漢の學風 (The invention of paper and its ramifications on the trend of scholarship in Later Han). *Tōhōgaku*, 79 (1990): 1–13.

Shimokawa Chieko 下川ちえこ. *Sesetsu shingo* ni mirareru joseikan 世説新語に見られる女性觀 (The gender view of women as seen from *Shishuo xinyu*). *Kagawa Chūgoku gakkai ho*, 12 (1984): 22–35.

Sima Qian 司馬遷. Huaji liezhuan 滑稽列傳 (Biographies of the *huaji*-ists). In *Shiji* 史記 (Records of the Grand Historian), vol. 10. Beijing: Zhonghua shuju, 1982.

——. Kongzi shijia di shiqi 孔子世家第十七 (Chapter 17: The hereditary house of Confucius). In *Shiji* 史記 (Records of the Grand Historian), vol. 6: 1905–47. Beijing: Zhonghua shuju, 1999.

——. Laozi Hanfeizi zhuan 老子韓非列傳 (Biographies of Laozi and Han Fei Zi). In *Shiji* 史記 (Records of the Grand Historian), vol. 3, *juan* 63. Beijing: Zhonghua shuju, 1999.

——. *Shiji* 史記 (Records of the Grand Historian). 10 vols. Beijing: Zhonghua Shuju. 1959, 1982 and 1999.

Sima Qian. *Records of the Grand Historian of China: Qin dynasty*. Trans. Burton Watson. Hong Kong / New York: Renditions / Columbia University Press, 1993.

Sivin, Nathan. *Medicine, philosophy and religion in ancient China: Researchers and reflections*. Aldershot: Variorum, 1995.

Smedley, Agnes. *Battle hymn of China*. New York: Alfred A. Knopf, 1943.

Snow, Helen Foster. *My China years*. New York: William Morrow, 1984.

Sohigian, Diran John. Contagion of laughter: The rise of the humor phenomenon in Shanghai in the 1930s. *positions*, 15 (1) (2007): 137–63.

——. The life and times of Lin Yutang. Ph.D. dissertation. Columbia University, 1991.

Solomon, Richard. *Chinese negotiating behaviour: Pursuing interests through 'old friends'*. Washington, DC: US Institute of Peace Press, 1999.

Spielmann, M. H. *The history of* Punch. London: Cassell, 1895.

Strachey, Lionel. *The world's wit and humor: An encyclopedia of the classic wit and humor of all ages and nations*. 15 vols. New York: Review of Reviews Company, 1905–12. http://openlibrary.org/a/OL6008530A/Lionel_Strachey (accessed 3 April 2009).

Stelmack, Robert M. and Anastasios Stalikas. Galen and the humour theory of temperament. *Personality and Individual Differences*, 12 (3) (1991): 255–63.

Sui Shusen 隋樹森, ed. *Yuanqu xuan waibian* 元曲選外編 (Supplement to selection of Yuan drama). Beijing: Zhonghua shuju, 1980.

Sun Ailing 孫愛玲. Daguanyuan zhong wenrou de "li" jian 大觀園中溫柔的 '理' 劍 (The gentle sword of principle in the Prospect Garden). *Honglou meng xuekan* 紅樓夢學刊, 2 (2000): 80–92.

Sun, Michelle C. Humor literature as a lens to Chinese identity. *East–West Connections: Review of Asian Studies* (published by the Asian Studies Development Program National Centers), 3 (1) (2004): 111–4.

Sun Weike 孫偉科. Hongxue zhong renwu pingjia de fangfalun pingxi 紅學 中人物評價的方法論評析 (Critique of the methodology of evaluating characters in Redology). *Honglou meng xuekan* 紅樓夢學刊, 6 (2008): 174–8.

Sun Xun 孫遜, ed. Honglou meng *jianshang cidian* 紅樓夢鑑賞辭典 (A critical dictionary of *Dream of the red chamber*). Shanghai: Hanyu dacidian chubanshe, 2005.

Ta hsüeh *and* Chung yung (The highest order of cultivation *and* On the practice of the mean). Trans. Andrew Plaks. New York: Penguin, 2003.

Tang zong hai rong chuan 唐宗海容川. Yijing jingyi 醫經精義 (Essential meanings from the medical classics). In *Zhongguo yiyao huihai* 中國醫 藥匯海, vol. 8. Comp. Cai Luxian 蔡陸仙. Beijing: Beijingshi Zhongguo shudian, 1941.

't Hart, Marjolein. Humour and Social Protest: An Introduction. In *Humour and social protest* (*International Review of Social History*, supplement 15), ed. Marjolein 't Hart and Dennis Bos. 1–20. Cambridge: Press Syndicate of the University of Cambridge, 2007.

Thorpe, Ashley. *The role of the* chou *("clown") in traditional Chinese drama: Comedy, criticism and cosmology on the Chinese stage.* Lewiston: Edwin Mellen, 2007.

Tiquia, Rey. *Traditional Chinese Medicine: A guide to its practice.* Sydney: Choice, 1996.

——. Traditional Chinese Medicine as an Australian tradition of health care. Ph.D. thesis, University of Melbourne, 2004.

Tobyn, Graeme. *Culpepers's medicine: A practice of Western holistic medicine.* Shaftesbury: Element, 1997.

Tsai Chih-chung [Cai Zhizhong] 蔡志忠. *Liezi shuo: Yu feng er xing de zhesi* 列子 說：御風而行的哲思 (Liezi said: The philosophical idea of riding on the wind). Beijing: Sanlian chubanshe, 1990.

Twain, Mark [Samuel Langhorne Clemens]. *Mark Twain's notebooks and journals.* Ed. Frederick Anderson, Lin Salamo and Bernard L. Stein. 3 vols. Berkeley, CA: University of California Press, 1975–79.

Wan Pingjin 萬平近. *Lin Yutang pingzhuan* 林語堂評傳 (A biographical commentary of Lin Yutang). Chongqing: Chongqing chubanshe, 1996.

Wang Bing 王冰. Chongguang buzhu Huangdi neijing suwen 重廣補注黃帝內經素問 (The Yellow Emperor's inner canon: Basic questions, with additional and expanded comments). In *Sibu congkan* 四部叢刊, vol. 63. Shanghai: Shanghai shudian, 1989.

Wang Chong 王充. *Lun heng* 論衡 (Critical essays). Changchun: Jilin renmin chubanshe, 2003.

Wang Jide 王驥德. *Wang Jide qulü* 王驥德曲律 (Wang Jide's Rules for dramatic lyrics). Ed. Chen Duo 陳多 and Ye Changhai 叶長海. Changsha: Hunan renmin chubanshe, 1983.

Wang, Jing. *The story of stone: Intertextuality, ancient Chinese stone lore, and the stone symbolism in* Dream of the red chamber, Water margin, *and* The Journey to the West. Durham, NC: Duke University Press, 1992.

——. *Brand new China: Advertising, media, and commercial culture.* Cambridge, MA: Harvard University Press, 2008.

Wang Jisi 王季思. Yuan zaju zhong xieyin shuangguanyu 元雜劇中諧音雙關語 (Homophonic puns in Yuan drama). *Guowen yuekan* 國文月刊 (Chinese language monthly), 67 (1948): 14–19.

Wang Shouzhi 王壽之. *Yuan zaju xiju yishu* 元雜劇喜劇藝術 (Comic art of the Yuan *zaju*). Hefei: Anhui wenyi chubanshe, 1986.

Wang Xiaobo 王小波. *Wang Xiaobo wenji* 王小波文集 (Collected works of Wang Xiaobo). 4 vols. Beijing: Zhongguo qingnian chubanshe, 1999.

Wang Xiaofeng 王小峰. Kuaile yu youmo 快樂與幽默 (Happiness and humour). Dai san ge biao, 27 December 2006. http://www.wangxiaofeng.net/?p=727. Trans. Raymond Zhou as "Chinese sense of humor? You've got to be joking", 17 January 2007. http://raymondzhou.ycool.com/post.2645834.html (accessed 9 June 2009).

Wang Xiaoming 王曉明. *Lu Xun zhuan* 魯迅傳 (Biography of Lu Xun). Shanghai: Shanghai wenyi, 1993.

Wang Yuchun 王玉春. Xue Baochai de shuangchong xingge yu duzhe de shuangchong pingjia chidu 薛寶釵的雙重性格與讀者的雙重評價尺度 (The double nature of Xue Baochai and the double evaluation measures used by readers). *Honglou meng xuekan* 紅樓夢學刊, 2 (2008): 66–74.

Wang Zao 汪藻. *Shishuo xulu* 世說敍錄 (Preface and notes on *Shishuo*). In Liu Yiqing 劉義慶, *Shishuo xinyu* 世說新語 *juan* 5. 1–28. Beijing: Zhonghua shuju, 1962.

Wang Zhiyong 汪志勇. *Handan ji* de xiju yishi duhou 《邯鄲記的喜劇意識》讀後 (A review of the comic consciousness of *Handan ji*). *Zhongwai wenxue* 中外文學, 13 (2) (1984): 157–9.

Watson, Karli K., Benjamin J. Matthews and John A. Allman. Brain activation during sight gags and language-dependent humor. *Cerebral Cortex*, 17 (2) (2007): 314–24.

Wells, Henry W. *Traditional Chinese humor: A study in art and literature.* Bloomington, IN: Indiana University Press, 1971.

Wild, Barbara, Frank A. Rodden, Wolfgang Grodd and Willibald Ruch. Neural correlates of laughter and humour: Review article. *Brain*, 126 (10) (2003): 2121–38.

Willis, Thomas. *Cerebri anatome, cui accessit nervorum descriptio et usus.* Amsterdam: Gerbrand Schagen, 1664, and London: Thomas Dring, 1681.

Wu Cheng'en 吳承恩. *Xiyouji* 西游記 (Journey to the west). Beijing: Renmin chubanshe, 1980.

Wu Jingzi 吳敬梓. *Rulin waishi* 儒林外史 (The scholars). Beijing: Renmin chubanshe, 1962.

Wujastyk, Dominik, trans. and ed. *The roots of Āyurveda: Selections from Sanskrit medical writings.* London: Penguin, 2003.

Xiao Dengfu 蕭登福. *Liezi tanwei* 列子探微 (Liezi analyzed). Taipei: Wenjin chubanshe, 1990.

Xu Jinbang 許金榜. *Yuan zaju gailun* 元雜劇概論 (An introduction to the drama of the Yuan dynasty). Jinan: Qilu shushe, 1986.

Xu Shen 許慎. *Shuowen jiezi* 說文解字. (Explaining simple and analysing compound characters). Yangzhou: Jiangsu guangling guji keyinshe, 1997.

Xu, Weihe 許衛和. The Confucian politics of appearance — and its impact on Chinese humor. *Philosophy East & West*, 54 (4) (2004): 514–32.

Xu Weihe 許衛和. Lun *Honglou meng* zhong 'yiyin' yici de chuchu jiqi youmo yu yiyi 論《紅樓夢》中"意淫"一詞的出處及其幽默與意義 (On the origin of the "lust of the mind", its humour, and significance in *Honglou meng*). *Hanxue yanjiu* 漢學研究, 25 (1) (2007): 341–70.

Xunzi 荀子. Ed. Geng Yun 耿芸 (Annotated by Yang Liang 楊倞). Shanghai: Shanghai guji chubanshe, 1996.

Yan Changke 顏長珂. *Xixiang ji* de xiju tese 《西廂記》的喜劇特色 (Characteristics of comedy in *The west chamber*). *Xiju yanjiu* 戲曲研究 (Opera research), 2 (1980): 212–26.

Yang Bojun 楊伯峻. *Liezi jishi* 列子集釋 (Liezi collected explanations). Beijing: Zhonghua shuju, 1979.

Yang Luosheng 楊羅生. Manshuo Xue Baochai de leng 漫說薛寶釵的冷 (An informal discussion of Xue Baochai's coldness). *Honglou meng xuekan* 紅樓夢學刊, 2 (2004): 219–34.

Yang Xiong 揚雄. Yangzi fayan wuzi 揚子法言吾子 (Proper words of Master Yang: My master [Chapter 2]). In *Sibu congkan chubian* 四部叢刊初編, vol. 59. Shanghai: Shanghai shudian, 1989.

Yang Yifang 楊依方. *Yang Yongxuan zhongyi zhenjiu jingyan xuan* 楊永璇中醫針灸經驗選 (Selected works of Yang Yongxuan on TCM and acupuncture practice). Shanghai: Kexue jishu chubanshe, 1984.

Yang Yong 楊勇. Shishuo xinyu *jiaojian* 世説新語校牋 (A new account of tales of the world with annotations). Jiulong: Xianggang dazhong shuju, 1969.

——. *Shishuo xinyu*: shuming, juanzhi, banben kao 世説新語：書名, 卷帙, 版本考 (*Shishuo xinyu*: A study of its title, divisions and editions). *Journal of Oriental Studies*, 8 (1) (1970): 276–88.

Yisu 一粟. Honglou meng juan 紅樓夢卷 (About Dream of the red chamber). Beijing: Zhonghua shuju, 1965.

Yu Jiaxi 余嘉錫, ed. Shishuo xinyu jianshu 世說新語箋疏 (An annotation and commentary of Shishuo xinyu). Beijing: Zhonghua shuju, 1983.

Yuasa, Yasuo. The body: Self-cultivation and ki-energy. Trans. Shigenori Nagatomo and Monte S. Hull. Albany, NY: State University of New York Press, 1993.

Zang Maoxun 臧懋循, ed. Yuanqu xuan 元曲選 (Selection of Yuan drama). In Xuxiu Siku quanshu 續修四庫全書, vols. 1760–62. Shanghai: Shanghai guji, 1995.

Zhang Facai 張發財. http://blog.sina.com.cn/s/blog_49b5a8160100bfds.html (accessed 4 June 2009).

Zhang Kebiao 章克標. Lin Yutang zai Shanghai 林語堂在上海 (Lin Yutang in Shanghai). Wenhui yuekan 文匯月刊, (October 1989): 34–9.

Zhang Li. The good person of Sichuan and the Chinese cultural tradition. Trans. Ann Huss. Frontiers of Literary Studies in China, 3 (1) (2009): 133–56.

Zhang Shouchen. Traditional comic tales. Trans. Gladys Yang. Beijing: Chinese Literature, 1983.

Zhang Shuxiang 張淑香. Xixiang ji de xiju chengfen 《西廂記》的喜劇成份 (Comic elements of The west chamber). In Yuan zaju zhong de aiqing yu shehui 元雜劇中的愛情與社會 (Love and society in Yuan dynasty zaju). 169–217. Taipei: Chang'an chubanshe, 1980.

Zhang Wenzhen 張文珍. Lun Xue Baochai de "su" 論薛寶釵的"俗" (On Xue Baochai's "conventionality"). Honglou meng xuekan 紅樓夢學刊, 3 (2003): 131–40.

Zhang, Yanhua. Transforming emotions with Chinese medicine: An ethnographic account from contemporary China. New York: State University of New York Press, 2007.

Zhao Fen 趙棻. Zhongyi jichu lilun xiangjie 中醫基礎理論詳解 (A detailed elucidation of TCM foundation theory). Fujian: Fujian kexue jishu chubanshe, 1981.

Zhejiang Provincial TCM Research Office 浙江省中醫研究所. Wenyi lun pingzhu 《溫疫論》評註 (On warm contagious diseases: Notes and commentary). Beijing: Renmin weisheng chubanshe, 1985 (original edition, Wu Youxing 吳有性, Wenyi lun 溫疫論, 1642).

Zheng 鄭氏. Nü xiao jing 女孝經 (Classic of filial piety for women). Beijing: Zhonghua shuju, 1991.

Zheng Kai 鄭凱. XianQin youmo wenxue 先秦幽默文學 (Pre-Qin humorous literature). Guangzhou: Jinan daxue chubanshe, 1993.

Zhongguo lidai xiaohua jicheng 中國歷代笑話集成 (Collected jokes from Chinese history). 5 vols. Ed. Chen Weili 陳維禮 and Guo Junfeng 郭俊峰. Changchun: Shidai wenyi chubanshe, 1996.

Zhou Mi 周密. *Qidong yeyu* 齊東野語 (Rustic words of a man from Eastern Qi). Shanghai: Huadong shifandaxue chubanshe, 1987.

Zhu Ying. Feng Xiaogang and Chinese New Year films. *Asian Cinema*, 19 (1) (2007): 43–64.

Zhuangzi 莊子. *Zhuangzi jishi* 莊子集釋 (Collected exegeses of Zhuangzi). Taipei: Shijie shuju, 1972.

Zhuangzi. *Basic writings / Chuang Tzu*. Trans. Burton Watson. New York: Columbia University Press, 1996.

Zhuangzi quanyi 莊子全譯 (Complete translation of the *Book of Zhuangzi*). Ed. Zhang Gengguang 張耿光. Guiyang: Guizhou renmin chubanshe, 1991.

Zhu Xi 朱熹. Zhuzi quanshu 朱子全書 (Collected writings of Zhu Xi). 27 vols. Shanghai: Shanghai guji chubanshe, 2002.

Zhu Yixuan 朱一玄. Honglou meng *ziliao huibian* 紅樓夢資料彙編 (Compilation of materials relating to *Dream of the red chamber*). Tianjin: Nankai daxue chubanshe, 1985.

Zong Baihua 宗白華. Lun *Shishuo xinyu* he Jin ren de mei 論世説新語和晉人的美 (On *Shishuo xinyu* and the aesthetics of the Jin). In *Xiandai wenxue lunwen xuandu* 現代文學論文選讀, ed. Li Yan 李棪. 165–85. Hong Kong: Dongya shuju, 1971.

Zou Zizhen 鄒自振. *Honglou meng* de si dui yishu bianzhengfa 紅樓夢的四對藝術辯證法 (Four pairs of artistic dialectics in *Dream of the red chamber*). *Honglou meng xuekan* 紅樓夢學刊, 3 (2001): 86–97.

Index